GENESIS

BELIEF

*A Theological Commentary
on the Bible*

GENERAL EDITORS

*Amy Plantinga Pauw
William C. Placher*[†]

GENESIS

MIGUEL A. DE LA TORRE

WESTMINSTER
JOHN KNOX PRESS
LOUISVILLE • KENTUCKY

© 2011 Miguel A. De La Torre

First edition
Published by Westminster John Knox Press
Louisville, Kentucky

11 12 13 14 15 16 17 18 19 20—10 9 8 7 6 5 4 3 2 1

Unless otherwise indicated, Scripture quotations are from the New Revised Standard Version
of the Bible, copyright © 1989 by the Division of Christian Education of the National Council of
the Churches of Christ in the U.S.A., and are used by permission. Scripture quotations marked JB
are from *The Jerusalem Bible*, copyright © 1966, 1967, 1968 by Darton, Longman & Todd, Ltd.,
and Doubleday & Co., Inc. Used by permission of the publishers.

Book design by Drew Stevens
Cover design by Lisa Buckley
Cover illustration © David Chapman/Design Pics/Corbis

Library of Congress Cataloging-in-Publication Data
De La Torre, Miguel A.
    Genesis / Miguel A. De La Torre. — 1st ed.
        p. cm. — (Belief)
    Includes bibliographical references (p.   ) and indexes.
    ISBN 978-0-664-23252-8 (alk. paper)
    1. Bible. O.T. Genesis—Commentaries. 2. Marginality, Social—Religious
aspects—Christianity. I. Title.
    BS1235.53.D4 2011
    222'.1107—dc23

                                                    2011023667

To
The Bible Faculty at the Iliff School of Theology

Contents

Publisher's Note

William C. Placher worked with Amy Plantinga Pauw as a general editor for this series until his untimely death in November 2008. Bill brought great energy and vision to the series, and was instrumental in defining and articulating its distinctive approach and in securing theologians to write for it. Bill's own commentary for the series was the last thing he wrote, and Westminster John Knox Press dedicates the entire series to his memory with affection and gratitude.

William C. Placher, LaFollette Distinguished Professor in Humanities at Wabash College, spent thirty-four years as one of Wabash College's most popular teachers. A summa cum laude graduate of Wabash in 1970, he earned his master's degree in philosophy in 1974 and his Ph.D. in 1975, both from Yale University. In 2002 the American Academy of Religion honored him with the Excellence in Teaching Award. Placher was also the author of thirteen books, including *A History of Christian Theology*, *The Triune God*, *The Domestication of Transcendence*, *Jesus the Savior*, *Narratives of a Vulnerable God*, and *Unapologetic Theology*. He also edited the volume *Essentials of Christian Theology*, which was named as one of 2004's most outstanding books by both *The Christian Century* and *Christianity Today* magazines.

Series Introduction

Belief: A Theological Commentary on the Bible is a series from West-minster John Knox Press featuring biblical commentaries written by theologians. The writers of this series share Karl Barth's concern that, insofar as their usefulness to pastors goes, most modern commentaries are "no commentary at all, but merely the first step toward a commentary." Historical-critical approaches to Scripture rule out some readings and commend others, but such methods only begin to help theological reflection and the preaching of the Word. By themselves, they do not convey the powerful sense of God's merciful presence that calls Christians to repentance and praise; they do not bring the church fully forward in the life of discipleship. It is to such tasks that theologians are called.

For several generations, however, professional theologians in North America and Europe have not been writing commentaries on the Christian Scriptures. The specialization of professional disciplines and the expectations of theological academies about the kind of writing that theologians should do, as well as many of the directions in which contemporary theology itself has gone, have contributed to this dearth of theological commentaries. This is a relatively new phenomenon; until the last century or two, the church's great theologians also routinely saw themselves as biblical interpreters. The gap between the fields is a loss for both the church and the discipline of theology itself. By inviting forty contemporary theologians to wrestle deeply with particular texts of Scripture, the editors of this series hope not only to provide new theological resources for the

church, but also to encourage all theologians to pay more attention
to Scripture and the life of the church in their writings.

We are grateful to the Louisville Institute, which provided fund-
ing for a consultation in June 2007. We invited theologians, pastors,
and biblical scholars to join us in a conversation about what this
series could contribute to the life of the church. The time was pro-
vocative and the results were rich. Much of the series' shape owes
to the insights of these skilled and faithful interpreters, who sought
to describe a way to write a commentary that served the theological
needs of the church and its pastors with relevance, historical accu-
racy, and theological depth. The passion of these participants guided
us in creating this series and lives on in the volumes.

As theologians, the authors will be interested much less in the
matters of form, authorship, historical setting, social context, and
philology—the very issues that are often of primary concern to critical biblical scholars. Instead, this series' authors will seek to explain
the theological importance of the texts for the church today, using
biblical scholarship as needed for such explication but without
any attempt to cover all of the topics of the usual modern biblical
commentary. This thirty-six-volume series will provide passage-
by-passage commentary on all the books of the Protestant biblical
canon, with more extensive attention given to passages of particular
theological significance.

The authors' chief dialogue will be with the church's creeds, practices, and hymns; with the history of faithful interpretation and use
of the Scriptures; with the categories and concepts of theology; and
with contemporary culture in both "high" and popular forms. Each
volume will begin with a discussion of *why* the church needs this
book and why we need it *now*, in order to ground all of the commentary in contemporary relevance. Throughout each volume, text
boxes will highlight the voices of ancient and modern interpreters
from the global communities of faith, and occasional essays will
allow deeper reflection on the key theological concepts of these biblical books.

The authors of this commentary series are theologians of the
church who embrace a variety of confessional and theological per-
spectives. The group of authors assembled for this series represents

more diversity of race, ethnicity, and gender than any other commentary series. They approach the larger Christian tradition with a critical respect, seeking to reclaim its riches and at the same time to acknowledge its shortcomings. The authors also aim to make available to readers a wide range of contemporary theological voices from many parts of the world. While it does recover an older genre of writing, this series is not an attempt to retrieve some idealized past. These commentaries have learned from tradition, but they are most importantly commentaries for today. The authors share the conviction that their work will be more contemporary, more faithful, and more radical, to the extent that it is more biblical, honestly wrestling with the texts of the Scriptures.

William C. Placher
Amy Plantinga Pauw

Preface

I am not a biblical scholar, nor do I claim to be. Instead, I am a social ethicist who focuses on praxis, specifically praxis that might contribute to the dismantlement of oppressive social structures. Although I am an ethicist who takes the biblical text seriously in constructing liberative ethical paradigms, it is important to reiterate that I have not been officially trained within the academic discipline of biblical scholarship. Does this mean that those of us who are men and women of faith cannot use the biblical text as the source and foundation for our moral analysis? Is commenting on the Bible off-limits to nonbiblical scholars? Has the text become the sole possession of academicians concentrating on hermeneutics? Heaven forbid! As crucial as those possessing Ph.D.'s may be in elucidating portions of the Scriptures, the Bible was not written by, to, or for the academy. First and foremost, it was written by believers, to and for the faith community. Interpreting the biblical text is not an academic discipline reserved for the expertise of biblical scholars; rather, biblical interpretations are reflections based on the real-life experience of ordinary believers. The danger of reading the Bible through the eyes of the academy is that we end with interpretations captive to the socioeconomic location of scholars doing the interpreting.

Biblical scholars, like the rest of us, unconsciously read their biases and presuppositions into the text. But what would happen if we were to purposely read the Bible, specifically the book of Genesis, from the margins? What would happen if we were to give an epistemological preference to the readings emulating from the disenfranchised and dispossessed? And what if we focused our reading so as to raise issues concerning which type of engaged praxis is congruent with the Scriptures? No doubt, the emphasis placed on the reading would differ from what has become a more normative interpretation. For example, while many may argue over the meaning of the word "day" in the creation stories (was the length of one day twenty-four hours, or was a day a million years), those experiencing dispossession seldom participate in such speculations. For the marginalized who read Genesis for hope and strength to struggle and survive one more day, such debates over the length of the original "day" become nonsensical. As interesting as solving cosmic mysteries may be, it remains a luxurious privilege the marginalized can seldom afford. While many who are privileged read the text either to answer such mysteries or to dismiss the Bible as an irrelevant ancient text in a modern world, the disenfranchised usually read the text to find ways to deal faithfully with lives marked by hardships and struggles. It is through this latter lens that in this commentary I will read the book of Genesis. Of course, this approach to reading the Bible is not novel. Other scholars have also sought to read the Bible from the margins; and it is to them, throughout this commentary, that we will continuously turn for guidance.

As mentioned, I am not a biblical scholar, even though I do use the tools of modern biblical scholarship to help understand the text while still maintaining a preferential hermeneutical option for those (ordinary people of faith and academicians) who read the Bible from the margins. Throughout Christian history individuals of faith have looked toward Holy Writ and written commentaries in their quest to score a moral life of discipleship. It is to this historic venture, that as author of this commentary, I commit.

Unlike most commentaries, this one intentionally and unapologetically provides a liberative ethical reflection on the biblical book of Genesis. Although important and at times useful to employ, I will be less interested in the biblical scholarly matters of form, authorship, historical setting, social context, and philology, which are often of primary concern in higher-critical biblical scholarship. While not ignoring such biblical scholarship, I will instead prefer the ethical emphasis found in the book of Genesis, using higher-critical analysis as needed for explication and aligning myself with those scholars and church leaders who share my commitment to justice and liberation. Hence I will not attempt to cover all of the topics of the usual modern biblical analysis. This book will provide passage-by-passage commentary on Genesis, with more extensive attention given to those of particular theological or ethical significance. I will make occasional reference to "standard" commentaries, but not to engage them as the chief dialogue partners. Instead, my chief dialogue will be with marginalized communities of faith trying to see the face of God in the midst of dispossession and disenfranchisement.

As author, I will approach the larger faith tradition with a critical respect, seeking to reclaim its riches and at the same time to acknowledge its shortcomings. My aim is to make available to readers a wide range of voices, specifically from the margins of U.S. society. As can be expected, I am grateful to those who have helped me in this process of writing this book. I am honored to have been invited to be part of this series by the editorial consultants: Amy Plantinga Pauw and the late William C. Placher. I am also grateful to Jon Berquist, former senior editor at Westminster John Knox Press, for all the assistance and guidance he provided; and to the present editor of the project, Donald K. McKim. Finally, a special thanks is given to my administrative assistant, Debbie McLaren.

Abbreviations

JB	*Jerusalem Bible*
KJV	King James Version
NIV	New International Version
NPNF	*Nicene and Post-Nicene Fathers*
NRSV	New Revised Standard Version
OBT	Overtures to Biblical Theology
OTL	Old Testament Library
RSV	Revised Standard Version

Introduction:
Why Genesis? Why Now?

Jacob, the patriarch, wrestles with God, demanding he be given a blessing (Gen. 32:24–32). But Jacob learns that the struggle to see God face-to-face has consequences. Not only does Jacob become a new person, being called Israel from that day forward, but he also limps away—an injury that will constantly remind him, for the rest of his days, of his encounter with the Divine. Likewise, there are consequences when we truly wrestle with the biblical text, struggling to see the face of God. Like Jacob, we too can receive a blessing, but usually at a cost. We can be renewed, for the text has proven to powerfully transform individuals' lives throughout the ages. Ideally, the transformation is for the better, but history has shown us that this is not always the case.

We find ourselves in a world where what we define as evil seems to prevail. War, genocide, violence, oppression, and abuse seem more the norm than the love, peace, and joy promised in Holy Writ. We are left wondering at times if God is truly present in this suffering world. We wrestle with a God who at times seems mute, demanding solidarity in the midst of struggle and a blessing in the midst of adversity. How can the Creator that is portrayed in Genesis seem so invisible during the troubling times in which we live—times filled with trials and tribulations? For many of us, especially those who live on the underside of history, we need to know that the God of Genesis, the God of beginnings, still accompanies us. We need to know that there is indeed a God with whom to wrestle. This is why a book like Genesis, the book that first introduces us to the God of all, is so important for such a time as this.

The narratives found in Genesis are testimonies from ordinary individuals who, like us, fall short of the glory of God; they raised key issues during their own time as well as ours. These timeless issues concerning injustice, oppression, migration, sexual abuse, disenfranchisement, and powerlessness continue to be key issues for Christian faith and life today. Parallels exist between the testimonies found in Genesis and the testimonies heard today at the margins of society, from those who are disenfranchised and struggling to survive. To read Genesis is to read the testimonies of "illegal" immigrants, of the sexually abused, of the outcasts, and of all those relegated to the margins of society. Their testimonies resonate with today's testimonies arising from among the disenfranchised. And while Genesis provides no easy answers or simplistic solutions for those marginalized today, it does provide an opportunity to wrestle with God and the text—a wrestling that can provide guidance, comfort, and dare I say hope for our own times.

To wrestle with the text is to be changed; but it can also humble us. The change might force us to abandon treasured presuppositions about the world and our place in it. It might force us to question what we always assumed the Bible said. It might even lead us to question the Bible or God. Change and renewal in our thoughts and in how we live is usually painful, leaving many of us to simply limp away in frustration at not fully understanding. Putting away our old selves to conform to the biblical teachings is usually a painful process, and at times can cost us our lives. Jacob's encounter with God occurred in the book of Genesis, and it is this particular book that this commentary focuses on in the hopes of also encountering the Divine. This is why we turn to Genesis. This is why it is important to do so now.

How I Am Reading Genesis

We all come to the Bible with certain presuppositions and assumptions. For this reason it is important that we recognize what we bring to the reading, suspicious of how our social location influences how we normalize the text's interpretations. So before turning attention to the text of Genesis, I will briefly introduce the book to the reader and explain how I will approach the text in this commentary.

Composition

The Greek translation of the first words of the Hebrew Scriptures, *bere'shit* (in the beginning), provides the name for the first book of the Bible—Genesis. The first five books of the Bible, Genesis, Exodus, Leviticus, Numbers, and Deuteronomy, are usually referred to within Christian tradition as the Pentateuch. These five books are bound together as a complete unit, and as such it is difficult to interpret any one of them apart from the other four. To read Genesis is to be cognizant that it is part of a larger narrative. Within Jewish tradition, these five books are considered the heart of the Bible and are commonly referred to as the Torah. Besides being central to Judaism, the Pentateuch was formative in the development of Islam and Christianity.

Genesis is written to answer certain sociotheological questions: (1) Who are we as a people (anthropology)? (2) What is our origin (cosmology)? (3) Are we alone, or is there something greater than us (spirituality)? (4) If there is something greater—a God if you will—is this the God of our particular tribe or a God that rules over all other gods and all other humans (sociology)? (5) Finally, who is this God and, more importantly, what is the character of this God who we say we believe in (theology)? Just as important, Genesis has a political thesis: The Creator of the universe has chosen the seminomadic Hebrew patriarchs, and their descendants, to take possession of a territory called Canaan, a land flowing with milk and honey, as their eternal inheritance—a thesis that even to this day is fraught with political ramifications. Regardless of the moral, spiritual, and ethical lessons that can be learned by reading Genesis, the reader should be mindful that one of the book's purposes is to provide moral justification for the eventual genocide of the promised land's original indigenous inhabitants as recorded in the book of Joshua. When Joshua assembles the people at Shechem after the successes of his military campaigns, he recites a sacred history connecting the Genesis narrative with the conquest of another's land given to the

Hebrews by God—a land that the Hebrews have not labored for, with cities they have not built, and vineyards they have not planted (Josh. 24:2–3). In Joshua's mind, Genesis justifies conquest.

Authorship

Tradition has it that Moses penned the Pentateuch, recounting the history from the creation of the earth to, and including, his own death. But rather than being penned by the hand of one author, the Pentateuch reveals itself on even a casual reading as a compilation of stories, folktales, records, songs, traditions, and legal matters spanning centuries. Biblical scholars tell us that the book of Genesis is mainly composed of two separate documents, brought together to create a narrative. These two documents, which make up the epic tradition, have come to be known as J and E. The J (Jehovist or Yahwist) document is considered to be the oldest source, dating to the tenth/ninth century BCE during the time of King David and Solomon of the southern kingdom of Judah. The E (Elohist) document, which parallels J, has been dated to the ninth/eighth century BCE and has come to be associated with the northern kingdom of Israel. It is believed that some time after the fall of the northern kingdom (722/721 BCE) a redactor or editor combined J with E.[1] A third and final document was eventually added to the JE document, P (Priestly), fashioned by a priestly redactor during the sixth/fifth century BCE from temple records that survived the Babylonian captivity.[2] While JE concentrates on narratives, P mainly consists of genealogical, liturgical, and legal material.

1. J and E represent the distinctive names, Jehovah and Elohim, respectively, used for God throughout the document. Jehovah is an artificial form resulting from adding the vowels of "Adonai" (Hebrew for Lord) to YHWH (Yahweh) to prevent the uttering of God's sacred name.
2. A fourth document in the Pentateuch, D, which stands for Deuteronomic, is primarily limited to the book of Deuteronomy, with little attestation in Genesis. Some date this source to the seventh century BCE and connect it to the lost book of the law found in the temple during the reign of King Josiah (622 BCE). It is important to note that the dates I have used to mark the composition of D, along with J, E, and P, are merely estimates and that biblical scholars continue to dispute these dates. Although I am willing for purposes of this commentary to accept these estimates, I have no desire to participate in this dating debate. Attempting to prove what cannot be proven with any certainty is a fascinating scholarly endeavor but will remain a luxury beyond the scope of this commentary.

It is important to note that the classical Documentary Hypothesis of four neat sources coming together to form the Pentateuch has been challenged by the Fragmentary Hypothesis, which recognizes multiple sources of the text, including several oral traditions that have served as the foundation for literal documents. Within the four major sources (J, E, D, and P) exist multiple ancient materials that, no doubt, were woven into the document—materials predating by centuries the final completion of the document. Some of these literary compositions, specifically the poetic works, are considered among the oldest. Several scholars have recognized G, which stands for *Grundlage,* a common groundwork, running from Genesis through Numbers and serving as the basis for the J and E narratives. G is dated from the eleventh/tenth century, a period from the judges to the united kingdom.

We are left wondering what unifying motif, theology, and/ or worldview was superimposed on the text as different sources and documents were brought together by the redactor(s). The completion of the Pentateuch in its final form can be dated, at the latest, to the end of the fifth century. This removes the completion of Genesis from the patriarchs and the events that surrounded them by at least 1,400 years.[3] Complicating the interpretive process is discerning the intentions of the redactor(s) or editor(s) of the text as it took final form. Did they, just as we do, read their own culture and identity into the biblical narrative?

While such theories of the authorship are fascinating, they will, for all practical purposes, remain beyond the scope of this commentary. Hence I will, for the sake of simplicity, simply refer to the "author." For our purposes, the question we will wrestle with is not if Abraham, Isaac, and Jacob are historical persons, for even if they are, it would be difficult based solely on the distance between them and when the biblical narrative was fashioned to ascertain much about who they really were, their lives, or how they lived. In the final analysis, no categorical conclusion can be determined. It remains a leap of faith to accept the literary figures and events in

---

3. The distance is still 900 years if we assume Abraham entered Canaan around 1850 BCE and Solomon ascended the throne in 970, with the J document coming together shortly thereafter.

Genesis as literal historical truths, especially when we recognize the text was not written as a history book, but as a testimony to the God who moves through history. What is important, for the faith community, is how the stories within Genesis serve as testimonies concerning the transcendent God who was present in their lives.

Myth or History

Debates attempting to prove the reliability of Genesis as factual history remain an intellectual luxury. For those caught in oppressive relationships, the story of Noah is not read to determine if he built an ark three hundred cubits long, but rather to seek the face of God and discern a divine word that can sustain the spirit in the midst of disaster. Marginalized communities seem less interested in proving the Bible than finding guidance as to what praxis, faithful to the biblical mandate, can be implemented to bring about a more just society. What can Noah's testimony about God teach us on how we are to view the webs of oppressive structures in which some find themselves, entangled due to the color of their skin, their sexual orientation, their economic station in life, their gender, or their ethnicity.

Hence the stories in Genesis are real. Not necessarily because they may have literally occurred, but because they reveal ethical certainties concerning God and God's call for love, mercy, and justice— even when the heroes of the story fall short of godly behavior. As important as it may be for the sake of scholarship to deconstruct the garden of Eden, more important for the faith community is to learn the lessons obtained because the garden of Eden existed for those who first uttered the story. To read Genesis from the margins is to read it prima facie, at face value. The goal is not to prove or disprove the narrative's validity; the goal is to learn from the faith-influenced testimonies of those within the narrative about the transcendent God's immediacy with God's creation, specifically humans. Genesis is written to reveal this God whom we claim to worship, as well as to reveal who we are before this God.

Plot Line

The Pentateuch starts with the creation of the earth and ends with the death of Moses on the plains of Moab. As a whole, the Pentateuch is the first part of a longer historical narrative ending in the middle of the Babylonian captivity (2 Kgs. 25:30). In total, this is a history covering approximately 3,400 years. Regardless if these numbers are accurate or not, they reveal that the majority of "recorded" time is concentrated in the Genesis narrative, which encompasses a story that spans about 2,400 years.[4]

All too often we read Genesis as a book that begins with the perfection of creation and then rapidly disintegrates in a moral and historical downward trend. Such a reading fits neatly with a theology that perceives the world as the domain of evil due to the fall of humanity. Yet Genesis seems more to be a testimony of the goodness of God's creation in spite of the shortcomings of humanity. Rather than a historical downward progression, maybe it would be more accurate to read Genesis as a story, like life, filled with high and low points, with successes and failures that give meaning to the human condition. The good news of Genesis is that God renews, regardless of how the story unfolds. There is a Creator of all who is present and initiates blessings.

The first eleven chapters of the Genesis narrative encompass universal cosmic events addressing how the world came to be formed, who formed it, why humans die, why violence between humans exists, how this Creator has the power to punish the wicked through the cataclysmic event of a worldwide flood, and why different languages and cultures exist. Starting with chapter 12 through the end of the book, the plot moves from the universal to the particular, focusing on the antecedents of the Jewish people—a barren couple, Abraham and Sarah, who are promised to birth a great nation from whom others will be blessed. In spite of obstacles that threaten the divine promise, the book bears testimony to God's faithfulness. These stories concerning this family and the nation that

---

4. These calculations accept the internal timeline of the biblical text as accurate, specifically the biblical dating of creation.

proceeded from them are to serve as an everlasting testimony to God's providence and sovereignty, so that the entire world can come to know the Creator of the universe.

Reading Genesis as Testimony

God uses weak, sinful people. The characters in Genesis are portrayed with brutal realism—warts and all. Noah was a drunk; Abraham pimped his wife Sarah and raped her slave Hagar; Jacob was a liar and deceiver; Reuben slept with his father's concubine; Joseph strengthened an oppressive empire; and Judah enjoyed the sexual favors of his daughter-in-law, who he thought was a prostitute. The patriarchs and heroes of the faith (mainly men) fell short of the glory of God, and yet they were used by God to bring about God's revelation to the world. Their testimonies are not that different from the testimonies we hear today in our churches from women and men who are just as weak and sinful.

Within the Latina/o church, as well as other marginalized faith communities, *los testimonios*, the testimonies, are an important component of the worship experience. They are central to the spirituality of Hispanics, for they allow the person to (1) voice her or his trials and tribulations to the faith community, thus giving the church the opportunity to be used by God to minister to the needs of the troubled soul; (2) be a witness to how God is moving within the faith community in spite of the struggles voiced; (3) create solidarity with the rest of the faith community, who become fellow sojourners through difficult times; (4) realize that despite the hardships faced, the believers within our midst are not alone, for God and their faith community are participants in their disappointments and victories; and finally (5) enter the reality of the metaphysical presence of the Divine in the everyday, a presence that can lead to deliverance and/ or physical or emotional healing.

In this commentary I will purposely read Genesis by employing this spiritual concept. The different stories that make up Genesis will be read as if they were the testimonies of those who encounter God. Through this methodology, Genesis can be enfleshed (incarnated) for the reader. Still, to hear testimonies is to recognize that while they are about God, they may not necessarily be godly. Testimonies are based on memory, at times faulty or self-serving memories that might be embellished to emphasize the truth of the message. As real and meaningful as the testimony may be to the one giving it, not all testimonies are inerrant.

I recall sitting in a Hispanic congregation and hearing someone rise to testify about God's loving mercies. Yet I was offended by the testimony. He said, "I thank God that he gave me a submissive wife who recognizes my headship within the family." This type of testimony is problematic, oppressive, and ungodly—and yet it is a testimony arising from the body of believers. Just because one is among the marginalized does not mean one's interpretation is from God. Still, even such a testimony can tell me something about how God is perceived. Some testimonies in Genesis are just as troublesome, supporting patriarchy, slavery, conquest, ethnic discrimination, genocide, and abuse. Our goal is not to shrink away from these difficult passages, but, like Jacob, to wrestle with them.

Presuppositions before Reading Genesis

No one reads Scripture objectively. We all read the Scriptures sub-jectively. All of us bring our biases and presuppositions to the text, reading into it our theology and worldview. To claim objectivity is to mask the power of making the subjective readings of some norma-tive for all. A healthy dose of hermeneutical suspicion is required so as not to fuse and confuse one's own subjective reading with the text. For this reason, it is crucial to be clear as to what I am bringing to the interpretive process.

First, as a Christian I read Genesis with the knowledge of the good news of Jesus Christ. As tempting as it may be to read the Hebrew Bible solely through the lens of Christ, we must resist the tendency of Christianizing Genesis so it can neatly fit our Christian faith. In this commentary my approach to exegesis recognizes that the Hebrew Bible, as sacred literature, is first and foremost sacred for Judaism, and as such cannot be subordinated to my Christian sensibilities.

Our goal is to discover God's character and God's relationship with humanity from what the text says, and not necessarily from whatever Christian theology I may read into the text. We must strive to avoid the bias that somehow the Hebrew Bible in general, and Genesis in particular, is incomplete or lacking without the New Testament. Obviously, such a reading is difficult if not impossible for Christians to do (especially this Christian); nevertheless, it should not diminish our effort to read the text in this manner. Hence the reader should not be surprised if I fail to provide tidy conclusions where the answer to every question raised by the Hebrew text is the New Testament Jesus.

Second, as a liberationist, that is, one who seriously engages in liberative ethics and theology, I approach Genesis from the margins. To read Genesis from the margins is to grasp God in the midst of struggle and oppression. Such a reading attempts to understand why God's people find themselves struggling for survival within a society that appears to be designed to privilege one group at the expense of others. Genesis becomes more than a narrative requiring scholarly analysis; it becomes a text of hope, a hope in a God whose essence is the liberation of all who are oppressed, all who subsist at the margins of society—regardless as to how hopeless reality remains. But to read Genesis from the margins, by its very nature, is to challenge how the dominant culture has historically been taught to interpret the text.

In short, the object of this commentary is not to sugarcoat or dismiss difficult passages, but like Jacob to wrestle with the text, seeking to see God's face—even if we end up limping away, not fully understanding what just happened. It is to this hermeneutical project that we now boldly turn our attention.

1:1–2:25

The Story of Beginnings

1:1–25

First Testimony of the Earth

On Sunday, October 23, 4004 BCE, some six thousand years ago, God created the heavens and the earth—at least according to James Ussher, archbishop of Armagh in Ireland, who made his calculations during the mid-seventeenth century.[1] Taking the biblical text literally, Archbishop Ussher was able to determine the precise day creation took place. He also demonstrates for us how problematic it becomes when the text is read contrary to the intention of the original authors—that is, literally. Using the biblical text to scientifically explain how our cosmos came into being does harm to the creation stories. The purpose of these texts is not to elucidate the how, the mechanics of creation; but rather to seek answers about the why, the ultimate questions facing humanity. To read the book of Genesis, especially the first eleven chapters, as history—rather than testimonies about the faith—at the very least leads to awkward interpretations (e.g., the day creation took place) and at worst to oppressive structures (e.g., the establishment of patriarchy).

Justo L. González warns us:

> In Genesis 1 we are told that God made the world in six days. . . .
> [T]he text does not tell us whether we are to interpret it literally or not. If you insist that the text must be taken literally, that is your privilege. . . . [Y]our position, as well as the position of someone who says that the text is to be taken as a metaphor, is based, not on the text itself, but on your interpretation of the

---

1. James Ussher, *The Annals of the World* [1658], updated by Larry and Marion Pierce (Green Forrest, AR: Master, 2003), 17.

11

text. If either you or the other person errs, the error is not in the text itself, but in its interpretation.[2]

The author of Genesis is not interested in pinpointing the exact moment of creation; rather, the author is attempting to convey certain metaphysical truths concerning the faith of its readers, in the hope of answering certain cosmic questions that arise from human existence. What then is the fundamental truth that the opening verses of Genesis wish to convey to the believer? "In the beginning . . . God created the heavens and the earth." With this simple declaration, several cosmic questions are answered. How did we get here? Is there someone or something greater than us? Who made all that I see? How did existence begin and who began it? And more importantly for the original readers, is my God powerful and capable enough to sustain me in the midst of dislocation and disenfranchisement? These are the questions that the author wrestles with, seeking answers to these cosmic mysteries. To ask of the text how the earth was created or the process by which reality came into being is to ask the wrong questions. Not how but who, not process but purpose— these are the concerns of the author.

The text tells us that the earth was a formless void and there was a great darkness over the watery deep. Like a mother hen brooding over her nest waiting for life to spring forth, God's spirit hovered over the waters. The good news is that God's spirit still hovers over the formless void of broken lives and the great darkness in which the marginalized find themselves. In the chaos that reigns—sexism, racism, classism, heterosexism, and all the other -isms—God's spirit still hovers. In the darkness of oppression we may not be able to see, feel, detect, or recognize the presence of God's spirit; still, the good news of the opening verses of the Bible is that God accompanies us. In the darkness when we wonder if our prayers go any higher than our ceilings, we can take comfort in knowing that we are not alone. The God of Genesis is not a distant deity but a God who is present, brooding over us like a mother hen.

2. Justo L. González, *Santa Biblia: The Bible Through Hispanic Eyes* (Nashville: Abingdon Press, 1996), 12.

Failure to understand the purpose of the opening verses of Genesis can lead to interpretations that have nothing to do with the author's intent. As Walter Brueggemann reminds us, the text was written by the P source, addressed to exiles, sometime around the sixth century BCE. The opening words of Genesis are meant to be theological and pastoral for real people exiled in Babylon and wondering if this God of Israel is more powerful than the surrounding Babylonian gods. The Priestly response is less concerned with the origins of the cosmos than it is with providing hope to these despairing refugees. The message that the author of these first verses in Genesis wishes to convey is that their God is indeed the Almighty who created all that is and, as such, is the God of life.[3] For those of us who have experienced exile from our homeland, we understand what it means to exist in a formless void stuck in a great darkness. Written for refugees, these two opening verses remind them and us today that our God is hovering over us, ready to begin a new work. The intention of the author was not to describe how the universe came into being, but rather to affirm the power of God.

Besides comforting us, these verses also challenge us. From the spirit comes the physical manifestation. Out of the deep watery chaos comes order and harmony. Because God is presented in the text as the first cause, existence has meaning. Although God's creative activity is different from human creative activity, to create provides a model for us based on a God who created in the darkness with nothing. We too who may have nothing are called to create.

Creation is understood as that which exists that is not God and, while separate from God, remains bound to God. This creation comes into being through the spoken word. Unlike the second creation story to be discussed later, in this first testimony of the earth all things are created out of

> I beg you, my child, to look at the heaven and the earth and see everything that is in them, and recognize that God did not make them out of things that existed. And in the same way the human race came into being.
> —2 Maccabees 7:28

---

3. Walter Brueggemann, *Genesis*, Interpretation (Atlanta: John Knox Press, 1982), 24–25.

nothing (*creation ex nihilo*) by God through God's spoken word. It is an expression of God's will manifested as praxis, God's free act that not only creates but sustains all that is created.

The author of this text wished to convey this truth to readers and wrote this account in the form of a hymn, a psalm, a song. Thus the author writes as a poet, not a scientist. The purpose is not to convey scientific or historical facts, but rather to convey truths about the character of this God of creation.

The importance of creation from nothing is picked up by Christians in the opening verse of the Gospel of John. "In the beginning was the Word [*logos*], and the Word was with God, and the Word was God" (John 1:1). If we read this passage in Spanish, we discover: "*En el principio era el Verbo . . . ,*" literally, "In the beginning was the Verb." For Spanish readers, Jesus is not the Word, but the Verb. Divinity as noun presents us with a static God; but divinity as verb—an action word—is a God whose very nature is praxis, to create. Rather than reflecting on a noun, Word, which becomes the basis of how we understand God (theology), those reading the Bible in Spanish concentrate on God as Verb, as action—as in "doing" theology. The act of creation defines for us a God whose character can be expressed by God's free activity of creating matter that is good. This creation becomes possible because our God is a verb, not a noun.

Because there were no eyewitnesses to creation, the belief that it was God who brought order to the dark chaos becomes an affirmation of faith, meaning that it can only be known and attested through faith. Neither God's existence nor God's creative act as the author of all that is can ever be proven. It is ludicrous to attempt placing God under a microscope to prove God's existence. Only through faith are we introduced to a God who is alive.

> I believe in God, the Father Almighty, the Maker of heaven and earth.
> —First line of the Apostles' Creed

Before the creation of human reality, we believe through faith that God already existed; and God will continue to exist, independent of any outside source, long after human reality comes to an end. Although God stands apart from God's creation, God remains relationally tied to it. Because God created all that exists, God is not limited to one minor tribe of people. God is the God of all, and there exists no other god that can be a rival. God, indeed, is the "I AM WHO I AM," a living God whose character, as manifested in creation, is to bring forth life. The God of our faith is the God of the living who is concerned with life and the forces (e.g., social structures) that threaten life.

For the first time, God speaks into emptiness; God speaks even when there is no one to listen. The first words uttered from God's mouth are: "Let there be light." As the words are spoken, the action occurs. There is light and God saw it was good, for there can be no life without the light on which it depends. The light is divided from the darkness, with the former called "day," and the latter called "night." Yes, God is responsible for light; but God, the Creator of all, is also responsible for darkness. As the prophet Isaiah reminds us, "I am Yahweh and there is none else; forming light and creating darkness, making peace and creating evil" (Isa. 45:6–7, my trans.). In the mind of the ancient author, God is the source of light and also the source of darkness, responsible for both peace and evil. Light and darkness, according to the psalmist, are alike to God (Ps. 139:11–12). God is present in the light of day and in the dark of night, on the sunny mountaintop of hope and in the twilight depth of despair. There is no darkness that can swallow up God or obscure God's vision, for Yahweh is Lord even in the darkness and God is over it as well as over the light. The good news is that in the very midst of darkness, the God of Genesis says, "Let there be light," and there is light! Both light and darkness are created by God; the first evening and morning occur. The first day expired. Yet there was no sun. The sun would not be created until the fourth day, leaving us to wonder what or who was emitting the light. On the second day God creates a vault to divide the waters above the vault from the waters below the vault. God called the vault "heaven." In the mind of the author, this vault was like an upside-down, translucent, bowl-shaped structure fastened to the earth, containing windows that open so water (rain) can fall from the heavens. The waters below the vault would create the oceans, lakes, rivers, streams, and brooks, all fed by subterranean waters after the land is called forth. Eventually, we will read of a worldwide flood caused by the gates of the heavens being opened and the subterranean waters bursting forth beyond their boundaries.

On the third day God brought the waters below the vault together to create a single mass, allowing dry ground to appear, floating on the waters. God called the dry ground "earth" and the waters "seas," and it was good. Then God performs a second creative act on the same day by calling forth vegetation—seed-bearing plants and fruit-bearing trees. Through this act a practical purpose is accomplished: the living creatures that are to follow will find nourishing resources that will sustain life. And as important as seed-bearing plants and fruit-bearing trees are, God also calls forth roses, lilies, daisies, and daffodils. Creation is not solely functional; it also has aesthetic value.

On day four God placed lights in the heavens to divide day from night and indicate festivals. A cosmic clock is created that dictates the passage of time, more specifically, the orderly and harmonious changing of the seasons. These lights in the vault of heaven would shine on the earth. Two great lights were created, one to govern the day and the smaller one to govern the night along with the stars. The psalmist will one day sing of this event: "By the word of Yahweh the heavens were made, and the starry hosts by the breath of God's mouth" (Ps. 33:6, my trans.).

On the fifth day God commanded that the waters teem with living creatures and that birds fly within the vault of heaven. God blessed these creatures and commanded that they be fruitful and multiply, that they be self-perpetuating. That is, God created and encouraged that all living creatures—the birds and the bees—engage in sexual activity in cooperation with God's creative work of bringing forth life. Sex, as part of creation, is also good because it is ordained by God.

On day six God created every kind of living creature—cattle, creeping things, and the beasts of the field to roam the earth. And it was good, it was and is all good; that is, what was created had a purpose to fulfill. Nothing created by God is bad or evil. Yet one of those creeping things was a serpent that later would tempt humanity. Was the serpent not good, even though the text states all that was created was good? This is an important question to be discussed later. For now, even the serpent, as part of God's creation, was good.

Theologians have distinguished the first three days of creation from the last three days. *Opus divisionis* (work of division) during the first three days creates symmetry with the *opus ornatus* (work of ornamentation) of the last three days. The division between the darkness and the light created on day one is balanced with the sun, moon, and stars that give off or reflect light on the fourth day. The division between the waters by creating the vault called heaven on the second day is filled with fish and birds on the fifth day. And the division between the water and the earth that is brought forth on the third day is filled with creatures to roam the land on the sixth day. The psalmist sings not only of the goodness of creation, including harmony in the words chosen to imagine God's creative act, but also of the harmonious order of said creative act that took place. In words and order of action, Genesis begins poetically.

FURTHER REFLECTIONS
Creationism

Outside Cincinnati, Ohio, in northern Kentucky, a state-of-the-art, 70,000-square-foot Creation Museum opened to much fanfare in 2007. Built at a cost of $27 million, it contains Disney-like exhibits that advocate the inerrancy of the creation story (singular, not plural). For $24.95 patrons can spend the day watching exhibits such as human children and dinosaurs playing in peace and harmony near Eden's rivers (since both were created by God on the sixth day). A frequently offered one-hour lecture, "Is Genesis Relevant in Today's World?" given by Tim Chaffey (whose highest academic degree is a Master of Divinity from Liberty Baptist Theological Seminary) justifies its reason for existence on the museum's official Web site:

> Our culture is quickly becoming a post-Christian society and it has rejected the authority of God's Word. Sadly, many in the church are following the world's example. The concentrated attacks on the book of Genesis have been a driving force leading to this current situation. This presentation explains that the solution to the problem is grounded in the Bible's first

book and will demonstrate that we can trust God's Word from its very first verse.[4]

Yet in spite of the Creation Museum's apologetics, anyone who reads the first two chapters of Genesis reads two creation stories penned by different authors living centuries apart. The tradition that Moses is responsible for writing the first five books of the Bible, the Torah, quickly becomes indefensible. A superficial glance of the first two chapters reveals two very different orders. The first story (1:1–2:4a) lists the order of creation as follows: day 0—formless void; day 1—light is created; day 2—the heavens are created; day 3—land and vegetation are created; day 4—the sun and moon are created; day 5—the living creatures in the water and air are created; day 6—the living creatures on the land and humans (both male and female) are created; day 7—God rested. By contrast, the second creation story (2:4b–25) lists what appears to be just one day of activity where everything was created in the following order: (1) there is land; (2) water surfaces on the land; (3) man; (4) Eden (plants); (5) animals; (6) woman.

Regardless as to how obvious it may appear that two very different stories concerning creation exist, within our modern times there is a cultural push within legislative state houses and local school boards to include the concept of creationism, based on the first creation story, within the school curricula, to be taught alongside evolutionary theories. This political activism is based on a religious movement that developed in the early twentieth century called fundamentalism, a populist response to the biblical criticism that was developing within the academy. Central to the tenets of the fundamentalist movement is the principle of inerrancy; that is, the Bible is without error. Because the true author of the biblical text is God, it is impossible for the Bible to contain any errors. If the Bible is found to be wrong in any aspect, then the entire text becomes unreliable as the authoritative foundation for Christian living. Thus, if the Bible states it took God six days to create the earth, then it took God

---

4. http://creationmuseum.org/whats-here/activities/ (November, 2010).

six days (seen by many as twenty-four-hour periods) to create the earth. Demanding that creationism, or its latest manifestation since the 1990s as intelligent design, be taught as scientific truth is waged on the public battleground—a struggle for the very relevance of the Bible in America.

In spite of the sensational 1925 Scopes trial, the attempt to make the teaching of creationism normative continues to this day. Those advocating a fundamentalist agenda want to reconcile the Bible with science in order to create a harmonious worldview, an endeavor undertaken by a small minority of scholars within academia. For them the earth, contrary to fossil evidence, is only six to ten thousand years old. To render the biblical text as a science book is problematic, for in the final analysis it leads to bad science, bad theology, and bad hermeneutics. Those concerned with advancing this fundamentalist agenda spend much time and effort discussing the meaning of the word "day" in the creation story. Was a day twenty-four hours long, or was a day a thousand, if not a million, years? Frankly, those on the margins of society do not seem to care.

The dominant culture usually looks for answers to questions that are simply unimportant to the social location of those living under oppressive structures. It is rare to find any biblical and theological scholars of color participating in the creationism debate. When a people live under repressive structures, they turn to the Bible for the strength to survive another day, not to figure out how long a day lasted in Genesis 1. The Bible is not read with the intellectual curiosity of solving cosmic mysteries. Rather, most people of color look to the text to find guidance in dealing with daily life, a life usually marked by struggles and hardships. Debates over the scientific validity of the Bible become a luxurious privilege for those who do not endure discriminatory structures. For many in the dominant culture the objective in reading the Bible is to answer such questions, usually simplistically.

Regardless as to how this debate unfolds, whether the biblical interpretation determined appeals to the fundamentalists or the liberals, the overall dominant culture reads the text through the lens of modernity, even while protesting the present-day ramifications of the Enlightenment.

"Does God exist?" becomes the overall quest of those residing within the dominant culture. In contrast, from the margins of
society the question becomes, "What is the character of this God
who we claim exists?" While the evangelistic mission of many Euro-
Americans is to convince the nonbeliever to believe, those who
reside on the underside of society see their evangelistic venture
to be that of convincing the undervalued (nonperson) of his or her
humanity based on the image of God that dwells within all humans.

1:26–27

Testimony of the First Humans

The first story of creation, as compiled by the P source, reaches
its climactic end on the sixth day with God's crowning creation of
"man." We are told that God said, "Let us create man in our own
image" (my trans.), leaving the reader to wonder who exactly is *us*.
For many Christian theologians and biblical scholars, the "us" is a
reference to the doctrine of the Trinity, thus neatly tying Genesis
1:26 with the proclamation in the two first verses of the Gospel of
John—that in the beginning was the Word (Jesus), the Word was
with God, and the Word was God. Through this Word all things
came into being. To emphasize this point, attention is drawn to the
Hebrew plural name (which may not necessarily be a proper noun)
for God, *'elohim*, the plural of *'el*. While such an interpretation may
resonate among Christians, for millennia Jewish readers of this text
did not subscribe to how Christians historically read their theology
into the sacred text. The "us" has been understood to allude to the
heavenly host of angels from whom God took counsel. "Us" simply
refers to the plural of majesty as reflected by the divine court made
up of the "sons of God" (6:2). But if this is so, are humans then created in some combined image of God and the angels? Other scholars, taking a more historical view, wonder if the usage of "us" might
be some ancient echo to a polytheistic past.

Creating man in God's own image reveals as much about God as
it does about humans. To be created in the likeness of God refers
to more than just the corporeal, especially since God as spirit has

no legs, arms, feet, and so on. Humans are metaphorically like God spiritually, mentally, emotionally, and physiologically. If we want to understand something about the reality of God, then it behooves us to look toward humans, who are the image or copy of the original. Yet this methodology might prove problematic. When we try to imagine God, most, due to millennia of religious art, picture God in a male body. The great Western masters have illustrated for us a white, bearded, and muscular elderly man as the manifestation of Divinity. Not surprisingly, most of us, along with the majority of biblical translations, anthropomorphize God as "he"; yet God as a "he" is responsible for establishing, sustaining, and advancing patriarchy within religion, specifically Christianity. There is a danger when we make God male.

If our goal is to read the Bible with liberative eyes, that is, through the eyes of the world's marginalized seeking within the text a message of liberation, then we must reread familiar passages demonstrating how centuries if not millennia of interpretations have been used to justify oppressive structures. In the case of these two verses, we need to debunk how they have been used to justify patriarchy.

Most translations of these two verses make clear that God created man in God's own image. For example, the NIV states: "Then God said, 'Let us make man in our image, in our likeness. . . .' So God created man in his own image, in the image of God he created him; male and

> If God is male, then the male is God.
>
> —Mary Daly
>
> *Beyond God the Father: Toward a Philosophy of Women's Liberation* (Boston: Beacon, 1973), 19.

female he created them." The KJV, the Living Bible, and the RSV, to name but a few, also emphasize man as being created in the image of God.

Yet the Hebrew word used for man is *ha'adam*, and it is this word that most English Bibles have translated as "man." But is this the correct translation for the word? The word *'adam* can be a reference to a proper name, as in the case of Adam, the partner of Eve, although some scholars argue that early Jewish interpretation of *'adam* as a proper name was due to a misinterpretation of the J text in Genesis

2, as well as subsequent chapters.[5] The word 'adam can also refer to
"man," a male-gendered individual, as opposed to the Hebrew word
'ishshah, translated as "woman," although some early Jewish exegesis
of the verse regarded the first human being as an androgynous earth
creature.[6] Finally, 'adam can be translated as "humanity."

The question before us is which of these three definitions for
'adam is the proper translation for these two verses. The answer is
found at the end of verse 27, "male and female God created them."
We can ask, was Adam the individual created male and female, containing the sexual organs of both genders? Or was the man created as
both male and female? Possibly, but more likely, the text is referring
to humanity, which comprises males and females. Hence a proper
translation of these two verses would be: "And God said, let us make
humanity in our own image, in the likeness of ourselves. So God created humans in the image of God, in the image of God God created
them, male and female God created them."

For humanity, consisting of male and female, to be created in the
image of God means that God is male and female; God is our Father
and our Mother. Elizabeth Cady Stanton echoes this understanding
of the Deity: "If language has any meaning, we have in these texts
a plain declaration of the existence of the feminine element in the
Godhead, equal in power and glory with the masculine. The Heavenly Mother and Father! 'God created man in his own image, male
and female.'"[7]

Scholars such as Paul Tillich and Paul Ricoeur remind us that we
can only use symbols to describe or understand God, connecting the
meaning of one thing recognized by a given community that is com-
prehensible (e.g., male or female) with another thing that is beyond
our understanding (e.g., God).[8] While symbols assist us in grasping the incomprehensible essence we call God, they are incapable of

---

5. Helen Schüngel-Staumann, "On the Creation of Man and Woman in Genesis 1–2: The History
and Reception of the Texts Reconsidered," in *Biblical Studies Alternatively: An Introductory
Reader*, comp. Susanne Scholz (Upper Saddle River, NJ: Prentice Hall, 2003), 84.

6. Ibid.

7. Elizabeth Cady Stanton, ed., *The Woman's Bible* (New York: European Printing, 1898), 20.

8. Paul Ricoeur, *Interpretation Theory: Discourse and the Surplus of Meaning* (Fort Worth: Texas
Christian University Press, 1976); and Paul Tillich, *Theology of Culture*, ed. Robert C. Kimball
(Oxford: Oxford University Press, 1959).

fully describing the reality of God. To take symbolic language literally (e.g., God is exclusively male or female) leads to the absurd (e.g., God has a penis or vagina), which borders on idolatry (the creation of hierarchies in relationships by who is closer to the divine ideal). To speak of God as male, as fire, or as mother is to speak of God in symbols that through analogies convey limited knowledge for understanding what God is like.

So God is male and female. God is not male and God is not female. God is everything between male and female, and God is beyond maleness and femaleness. Using a Hindu Arthanareesvara image, Padma Gallup attempts to elucidate this concept: "If the Godhead created humans in its image, then the Godhead must be a male/female, side-by-side, non-dualistic whole."[9] The radical nature of the Hebrew God as described in the book of Genesis is that, unlike the neighboring Canaanite gods, Yahweh has no bodily form, hence no gender. The gods of the people surrounding the Hebrews were often depicted in small statuettes about the size of a human hand. If these gods were female, they were usually depicted with large pendulous breasts, broad hips, and prominent vaginas. Some of the male god statuettes were depicted with large protruding and erect penises. Even though this was the norm for fertility gods, the God of the Hebrews, who was also responsible for creating and sustaining all that has life, had neither breasts nor penis. Against this background, it was considered blasphemy to make any graven image of the true God (Exod. 20:4), for such a God was beyond the imagination of finite minds.

To make an image of God, either as a statue or a painting, was prohibited because once God was given a male body (or a female body for that matter), God's transcendence was pierced, reduced to less than God is. God can never be contained in any type of depiction created by humans, for to create God in our own image is to create a God that is superfluous. Making God a "he" has little to do with maintaining theological political correctness; it has more to do with reading our sexism into the biblical text. If male and female are

9. Padma Gallup, "Doing Theology: An Asian Feminist Perspective," *Commission on Theological Concerns Bulletin* 4 (Christian Conference in Asia 1983): 22.

created in God's image, women cease being an appendix to the creation story; in the second version (Gen. 2) women are created in the image of man. To refer to God as a "he" or even as a "she" is to deny the Deity of its mystery, reducing God to a controllable concept that can be used to justify oppressive structures. Thus by gendering God we participate in blasphemy.

If both male and female, or better yet, all of humanity, are created in the image of God, then the worth and dignity of all humans are affirmed. This humanity created in the image of God comprises both an "I" and a "Thou." The diversity of creation as expressed in humanity, it is presumed, becomes an act of divine love, a love that seeks companionship, a love that exists for others. Being human can never occur in isolation, apart or disconnected from others. Unlike the rest of creation, these humans exist in relationship to God, to creation, and to one another. It is these reciprocal relations that define humans, as such relationships provide opportunities for self-realization. To become an island unto oneself is to deny one's humanity.

To be in right relationship with God is to be in right relationship with creation and other people. According to Justo González, God's very nature is being-for-others, love. To be human in the image of God is to also be-for-others. If God is love, whose very essence expresses concern for others, then to be created in the image of God means that humans are a product of love expressed as being-for-others.[10] The alternative of being-for-others, prevalent in salient individualistic Western cultures, is being-alone, being-without-others, which is contrary to God's will in creating. Only through relationships with others can we expect to have our consciousness raised concerning the conditions the rest of humanity is forced to endure. Being-for-others becomes possible as we become conscious of others. But when we cut ourselves off from the vast majority of humanity, which happens to be marginalized and disenfranchised, refusing to hear their cry or see their condition, we cease being-for-others. In a very real sense, we cease being human. Hence salvation and liberation—that is, becoming human—are as much for those complicit with oppressive social structures as they are for the dispossessed.

10. Justo González, *Mañana: Christian Theology from a Hispanic Perspective* (Nashville: Abingdon Press, 1990), 131–38.

Of all creation, God only speaks to humans. If the doctrine of the *imago Dei*, the image of God, answers the question, Who are we? then God's first instructions answer the question, Why are we here? Together, man and woman as humanity are to rule over creation. But how does one rule over creation? After all, to "rule," to "subdue," to "have dominion over" are disturbing terms reflecting a more patriarchal, totalitarian hierarchy.

If we did not create the earth, and if the earth belongs to God, then the word "rule," as we have come to define it, might be problematic unless we understand ruling God's earth as stewardship, not as human preeminence. To define rule as domination ignores how the exploitive consequences of plunder have wrought havoc and chaos upon creation. To rule is to rule for the welfare of creation, not placing oneself over and above creation but rather remaining cognizant that one is part of creation. To rule to satisfy self-interest only invites the destruction of God's creation. To rule justly, or to be faithful stewards, requires seeking harmony not only with creation but with one another. To disproportionately extract more of the earth's resources to the detriment of others who are more vulnerable, or at the expense of the earth itself, is to move away from and against God's design of creation.

> One can rule by "careless" domination; one can rule by subjecting everything to oneself; one can rule by assuming that everything that isn't oneself is good and has value only as it helps oneself. The first is brutish, the second is arrogant, the third is cynical. That kind of rule, in the creation as in a family, is a kind of ruling that is catastrophic. It ultimately destroys the ruler.
>
> —Joseph Sittler
>
> *Evocations of Grace: The Writings of Joseph Sittler on Ecology, Theology, and Ethics,* ed. Steven Bouma-Prediger and Peter Bakken (Grand Rapids: Eerdmans, 2000), 204–5.

1:28a

Testimony on the Blessing of Sex

During creation, God formed humans in God's own image with the capacity to engage in sexual activity. Once humans were created,

God's first instruction to them was to have sex! Not only is a sexual relationship the first gift given to humans by God, it was a gift that God blessed and declared "good" (1:31). But to say that sex is good is an understatement. Sex is great! It is great because it fosters intimacy within relationships that serves as the basis for healthy and just communities. As such, the first words God addresses to humans, the very first instructions given—even before forbidding eating fruit from the tree of knowledge of good and evil—was to engage in sex. God instructs this new human creation to "be fruitful and multiply," a goal that can be achieved only through copulation. Procreation allows humans to participate and continue in God's creation, for like God, humans have the ability to create new life.

Nevertheless, pronouncements that the sole purpose of sexual intercourse is reproduction are both problematic and damaging. It would be an error to conclude that reproduction is sex's sole and ultimate purpose; for while sex is the source for future generations, it is also the source of extreme pleasure.

> To indulge in intercourse without intending children is to outrage nature.
> —Clement of Alexandria, *Christ the Educator* 2.10.95.

Yet, since the founding of Christianity, an attempt has been made to equate sex with the forbidden fruit. For Augustine sex became the reason for Adam and Eve's expulsion from the garden. Adam covered his genitals with fig leaves not out of a sense of modesty, but rather because Adam, according to Augustine, was sexually aroused. By linking shame and sex to the Christian doctrine of the fall, Augustine argued that the aroused sexual organs of humans signify human will toward the flesh, over and against the spirit.[11] The erect male sex organ symbolized man's rebellion to God, hence, for Augustine, redefining sex as the cause for expulsion from paradise. To desire or participate in sex today links us to Adam, who chose the things of this world rather than the spiritual realm of God.

Augustine's interpretation of the role sex played in the garden reduced sex to an act involving nothing more than the genitals, with

11. Augustine, *City of God* 14.19, 21.

an emphasis on who one engages in sex and the sexual act itself. Sexual ethics is reduced to a fear-driven discourse. Have sex and you will get someone pregnant, you will die of AIDS, you will catch some sexually transmitted disease, or, if female, you will get pregnant or be seen as a "fallen" woman unable to marry a godly man. Yet this verse in Genesis states that sex is blessed by God. Rather than a "just say no," knee-jerk reaction to sexuality, this verse encourages creation's focus on relationships where sex can and should occur.

Frustrating our ability to interpret a pro-sex, pro-body reading of this verse is that for the past two thousand years Christianity created a false dichotomy between the sacred (the spirit) and what was defined as profane (the body). Crucial to Christian thought is the concept that the soul and the flesh struggle against each other for supremacy of the individual. Early Christian writers were highly influenced by this antagonistic body/soul dualism, stressing the danger new believers faced if they succumbed to the mortal body, as opposed to the immortal soul. That which is of the flesh was conceived as being corruptible, while only that which is of the spirit could expect to inherit the eternal. Or as Paul reminded us, "flesh and blood cannot inherit the kingdom of God, nor does the perishable inherit the imperishable" (1 Cor. 15:50). Even though some will argue that the way Paul defined flesh and spirit does not necessarily support the argument in favor of the flesh-spirit divide, this divide still became a salient characteristic of Christianity, with Paul's words being appropriated to justify this divide.

This understanding of a flesh-spirit divide is foreign to the Hebrew Bible; nevertheless, it became a prominent feature of early Christianity through the influence of Neoplatonic thought and Stoic philosophy and its proclivity for devaluing the body. The emphasis on obtaining inner peace through the human will's ability to control passions contributed to the overall pessimism regarding desire, specifically sexual desire. For the Stoics in particular, marriage became the means by which self-control was practiced. The rational reason for engaging in sex became procreation. While many modes of understanding gender and sexual reality developed during Christianity's early years, the body/soul cosmic split was among the most prevalent characteristics of that era. As the early Christian scholar

Tertullian succinctly stated: "Flesh is an earthly, spirit a heavenly, material."[12]

To argue that the flesh is inherently sinful alienates believers from their bodies and, in turn, from their sexuality. Redemption came to be understood as a flight from the body—the material toward the spiritual—an understanding that continues to influence faith communities today. For those seeking spiritual purification, hope for spiritual wholeness was, and continues to be, found in the process of freeing oneself from the sinful influences of one's body or, for Christians, crucifying one's sinful flesh to Jesus' cross. Earthly pleasures like sex are forsaken in remembrance of Christ's ultimate sacrifice.

> I must disfigure that face which contrary to God's commandment I have painted with rouge, white lead, and antimony. I must mortify that body which has been given up to many pleasures. I must make up for my long laughter by constant weeping. I must exchange my soft linen and costly silks for rough goat's hair. I who have pleased my husband and the world in the past, desire now to please Christ.
> —Jerome
>
> Letter CVIII:15, to Eustochium about her mother, Paula (347–404) (NPNF 2/6:203).

What develops from this body/soul dichotomy is a very anti-body perspective, where the body, in and of itself, is evil. But contrary to the body/soul dichotomy constructed by Christianity, this verse stresses that God blesses sex and declares it good.

Not only is this first couple to engage in sex while in paradise, be fruitful, and multiply, but they are also to "fill the earth." Hence, before their first rebellion against God, God already declared that God's will was for them to fill the earth. Ironically, in order for them to obey God's instructions, they eventually would have to leave the garden. As long as they remained in the garden, they could not fulfill God's will. In effect, their future rebellion must have been expected. By rebelling against God, the man and the woman quickened God's ultimate aim of getting them to leave the garden. In a way, sin may be needed to push humanity forward, striving to reach their full potential as they continue to seek the face of God.

12. Tertullian, *To His Wife* 1.4.

1:28b

Testimony of Dominion

Immediately after creating man and woman, God instructs them to be fruitful and multiply (by engaging in sex), and to fill the earth and conquer it. Paradoxically, to fill the earth and conquer it means that they must eventually leave Eden—continuing the process of creation through procreation and labor. According to the text, humans are to have dominion over the fish of the sea, the birds of the air, and all living animals that roam the earth. They, both man and woman, are called to exercise dominion over all things, to jointly subdue and subjugate creation. Yet, since ancient times, conquest has been a male venture. Patriarchy, and its imposition on all human social structures, has worked against the instructions of God for gender equality in domesticating the earth.

Although the verse calls for male and female to jointly have dominion over creation, still it remains problematic. The Hebrew word for "have dominion," *radah*, connotes the absolute power held by the sovereigns of the ancient world. Historically, we have come to read this verse as permission to use and abuse creation, similar to how the ancient rulers used and abused their subjects. Man, like the ancient king, is ordained to rule over all. This understanding of humans occupying the pinnacle of creation has been echoed throughout Christian history, most recently by Pope John Paul II, who stated, "Everything in creation is ordered to man and everything is made subject to him."[13]

To some degree, biblical passages such as this one have justified human domination of nature, specifically the subjugation of nature to a Western Christianity that contributes to the present ecological challenges facing humanity. The eschatological belief that human destiny resides with God in heaven, and that the earth is but a place we sojourn through in order to reach that destiny, has encouraged, at the very least, a neglect of our environment. This view was best articulated by James G. Watt, secretary of the interior during the Reagan administration. As the secretary of the interior, it was Watt's responsibility to safeguard U.S. natural resources and protect the

---

13. Pope John Paul II, *The Gospel of Life* (New York: Random House, 1995), 61.

environment. Carrying out his official governmental responsibilities through a Christian dispensationalist lens led him to conclude, "My responsibility is to follow the Scriptures which call upon us to occupy the land until Jesus returns." For Watt, Jesus is coming soon to rescue the faithful from an earth destined for total destruction. Any attempt to preserve or safeguard the earth is in effect a waste of time, energy, and resources.[14]

Former Secretary Watt is one among many Christians who accept this eschatological worldview. Many Christians today accept the events depicted in the popular *Left Behind* futuristic novel series, written by Tim LaHaye and Jerry B. Jenkins, as Christian prophecies rather than fiction. For these Christians, who accept as truth a dispensationalist view of the "end times," the destruction of the earth is a welcome event because it ushers in Jesus' "second coming" when he will rapture (take away from the earth) those destined to be saved from the apocalypse of a depleted planet. If the world will come to a conflagration, and such an end is close at hand, why worry about the environment?

Just as sexism teaches that a woman finds value, self-worth, and actualization through a man, so too does land require human action as labor to become "developed."

> Once the land had been won, it was treated like a fallen woman. . . . The wilderness, once conquered, was no longer wild, the virgin land, once used, lost her innocence. . . . We treat the land neither reverently, as our mother, nor chivalrously, as a virgin, but contemptuously, as if she were no better than a whore. We rape her. And when we are done, we leave her *and our wastes* behind.
>
> —Mark Gerzon
>
> *A Choice of Heroes* (Boston: Houghton Mifflin, 1982), 20–21.

Land as commodity, as thing, is land as whore. Modernity has taught us to see land as an item to be used, enjoyed, and abused, a gift from God needing domestication. Virgin land is "undeveloped" or "empty." Its value lies only in anticipation of how humans intend to domesticate it.

---

14. Bill Prochnau, "The Watt Controversy," *Washington Post*, June 30, 1981.

This exclusive approach to using land led to an inhumane reading of Genesis 1:28. To claim that this verse justifies domination is to misread the passage. Larry L. Rasmussen reminds us that no word for nature as a separate realm from humans or creation exists in Hebrew, mainly because of the absence of a human-nature dichotomy. Humans are part of, not separate from, nature. This understanding has prevented rabbinical interpretations of this passage from defining "domination" as a form of exploitative subjugation. Rather than rulers of the earth, we are called to be *shomrey 'adamah* (guardians of the earth [in the sense of land, soil]).[15]

The creation story does not make us conquerors; it makes us stewards. The eighteenth-century Quaker William Penn probably said it best, "For we have nothing that we can call our own; no, not our selves: For we are all but Tenants, and at Will too, of the great Lord of our selves, and the rest of this great Farm, the World that we live upon."[16] As caretakers of "this great Farm," humans are responsible before God to protect and preserve the planet's resources so that all of the earth's inhabitants can partake of its fruits. While the concept of stewardship may appear more politically correct than dominion, both concepts remain rooted in an anthropocentric view that keeps humans at the pinnacle of the creation order, reinforcing a hierarchy of humans over, and at times against, nature.

What we can say about this verse is that it is against the aim of creation for one people, at the expense of others and due to their military superiority, to force the majority of the planet's resources to flow toward their borders for their exclusive use. Creation as gift means that all living creatures have a basic right to its resources. To hoard the planet's resources upsets the delicate balance between life and the resources needed to sustain life. To interpret this verse to justify domination of the earth and all that it holds encourages a Christianity that views the environment as an incessant means of satisfying the wants and desires of those with the military superiority

15. Larry L. Rasmussen, *Earth Community, Earth Ethics* (Maryknoll, NY: Orbis, 1996), 231.

16. William Penn, *More Fruits of Solitude Being the Second Part of Reflections and Maxims, Relating to the Conduct of Human Life*, 339:18 (Electronic Text Center, University of Virginia Library, http://etext.virginia.edu/etcbin/toccer-new2?id=PenSoli.sgm&images=images/modeng&data=/texts/english/modeng/parsed&tag=public&part=all).

to hoard the planet's resources. Humans, viewing themselves as the center of the created order, have historically perceived the environment as an unlimited storehouse of raw materials, provided by God for human convenience. Thus the resources of the earth have been sacrificed in the quest for economic growth.

Lawrence H. Summers, former World Bank chief economist, captures the theological concept of subduing and domesticating the earth's resources in an internal agency memo:

> Just between you and me, shouldn't the World Bank be encouraging *more* migration of the dirty industries to LDCs [Less Developed Countries]? . . . The measure of the costs of health impairing pollution depends on the foregone earnings from increased morbidity and mortality. From this point of view, a given amount of health impairing pollution should be done in the country with the lowest cost, which will be the country with the lowest wages. I think the economic logic behind dumping a load of toxic waste in the lowest wage country is despicable and we should face up to that. . . . I've always thought that underpopulated countries in Africa are vastly *under*polluted, their air quality is probably vastly inefficiently low compared to Los Angeles or Mexico City.[17]

Our present global economic structures reduce humans to their economic value, with those of Eurocentric descent possessing an economic privilege that is worth more than those who are disenfranchised.

> We cannot criticize the hierarchy of male over female without ultimately criticizing and overcoming the hierarchy of human over nature.
> —Rosemary Radford Ruether
>
> *Sexism and God-Talk: Toward a Feminist Theology* (Boston: Beacon, 1983), 73.

Still, because the resources of our planet are not limitless, humans must create a harmonious relationship with nature, as with other humans. To exploit the planet's resources is to exploit the planet's marginalized, for both are interconnected.

17. Susan George and Fabrizio Sabelli, *Faith & Credit: The World Bank's Secular Empire* (Boulder, CO: Westview Press, 1994), 98–100.

It is difficult, if not impossible, to speak of one without mentioning the other. Leonardo Boff has given voice to the cry of the oppressed, linking it with the cry of the earth. He insists that the logic and justification that lead the powerful and privileged to exploit and subjugate the world's marginalized is the same logic and justification that plunders the earth's wealth and leads to its devastation.[18]

The exploitation of the earth is partly due to the belief that its resources belong to humans. Yet the psalmist boldly proclaims, "The earth is the LORD's and all that is in it, the world, and those who live in it" (Ps. 24:1). The God who notices the fall of a sparrow is concerned with all of creation. Karen Backer-Fletcher insists that for Christians the incarnation, God becoming flesh, is the act of Divinity joining the dust of the earth to reconcile the broken relationship between God and creation, with humans, as creatures of dust, being part of creation.[19] Thus God's instructions to humanity in this verse must imply environmental responsibilities.

To continue to insist on exploiting the earth's resources and, by extension, exploiting the earth's inhabitants perpetuates our refusal to recognize the damage being committed to the environment. To subdue and subjugate the earth is the ultimate form of oppression, for it brings destruction to life (including human life) on this planet. If liberation and salvation are to come to the earth's disenfranchised, then they must also come to the earth. The earth needs to be saved in order for individuals to also receive salvation. If nature is wasted, depleted, and destroyed, then individuals will not be able to control their destiny. Such a sin cannot be easily atoned, for we are not gods that can resurrect extinct species. This calls for radical changes in the political sphere, changes that if not taken can lead to the domination of all due to limited resources that would continue to be controlled by the wealthy few.

18. Leonardo Boff, *Cry of the Earth, Cry of the Poor*, trans. Phillip Berryman (Maryknoll, NY: Orbis, 1997), xi.
19. Karen Backer-Fletcher, *Sisters of Dust, Sisters of Spirit: Womanist Wordings on God and Creation* (Minneapolis: Fortress Press, 1998), 19.

1:29–30
Testimony of the Animals

The biblical text teaches us that God is the Creator, who brought all of existence into being in just six days. But God is more than simply a Creator; God is also a provider and sustainer. God provided all the seed-bearing plants and trees with seed-bearing fruit to be food for humans. Additionally, God provided all of the wild beasts, the birds of the heaven, and all the living reptiles on the earth foliage and herbs as food. The psalmist sings to the glories of creation, capturing God's role of maintaining life. "[All creatures] look to you to give them their food in due season; when you give to them, they gather it up; when you open your hand, they are filled with good things" (Ps. 104:27–28). We can behold the birds of the air that neither reap nor sow, and yet they are provided for.

Many indigenous religions maintain a sacred respect for creation, lost and historically abused by many Western Christian groups. All that has life is sacred before the Creator of all life, making it difficult to limit spiritual worthiness and well-being to just humans. George "Tink" Tinker reminds us that "in the Native American world, we recognize that interrelatedness as a peer relationship between the two-leggeds and all the others—four-legged, winged, and other living, moving things. This is the real world within which we hope to actualize the ideal world of creational balance and harmony."[20] Earth-centered religions, rooted in the abode of ancestors, are unlike Western religions, which emphasize a heavenly place. The earth provides all that is needed to live a full and abundant life. Like the oceans that are able to support and sustain all life that exists in their waters, so too is the land able to support and sustain all life that exists on it. This abundance becomes evident as humans learn to live in harmony with nature. Shortages occur when humans attempt to impose their will on the fair and natural distribution of nature's resources according to the needs of the people.

---

20. George "Tink" Tinker, "The Bible as a Text in Cultures: Native Americans," in *The Peoples' Bible: New Revised Standard Version with the Apocrypha,* ed. Curtiss Paul DeYoung et al. (Minneapolis: Fortress Press, 2009), 50.

The natural distribution of the earth's resources is disrupted by our choice to eat our fellow living creatures. It is interesting to note that the original intent of creation, as elucidated in these verses, was for all that has life, including humans, to be vegetarians. Killing in Eden, even for food, was considered incongruent with paradise's primeval peace as designed by God. No blood was shed, and no survival of the fittest existed in this idyllic garden. There was truly peace on earth and goodwill toward humans. Since the expulsion from the garden, an attempt to return to Eden has captured the religious imagination. The messianic vision of the future becomes modeled on the past, with the wolf cohabitating with the lamb, the leopard sleeping with the kid, the cow and bear becoming friends, the lion eating straw like the ox, and the child playing with the asp (Isa. 11:6–8).

> These principles of divine ownership (men have possessions but not the ultimate title [of the land]) and of social equity or "commonwealth" are fundamental in the Christian world view. This is why almsgiving in Christian ethics and moral theology has always been treated under the heading of justice, *not of mercy*. In some measure, then, to give to a neighbor in need—to share with him—is actually *giving him what is his own*.
>
> —Joseph Fletcher
>
> *Moral Responsibility: Situation Ethics at Work* (Philadelphia: Westminster Press, 1967), 190.

But why wait for some messianic future to begin modeling our behavior on Eden's paradigm? When we consider the damage humans inflict on the earth because they choose to be carnivorous, it makes sense that the original order of vegetarianism (if not veganism) should be seriously reconsidered. Today, if anyone truly wishes to reduce their carbon footprint and contribute to relieving global hunger, probably the greatest contribution one can make is to become a vegetarian. According to the Food and Agriculture Organization of the United Nations, in a 2006 study titled "Livestock's Long Shadow," our livestock sector is one of the top two or three most significant contributors to the most serious environmental problems faced at every level of society, from local to global, impacting climate change, degradation, air pollution, water pollution, water shortage, and loss of biodiversity. For example, the methane released by cows and pigs, while less prevalent in the air than carbon dioxide, is 23 times more potent as a heat-trapping gas, making livestock responsible for 18 percent of the world's greenhouse gas problem. Additionally, the land used by cows grazing could feed more of the world's population if it were used for crops. According to the study, grazing takes up 26 percent of the land on earth that is not covered by ice, 30 percent if you count the land used to grow feed for the animals.[21]

Besides helping our environment, moving closer to the Eden model can reduce global hunger. If everyone on earth ate like Americans, current food supplies would be able to feed only 2.5 billion people, or about half the world's population. However, if we all ate a subsistence diet, getting only the calories we need, current annual food production could feed 6 billion people. If I consume 5,000 calories daily and my neighbor consumes none, then shouldn't I reduce my intake to about 2,500 daily calories to make it possible for those who receive none to get something? Eating less and consuming more vegetables and fruits, as did the first humans, can substantially reduce global hunger.

> A 10% decrease in beef consumption in the United States, for instance, would release enough grain to feed 60 million people in the less developed nations.
> —Daniel Chiras
>
> *Environmental Science*, 8th ed. (Sudbury, MA: Jones & Bartlett, 2009), 190.

Adopting vegetarianism as found in Eden is not a panacea, but it can contribute to reducing global hunger in underdeveloped nations, and definitely reducing obesity in developed nations such as the United States. If Christians maintain that the body is indeed the temple of God's Holy Spirit, then abusing the body through ingested pollutants is akin to desecrating the temple. Obesity has become an eating disorder afflicting a substantially large portion of Americans. Abusing bodies is sinful behavior. A move toward vegetarianism leads to a healthier lifestyle and uses fewer resources. In effect, becoming a vegetarian can be understood as a social justice act.

21. "Global Warming Culprits: Cars and . . . Cows," *ABC News*, December 13, 2006.

1:31–2:4a

Testimony about the Sabbath

Everything that exists came from God; and with each new day of creation God pronounced it good (1:10, 12, 18, 21, 25). But now, when God saw all that was, the full completion of creation, God determined it to be *very* good, to be perfect. No dichotomy between the goodness of God and the wickedness of the earth exists in the creation story. The earth and all it contains is good because it is derived from God. A common danger exists of disparaging humans and the earth when comparing them to God. Many religions have so demonized matter—as represented by God's good creation—that nothing good can be found in the physical world or among human flesh, and yet neither is inherently evil. While humans may fall short of the glory of God, this does not mean that humans are naturally bad. Humans and the earth are good because God said so, and as such should be celebrated. God does not stand against a supposed wicked earth and its inhabitants; rather, God stands in solidarity with creation, deemed to be good in God's eyes.

To say that all of creation is indeed "very good" assumes that there is nothing intrinsically evil with the original creation. Unlike other creation myths, the biblical creation story has no duality between good and evil beings active in creation, hence explaining the existence of both. God solely creates without any assistance or consort. But if Eden is pristine, we must wonder from where the tempting serpent came. Obviously, God created it as good. Although this passage does not deal with the concept of evil (which we will look at more closely in the commentary on chap. 3), it does set the stage for what will prove to be a theological incongruency. Is God responsible for creating evil? Or more directly, does evil also come from God?

The text informs us that all the elements of heaven and earth were completed. For some scholars not only was the earth completed, but so too was the host of heaven, along with the angels and other creatures that fill it. In any case, on the seventh day, one day after the completion of the heavens and earth, God rested. God blessed the seventh day and made it holy, a time to celebrate the goodness of God's creation, a foretaste of eternal fellowship with the Creator.

Although it is sometimes assumed that the high point of the creation is the arrival of humankind as described in Gen. 1:26–28, in truth the crowning moment of the making of the world does not arrive until the seventh day on which God "rested." In this way the Sabbath is connected with and rooted in the creation of the world.
—Johanna W. H. van Wijk-Bos

Making Wise the Simple: The Torah in Christian Faith and Practice (Grand Rapids: Eerdmans, 2005), 94.

Later, in Exodus, when God gives Moses the Ten Commandments, the fourth one will echo back to the Genesis creation story: Remember the Sabbath and keep it holy. The word "Sabbath" comes from the Hebrew noun based on the verb meaning "to cease, to desist from, to terminate," referring more to the act of ceasing to create than to some exhausted God needing to rest. To associate rest with the Sabbath is more a postbiblical interpretation than how the term was understood by the text's original readers. Although the commandment to keep the Sabbath holy was meant for the Jews, the placement of the commandment's origins in Genesis makes this an obligation on all of humanity, not just the future nation of Israel. In the commandment, God instructs humans to work six days; but on the seventh they and their servants are to engage in no work whatsoever (Exod. 20:8–10). The poor and the rich, regardless of status, equally share in the act of resting.

But how do we actually keep this seventh day holy? A difference exists between taking a day to rest and institutionalizing and codifying the Sabbath with rules and regulations. Soon after the commandment was given, a fence was erected around the Torah to serve as a protective barrier that would assure compliance. This fence directed the faithful as to what could or could not be done on the Sabbath so it would be properly observed. For example, candles were to be lit prior to sunset rather than at sunset lest the appropriate time accidently pass and the Sabbath become defiled. Later, added rules border on the absurd. Even to this day, some religious traditions consider watching television, playing cards or games, hearing music, or enjoying a good joke sinful if conducted on the Sabbath. Jesus also struggled with the codification of the Sabbath in his own day, being chastised by the religious leaders for curing a man with a withered hand on the Sabbath (Matt. 12:9–14). Yet he reminds us that the Sabbath is made for humans, not humans for the Sabbath (Mark 2:27).

All too often, when we read this commandment, or study the Genesis story of the establishment of the Sabbath, we place the emphasis on taking a day off, mainly because we have become accustomed to reading the biblical text through the eyes of white middle-class America. Taking a day off from our busy schedules is especially pleasing due to our overworked lives. But as tempting as it may be to focus on the Sabbath, Justo González cautions us about ignoring how our social location influences how Scripture is interpreted. He recounts a sermon he heard at a church composed mainly of the undocumented and day laborers. The minister began by asking how many within the congregation worked six days last week. Five days? Four days? Few in the congregation were able to raise their hands to any of these questions. The preacher then asked how many would have wanted to work six days last week but were unable to find employment. Almost every hand went up. To this response, the minister asked, "How, then, are we to obey the law of God that commands that we shall work six days, when we cannot even find work for a single day?"[22]

When the poor read the biblical text through their own eyes, they teach those with middle- and upper-class privilege that God's commandment is more than the capricious imposition of a Deity to choose one day in seven to do nothing. Rather, God establishes symmetry and balance in the created order, a rhythm, in this case between work and rest. Working six days is counterbalanced with resting one. When we read this text from the position of economic privilege, we assume the privilege of being employed, ignoring the segments of our society that lack opportunities for gainful employment due to their race, ethnicity, gender, or class. By imposing on the text our assumptions of class privilege, we are oblivious to the first part of the Genesis story—God worked for six days.

Only when we begin to read the Bible from the margins are we challenged and confronted with how much our present economic

22. González, *Santa Biblia*, 59–60.

structures benefit by ignoring that God worked six days and wants us to do likewise. For our economy to work at top efficiency, an "acceptable" unemployment rate must be maintained. A healthy unemployment rate assures the existence of a reserve army of underskilled and undereducated laborers that would keep wages depressed. Generally speaking, whenever the unemployment rate drops too low, the stock market gets jittery and begins a downward turn because full employment is bad for business. Full employment means that companies would have to pay higher wages in order to attract and retain employees. Paying higher wages, an expense, negatively affects corporate profits, reducing the bottom line. When we consider that those who are unemployed are disproportionately people of color, those living on the margins, we begin to realize that our economic system is structured so that certain segments of the population are unable to keep God's commandment, "Six days you shall labor." To read these verses concerning the Sabbath in Genesis is to provide a biblical critique as to how we, as a nation, economically organize ourselves.

2:4b–7

Testimony of Adam

There are two creation stories in Genesis, the second one beginning with 2:4b. These two accounts are penned by different authors and are separated from each other by about four centuries, with this second creation story being the older of the two. The first creation story is attributed to the P source, while J is believed to be responsible for the second. What the reader might first notice is the different style and vocabulary employed in the two accounts. The first account sounds more like a psalm or a liturgical song, while the second account sounds more like a parable. Also, the order of creation is quite different in each of the stories. Unlike the first creation story, which began with God's spirit hovering over the waters, the second one begins in the desert, a barren earth with no wild bush or wild plant, an earth that has yet to experience rain or anyone to till its soil. While the first creation story concentrates on how the universe came into being, the second creation story is centered on the forming of man (not necessarily woman) and meeting his needs. One can also note that it takes God six days to bring the world into being in the first account; the second account mentions only one day of creation. Also, unlike the first creation story in which God *creates* (*bara'*) by simply speaking and reality comes into being, this second story provides us with a more anthropomorphic God—a God who *makes* (*yatsar*) from the ground's dust. This is a God who also breathes into nostrils, plants a garden, takes man's rib, walks in the garden, and converses with humans.

> The "earth is his mother"; he comes out of her womb. Of course, the ground from which man is taken is still not cursed but the blessed ground.... Man does not "have" a body; he does not "have" a soul; rather he "is" body and soul.
> —Dietrich Bonhoeffer
>
> *Creation and Fall: A Theological Interpretation of Genesis 1–3*, trans. John C. Fletcher (New York: Macmillan, 1959), 46.

Unlike the first creation story in which on the sixth day God creates male and female in God's own image, this second creation story starts with God forming man (not woman) to till the ground. Man has an occupation before man is even created. Like a potter, God fashions man from the soil's clay. Hence man (*'adam*) comes from the ground (*'adamah*) that he is called to till. Yet, later in the story, we are told that man's punishment for disobedience is to till the ground (3:23). Regardless of this inconsistency, man remains a literal creation of his environment, the dust of the earth, intimately formed from the hands of God. Humans, who are of the earth, are unable to claim equality with their Creator.

We come from dust, and when we die, to the dust we shall return (3:19).

We have always assumed that Adam, the first "man," was male. However, some feminist biblical scholars, like Phyllis Trible, have questioned this assumption. Trible insists on interpreting God's first created human, called *ha'adam*, a generic term for humankind, as androgynous (incorporating both sexes). God would eventually take a rib of this androgynous creature and form woman; hence the sexes are divided and the one becomes two. While the first act, according to Trible, was the creation of androgyny, the final act becomes the creation of sexuality (2:23).[23] One became two, and from that point forward, through sexual union, two will again become one.

The idea that the first earth creature was androgynous echoes Plato's *Symposium*, where Aristophanes claims that primeval humans were "not two as they are now, but originally three in number; there was man, woman, and the union of the two, having a name corresponding to this double nature, which had once a real existence, but now lost, and the word 'Androgynous' is only preserved as a term of reproach."[24] This creature had four hands and feet, and two faces and two privy members. The male, female, and hermaphrodite creature was three as the sun, moon, and earth are three. They were powerful and dared to attack the gods. Sensing a threat, the gods bisected them to diminish their strength. This partition into two caused the now divided creature to enter a quest to find its "other half" to reconstitute the primeval unity of one. Or, as Aristophanes recounts it, "each desiring his other half, came together, and throwing their arms about one another, entwined in mutual embraces, longing to grow into one."[25]

Besides questioning this first human's gender, we should also question its race. Genesis is silent concerning the race of the first man, maybe because it does not matter. Nevertheless, most of our images, whether they be on our churches' stained-glass windows, or in our pictorial books, depict the first man and woman as white, which raises the question that if they were white, where did black people (or any other race for that matter—brown, red, yellow, or any combination thereof) come from? But why assume that the first man was white? Some have argued that the substance God used to form man was the soil of the ground. Now, if the richest and most fertile soil is black, and God chose the best soil for God's ultimate creation, wouldn't the skin of that creation resemble the ingredient used? Maybe the question we should be asking is, where do whites come from?

23. Phyllis Trible, "Eve and Adam: Genesis 2–3 Reread" (1973), in *Biblical Studies Alternatively: An Introductory Reader,* comp. Susanne Scholz (Upper Saddle River, NJ: Prentice Hall, 2003), 94–96.
24. Plato, "Symposium," *The Philosophy of Plato,* ed. Irwin Edman (New York: Simon & Schuster, 1928), 353.
25. Ibid., 355.

But then again, these are the wrong questions to ask from the text. To do so will only produce wrong answers. While we have no idea what color the first humans were, the Bible does record the presence of Africans in Genesis and beyond. Unfortunately, reading the text for centuries through Eurocentric eyes has made them invisible. For example, in Genesis 10:8–12, the founder of civilization in Mesopotamia, Nimrod, is called the son of Cush. Cush is the most commonly used term in the biblical text to designate a person's black color. "Cush" was the name given by the Egyptians to the people living south of them. The Hebrews picked up this term and used it to refer to the people from the interior regions of Africa. When the Hebrew biblical text was translated into Greek (the Septuagint), the most frequent translation for Cush was *Aithiops,* which literally meant "burnt face." While *Aithiops* is translated into English as "Ethiopian," the term was also used to refer to Africans of dark skin pigmentation with African physical features (wide nose, hair texture, and so on).

In the Hebrew Bible, Cush is usually Ethiopia; however, the term was also used to refer to the Egyptians. In short, Cush (Ethiopia), Nubia, Put (Phut), and Egypt were not always distinct geographic entities, but can be understood as referring essentially to the ancestors of the same people group, Africans. By defining the terms that reveal the presence of Africans in the Bible, we quickly discover their major contributions. Besides Nimrod and Moses' Cushite wife, we also discover that the prophet Zephaniah is the son of Cushi. The Hebrew word *Phinehas,* a derivative from the Egyptian word *Pa-Nehsi,* means Nubian or Negro. Phinehas is also the proper name of Aaron's grandson (Moses' grandnephew), the high priest Eli's son (during the prophet Samuel's youth), and numerous Jews in postexilic times.[26] Why call a child "Negro" if he or she was not black? Other biblical characters who most certainly were African were: Hagar, Sarah's maid and Abraham's concubine (Gen. 16), Jeremiah's benefactor Ebed-melech (Jer. 38–39), the Ethiopian king Tirhakah

---

26. Charles Copher, "The Black Presence on the Old Testament," in *Stony the Road We Trod: African American Biblical Interpretation,* ed. Cain Hope Felder (Minneapolis: Fortress Press, 1991), 146–64.

(Isa. 37:9), the queen of Sheba (1 Kgs. 10), Simon of Cyrene (Matt. 27:32), and the Ethiopian eunuch (Acts 8).

The text tells us that after God formed man, God breathed into his nostrils the breath of life, bringing him to life. With this divine act, man became a living being. This act answers the ancient question, where do we come from? The answer: all human life, and as we will soon see all life, comes from God, who forms us and gives us God's spirit. God is the source of life, and as such is the God of life. If God was to withhold God's breath, we would cease to exist. As the psalmist reminds us: "You [God] give breath, and they are created; you keep renewing the face of the earth" (Ps. 104:30, my trans.). The breath of life God breathed into the clay creature's nostrils is referred to in Hebrew as *ruah*, a word that also means "wind" and "spirit." God's spirit is what gives us life and is what continues to dwell within us.

Man is completed when he possesses a soul. The Hebrew word used for living "being" is *nephesh*, which can also be translated as "soul." The word had psychical uses expressive of desire, emotions, feelings, and appetite.

> The biblical narrative provides a picture of the divinity directly offering an image and likeness of the divine self in the soul and body of woman and man.
>
> —Dwight N. Hopkins
>
> *Being Human: Race, Culture, and Religion* (Minneapolis: Fortress Press, 2005), 126.

It is important to note that throughout Genesis, as well as the entire Hebrew Bible, the later philosophical sense of the soul (*nephesh*) as a noncorporeal entity that survives the body after its death did not exist. The use of this term connoted personal, temporal physical life being lived in the present.[27] For this reason, when the biblical text speaks of resurrection, it is always a physical, bodily resurrection—not the rising of some spiritual being. It is not the soul that lives on, but the body and all it encompasses that will arise from the dead and live. The prophet Daniel, commenting on the day of resurrection, reminds us

---

27. Suzanne Noffke, "Soul," in *The New Dictionary of Catholic Spirituality*, ed. Michael Downey (Collegeville, MN: The Liturgical Press, 1993), 909.

that "many of those who sleep in the dust of the earth shall awake, some to everlasting life, and some to shame and everlasting contempt" (Dan. 12:2).

Unfortunately, Christian theology soon created a dichotomy between the flesh or body (the profane) and the soul or spirit (the sacred), with the latter being superior to the former. This dichotomy had devastating implications for the future development of Christianity. Many Christians have come to believe that the soul and the flesh were forced to struggle against each other for supremacy of the individual. Early Christian writers were highly influenced by this antagonistic body/soul dualism, stressing the danger new believers faced if they succumbed to the mortal body. That which is of the flesh was conceived as being corruptible, while only that which is of the spirit could expect to inherit the eternal (1 Cor. 15:50). Spiritual development in the early Christian church came at the expense of the body, in which nothing good was believed to dwell. Paul illustrated this point: "For I know that nothing good dwells within me, that is, in my flesh. I can will what is right, but I cannot do it. . . . Wretched man that I am! Who will rescue me from this body of death? . . . So then, with my mind I am a slave to the law of God, but with my flesh I am a slave to the law of sin" (Rom. 7:18, 24, 25).

In the early church, the flesh became inherently sinful, alienating believers from their bodies. Redemption came to be understood as a flight from the body—the material toward the spiritual—an understanding that continues to influence the faith community today. For those seeking spiritual purification, hope for spiritual wholeness was, and continues to be, found in the process of freeing one's self from the sinful influences of one's body. Earthly pleasures are forsaken in remembrance of Christ's ultimate sacrifice, or as Paul reminds us, "those who belong to Christ Jesus have crucified the flesh with its passions and desires" (Gal. 5:24). Unfortunately, what developed from this body/soul dichotomy is an anti-body perspective from which the body is considered as evil.

God breathed life into human bodies, bodies created by God, indicating God's view of the body. The body is not the focus of all evil, but it is good because God formed it with God's own hands. For Christians the theological concept of the incarnation, God taking on flesh, only demonstrates the high regard God holds for the body. The body is so good that even God takes on bodily form through Jesus Christ.

2:8–17

Second Testimony of the Earth

God then planted a garden in Eden, located somewhere in the east, and placed God's first creation, man, in the garden. The Hebrew word for Eden, *'eden,* has also been used in the Scriptures to refer to delicacies and delight. No doubt the word conjured up images of paradise, a garden of delight both beautiful and fruitful, for the ancient reader of the text. The prophet Ezekiel would later refer to Eden as God's garden, as opposed to a garden planted for the first man. It is located on God's holy mountain from where the primal human was thrown down and driven out by a guardian cherub (Ezek. 28:13–16).

Although we do not know where this garden was located, the writer seemed to have some idea, locating it where the river that flowed through the garden divided into four: the river Pishon, which encircled the land of Havilah (Arabia or India?), where there is gold, onyx stone, and bdellium (an aromatic resin); the river Gihon, which encircled the whole land of the Cush (Ethiopia or the land of the Kassites?); the river Tigris, which flows east toward Ashur; and the Euphrates. While the Tigris and Euphrates are identifiable, the first two rivers mentioned, the Pishon and Gihon, are not. Additionally, the two identifiable rivers do not have, nor have they had, a common source as indicated by the text (2:10), so even they are in question. Hence any attempt to pinpoint Eden based on the text is pure speculation. Some scholars have hypothesized that the four mentioned rivers, like the four corners or directions of the earth, represent in the ancient mind the four rivers that encircled the then-known world, with the Pishon identified with either the Indus or Ganges and the Gihon identified with either the Nile or the Nubian Nile.

Regardless of where Eden is located, what makes the mention of the four rivers interesting is that the author attempted to locate the story within his or her known physical world. The garden of Eden, whether real or mythical, is connected to our physical earth.

From the barren ground, God caused an oasis to spring up, containing every kind of tree with desirable fruit that was pleasing to the eye. This garden is planted by God to serve as a gracious gift for the man; thus it becomes Adam's garden. In the middle of the garden, God planted two trees: the tree of life and the tree of death, called the tree of the knowledge of good and evil, because, as we shall soon see, whoever eats from it would die. Archie C. C. Lee observes that "the two trees, the fruits of which are forbidden to Adam and Eve, represent the two aspirations of human beings— a longing for knowledge and a quest for immortality."[28] Not much is said about these trees outside of what appears in the second and third chapters of Genesis. The tree of life, for Christians, reappears as a reward for the faithful to feed on at the end of the biblical story in the book of Revelation (Rev. 22:14). When the new Jerusalem is established, trees of life will appear on both banks of the river of the water of life that will rise from the throne of God. And the leaves from these trees of life will be for the healing of the nations (Rev. 22:1–2).

Unlike the first creation story, in the second story God is more present in the everyday life of the man, making him a partner in God's work. Man was placed in the garden to attend to it, to till its soil and bring forth its fruit. The ancient question, "Why do I exist?" is answered: to partner with God on a task of maintaining the integrity of the planet. We transcend our individual self when we live into our role of serving as custodian to God's creation, not just to till the ground but to keep the planet productive.

> Attempts to locate a geographical site of Eden are as foolish as trying to identify the spot on the road from Jerusalem to Jericho where the traveler was attacked by robbers in the parable of the Good Samaritan.
>
> —Alan Richardson
>
> *Genesis 1–11: The Creation Stories and the Modern World View* (London: SCM Press, 1953), 62.

---

28. Archie C. C. Lee, "The Chinese Creation Myth of Nu Kua and the Biblical Narrative in Genesis 1–11," in *Voices from the Margins: Interpreting the Bible in the Third World,* ed. R. S. Sugirtharajah (Maryknoll, NY: Orbis, 1995), 375.

To imagine an idyllic world absent of work contradicts the biblical text. Within the paradise called Eden, humans were intended to labor, not to sit idly and simply pick fruit whenever they were hungry. Work is not a curse, regardless of what we may think. Human labor is part of the divine economy. Together, God and humans are responsible for preserving the earth; God sustains and humans maintain. Adam, who is derived from the soil, has a special relationship with God's creation. Adam literally receives life from the soil; he is not just formed from it, but depends on its produce to survive. And, while it may appear that the author assumed that the natural occupation of humans was farming, one can argue that any labor, including farming, that makes this earth and its inhabitants better answers the question, "Why do I exist?" Today, to engage in business practices that make money on the backs of others, without contributing to the betterment of the planet, demonstrates how far we have fallen from the original purpose of human existence. One needs to just observe the "creative financing" employed by Wall Street that brought about the 2008 great recession, which enriched some who produced nothing at the expense of many who work hard each and every day, to provide proof for this proposition.

Adam was created to live in and attend to paradise. He was allowed to eat the fruit of any of the garden's trees, except for the tree of the knowledge of good and evil, for if he did, he would surely die. But how can humans know good or evil, or even death, if they do not partake of the forbidden fruit? It is important to note that "good and evil" here refer to the wisdom obtained through experience rather than any understanding of a moral code. Why would God deny humans experiential knowledge? Is God commanding that the first human remain ignorant and simply trust God with childlike innocence? But to eat from this tree is to experience life, all its pleasures and all its pains. To eat from this tree is to become fully human. Eating from the tree moves humans from the childlike innocence of the garden toward maturation that experiences and understands knowledge and wisdom. If God did not want humans to taste the fruit of knowledge, why then did God plant this tree? To tempt humans? To demarcate God's ultimate authority?

To complicate the story further, God said that death will come on the day the forbidden fruit is eaten. Yet, as we will soon discover, death did not come on that day. Indeed, both Adam and Eve lived for several centuries after eating from the forbidden tree. Was this the kind of hyperbole most parents use when speaking to children to scare them into obedience? If you take candy from a stranger, you will die. We can interpret the passage to say it meant spiritual death, but the danger with such interpretations is that we read our theology into the text so as to save God from what God purportedly said.

Furthermore, it is important to remember that woman is not yet created, so she did not get to hear God's admonishment. Her information about the consequences of eating from the tree was secondhand. We are left wondering who eventually told her about the prohibition. Was it Adam? Was it God? Or did anyone even bother to tell her? This may be why she thought that even touching the tree would also cause death (3:3). Regardless, the text wants the reader to know that disobedience, rebellion against God's instructions, has consequences—in this case, death, a death that does not take place on the day of rebellion. Strangely, the tree of life is not mentioned in God's admonition, leaving one to wonder if the first humans could have eaten from this tree without any consequences.

One could assume that living in paradise would be innocent bliss. Not so, says Søren Kierkegaard in *The Concept of Dread* (1844). Writing under the pseudonym Vigilius Haufniensis (Watcher of the Marketplace), he attempts to understand Adam's state of mind prior to his rebellion against God and his subsequent expulsion from the garden of Eden. Although Adam may be living in a state of peace and tranquility, he is simultaneously living in a state of dread. (And so are we.) But what exactly does Adam dread? He dreads nothing— literally no thing. Adam dreads the freedom he possesses because of the possibilities it offers. He does not dread what is, but what could be, what he can do with the freedom he has. We can experience Adam's dread every time we look over a cliff. Although we may fear losing our footing and falling, we also dread voluntarily hurling ourselves into the chasm; or as Kierkegaard would say, "One may liken dread to dizziness. He whose eye chances to look down into the

yawning abyss becomes dizzy" (with the yawning abyss symbolizing our freedom).[29]

> **Boredom is the root of all evil. The history of this can be traced from the very beginning of the world. The gods were bored, so they created man. Adam was bored because he was alone, and so Eve was created. Thus boredom entered the world and increased in proportion to the increase in population. . . . Consider the consequences of this boredom. Humanity fell from its lofty heights, first because of Eve, and then from the Tower of Babel.**
>
> **—Søren Kierkegaard**
>
> *Either/Or*, trans. David F. Swenson and Lillian Marvin Swenson, 2 vols. (Garden City, NY: Doubleday Anchor Book, 1959), 1:282.

It is the forbidden fruit that one imagines tastes sweeter. When God forbids Adam to eat from the tree of the knowledge of good and evil, Adam enters a state of dread because he is awakened to the possibility of freedom. The knowledge that he can disobey God arouses a desire to do so, for there is nothing prohibiting him from sinning but himself. The future that does not yet exist, the future that is nothing, Adam must create by his actions, his praxis—so unlike the past, which was already created for him. In a sense, Adam creates who he is in the future and dreads not finding himself there. He dreads failing in the creation of self. Dread becomes the fear of Adam's (and our) freedom. As Jean-Paul Sartre reminds us, "Man is nothing else but what he makes of himself"; thus "we are condemned to be free."[30]

2:18–23

Testimony of the Woman

God noticed that man was alone, and it was not good. In the idyllic garden of perfection, God was not enough. Man needed more than just a relationship with his Creator; man needed a partner, someone with whom there could be intimacy. Humans are social creatures.

---

29. Søren Kierkegaard, *The Concept of Dread* (1844), trans. Walter Lowrie (Princeton: Princeton University Press, 1957), 55.
30. Jean-Paul Sartre, *Existentialism*, trans. Bernard Frechtman (New York: Philosophical Library, 1947), 18, 27.

From the beginning, humans, as relational beings, are meant to be in community, to exist with and for others. Humans were conceived by God to be in relationship with their Creator, and as an extension of that relationship, they were created to be in relationship with each other. To be alone, apart from a community, is not good. Alone, humans (especially infants and children) can neither physically nor psychologically develop or survive.

God decides to create a "helper" to serve as man's partner, so he would not be alone. But God does not immediately create woman; God first creates the wild beasts on the land and the birds of the heavens. In the first creation story, God simply spoke and things came into being. Here God is portrayed as an artisan, forming creatures from the clay of the earth. God then brings all these creatures to life and parades them before man, who proceeds to name them, thus indicating man's dominance over them. Naming establishes conceptual order to human reality. Whatever man called the creature, it became more than just the animal's name; it located the creature within its relationship to man, specifically how the creature would be a helpmate and serve man. In other words, the animals were objectified. Nevertheless, there is a storytelling quality to the narrative as all the animals come before man for his approval and christening; then trotting off, they live in blissful harmony within the garden among all the other creatures created by God.

None of the animals God created from the dust of the ground (the same substance used to form man) made for a suitable mate (suggesting bestiality?). So God decides to create a woman from the same flesh as man, to serve as the perfect helpmate. Unfortunately, this version of the creation of humanity has proven to be more problematic than the earlier version of 1:27, for it has been and continues to be used to justify women's subjugation to men. It has led theologians like John Calvin to conclude that "the vulgar proverb, indeed, is that [woman] is a necessary evil . . . but the voice of God . . . declares that woman is given as a companion and an associate to the man, to assist him to live well."[31] However, the Hebrew word used

---

31. John Calvin, *Commentaries on the First Book of Moses Called Genesis*, trans. John King, 2 vols. (1843–1845; repr. Grand Rapids: Eerdmans, 1948), 1:129.

in the text for "helper," *'ezer*, is derived from the root word mean-ing "support" or "help." Throughout the Bible, the use of *'ezer* does not imply subordination or inferiority for the one who is doing the helping. For example, God is referred to as the "father [who] was my *'ezer*" (Exod. 18:4). The psalmist proclaims God as being the "*'ezer* of the orphan," and declares, "The LORD is on my side to help [*'ezer*] me" (Pss. 10:14; 118:7). Nowhere in the biblical text where God is referred to as our *'ezer*, our helper, does the term imply subservience. Why then do we assume it does when referred to a woman? A bet-ter translation for *'ezer* might be "companion," thus reinforcing the hierarchical-free relationship originally intended in creation.

Still, throughout history Jews and Christians have argued that the creation of woman was secondary, hence placing her at a lower status than man. Because woman is the last to be created, she is infe-rior to man, who was created first. For centuries, a natural hierar-chy has been assumed to be related to the order of creation. God creates natural dualism: spirit-flesh, rational-emotional, subject-object, and male-female. Because man is closer to the spirit, according to this misogynist logic, he is a ratio-nal subject ordained to rule. Following this same reason, because woman is closer to the flesh, she is an emotional object ordained to be ruled. Thus sub-jecting woman to man becomes the natural manifestation of subjecting passion to reason.

> The Apostle has made known to us certain three unions, Christ and the Church, husband and wife, spirit and flesh. Of these the former consult for the good of the latter, the latter wait upon the former. All the things are good, when, in them, certain set over by way of pre-eminence, certain made subject in a becoming manner, observe the beauty of order.
>
> —**Augustine of Hippo**
>
> *On Continence* 23 (NPNF 1/3:388).

But others insist that the last will be first. Creation is not a linearly declining process ending with the creation of woman; rather, it is a circular process, where both ends equally come together at the pin-nacle of the circle, at the pinnacle of creation. The creation of man at one point of the circle is at the same spot as the creation of woman at the end of that same circle. Thus the circle is closed with the forming of woman. Woman here is not seen as some sort of afterthought, but as the culmination of creative activity.

It is important to note that the man had no part in the creation of the woman; this was solely a divine act. The man does not get to see how God makes the woman; hence the miracle of life remains a mystery. Instead, God caused the man to fall into a deep magical sleep. While the man slept, God took one of his ribs and enclosed it in flesh to build the woman. The word translated as "rib," *tsela'*, is usually translated in other biblical verses as "side"; hence God creates woman from man's side. For the first and only time, a man "births" a woman, appropriating the woman's biological function of birthing new life.

Regardless of how we reread this text to highlight its liberating message, the fact remains that these verses have successfully been used throughout history to subjugate women, no matter how much we care to protest its historical misuse. Paul would eventually use this verse to require the subjugation of women, manifested in the veiling of their heads: "A man ought not to have his head veiled, since he is the image and reflection [or glory] of God; but woman is the reflection [or glory] of man" (1 Cor. 11:7).

Women as the glory of man would lead some to think that women's salvation would rely on men or on becoming like men. For example, in the last verse of the gnostic *Gospel of Thomas*, Peter voices the unworthiness of Mary because she is not male. Capturing the sentiments of the time, women's worthiness could only occur if they abandoned their gender and sexuality. "Simon Peter said to [the disciples]: 'Let Mary leave us, for women are not worthy of life.' Jesus said, 'I myself shall lead her in order to make her male, so

> There Adam slept, and God formed the body of woman from one of his ribs, signifying that she should stand at his side as a companion and never lie at his feet like a slave, and also that he should love her as his own flesh.
>
> —Christine de Pizan
>
> *The Book of the City Ladies* (1405), quoted in *A Reformation Reader: Primary Texts with Introductions*, ed. Denis R. Janz, 2nd ed. (Minneapolis: Fortress Press, 2008), 16.

that she too may become a living spirit resembling you males. For every woman who will make herself male will enter the kingdom of heaven.'"[32]

Creating woman from the rib of man leads liberationist theologian Rosemary Radford Ruether to conclude:

> This story of creation of the man, and then the woman from his rib, is even more androcentric than Gen. 1:27. Although Eve is a member of the same flesh (species) as Adam and hence able to be a partner with him in a way the animals are not, this is hardly an egalitarian partnership. . . . The man is both a male individual and the physical source of the woman. She is not denigrated as evil, but neither is she a free-standing person in a companionship of social equals. His priority and her derivative origin from him locate her as both an extension of him and partner to aid him in procreation and family life. She is "of him" and "for him" in a way that disallows the possibility that she can be "for herself," as he is for himself.[33]

When God presented the woman to man, the man was overjoyed. This new creature was bone from his bone and flesh from his flesh. He called (thus implying authority over) the new creature "woman," for it was taken from man. Although the words "man" and "woman" in Hebrew are not derived from the same root and the origin of these words is uncertain, it is generally accepted that the basis for the root word for "woman" is derived from the Assyrian word *anašui,* which means "to be weak, sick."[34] Still, as problematic as this passage may be, in his response to woman, man discovers himself, as both become able to transcend their base, self-centered instincts to become community, each for the other.

32. *The Gospel According to Thomas* 50.114, trans. Thomas O. Lambdin, in *The Nag Hammadi Library,* ed. James M. Robinson, rev. ed. (San Francisco: HarperSanFrancisco, 1988), 138.

33. Rosemary Radford Ruether, *Women and Redemption: A Theological History* (Minneapolis: Fortress Press, 1998), 26.

34. Otto J. Baab, "Sex, Sexual Behavior," in *The Interpreter's Dictionary of the Bible,* vol. 4, ed. George Arthur Buttrick (Nashville: Abingdon Press, 1962), 297.

FURTHER REFLECTIONS
Lilith

The appearance of two creation stories in Genesis led early rabbinic readers of the text to imagine that Adam had two separate wives.[35] Adam's first wife, who arose from the dust of the ground in 1:26, was called Lilith. Being created at the same time as Adam, she insisted and demanded total equality. Her "sin," which serves as a warning for all wives, was her refusal to submit to the man's authority. Not surprisingly Adam rebuffed her attempts to treat her as an equal, so Lilith left Eden. But God sent three angels (Senoy, Sansenoy, and Semangelof) to bring her back to the garden. They caught up to her at the Sea of Reeds, attempting to persuade her to return. In spite of their efforts, Lilith refused unless she could be treated as an equal. The angels, frustrated, cursed her. From that day forward, one hundred of her demon children are destined to die each and every day. She countered the angels' curse by vowing to prey on women in labor and their babies.

After this, she labored to get Adam and Eve expelled from the garden. Some interpreters of the text have even said she was the tempting serpent. Since her success in getting humans to rebel against God, she has continued her attacks on humanity, being blamed for the death of small children. To this day, whenever a woman has a stillborn birth, or whenever an infant dies in its cradle, Lilith is to blame. Many pregnant women, to ward off her influence, wear amulets bearing the names of the three angels sent to fetch her back to Eden.

Lilith appears only once in the biblical text. Isaiah 34:14 describes God's prophetic judgment on Edom. Her brief mention finds her in the company of unclean animals in what will become a wasteland. Hence she is believed to haunt deserted and desolated places, where the hyenas and satyrs make their home. She wandered the earth until meeting Sammael, head of the fallen angels, whom she

---

35. Babylonian Talmud, *Erubin* 100b; *Niddah* 24b.

married.[36] The Talmud describes her as having long hair and wings.[37] By the medieval period, Lilith was identified as the grandmother of the devil and the patroness of witches. Men who sleep alone must beware they are not stalked by this she-devil.

According to 2:18, God realized that it was not good for man, Adam, to be alone, hence the second story of creation and the forming of Eve. Unlike Lilith, Eve was not created equal to man, but came from man; that is, she was birthed by man. According to Mary Daly, "language for millennia has affirmed the fact that Eve was born from Adam, the first among history's unmarried pregnant males who courageously chose childbirth under sedation rather than abortion, consequently obtaining a child-bride."[38]

So from Adam his second wife springs forth; and from her, humanity. Adam's first wife, Lilith, meanwhile refused to submit to Adam's authority, and as punishment was made sterile. She demanded equality and instead was demonized, maybe as a warning to Eve not to follow in her footsteps. Judith Plaskow attempts to de-demonize this "uppity woman":

> Adam was happy now [with his second wife], and Eve, though she occasionally sensed capacities within herself that remained undeveloped, was basically satisfied with the role of Adam's wife and helper. . . . After this encounter [repelling an attempt by Lilith to reenter Eden], seeds of curiosity and doubt began to grow in Eve's mind. Was Lilith indeed just another woman? Adam had said she was a demon. Another woman! The very idea attracted Eve. . . . [H]ow beautiful and strong Lilith had looked! How bravely she had fought! Slowly, slowly, Eve began to think about the limits of her own life within the garden.[39]

---

36. The Jewish folktales and legends concerning Lilith spread during the Middle Ages; specifically in the anonymous work *Alphabet of Ben Sira* composed in an aggadic midrash style. For the complete story, see David Stern and Mark J. Mirsky, *Rabbinic Fantasies: Imaginative Narratives from Classical Hebrew Literature* (New Haven: Yale University Press, 1990), 183–84.

37. Babylonian Talmud, *Erubin* 18b, 100b; *Niddah* 24b; *Shabbath* 151b.

38. Mary Daly, *Beyond God the Father: Toward a Philosophy of Women's Liberation* (Boston: Beacon, 1973), 195.

39. Judith Plaskow Goldenberg, "Epilogue: The Coming of Lilith," in *Religion and Sexism: Images of Woman in the Jewish and Christian Traditions*, ed. Rosemary Radford Ruether (New York: Simon & Schuster, 1974), 341–42.

2:24–25

Testimonies of the First Man and Woman

For this reason, a man will leave his father and mother, from whom his own bone and flesh was formed, cleave to his wife, and the two will become one flesh. Genesis provides a definition for the ideal marriage before it becomes institutionalized and before the first human rebellion (or fall) occurs. This ideal marriage is presented not as a covenant, which is more apropos for business contractual transactions, but as a familial relationship rooted in the action "clings to" or "cleaves to" (KJV, RSV), that is, sexual intercourse. We are told that this familial bond created between the two is to be stronger than the previous relationship existing between parents and child. It is interesting to note that the man leaves a father and mother, even though Adam as the first man supposedly had no father or mother. No mention of the woman's parents is made, thus reinforcing the concept of her independence from patriarchal structures, which unfortunately will soon radically change with the first rebellion.

Although the passage may provide a paradigm for an ideal marriage, we must use caution in assuming that the "cleaving" that took place between the first man and the first woman was a marriage as we understand it today. Marriage was neither required in the biblical text nor universally accepted throughout early Western Christendom as a prerequisite for sex. Before marriage was elevated to a sacrament during the Council of Trent (1563), it was not regarded as sacred. The ideas that marriage had to be licensed by the state and sanctioned by the church are modern innovations. Marriage was mainly a civil arrangement void of clergy-officiated ceremonies. The definition of marriage has always been evolving, from an understanding of marriage along the lines of property rights, to marriage as a means for procreation, to a family-dominated arrangement designed to protect wealth, to more recently as a response to attraction, love, and mutual respect. In fact, what we call the traditional marriage is quite a modern invention (since about the seventeenth century). Our modern definition of the traditional marriage based on love, trust, vulnerability, and commitment is really not traditional; it is also not biblical. However, in this verse in Genesis we do find the seed of mutuality and vulnerability on which our present ideal understanding of the concept of marriage can be based.

Ironically, what has come to be called "the biblical definition of a traditional marriage" is not rooted in the biblical text. Biblical marriage, as it came to be defined after the first rebellion, meant male ownership of women who existed for sexual pleasure. Upon marriage, a woman's property and her body became the possession of her new husband. As the head of the household, men (usually eighteen to twenty-four years old) had nearly unlimited rights over wives and children. A woman became available for a man's possession soon after she reached puberty (usually eleven to thirteen years old), that is, when she became physically able to produce children. The familial relationship based on mutuality and vulnerability as described in 2:24 and 25 differs significantly from how the Bible came to define marriage.

Furthermore, the biblical understanding of the purpose of marriage has been reproduction, even to the point that a man could dissolve his marriage if his wife failed to bear him heirs. Besides reproduction, marriage within a patriarchal social order also served political and economic means. Marriages during antiquity mainly focused on codifying economic responsibilities and obligations. Wives were chosen from good families not only to secure the legitimacy of a man's children, but to strengthen political and economic alliances between families, clans, tribes, and kingdoms. To ensure that offspring were legitimate heirs, the woman was restricted to just one sex partner, her husband. Meanwhile, the husband maintained the right to have multiple sex partners—wives, concubines, war booty, sexual slaves, even prostitutes.

This concept that a man would leave his father and mother and cleave to a woman can inform how our modern society might define a healthy marriage, but it should not be limited to the civil institution of marriage. It becomes a biblical pattern for all who cleave to each other to become one for the purposes of establishing a familial relationship. "Familial," that which is of or common to a family, is relation-centered. At its very core, a familial relationship is based on mutual commitment and vulnerability. It serves as a corrective measure to the hyper-individuality salient within Euro-American

Western culture by reinforcing the family, not the individual, as the basic social unit of society. Generally speaking, the familial relationship is not limited to two individuals forming a bond to become one flesh; it can also encompass children, siblings, elders, and all others who we term extended family. Thus not all familial relationships are sexual, nor should they be.

But through the cleaving that took place between the first man and the first woman, sex bonded such relationships. Sex is so great that it occurs within humanity's innocence, within the garden of Eden, before the first rebellion and the "fall." When two choose to become one flesh within a familial-based relationship, where mutual sexual pleasure can be epitomized, the opportunity to create intimacy exists. This sexual pleasure is not only abundantly satisfying; it also opens us up to the possibility of communing with God: at its best, sex creates a feeling of security, fulfillment, and ultimate love due to the process of two becoming one mind, one flesh, and one spirit.

As important as becoming one flesh may be, creating a familial relationship does not necessarily signify marriage. Although church weddings are religious rituals and celebrations that publicly proclaim the existence of a familial relationship, these events do not create family—people do. Church weddings serve to bless a relationship. If a sexual relationship fails to meet the deepest physical, emotional, spiritual, and intellectual needs of both partners, there may be a marriage, because a ritual occurred in a church building, but there is no family.

Man and woman are called to become "one flesh." The word used for "one" in Hebrew is *'ehad*. In this passage, *'ehad* connotes a union of separate entities, even though this sense is not endemic to *'ehad*. Nevertheless, it is curious that this is the same word used in the Shema, "Hear, O Israel: The Lord is our God, the Lord is one [*'ehad*]" (Deut. 6:4, my trans.). The union of two individuals in marriage patterns itself after the essence, the oneness of God. For Christians, the theological concept of the Trinity, developed in the late second century by Tertullian,[40] creates a model that can be emulated with familial relationships. According to this particular doctrine,

40. Tertullian, *Modesty* 21.16.

God is one and yet has been revealed to humanity as Yahweh, Jesus Christ, and the Holy Spirit. The doctrine maintains that these manifestations of God are coequal in the sharing of substance, power, and importance. In spite of the fact that many Christians attempt to view Divinity in hierarchical terms—placing the Father first, followed by the Son, and finally the Holy Spirit—the actual doctrine insists that the Trinity exists within a nonhierarchical model.

Regardless of whether one accepts or rejects this doctrine, what it represents can be useful in understanding the proper healthy relationship between two individuals. While many have tried to explain the Trinity, trying to solve it as if it was some cosmic puzzle, marginalized communities of color have instead emphasized the Trinity along the terms of communal relationships. Whatever we wish to say about God, God's character is relational, based on the act of sharing. Trinity symbolizes the sharing of authority. This paradigm of being one can become the model for humans, specifically the two who become one flesh. Although there was no marriage ceremony or ritual recorded taking place for the first man and woman, the relationship between the first man and woman can nevertheless inform modern-day marriages or any other relationship where the two, cleaving to each other, become one flesh. For two to be one means that the ideal familial relationship or marriage must exist without any hierarchical structures.

In other words, the relationship of oneness was originally intended to be nonpatriarchal. It is with divine judgment, after the human's first rebellion, that this relationship becomes perverted and patriarchal.

Can this one flesh ever be dissolved? When the Pharisees attempted to trap Jesus on the question of divorce,

> Born to mutuality and harmony, a man and a woman live in a garden where nature and history unite to celebrate the one flesh of sexuality. Naked without shame or fear, this couple treats each other with tenderness and respect. Neither escaping nor exploiting sex, they embrace and enjoy it. . . . In this setting, there is no male dominance, no female subordination, and no stereotyping of either sex.
>
> —Phyllis Trible
>
> *God and the Rhetoric of Sexuality*, OBT (Philadelphia: Fortress Press, 1978), 161.

he answered them by first quoting Genesis 2:24, and then stating, "what God has joined together, let no one separate" (Matt. 19:3–9). For Jesus this verse brings God into the equation of marriage, and expands the importance of the union by prohibiting divorce. The oneness between couples becomes the same oneness we are called to share with God. Elsewhere Jesus reminds us that not only do we have the capacity to become one with each other, but also one with God (John 17:21–23). In a sense, the familial relationship between two individuals is based on the oneness we can experience with our God.

This is why Jesus states that anyone who divorces his wife or marries a divorced woman commits adultery (Matt. 5:32). Divorce is painful because it tears apart the flesh that was made one in God. While it is hard to imagine the admonition against divorce being liberating in modern days, Jesus' pronouncement against divorce was liberating for women who, trapped within a patriarchal social order, were financially vulnerable when their husbands easily divorced them for the most trivial of matters. Still, circumstances exist where divorce may be the more liberating recourse. As injurious as divorce can be to the soul and body, it can also at times be the means by which the soul and body might be saved. The destruction of a human, created in the image of God, is a sin that can be manifested through spousal abuse, whether it is physical, emotional, or psychological. For some, their alternatives are choosing to stay within an abusive relationship or divorce, neither one being ideal. But when divorce leads to saving and/or restoring a person's worth and dignity, then divorce might very well be the better of the two alternatives.

The text gives the example of a male and female becoming one flesh, but is this example normative for everyone? The early rabbinical writers seem to have thought so. Rabbi Akiba wrote, "*And he shall cleave*, but not to a male; to his wife."[41] This leads us to wonder if two males or two females can cleave to each other and become one flesh. Maybe this is the wrong question to ponder. The question may not be if two same-gender loving partners can cleave to

---

41. Babylonian Talmud, *Sanhedrin* 58a.

each other and become one flesh, for they have always done so, and continue to do so. Maybe the question is how we might understand this verse in light of the reality of what is occurring more openly today with several states legalizing same-sex marriages. True, the story is about Adam and Eve, not Adam and Steve, as opponents to same-sex marriage want to remind us, although Augustine, due to his misogynist views, thought it would have been better for God to place another man, instead of a woman, in the garden with Adam.[42] Still, the story exists to answer important human questions, including what should be the basis for developing a familial sexual relationship, not who that relationship should be with. Because same-gender loving people have created familial relationships by cleaving to each other and becoming one flesh, it might be better to ponder why a portion of the faith community opposes this.

Historically, the purpose of marriage was to procreate, to be fruitful and multiply. Hence religious leaders saw any act that prevented procreation from occurring to be contrary to the will of God and the purpose of marriage. Not surprisingly, certain sexual acts that did not inseminate a woman (i.e., oral, anal, masturbation, sex during a woman's menstrual cycle, use of contraception, or

> I can stand before [my wife], totally naked, and feel no shame whatsoever. Even though I am unable to hide my sagging excess weight, stretch marks, wrinkles, and grayness, I can stand totally vulnerable and exposed to her gaze without fear of ridicule or abandonment. I stand before her not just physically naked, but also emotionally, intellectually, and psychologically naked. And the good news is that she can do likewise. We are able to stand fully transparent before each other because for years, during good times and bad, we have created a familial relationship based on vulnerability. For only when two are totally vulnerable to each other and are able to stand naked—warts and all— are they truly free to fully share themselves with each other in body, spirit, and soul.
> —Miguel A. De La Torre
>
> *A Lily Among the Thorns: Imagining a New Christian Sexuality* (San Francisco: John Wiley & Sons, 2007), 8.

42. Augustine, *The Literal Meaning of Genesis* 9.5.9.

sex with a woman past menopause) were considered an abomination. Indeed, if a woman was unable to produce a child, preferably a male child, the husband had an obligation to divorce her and procure a more fertile replacement. Not surprisingly, same-gender sexual relationships, because they do not lead to pregnancy, were also considered an abomination. If we define the purpose of marriage to be procreation, then, yes, same-sex marriage should not be allowed. But if marriage is more than simply having children, if marriage is to become one flesh by creating a familial relationship, then the race, faith, ethnicity, or gender of the participants ceases to be important.

Both the man and the woman were naked, and yet they felt no shame. For the ancient Hebrew mind, nakedness was a metaphor for vulnerability (as it is for many today). That they were able to stand stark naked before each other, totally vulnerable, and yet not be ashamed goes beyond their innocence concerning sexuality. After all, if they "cleaved" to each other in the previous verse, they were no longer all that innocent. The beauty of this verse is the affirmation that after cleaving to each other, after becoming totally vulnerable in each other's presence, they still felt no shame.

3:1–11:9

The Story of Rebellion

3:1–5
Testimony of the Serpent

Did the serpent actually speak? Ethicist Allen Verhey tells the story of an exchange that occurred during his ordination process. During the exam period, when any delegate to the classis could question him, an elder of one of the Reformed churches stood up and prefaced his question by observing that it says in Genesis 3 that the serpent spoke. Then he asked, "Do you think the serpent spoke?" No doubt the inquisitor was testing to see if Verhey interpreted the Bible literally. Instead, Verhey proceeded to explain that it is probably inappropriate to ask whether the serpent really spoke, concluding, "If we ask the wrong questions of Scripture, we will get the wrong answers—and then we should blame not Scripture but our questions." All too often we approach the Scriptures in general, Genesis in particular, with the wrong questions. Did creation actually take seven literal days? Were Adam and Eve historical figures? Did the serpent speak?

According to a popular anecdote, theologian Karl Barth, at the end of one of his lectures, was asked a similar question by a woman in the audience. "Did the serpent in Genesis actually speak?" Barth replied that it did not matter whether the serpent spoke, but what the serpent said. Some, like the ancient historian Josephus, insist that all living creatures in Eden shared a common language and thus were able to communicate with one another and with humans.[1] But it matters little if the serpent, or any other animal for that matter,

---

1. Josephus, *Antiquities of the Jews* 1.1.4.

actually spoke. What is important is that a trickster slithered into paradise as the most subtle of all the wild beasts God created.

In the interpretations given by the early church fathers, the serpent has come to personify evil. If they are correct, where does this evil come from? Did evil exist prior to humans? If God is the creator of all, did God create evil? Is the biblical faith based on some sort of spiritual duality between the forces of good represented as God and the forces of evil represented by Satan disguised as a serpent? The answer to the origin of evil is simple: we do not know. The Genesis account completely ignores these questions, and to ask these wrong questions of the biblical passage is to elicit wrong answers. All that we can say is that the serpent is still speaking.

God as absolute good is a theological proposition read into the Scriptures, even though it is not necessarily supported by a close reading of the text. A theological dichotomy that neatly separates absolute good from absolute evil is challenged by the biblical text and by existentially and morally comparing such a position with the realities of human life. Who has not faced, or will face, tragedy, misery, illness, and death? The phrase "life is unfair" captures a reality that leads us to question if any sense of cosmic justice and mercy exist. Human-inspired depraved acts and natural disasters randomly claim thousands of innocent lives each year. Many have referred to this dilemma as the theodicy question. How can an all-loving, all-powerful God allow evil to occur? Or in the case of this particular biblical passage, how could God allow the serpent to exist? What parents would allow a child to unjustly suffer if they had the power to prevent evil, like the serpent, from touching or hurting their child?

Jesus will one day ask, "Is there anyone among you who, if your child asks for bread, will give a stone? Or if the child asks for a fish, will give a snake? If you then, who are evil, know how to give good gifts to your children, how much more will your Father in heaven give good things to those who ask him!" (Matt. 7:9–11). Yet, reading the morning paper, one finds stories about inclement weather wiping out entire families, innocent children perishing at the hands of child molesters and murderers, and God-fearing people dying in freak accidents. When we consider the billions of senseless deaths, tragedies, and atrocities that define human history, history seems to deny more than confirm the paternal love of a caring and merciful God. One is forced to ask, Where is God? Comparing Jesus' words with the reality of evil in our global economy seems to indicate that earthly parents, rather than God, know better about how to care for their children. It is God who appears to be giving the tens of thousands who die each day of hunger and preventable diseases a stone when they are begging for some bread, or hands them a snake when they are praying for some fish.

Seeing the serpent as evil may have more to do with the imposition of Christian theology on the text than its possible purpose—to serve as a literary device to introduce a new reality to the story. We are never told that the serpent is evil, only that it is subtle and crafty. Whatever the serpent may have originally meant to the early readers of the text, two thousand years of Christian instruction have interpreted it as the manifestation of evil, although it is not described as such by the text. The introduction of the serpent as the symbol for evil becomes a theological attempt to justify God while legitimizing evil. For Christians, the serpent as personifying evil, to a certain extent, tries to save God from appearing as the source of the evil that is so much a part of the reality of human suffering and death.

The Scriptures attempt to convince us that God is worthy of our worship despite the presence of evil, even though the most troubling conclusion derived from the Judeo-Christian biblical text is the discovery of a God who is the cause and author of all that is good— *and all that is evil.* As the prophet Amos reminds us, "Does evil befall a city, unless the LORD has done it?" (Amos 3:6 RSV). The prophet Isaiah understands God to say, "I form the light, and create darkness; I make peace, and create evil. I the LORD do all these things" (Isa. 45:7 KJV). This is a God who sends evil spirits to torment individuals, as in the case of Saul (1 Sam. 18:10), Jeroboam (1 Kgs. 14:10), and Job (Job 1:12; 2:6). Contrary to popular opinion, this Genesis account does not introduce its readers to Satan in the form of a serpent, representing the Prince of Darkness and archenemy of God, whose primordial spiritual warfare continues to manifest itself in our times. Rather, this concept was developed over centuries of Christian history as evil came to be personified and given a name.

Nevertheless, one of the better-known manifestations of Satan within Christendom is portrayed as the tempting serpent in the garden of Eden. Although accepted by most Christians as true, this particular interpretation of the text would have been considered foreign to the ears of earlier Jewish biblical commentators. The early Christian fathers started reading Satan into this Genesis passage when influenced by the book of Revelation, specifically 12:9 and 20:2, where the primeval serpent, the great dragon, was identified as Satan. Justin Martyr, Christian apologist of the second century, would be among the first theologians to make the connection between the serpent in the garden and Satan. He believed that Satan, disguised as the serpent, participated in the fall of humanity by deceiving the woman in the garden of Eden, and through her, Adam.[2] Tertullian, an apologist of the third century, argued that because of Satan's deception of Adam, the entire human race, through Adam's seed, became infected with damnation.[3]

> **Because Satan sees that Adam is the more excellent, he does not dare assail him; for he fears that his attempt may turn out to be useless. . . . Satan, therefore, directs his attack on Eve as the weaker part.**
>
> —Martin Luther
>
> *Luther's Works*, vol. 1: *Lectures on Genesis: Chapters 1-5*, ed. Jaroslav Pelikan, trans. George V. Schick (St. Louis: Concordia Publishing House, 1958), 151.

These early church fathers would develop a theology making it necessary for God as Christ to become a sacrifice for the victory earned by the serpent in the garden. Jesus must offer his life not to God but to Satan, in substitution for the souls of humanity that belong to Satan because they followed him as serpent. According to this theological line of thinking, through the first Adam all humans inherited death; through the second Adam (Christ) humanity inherited the promise of everlasting life. Hence the serpent in the garden, responsible for leading humanity in its fall, is conquered through the death of Christ, with the serpent losing his hold on the souls of Adam and Eve's descendants.

---

2. Justin Martyr, *First Apology* 28; and *Dialogue with Trypho* 94.2.
3. Tertullian, *The Soul* 39.

But what happens to our theology if the serpent is not Satan? If there is no physical Satan, he must be created to protect God from being the author of evil. The serpent must be reread as the story of Satan, Lucifer, the evil one, or simply the devil to protect God. Satan's physical existence is not our main concern. What is important is the end result that evil became a historical entity we now call Satan. Still, seeing the serpent as Satan is theologically problematic. Radical monotheism makes it difficult to develop a demonology. As troublesome as it may be to conceive of God as being the author of malevolent acts, more so is the creation of another supernatural being in competition with God within a monotheistic religion.

Whether the serpent is evil or not, two thousand years of Christian theology portraying the serpent as the personification of evil have provided interesting observations concerning such an interpretation that can still be instructional. For example, it is interesting to note that when the serpent encounters the woman, she is not repulsed by evil; but then, evil usually seems plausible and attractive at first. This evil entity tempts the woman to disobey God's only command by inflicting doubt, making it seem as if God is prohibiting her from fully living her life and enjoying all of the available fruits life (not God) has to offer. The serpent succeeds in presenting God as a God of don'ts. Negative images of God, then and now, continue to be responsible for turning people away from God. Unfortunately, most of these negative images are disseminated by those who call themselves followers of God. We who are believers often play the role of the serpent when we describe God as some autocratic patriarchal scorekeeper who is only interested in denying us the freedom to live abundant lives, quick to punish us if we step out of line.

The serpent is the first creature in the biblical text to objectify God, talking about God rather than to or with God. Keeping God from the discussion, it is able to tempt the woman with a forbidden fruit. Although the biblical text fails to tell us the type of fruit borne by the tree of the knowledge of good and evil, Eurocentric artists throughout the centuries have imagined the forbidden fruit to be an apple. I, however, a son of the Caribbean, imagine Eden to be the perfection of a tropical island; hence, when I read the creation story through my own eyes, I envision the fruit to be a mango. Regardless as to what the fruit was, it is not the act of eating the forbidden fruit that is the sin; rather, the sin is rooted in the central idea of usurping God's authority as Creator.

But what if the early church fathers were wrong? What if the serpent is not the incarnation of Satan, but simply a literary device to move the story along? Then maybe the serpent can be seen as a trickster, a creature that can raise consciousness. It is interesting to note that the serpent never directly suggests eating the forbidden fruit, but through questions reinforces the already existing desire within humans. "Did God really say that to eat the fruit meant death?" asks the serpent (3:1, 4). The serpent, constantly portrayed as a liar, does not lie, but it also does not tell the truth. The serpent, in a way, was truthful in stating that eating the forbidden fruit would make humans godlike, being able to distinguish good from evil. But how humans defined "godlike" was probably very different from how the serpent was defining it. This is why the serpent can best be understood as a trickster figure, not necessarily evil, but shaking up the foundations of the cosmos nonetheless. The opening of the eyes of humans by eating the fruit of the tree may lead to expulsion; but in a way it also is what defines our humanity, our independence, our free will.

> Yet like God, the woman is an explorer. She seeks the good, fruit that is good. . . . The commentators cry for her blind obedience, her trust. But mature trust grows out of experience. How can the woman discriminate between God's words and the serpent's words until she has the experience of failure or the discrimination she seeks? . . . She seeks, reasonably, to be in a position to make a choice. Or, alternatively, she merely responds to her programming: to eat the good food, and to be like God! . . . Eve does not "sin"; she chooses reality over her naive, paradisiacal existence. Her choice marks the emergence of human character.
> —Danna Nolan Fewell and David M. Gunn
>
> *Gender, Power, and Promise: The Subject of the Bible's First Story* (Nashville: Abingdon Press, 1993), 30–31.

FURTHER REFLECTIONS
Satan

The serpent in the garden of Eden has become one of the better-known depictions of Satan within Christendom. Although most Christians accept that Satan appeared as a serpent in Eden, the text never presents the serpent as the evil one. As previously mentioned, Justin Martyr, a second-century apologist for the Christian faith, is among the first to argue that the prince of demons participated in the fall of humanity.[4] According to Irenaeus of Lyons, the second-century Roman apologist: "For as by the disobedience of the one man who was originally molded from virgin soil, the many were made sinners, and forfeited life; so was it necessary that, by the obedience of one man, who was originally born from a virgin, many should be justified and receive salvation."[5] Christ's death, according to the third-century apologist Origen, was "not only an example of death endured for the sake of piety, but also the first blow in the conflict which is to overthrow the power of that evil spirit the Devil, who had obtained dominion over the whole world."[6]

For Christians, the serpent in the garden, responsible for leading humanity in their fall, is conquered through the death of Christ, with the serpent losing his hold on the souls of Adam and Eve's descendants. As taught by Athanasius of Alexandria, the resurrection fulfilled the promise of the incarnation, for by God's self-sacrifice in Jesus Christ human beings might restore the *imago Dei*, the image of God, in their souls and reclaim their divine relationship with God. Yet ironically Satan is never mentioned in the book of Genesis. Indeed, the manifestation of a diabolical evil entity is relatively absent from the entire Hebrew Bible. The word *satan* appears twenty-seven times as a noun and six times as a verb throughout the Hebrew Bible. "The *satan*," used with a definite article (*has-satan*), connotes "adversary(ies)," "opponent(s)," "accuser(s)," or "slanderer(s)." For example, when the Philistines were preparing to attack Israel, they became concerned about bringing David along

---

4. Justin Martyr, *First Apology* 28; and *Dialogue with Trypho* 94.2.
5. Irenaeus, *Against Heresies* 3.18.7.
6. Origen, *Contra Celsus* 7.17.

lest "he become an adversary [*satan*] to us in the battle" (1 Sam. 29:4). We also read about King Solomon's message to Hiram, king of Tyre, in which he comments about the absence of warfare, a time when "there is neither adversary [*satan*] nor misfortune" (1 Kgs. 5:4). Even God can be a *satan*, as illustrated in the story concerning the prophet Balaam, who incurred God's wrath for undertaking a journey. The text tells us that "the angel of the Lᴏʀᴅ took his stand in the road as his adversary [*satan*]" (Num. 22:22). Please note that later in this commentary we will see how at times the term "the angel of the Lord" morphs into God.

In the Hebrew Bible anyone or any creature can be a *satan*, an adversary. But at some point the concept illustrated by the word *satan* in the Bible was personified into the being we have come to know as Satan. This being appears to be mentioned eighteen times in the Hebrew Bible, limited to only three books: once in 1 Chronicles (21:1), three times in two verses in Zechariah (3:1–2), and fourteen times within the first two chapters of the book of Job. Psalm 109:6 is another possibility, but it remains ambiguous. The same ambiguity can be found in the story of Balaam (Num. 22:22–35). But even if the word *satan* is not referring to the proper name Satan, it is referring to an office or role occupied by some being.

It is not until the intertestamental period, the period between the end of the Hebrew Bible's writings and the start of the writing of the New Testament, that the personification of Satan, along with a sophisticated demonology, develops. During these roughly three hundred years, highly influenced by the Babylonian captivity and its Persian influence, that Satan along with a quasi-mythological army of demons and fallen archangels captured the religious imagination and moved the Judeo-Christian discourse uncomfortably away from monotheism. To read Satan or the devil as part of the Genesis story is to read one's theology and ethical understanding of evil into the garden of Eden. While such an interpretation may be helpful in trying to understand from where evil originates, we must remain cognizant that this particular biblical interpretation of the serpent as Satan is foreign to the ears of earlier Jewish biblical commentators.[7]

---

7. For a complete analysis of the development of the concept of Satan, see Miguel A. De La Torre and Albert Hernandez, *The Quest for the Historical Satan* (Minneapolis: Fortress Press, 2011).

3:6–11
Testimony about the First Rebellion

The fall assumes theological truths about human nature that cannot be proven, but rather must be accepted through faith. Was human nature prior to the fall one of innocence? If so, does the fall condemn all of humanity because of the action of the first humans? Are we thus destined to be sinners because of that first act? Rather than assume, or read into the Scriptures, certain theological propositions, regardless of whether one accepts these as truths, a more neutral approach is to recognize what the text explicates: that humans rebel against God's authority. Hence, rather than using the term "the fall," and all the theological assumptions that term connotes, I find it more accurate to refer to this human disobedience as the first rebellion, one of four major rebellions (and a multitude of minors) that Genesis addresses. Rebellion becomes a continuous story, repeated throughout Genesis 1–11 (specifically in 4:1–16; 6:1–4; and 11:1–9), but most pronounced in this particular story. One rebellion is not more horrific than the others; rather, they all are part of the same overarching story.

While rebellion against God can be horrendous, as in the taking of human life, we are left wondering what was so terrible about eating from the tree that provides wisdom. The book of Proverbs reminds us that we are to pursue wisdom (Prov. 4:5), which is given to us by Yahweh (2:6) to protect us (4:6). Only fools spurn the wisdom (1:7) that will keep them from the way of evil (2:12). Because wisdom is supreme (4:7), we are not to forsake it (4:6); it is more precious than rubies (8:11) and better than gold (16:16). If the pursuit of wisdom is an honorable venture for the righteous, which one of us then, if provided the opportunity, would not also partake from the forbidden fruit? After all, the entire biblical text places a high value on wisdom.

Wisdom should be sought, but at the expense of disobeying God? No doubt the rebellion is based on human defiance, the exchanging of God's trust and grace for knowledge, a point we should not underestimate. Still, why did God make the object of disobedience such a worthy goal to pursue? Could it be that gaining knowledge about good and evil are acts of maturation? What parent does not want to train their child to discern between good and evil? Is partaking from the tree how humans move from childhood to adulthood? If so, could it be that God wanted humans to partake of the fruit to gain wisdom? If humans were indeed intended to eat from the tree of knowledge, did God play the trickster? After all, isn't God as ultimate Creator in charge of all that exists in God's garden? If all that was created comes from God, is the serpent but a side of God, the trickster side? And if so, is God teaching us that the pursuit of wisdom is always a painful course fraught with frightful consequences?

Maybe the "Freedom Is Not Free" bumper stickers supporting war contain a kernel of truth. Freedom and wisdom are seldom given; one must struggle for them. One must be willing to die for them. Could it be that disobeying God was a necessary evil? The actions that the first humans took meant they were no longer children, but like all adults would be held accountable for their acts. Once they are mature enough to grasp wisdom, they can never return to their former childlike state. They now know that death exists, and one day they will return to the dust from which they came—a dreadful realization. As children grow up and leave the security of their parents' home to enter the real world and make lives for themselves, with all the joys and hardships life entails, so too are the first humans ready to enter the world beyond the safety of the garden planted for them by God. Future theologians, like Peter Abelard in the twelfth century, would argue that since this is the best of all possible worlds, the fall was necessary because it created a need for atonement. God's atonement created a deeper and richer love for God than would have been possible if no fall had occurred.

Genesis informs us that the woman took this first step when she saw that the fruit was aesthetically pleasing. Desiring the knowledge that the tree could provide, she ate the forbidden fruit and gave some to her partner to eat. This was not an innocent mistake. The woman willfully acted in the hope of obtaining knowledge. According to Rebecca Todd Peters, "Feminist interpretations of this story have reclaimed Eve as not only the mother of all living, but as the mother of wisdom, a seeker of knowledge. Rather than live in a paradisiacal

> Den dat little man in back dar, he say women can't have as much rights as men, cause Christ wan't a woman! Whar did your Christ come from? Whar did your Christ come from? From God and a woman! Man had nothin' to do wid Him. If de fust woman God ever made was strong enough to turn de world upside down all alone, dese women togedder ought to be able to turn it back, and get it right side up again! And now dey is asking to do it, de men better let 'em.
>
> —Sojourner Truth
>
> "Ain't I A Woman?" Speech delivered at the Women's Convention in Akron, Ohio, 1851, as recorded by Frances D. Gage in *History of Woman Suffrage: 1848–1861*, ed. Elizabeth Cady Stanton, Susan Brownell Anthony, Matilda Joslyn Gage, and Ida Husted Harper, vol. 1 (Rochester, NY: Charles Mann, 1889), 116.

setting without knowing the difference between good and evil, Eve sought 'wisdom'; she chose to 'know.'"[8]

Eve's act of sharing the fruit with her partner has earned her the eternal reputation of temptress.

Dietrich Bonhoeffer, echoing centuries of Christian theology, simply states that "Eve falls first. She falls as the weaker one, as the one partly taken from man."[9] Because men have theorized that women led them toward rebellion against God, gender had to be regulated. One of the major themes within Christian thought is that women, represented by Eve, are the cause of sin and consequently the reason *man*kind was led astray from God's perfect will. Her moral inferiority is proven through Eve's initial role in causing sin. Like their mother Eve, women throughout the ages are the incarnation of temptation, specifically sexual temptation. Eve's action relegates all women to be subjugated to their men; they are the cause of human sin and cosmic evil, and thus cannot be trusted or placed in an authoritative role. Her supposed involvement in causing the fall makes her the counterpoint to Mary, the mother of Jesus, who serves as the medium by which the agent of the world's redemption entered history. Mary, as the eternal virgin, becomes the ideal model for all women to emulate. Women must then choose

8. Rebecca Todd Peters, *In Search of the Good Life: The Ethics of Globalization* (New York: Continuum, 2004), 46–47.

9. Dietrich Bonhoeffer, *Creation and Fall: A Theological Interpretation of Genesis 1–3*, trans. John C. Fletcher (New York: Macmillan, 1959), 75.

between the false dichotomy of mother and temptress or between virgin and whore.

Yet we need to remember that the woman was not alone. Her partner plays a passive role, remaining silent, neither intervening nor resisting. Once the fruit is handed over to him, he does not hesitate, but willingly partakes, even though the prohibition of eating from the tree of the knowledge of good and evil was given to him, not to the woman (2:16). Phyllis Trible points out that "the man does not theologize; he does not contemplate; he does not envision the full possibilities of the occasion. His one act is belly oriented, and it is an act of quiescence, not of initiative. The man is not dominant; he is not aggressive; he is not a decision maker."[10]

While some celebrate our free will as an important indicator of our humanity, others see it as excessive self-centeredness, pride. Two thousand years of Christian history have taught us that the original temptation of humanity is the pride of attempting to become God. The plucking of the forbidden fruit was motivated by human pride. Pride, one of the seven deadly sins, becomes from this point forward the main cause of humanity's oppression. The ethicist Reinhold Niebuhr would further develop this historical understanding by concluding that the human condition—pursuit of pride, not wisdom—is the original sin that has doomed humanity ever since the fall.[11]

In a sense, Niebuhr is correct. Self-centeredness is the endeavor of replacing God with humans, expressed today as the drive for power and privilege. However, as Valerie Saiving Goldstein points out, Niebuhr's analysis of the human condition is really an analysis of the male condition. (I would add to her observations that Niebuhr's analysis is of the Eurocentric male condition.) She argues that if sin is described as pride, then it must follow that love, defined as self-sacrifice, becomes redemptive.[12] She goes on:

---

10. Phyllis Trible, "Eve and Adam: Genesis 2-3 Reread" (1973), in *Biblical Studies Alternatively,* comp. Susanne Scholz (Upper Saddle River, NJ: Prentice Hall, 2003), 98.

11. Reinhold Niebuhr, *The Nature and Destiny of Man,* 2 vols. (New York: Charles Scribner's Sons, 1941), 1:186–204.

12. Valerie Saiving Goldstein, "The Human Situation: A Feminine View," *Journal of Religion* 40, no. 2 (1960): 100–101.

> For the temptations of woman *as woman* are not the same as
> the temptations of man *as man*, and the specifically feminine
> forms of sin—"feminine" not because they are confined to
> women or because women are incapable of sinning in other
> ways but because they are outgrowths of the basic feminine
> character structure—have a quality which can never be
> encompassed by such terms as "pride" and "will-to-power."[13]

But women, and I would add communities of color, should not
base their theology on an interpretation where the sin of humanity
is pride. Those who the dominant culture privileges may have
sufficient power and economic resources to set themselves up as
gods, but this status is achieved at the expense of those who live on
the periphery of society.

Some within the dominant culture may repent with Niebuhr
for their sin of pride, their desire to become like gods, and instead
attempt to live a more humble life; nevertheless, how can those
who cannot be gods repent? Repentance of pride may prove to be a
healthy step for those privileged by the dominant culture, but it can
prove deadly for the marginalized, increasing their oppression and
subjugation. The danger occurs when those with the power to define
what conversion entails impose on the wretched of the earth, made
wretched by the sins of the privileged, the requirement of being
"saved" in similar fashion and with similar feelings and emotions.

One size does not fit all. It was, and continues to be, assumed
that the salvation needed by those on the margins, who are seen as
deprived and inferior, is the same salvation for which those from the
dominant culture yearn. It is oppressive to preach to the marginalized
about self-denial and submission when the disenfranchised should
instead be hearing about pride in self and assertiveness. For those
who are already humble, there is no need to preach humility. The
human condition of the marginalized is nonpersonhood, making
salvation the transformation from nonpersonhood to personhood.
This explains the Gospel's Magnificat, "[God] pulled down the
powerful from their thrones, and exalted the humble ones; God has
filled the hungry with good things, and sent the rich away empty"

13. Ibid., 108–9.

(Luke 1:52–53, my trans.). It is the privileged who need to come to terms with their spiritual wretchedness due to their pride. It is the wretched who need to come to terms with their infinite worth by developing their pride.

Once the man and woman ate from the tree, their eyes were opened to their nakedness.

The first discovery they made once their eyes were opened was their vulnerability, for they were more than just physically naked, they were also emotionally and psychologically naked. They are left to make amends by creating clothing to cover their nakedness. But human attempts to cover up their vulnerabilities fall short of the mark. Fig-leaf clothes do not last for long.

For some, like Augustine of Hippo, sex was the forbidden fruit that the first humans tasted. The reason Adam covered his genitals with fig leaves, according to Augustine, was not due to modesty or shame, but rather because Adam's penis was erect. Augustine succeeds in linking shame and sex to the fall of humanity. Both Adam's erect penis and that of all men who follow him signify our will toward the flesh, over and against the spirit.[14] Adam's uncontrollable penis symbolized his rebellion against God, making sex the cause for expulsion from paradise. An erect penis, philosopher Michel Foucault reminds us, "[becomes] the image of man revolted against God." The Christian problem with sex becomes desire itself.[15] Sex, within Christian tradition, symbolized the choice for the material things of this world over against the

> "And they knew that they were naked," etc. Even of the one precept which they have possessed they have stripped themselves. "And they sewed the leaves of the fig (*te'enah*) together." R. Simon b. Yohai said: That is the leaf which brought the occasion (*to'anah*)—for death— into the world. R Isaac said: Thou hast acted sinfully; then take thread and sew!
> —*Midrash Genesis Rabbah* 19:6
>
> Translated under the editorship of Rabbi Dr. H. Freedman and Maurice Simon, 1939

---

14. Augustine, *City of God* 14.19, 21.
15. Michel Foucault, *Religion and Culture: Michel Foucault,* ed. Jeremy R. Carrette (New York: Routledge, 1999), 186.

spiritual things concerning the kingdom of heaven. Unfortunately, this type of interpretation has created a strong anti-body perspective from which sex is associated with shame, negatively influencing human development and relationships for the past two millennia, a perspective still prevalent in many circles within the Christian church.

Naked and vulnerable, the woman and man hear God walking in the garden in the cool of the day and hide among the trees. They may have hoped to become gods; but now they find themselves naked, cowering in the bushes before the one and only Almighty God. The consequence of rebelling against God (not sex) is shame, to hide oneself. Disobedience means trying to hide from the all-seeing eye of God, a futile task that only demonstrates alienation from God. But even as the humans hide, God calls out to them, asking where they are. The man responds that he heard God approaching and he was naked, so he hid.

"Who told you that you were naked?" God asks. Did God not know what had occurred? To ask the question indicates that the trust undergirding God's relationship with humans had been broken. It was obvious that the humans ate of the forbidden tree; they disobeyed God. Still, God asks humans what happened, not because God did not know the answer; but by their own mouths, they, and we, are convicted (2 Sam. 1:16; Job 15:6).

FURTHER REFLECTIONS
Original Sin

Sin, manifested individually or corporately, is such a part of the human condition that theologians have been led to argue for the concept of original sin. According to this doctrine, we are all born with a "stain" on our very souls, creating a need for divine atonement. Although the tenet of original sin does not explicitly appear in the biblical text, the account of human rebellion, known as the fall (Gen. 3), provides tacit substance for speculation on the provenance of sin. During the Babylonian captivity, Hebrew thought was exposed to Persian ideology, specifically the prevalent dualism between good and evil. In the postexilic period two theories emerged to explain the origins of sin. Many linked sin's origin to some diabolical force that coerced its way into the human condition (i.e., the devil), while others believed sin was inherited.

After the Christ event, the Apostolic Fathers barely mentioned the concept of original sin. Eventually, Tertullian made an argument linking Adam's soul with his progeny. All souls, according to Tertullian, were contained in the original soul that God breathed into Adam. Hence all souls are stained due to Adam's primeval sin.[16] This doctrine, known as traducianism, became the harbinger for our modern concept of original sin. Eastern Greek Fathers, along with Tertullian, advocated free will. Still, they viewed original sin as a wound inflicted on human nature. Only in a mystical sense, according to Gregory of Nyssa, do we share in the rebellious act of Adam.[17] Gregory believed that sin was contracted through paternal transmission, with copulating being the means.[18] The British monk Pelagius, realizing the pessimistic effect that a negative view of human nature could have on moral behavior, rejected any propensity toward sin by heavily emphasizing the notion of free will disconnected from the influences of the fall.[19]

But Augustine of Hippo impugned Pelagius by stating, "all sinned, since all were that one man [Adam]."[20] Sin is transmitted through the theory of "seminal propagation." Within the father's semen exists a generic spiritual substance (*fomes peccatum*) that is generationally transferred. While prior thinkers emphasized solidarity with Adam, Augustine formulated a doctrine of original sin connecting Adam's rebellion to humanity's complicity. Rather than emphasizing free will, with an inclination to do evil, Augustine insisted that we are born from our mothers' infected wombs as sinners in need of redemption.

The cornerstone of Augustine's biblical defense was Romans 5:12, where he misinterprets "because all sinned" as "in whom all

---

16. Tertullian, *The Soul* 39.
17. Gregory of Nyssa, *On the Beatitudes* 6 (PG 44, 1273).
18. Idem, *Against the Manichaeans* 8 (PG 39, 1096).
19. Robert F. Evans, *Pelagius: Inquiries and Reappraisals* (New York: Seabury, 1968), 82–83.
20. Augustine, *On the Merits and Remission of Sins* 1.10.11.

sinned," thus asserting that all humanity, in Adam, is in sin because Adam's sin is in all humans.[21] Despite Augustine's misinterpretation of the text, the fifth session of the Council of Trent (1546) reaffirmed the reality of original sin, its transmission from Adam, and its consequences for the body and soul. Protestants like Calvin continued within Augustine's understanding of original sin. In his *Institutes*, Calvin writes that original sin is "a hereditary depravity and corruption of our nature, diffused into all parts of the soul, which first makes us liable to God's wrath, then also brings forth in us what Scripture calls 'works of the flesh.'"[22]

Because original sin has been associated with sex for most of Christian history, sex has been viewed as a sinful act, even within marriage. By associating original sin with sex and its means of transmission, Christianity developed unhealthy understandings of sex; among its many negative consequences, it scapegoats women as the primary seducers of chaste men. Like Eve, the first woman, men are led to sin by all women, who are in reality temptresses. When we consider Christian societies' unhealthy history concerning sexuality and gender, maybe the concept of original sin has done more harm than good in trying to explain humanity's tendency toward evil.

3:12–20

Testimony about the Wages of Sin

What is it about the blame game that is so alluring that it leads humans away from taking responsibility for their actions? The futile attempt to evade responsibility for one's actions only makes repentance and restoration impossible to achieve. This human tendency of passing the buck first occurs in the garden. When God asked the man if he ate from the forbidden tree, he responded that the woman given to him by God gave him the fruit. Hence it is the woman's fault. The moment Adam blamed his companion, the trust and solidarity existing between them was broken. Both the man

---

21. Ibid., 3.14.
22. Calvin, *Institutes* 2.1.8.

and the woman now became totally vulnerable and unsafe before each other. No longer could the woman ever fully trust the man. At this very moment, male supremacy and patriarchy begin to take shape. And while the man attempts to shift the blame toward the woman, she, according to the man's response, is not solely to blame, for ultimately the man is implying that it is God's fault for giving the woman to him.

When God questions the woman, she in turn blames the serpent that beguiled her. Unfortunately for the serpent, it has no one to whom to pass the buck. Besides, until now, God does not even bother communicating with this beast. Maybe if God did, the serpent might have laid the full blame on God. After all, why did God plant the tree of temptation in the garden in the first place? Perhaps to test humans, to flex God's authority, to hope that humans would rebel and thus gain maturation? Regardless, it would appear that the buck stops with the serpent. While it may be true that the serpent was the instigator, the fact remains that all three pay the "wages of sin." Instigator and follower, regardless as to how passive the follower might have been, are held accountable for their actions, paying the consequences.

> But to trace the causes of evil in the instance of the first man, who is depicted as already in full command of the use of his reason, is neither necessary nor feasible, since otherwise this basis (the evil propensity) would have had to be created in him; therefore his sin is set forth as engendered directly from innocence. We must not, however, look for an origin in time of a moral character for which we are to be held responsible.
> —Immanuel Kant
>
> *Religion within the Limits of Reason Alone,* trans. Theodore M. Greene and Hoyt H. Hudson (New York: HarperCollins, 2008), 38.

God begins by cursing the serpent. It will be cursed among all animals, crawling on its belly and eating dust (did the serpent once have legs—lost after the first rebellion?). The seed of the serpent and that of the woman will become eternal enemies, with the latter bruising its head and the former retaliating by striking the heel of the woman's seed. For Christians reading their theology into the text, the seed of the woman is Jesus Christ, who will crush Satan (the head of the serpent), who in turn will retaliate by crucifying Christ (striking the heel of the woman's seed). This becomes for Christians the first mention of the coming Redeemer, what early commentators termed *Protoevangelium*.

Even though the passage is not considered prophecy and speaks of an ongoing enmity, the early interpreters of Christianity read these verses as an allusion to Satan's cosmic defeat. The apostle Paul, probably with this passage in mind, would eventually write, "The God of peace will shortly crush Satan under your feet" (Rom. 16:20). Of course, the early author of the text had no messianic notion in mind while penning this passage. The original readers understood these verses as a metaphor to explain the origins of good and evil people. "Seed" is read in its more collective meaning of humanity, hence helping explain why there are good and bad people in the world. A broader interpretation would also include good and evil things.[23]

What the text does reveal is that what was once a blessing now becomes a curse. As God responds to human rebellion, God speaks descriptively, not prescriptively, about the consequences of living with the knowledge of good and evil. The woman's pain during childbirth would be multiplied. What was once a blessing, to be fruitful and multiply, is now cursed with pain and sorrow. Furthermore, she would live her life desiring her husband while he dominates her. Her role comes to be defined in relationship to the man. God does curse the soil because of the man, although God does not curse the man, who nonetheless must till the ground. Humans will suffer to make the earth yield its fruits. They will work hard to gather thorns and thistles. By the sweat of their brow they will eat bread. What was once ordained in paradise, to tend to the garden, now becomes a cursed drudgery.

Hence this passage provides the ancient reader with answers to more cosmic questions. Why is the earth at times the enemy of humans, producing droughts, floods, tornadoes, hurricanes, blizzards, and so on? Why must humans work? Why does hard work produce thorns and thistles for so many? Another important cosmic question is answered: Why must we die? The text provides us with the oldest assessment of the human condition: humans will live a life

---

23. Mark Adam Elliott, *The Survivors of Israel: A Reconsideration of the Theology of Pre-Christian Judaism* (Grand Rapids: Eerdmans, 2000), 314–15.

of hard labor and then die, returning to the soil from whence they came. The ground will eventually reclaim what was formed from it. Meanwhile, we humans struggle not just to provide for our needs but also vainly against the inevitable—that one day we shall be food for worms. No wonder Qoheleth would eventually conclude:

> Naked from my mother's womb [I] came, as naked will [I] depart; nothing to take after all [my] labor. . . . For anyone who is chosen among all that live, there is still hope. Better a living dog than a dead lion. For the living at least know that they will die, the dead know nothing; nor do they have any more reward, their memory is forgotten. So too their loves, their hatreds, their jealousies—all these have perished, never again will they take part in whatever is done under the sun. (Ecclesiastes 5:15; 9:4–6 [my trans.]).

The perversion of creation brought about by rebellion becomes subjugation for all who are involved. Equality is replaced with oppression; the fellowship originally established is turned into alienation; the harmony enjoyed now becomes discord. To grow up and leave the security of childhood as experienced in the garden is to fully understand the consequences of knowing good and evil. Still, the good and the bad are what define human experience. We may no longer live in the garden, but our task is to return to it—with eyes wide open. We journey back to the garden when we strive to undo the consequences of rebellion, when we work against oppression, alienation, and discord by seeking equality, fellowship, and harmony.

While the "wages of sin" are being elucidated, the message of hope is pronounced. Finally, the first woman gets a name. Just as man previously named the animals to establish his rule over them, he now names his companion: *hawwah*—Hava—the Hebrew word related to the verbal root for "living," because she is the mother of all who live. In English we know her as Eve. Adam and Eve, soil and life, is from where existential humans emerge, and on which they depend. Paradoxically, during judgment, Adam believes in redemption. The name he gives Eve, as the mother of all who live, becomes a seed of hope in the midst of God's verdict of death. Grace abounds even during cursing.

3:16

Testimony about Women's Domination

Prior to human rebellion against God's will, we are told by the text that "the man and his wife were both naked, and were not ashamed" (2:25). The ideal relationship, as previously mentioned, is for two to stand before one another, totally naked and vulnerable, and yet feel no shame from what each partner sees in the other. Yet the biblical text has been used over the millennia to justify the domination of women due to their so-called duplicity and deceit.

> For evil are women, my children, as since they have no power or strength over men, they use wiles by outward attraction, that they may draw him to themselves. And whom they cannot bewitch by outward attraction, him they overcome by craft. . . . For a woman cannot force a man openly, but by a harlot's bearing she beguiles him.
>
> —*Testament of Reuben* 5:1–2, 4–5
>
> *The Testaments of the Twelve Patriarchs*, trans. Robert Henry Charles (London: Adam and Charles Black, 1908), 12.

The unquestionable principle of women's subordination in all of the Abrahamic faiths became so normalized within the fabric of societal structures that for anyone to raise concerns about the status quo was to be dismissed, if not persecuted, as a radical who hates God, men, and country (the *father*land).

Any examination of the biblical justification of patriarchy must begin with Genesis: "To the woman [God] said, 'I will greatly increase your sorrow in your childbearing, you shall bear children in sorrow, and your desire shall be for your husband, and he shall rule over you'" (my trans.). Reading through the eyes of patriarchy, the passage is quite straightforward for men: "Woman, you will desire me and I will rule, dominate, and be a master over you!" Her desire for man makes her dependent on man. Women were taught throughout history that it was their duty to submit to their deserved punishment because all women share in Eve's rebellion. God ordained that the proper role within marriage is to be one of domination and submission with the man on top and the woman on the bottom. During the 2000 gathering of the Southern Baptist Convention, the *Baptist Faith and Message* was amended to reflect this patriarchal interpretation concerning the subordinate role of women within a marriage relationship:

> A husband is to love his wife as Christ loved the Church. He has the God-given responsibility to provide for, to protect, and lead his family. A wife is to submit herself graciously to the servant leadership of her husband even as the church willingly submits to the headship of Christ. She, being in the image of God as is her husband and thus equal to him, has the God-given responsibility to respect her husband and to serve as his helper in managing the household and nurturing the next generation.[24]

The Southern Baptist Convention, along with many other denominations and faith traditions, can advocate women's domination by shrouding the concept within the velvet glove of politically correct words like "servant leadership." Yet the fact remains that for many who are religious, ever since the woman first ate from the forbidden tree and gave some to the man to eat, God condemned women to be subservient to men, illegitimizing female actions toward empowerment as unbiblical.

However, the words spoken by God in Genesis 3:16 occurred after the first rebellion and before the expulsion of the man and woman from paradise. Hence the question that should be raised is whether it is God's will for women to be ruled over by men, or whether God simply foretold what the consequences of rebellion would be for humanity, specifically women, in this verse. If we examine the next two verses concerning the punishment of the man, light might be shed on this question. In them, God turns to the man and curses the ground. The man will now need to till the cursed soil with the prospect of producing only "thorns and thistles." Gone forever is the garden of Eden and the effortless fruits that came forth. Only through the sweat of the brow will Adam and his family be fed. To work and labor in sorrow was not the ideal for Adam and all of his descendants.

Likewise, we should ask if it is God's will that women be ruled over by men. Again, using the same reasoning, the answer must

---

24. "The Family," *Baptist Faith and Message*, XVIII.

be no. It is God's will to return women to the garden, where they "were both naked, and were not ashamed," where the relationship between the man and the woman was vulnerable yet safe, because no power difference existed between them. Genesis 3:16 does not describe God's curse on women, nor does 3:17 describe God's curse on men. God's will for human relationships is not that men rule over women; but rather 3:16 illustrates the first consequence of rebellion, when the will of humans replaces God's will, perverting all relationships. They may have wanted the power that came with being God, but instead they fell into a state where social structures are created to deny them the power they sought: subservience to economic structures (agriculture as a way of surviving) for men, and sexist relational structures for women.

It is not that God ordains, approves of, or condones these new structural relationships, but rather that their development is part of the natural evolution begun with humanity's rebellion. Eden is perverted by hierarchical structures among humans. The idyllic idea of being naked and feeling no shame was distorted by the establishment of male superiority. The original relationship established by God prior to human rebellion was replaced with the curse of patriarchal relationships. Rather than finding equality within the image of God (1:26), humans found inequality in the patriarchy established as rebellion's first consequence. Not only is the oppressed woman forced to wear the mask of inferiority, but so too must the oppressor, man, wear the false mask of superiority—always fearful the mask might slip and reveal his true nature of vulnerability. Throughout history in their writings male theologians have constructed such masks for men to wear. For example, Martin Luther writes: "The male is like the sun in heaven, the female like the moon, the animals like the stars, over which sun and moon have dominion. In the first place, therefore, let us note from this passage that it was written that this sex may not be excluded from any glory of the human creature, although it is inferior to the male sex."[25]

The perversion that now exists between the relationship of men and women creates greater alienation between God and humans. The

25. Luther, *Lectures on Genesis: Chapters 1–5*, 69.

great error and continued danger is that we read the consequence of sin as if it were God's will and the divine norm for humanity.

Just as the blessing of being equally created in God's image was perverted with the inclusion of patriarchy, so too was the blessing to be fruitful and multiply (1:28) perverted to include pain and even death. God's pronouncement concerning the consequences of rebellion now includes pain during childbirth, leaving one to wonder if there had been no rebellion would childbirth have been a painless process. Regardless, sex roles are established. Women are relegated to the home, the private sphere—childbearing and rearing; while men are relegated to the fields, the public sphere—food producing and gathering. Because men are operating in the public sphere, its importance over and above the private sphere is presumed.

> In every human society the male's need for achievement can be recognized. Men may cook, or weave or dress dolls or hunt hummingbirds, but if such activities are appropriate occupations of men, then the whole society, men and woman alike, votes them as important. When the same occupations are performed by women, they are regarded as less important.
> —Margaret Mead
>
> *Male and Female* (1949; repr. New York: New American Library, 1959), 125.

FURTHER REFLECTIONS
The Genesis of Oppression

Sexism is but one aspect of what it means to be a white man with economic privilege in the United States. Gender, race, and class domination do not exist in isolated compartments, nor are they neatly relegated to uniform categories of repression. They interact, overlap, and conflict with one another. The initial oppression of women as found in the Genesis story becomes a prelude for all forms of oppression, where all who are nonwhite males possessing economic privilege are relegated to a feminine space so as to be housebroken. All forms of oppression are identical in their attempt to domesticate those who fall short of the privileged white male ideal. The sexist, who sees women playing a less productive role than men, transfers to the nonelite white male effeminate characteristics, placing him also in a feminine space. For this reason, women must be kept in their place, because once they are liberated, all types of other groups would want to also be liberated.

To be a white privileged man within the center of world economic power implies both domination and protection of their subordinates—women as well as nonwhite males. It becomes the white man's historic responsibility, his "burden," to educate and Christianize those below his superior standards. Women, nonwhites, and poor whites all fail to reach the exalted white man's station in life, because they lack what it takes to be a real man, a gift given to them by the ultimate Man, God.

When white privileged men gaze in the mirror, they recognize themselves through the distancing process of negative self-definition: "I am what I am not." I am not an emotional woman, therefore I am a rational man. I am not a lazy black person, therefore I am industrious. I am not an uncivilized Latino, therefore I am civilized. The formation of the white privileged man's ego constructs an illusory self-representation by ascribing femininity to all who fall short of their ideal self-delusion. Show me a sexist and I will show you a racist. Seeing those who do not live in white neighborhoods or attend their schools as second class or "less-than" facilitates relegating them to a feminine (whether they be female or male) role, so as to justify their subjugation. Seeing how these white privileged males are constructed as superior in the mirror of negative self-definition helps us better understand the underpinnings for the biblical justification for colonialism and imperialism.

It is naive to think that structures of oppression along gender, race, class, and sexual orientation function as isolated compartments. In a very real sense, the oppression of women is more than simply a sexist act. It serves as a paradigm for the subjugation of all people groups that fall short of the white male ideal. The curse levied on Eve in Genesis 3:16, that she will yearn for the man and he will rule over her, is not limited to women. All males who are colonized, either foreign or domestic, yearn to be *like* the one designated as superior while simultaneously they are being ruled over—more economically than politically. When we consider that the vast majority of the world's resources flow to the Eurocentric few, those relegated to the global South, including those impoverished spaces within industrial nations, it becomes obvious the extent to which those who fall short of the white privileged male ideal are domesticated like women.

To justify the subjugation of women through an apologetic reading of Genesis 3:16 goes beyond some ignorant sexist interpretation of the biblical text. It provide us with a blueprint on establishing racist, elitist, classist, and imperialist structures through the advocacy of sexist paradigms.

3:21–24
Testimony about Expulsion

Adam and Eve are expelled from paradise. In a sense they are the first refugees, forced to leave the land from which they were formed, under the sky that witnessed their coming into being. Only those torn from their homeland can relate to the gut-wrenching pain of being expelled from all that one knows. It matters little if the fault of expatriation was one's own, or due to political and social forces beyond one's control, the end result is the same—despair, distress, dispossession, and disenfranchisement. To be expelled is to become marginalized, possibly generations away from reestablishing oneself.

Many who today are refugees, like the Jews taken in captivity to Babylon (587 BCE), are forced to deal with the incomprehensible pain of being torn from one's own Eden. In Babylon, out of their pain, the Jews questioned the sovereignty of a God who would tear God's people from their homes and plant them in an alien land. With the psalmist (Ps. 137), all who are expelled from their land sing about their inability to sing a song:

> By the rivers of the Potomac, we sat and wept when we remembered our *patria*. On the midst of the willows we hung our *congo drums* and *maracas*. There, our captors asked us for the words of a song, and our plunderers joyfully said, "Sing us a *mambo*." How shall we sing our *rumba* in a pagan land? If I

forget you my homeland, may my right hand wither, may my
tongue cleave to my palate if I do not remember you—if I do
not bring up *mi tierra* as my greatest joy.

A major concern for those in exile, whether they are Adam and
Eve, the Jews in Babylon, or the many today who find themselves
in foreign lands, is their status as deportees. Does removal from
their homeland, by which their identity is constructed, indicate
a divine rejection, voiding any future participation in God's plan?
Does resettlement in a foreign land mean assimilation to a culture
perceived as inferior to one's own?

The *galut*, the Hebrew word for forced removal, is more than just
the result of international forces. To the one being plucked up and cast
into the Diaspora, *galut* becomes a religious condition which forces
the displaced person to ask the basic theodicy question: How can a
loving and powerful God allow such unbearable pain to befall God's
people? Hence the deeply political Psalm 137 is also deeply religious.
For Adam and Eve cast out of Eden, the captive Jews in the foreign
land of Babylon, and those of us who are refugees today, faith is a
means of coping with the existential situation of dislodgment, giving
meaning and hope to the shame and humiliation of displacement.

Yet in the midst of *galut*, God preserves human life. In spite of
human rebellion, humanity is still accepted by God. Expulsion does
not mean ultimate rejection. Because of God's mercy, God makes
Adam and Eve new garments to cover their shame, a shame brought
about by violating God's command. God makes these new garments
from the skins of animals. Garments made of skins provide a
testimony of hope that God is still involved in the affairs of humans.
Even when they are forced to leave the presence of God, God does
not leave their presence.

To obtain the skins, however, death had to enter paradise as the
first animal is slaughtered. The consequence of rebellion is death,
the spilling of blood. But why did the animal have to die for what
Adam and Eve did? This is one example of the unfairness of life.
Our rebellion usually causes consequences that do not necessarily
touch us but are devastating, if not deadly, for some other part of
creation. How many of the poor must offer up their lives as living

sacrifices so that the rich can live life abundantly? How many of the disenfranchised must be crucified so that the privileged can be saved in this world? The sin of wanting to be like gods usually means that the humble, like the unfortunate animal in paradise, must be slaughtered for the sake of covering the shame of those who aspire to be lords.

We are told in the expulsion story that God becomes concerned that the man, becoming like the Deity and possessing the knowledge of good and evil, might stretch out his hand and pick the fruit from the tree of life and thus live forever. So God expels the man from the garden of Eden to till new soil. It is curious, in spite of the shared participation in rebellion by the man and the woman, that the text leaves out the woman here. The text states that the man (singular form) became like God and that the man may try to obtain immortality, thus the man must be banished from the garden. We know that both Adam and Eve are expelled. So why the switch from referring to the couple to referring to just the man? Could it be that one of the consequences of rebellion is the invisibility of the woman? Does saying "the man" assume the woman is present under the man's domain? Regardless as to why the woman is excluded at this point in the story, a final cosmic question is answered: "Why aren't we immortal?" If Adam and Eve were truly like God, they would be immortal.

So God posts cherubim with whirling flaming swords as sentinels to guard the way to the tree of life. The cherub is usually portrayed as having a human-beast, sphinx-type appearance with wings (Ps. 18:10); "cherub" becomes the second most common word for a heavenly being, after *mal'ak* for "messenger" or "angel." Besides guarding the garden of Eden, their golden image is hammered, with extended wings, on top of the ark of the tabernacle (Exod. 25:18–20). Wooden images of cherubim, overlaid with gold, are later placed by King Solomon in the temple's holy of holies and carved onto the temple's walls and doors (1 Kgs. 6:23–35). It is believed that God is enthroned between the cherubim (1 Sam. 4:4; Isa. 37:16). The cherubim in Genesis 3 serve as barriers to the tree of life. Apparently, such heavenly creatures are empowered to constrict the actions of humans.

Eternal life, due to God's sentries, cannot be achieved through one's action, for humans are barred from eating from the tree of life. How then does one get to eat from this tree and obtain life eternal? Christians need to discover who owns the tree of life, and only then petition the owners for entrance. Jesus reminds us that blessed are the poor, for theirs is the kingdom of God (Luke 6:20). God's kingdom, and all that is in it, including the tree of life, is owned by the poor. This might explain why Jesus would later state that what we do, or fail to do, to the very least of these—the hungry, the thirsty, the alien, the naked, the infirmed, and the imprisoned—we do to him. Entrance into the kingdom, prepared since the foundation of the earth, is not based on correct doctrine, or membership in a certain church or denomination, or even the recital of some sinner's prayer. Entrance into the kingdom, according to Jesus, is based on what we do, or fail to do, to the least of these; eternal life is based on our praxis, our actions (Matt. 25:31–46). In short, no one can take up residency in the kingdom of God, where the tree of life is found, without a letter of recommendation from the poor and marginalized among us.

This does not mean we get to eat from the tree of life solely due to our good works. As the prophet Isaiah reminds us, all of our good works are but filthy rags before the Lord (Isa. 64:6). Although we are not saved by our works, lest anyone should boast (Eph. 2:8–9), our works remain the outward expression of an inward conversion. If there is no praxis, then it indicates a lack of commitment to the faith. As James reminds us, "someone will say, 'You have faith and I have works.' Show me your faith apart from your works, and I by my works will show you my faith. You believe that God is one; you do well. Even the demons believe—and shudder. Do you want to be shown, you senseless person, that faith apart from works is barren? . . . You see that a person is justified by works and not by faith alone" (Jas. 2:18–20, 24).

Salvation lies in the future. For now, humans are forced to leave paradise. The good news for us is that God follows them. Not only do humans become refugees, but so does God, who, due to human rebellion, also leaves the garden of Eden.

No longer does God walk in the garden in the cool of the day conversing face-to-face with God's creation. No longer does God observe the lion sleeping with the lamb. Although we usually focus on humans' expulsion from Eden, we should remember that God too, so as to be the preserver, chooses to become self-exiled from paradise. We, in the loneliness of being a stranger in a strange land, are not alone.

> So it is easy to overlook the fact that when God closes the door to the garden of Eden, God is outside and not inside the garden. . . . [T]he upshot of the sequel to the human eating of the tree of knowledge of good and bad is that God henceforth is in it with them, accompanies them into the world of broken relation, disparity of power, and violence that has been brought about.
>
> —Johanna van Wijk-Bos
>
> *Making Wise the Simple: The Torah in Christian Faith and Practice* (Grand Rapids: Eerdmans, 2005), 247.

4:1–16
Testimony about the Second Rebellion

The consequence of the first rebellion was alienation from God. In the account of the second rebellion, humans become further alienated from one another. Another consequence of the first rebellion is that woman, symbolized by Eve, becomes subjugated to two masters, Yahweh and man. Yet, in the midst of patriarchy, she finds a glimmer of hope by proclaiming her pride in her ability to create new life, in the creation of a new man. She gives birth to two boys, possibly twins; but it is the firstborn, Cain, on whom she places her hope that he will restore creation, a hope soon abandoned. The stable family Eve rejoices over will eventually slide into dysfunctional relationships ending in even greater alienation than the original expulsion from Eden. Maybe this family's dysfunctionality was rooted in Eve's obvious favoritism for her firstborn, Cain. Or maybe it was due to God's favoritism for her second-born, Abel. Whichever the case, the stage is set for a deadly rebellion within the first family.

We can detect Eve's favoritism for Cain by the name she gives her second-born. The word *hebel* (Abel) can be translated as "vanity," "vapor," or "nothing," words that indicate that this child is less than impressive. The name probably signifies either the fragility of the person or refers to his life span, which will be as transient as vapor. Regardless of why the child is named Abel, the biblical account begins with the entrance of discrimination in the world, a system where some are privileged over others. Nevertheless, in spite of the privilege shown to Cain, his name will come to be associated with evil, signifying the earth's first malefactor, due to his participation in fratricide.

Scholars believe that this section of Scripture was a product of J, written during the early monarchy of Solomon. Could it be that the author is celebrating how God rejects primogeniture—the right of the firstborn's inheritance? Does God overlook the firstborn when God decides whom God chooses to favor? This is a motif that will be repeated throughout Genesis, specifically in the stories of Jacob and Esau, as well as with Joseph and his brothers. The most significant reason for J to include these stories might be to indirectly comment on the events of J's own time, specifically the kingly anointment of David and Solomon, who like Abel were not the firstborn, and yet God, according to the writer of the text, also chose them. The first surely became last and the last became first.

The narrative unfolds with both sons bringing their offerings to God, even though nowhere in the story does God make such a request. Cain, the first human born and the first to cultivate the ground God cursed, approaches God with the produce that the land yielded. Abel, a herdsman, brings the finest unblemished livestock as an offering to God. We are never told why God regarded Abel's sacrifice favorably. Maybe God is more carnivore than herbivore? Or maybe the text is simply revealing, through the brothers' rivalry, the historical tension existing between two lifestyles of the ancient and present world—farming and shepherding. If so, is the text concluding that a nomadic pastoral life is superior to a life in an agricultural community? Regardless of the reasons why God chose sides, a bloody chain of events is to follow. Still, God's silence as to why one brother's sacrifice was acceptable and not the other's portrays a God who seems capricious, if not whimsical. To save God from such a characterization, many of us read our theology into the story—a theology elucidated by Christians in the book of Hebrews: "Through faith Abel offered God a better sacrifice than Cain, and for that he was proclaimed righteous when God bore witness of his offering" (Heb. 11:4, my trans.).

Although the text is silent about the motivation of those bringing sacrifices to a God who has not requested any, we assume that when Abel stood before the Lord of creation, he did so with a sincere and contrite heart. By contrast, we assume that the reason Cain's sacrifice was not acceptable to the Lord lay within his person. The type of sacrifice offered up to God is unimportant. What is important is the faith of the one making the offering. The prophet Isaiah quotes God as stating: "What to me is the multitude of your sacrifices? . . . I have had enough of burnt offerings of rams and the fat of fed beasts. I do not delight in the blood of bulls, or of lambs, or of goats. . . . Bringing offerings is futile; incense is an abomination to me. . . . Remove the evil of your doings from before my eyes; cease to do evil, learn to do good; seek justice, rescue the oppressed, defend the orphan, plead for the widow" (Isa. 1:11, 13, 16–17). It seems as if God rejected Cain's offering because Cain chose not to live faithfully by doing justice. Instead, he set up religion and offered religiosity.

> We need someone to be a prophet for us, too, and call us to conversion and not let us set up religion as something untouchable.
> —**Archbishop Oscar Romero**
>
> *Oscar Romero: The Violence of Love*, ed. and trans. James R. Brockman (Maryknoll, NY: Orbis, 2004), 143.

Cain could also have approached God humbly, a difficult task for those born as favorites or showered with privilege. Still, God encourages Cain, "Why are you angry, and why has your countenance fallen? . . . If you do not do well, sin is lurking at the door; its desire is for you, but you must master it." Here sin is mentioned for the first time in the biblical text, personified as some dangerous crouching beast. Nevertheless, God believed Cain could have entered into a right relationship with Abel and with the Divine. But Cain allowed sinful impulses and desire to master him. There is no Satan to blame or predestined fate to curse: Cain chose his path willingly. Privileged Cain is called to control his appetites, appetites that if acted on would bring violence on the one living on his underside, the one not privileged in this world. As Erasmus points out, Cain had free choice, he was able to overcome the evil temptations before him. He could have been rewarded if he chose to do what is good. Instead, by choosing to do evil, he would pay the consequences of his actions (punishment).[26] While Cain is responsible for choosing evil, we are still left wondering how a God of love could have created creatures like Cain with such a capacity for hatred that it could lead to murder.

The faithful bear testimony not through words but by the lifestyle they live. This testimony of praxis contrasts over and against those who rely on their privilege. Nothing needs to be said by those hungering for justice, for their very presence serves as condemnation. The very existence of the disenfranchised shames those who are privileged. The disenfranchised must be made invisible, or to the extreme, they must be killed. Whether Cain intended it or not, he, like his parents, becomes "like God," wielding the power of life and death over others. When we act out of hatred, we oppose God's call to love. When we act out of pride, we oppose God's call to be humble. And when we act out of selfishness, we oppose God's call of self-giving. All individuals, as well as all institutions—whether they are political, economic, or social—exist under the sway of sinful, if not deadly, behavior.

Death enters history. Sin occurs among humans of flesh and bone who enter the world as we do. God once asked Adam where he was. Now God asks Cain, where is his brother? Cain responds by lying, adding his own question for God: "Am I my brother's keeper?" Hence humans ask God the very first ethical question, a question that will take the rest of Genesis, if not the rest of the Bible, to answer. Am I my sibling's keeper? For the reader of the biblical text, the answer is an unequivocal yes; we are responsible for our siblings. But who is my brother? Who is my sister? If we are indeed the children of Adam and Eve, then are we not all brothers and sisters? All murder is fratricide, for we are all brothers, we are all sisters.

When God asks, What have you done with your brother? the

---

26. Desiderius Erasmus of Rotterdam, *De Libero Arbitrio*, ed. and trans. E. Gordon Rupp (Philadelphia: Westminster Press, 1964), 54.

question reveals God's preferential option for those abused and murdered—then and now. Those made invisible so that the few can enjoy their privilege are still important to God. God continues to ask those who are privileged: What have you done to your sisters and brothers? Those who live on your margins? Those who die dispossessed for your benefit? Their cries continue to rise up to God's ear.

Maybe Cain did not understand what murder was? After all, up to this point there had been no death. He might have noticed the death of animals, especially those that Abel offered up to God—but the death of a human? Could humans also die like animals? Could Cain have been surprised by the resulting death of Abel when he struck him in anger? Cain saw Abel's blood ooze from his dying body; today blood is spilled without those who benefit from the deaths needing to witness the consequences of their acts. Blood is not just spilled in the physical act of striking another; it is also spilled through economic policies that bring early death to the poor. How is our lifestyle of consumption contributing to the death of others? In today's world, Cain's sin of becoming God is repeated when the few also exercise their power of life and death over the many, especially when they appropriate the bulk of the world's resources, resulting in an institutional violence that is just as deadly as striking one's brother or sister with a stone. How many must die early deaths so that a small portion of the world's population can live in splendor, enjoying the vast majority of the world's resources? Like Cain, are we today also surprised when the world's dispossessed die throughout the world for lack of basic needs? We may never

> We shall not be able to shed light on the question: Where is God? unless we are able to answer the Lord's challenge: "Where is your brother?" (Gen 4:9). In this way we hasten history . . . we cause the kingdom to come; we cause the *kairos* to arrive, not as something fated but as the result of the free acceptance of God's gift. Acting "as free people" (1 Peter 2:16), by our behavior we "wait for and hasten the coming of the day of God" (2 Peter 3:12).
>
> —Gustavo Gutiérrez
>
> *The God of Life*, trans. Matthew J. O'Connell (Maryknoll, NY: Orbis, 1991), 118.

know what might result from our actions, but Cain warns us that all actions, those committed in the heat of anger or in the banality of the everyday, have consequences—at times, deadly consequences.

The ground, once cursed by God, now curses Cain, who becomes the first man born of humanity ever to be cursed by God. He, like his parents before him, becomes a refugee, the first to wander the earth, unable to set roots because the ground refuses to yield him any produce. As all who are strangers in a strange land know, to be an alien is to live at the mercy of whoever belongs to the dominant culture. No wonder Cain cries out for mercy, fearful that whoever he meets might kill him. God shows great leniency and tenderness by protecting Cain. Fearful that someone might kill him, Cain begs for protection and God complies by placing a mark on him. But if there are now only three people in the world, Cain and his parents, who does Cain fear might kill him? And where did he find a wife? Obviously, such questions are unimportant to the author, who is more concerned with Abel's testimony.

A disturbing interpretation concerning Cain's mark is its association with blackness. According to rabbinical tradition, Cain's mark was him becoming black.[27] Black people, as descendants of Cain's line, became the children of sin and murder. But such a conclusion must assume that Cain was white before he was cursed with blackness. This view is not limited to the rabbinical text, but also becomes the religious foundation of white supremacy. Cain's mark came to mean that servitude was the consequence of making Cain black—hence justifying slavery. If Cain was originally white, then so too were his parents, Adam and Eve; and since they were created in the image of God, then God is also white. But as previously mentioned, if God used the best soil to create Adam, and the richer the soil the blacker it is, would it not be reasonable to assume that Adam's skin would resemble the ingredient used? So if Adam and Eve were black, as were their children Cain and Abel, then could not the mark just as easily be that God made Cain white? Obviously, we have no idea what the color of the first humans was, nor is it important. The biblical text is silent on this topic. It only remains

27. *Midrash Genesis Rabbah* 22:6.

important to those wishing to justify the superiority of their own race. White supremacists have read their social context into the text and assumed the first humans were white.

Abel's testimony reveals to us a God who is a provoker, accuser, kinsman-redeemer (of blood), prosecutor, judge, punisher, savior (spare life), and protector (kinsman-redeemer for the murdered and murderer).[28] The story leaves us questioning what appears to be God's darker side. Is God some trickster that creates a situation and rejects Cain's offering for no good reason, just to see how he will react? And why pick on Cain and not Abel? Would the results have been different? The text leaves us with no clear answers to these questions, except to wrestle more with the text.

4:17–5:32

Testimonies from the Ancestors

Ancestors testify as to where we came from so that we can understand where we are going. Unfortunately, hyperindividualistic cultures seem to disregard, if not outright ignore, the stories of those who came before us. By contrast, the biblical text, in this section, presents two linear genealogies. These two lists are the first of about two dozen that appear throughout the biblical narrative. The most extensive genealogy is found in 1 Chronicles, spanning nine chapters (1:1–9:44), starting with Adam and concluding with the descendants of King Saul. There exists debate if some of these genealogies are lists of individuals or names of ethnic people groups or geographic areas, as exhibited in Genesis 10. Although genealogies are usually neglected by the modern reader of the Bible, they do provide powerful testimonies concerning God and God's people.

With the birth of each new generation comes the hope of renewal and restoration—an overturn of the Genesis 3 curse. The first genealogy (4:17–25) focuses on Cain and six generations of his descendants. The advancement in civilization and urban culture

---

28. A kinsman-redeemer is a legal term used to describe the process of recovering for the original owner what has been alienated by kinfolk. God as kinsman-redeemer saves the life that has legally been forfeited.

(creation of cities, rise of nomads, creation of music, and the development of metallurgy) is attributed to Cain's descendants. It is difficult to miss the subtle bias against cities and their advancements in civilization, for after all they were founded by Cain and his descendants, thus binding sin with urban life, a difficult teaching for those of us who are unashamedly urbanites. Still, we should pay heed to the warning. As culture progresses and humans learn to master their environment, the danger of a correlating increase in human violence exists. This link seems to convey that civil "men," who learn to dominate their setting and advance the human condition, can still fall short of being and acting humane. God seems to cease to be needed as humans become gods of their surroundings.

Cain's genealogy ends with the first poem of the biblical text, Lamech's self-sufficient song, boasting that if Cain was to be avenged sevenfold, then he is to be avenged seventy-sevenfold. And while Cain expressed remorse, Lamech's braggadocio celebrated his vengeful triumph. But vengeance has a way of threatening any cohesive community. For this reason, God reminds us through the Torah that "vengeance is mine" (Deut. 32:35). For Christians, the seventy-sevenfold vengeance claimed by Lamech, and the spirit that prompted it, is reversed by Jesus through his admonishment to Peter to forgive seventy-seven times (Matt. 18:22).

According to the *Midrash*, in his old age Lamech was blind and led around by his son, Tubal-cain. The boy, seeing Cain at some distance, mistook him for a beast (due to God's mark). The boy told Lamech, the inventor of war instruments, to shoot his bow toward Cain, which Lamech did. Upon discovering he had killed his ancestor, he struck his son and either accidently killed him or lamed him. Regardless, this rabbinical interpretation of the text serves as the basis for his raucous song.[29] It is interesting to also note that the appearance of a more benign Lamech in the second genealogy of Seth is probably a result of each genealogy coming from different documents (the first is considered to be J, while the second is probably P) rather than the assertion that Lamech is the same name

---

29. *Midrash Tanhuma: An English Translation of Genesis and Exodus*, ed. and trans. Samuel A. Berman (Hoboken, NJ: KTAV Publishing House, 1996), 32–33.

given to two different men. Finally, the mention of Lamech's two wives (the only time women are included in the list of begetters in the book of Genesis) might indicate that he was the first to practice polygamy in contrast to the monogamist pattern established in Genesis 2:24. According to *Midrash Genesis Rabbah* 23:2, one wife, Adah, drank a potion to make her sterile so that she could keep her figure; while the other wife, Zillah, served the role of procreation. As their names imply, Lamech "luxuriated" in Adah's body, and used to sit in the "shade" of Zillah's children.[30] Still, regardless of this telling rabbinic interpretation about the demeaning usage of women, Adah, according to the biblical text, did eventually give birth to Jabal (4:20).

Probably the most difficult question raised in Cain's genealogy is: Where did Cain find a wife? Is Cain's wife a sister not mentioned? If so, is humanity a product of incest? Martin Luther seemed to think so,[31] as do many fundamentalists. Or in the beginning, did God create humanity, not just one couple? If so, then we are not all descendants of Eve and Adam. During the so-called Age of Exploration of the 1500s, a similar proposition concerning a pre-Adam race was advocated. As Europeans conquered Asia, Africa, and the Americas, they encountered "savages" whom they forced into slave labor. As "beasts," they were considered to be a soulless subhuman race, akin to animals of burden descended from another type of "Adam." If they too were descendants of Adam, then we are all brothers and sisters because we are all his descendants. But by advancing the proposition that a pre-Adam race existed, from where Cain's future wife comes, then those participating in slavery were able to find biblical shelter from the accusation of enslaving their sisters or brothers in Adam. To be outside Adam's family is to be outside the human family, forfeiting any claim in possessing property rights or any type of human rights.[32]

---

30. See also Jerusalem Talmud, *Yebamot* 6:5.

31. Martin Luther, *Commentary on Genesis*, trans. J. Theodore Mueller, 2 vols. (Grand Rapids: Zondervan, 1958), 1:111–12.

32. See Olive Patricia Dickason, "The Concept of *l'Homme Sauvage*," in *Manlike Monsters on Trial: Early Records and Modern Evidence*, ed. Marjorie M. Halpin and Michael M. Ames (Vancouver: University of British Columbia Press, 1980), 71, 74.

Adam and Eve were white, and therefore *impossible* that *they* could be the progenitors of the kinky-headed, black-skinned negroes of this day. . . . That the negro being created before Adam, consequently he is a *beast* in God's nomenclature; and being a beast, was under Adam's rule and dominion, and, like all other beasts or animals, has no soul.

—Ariel

Ariel (Buckner H. Payne), *The Negro: What Is His Ethnological Status?* 2nd ed. (Cincinnati: Self-Published, 1867), 45.

Besides questions as to where Cain's wife came from, another concern is that Cain does not live out the curse from God to be "a wanderer over the earth" (Gen. 4:12); after all, he is credited with founding the city of Enoch.

In contrast with the first genealogy of Cain, the second genealogy (5:1–32) focuses on the descendants of Adam, through his son Seth, born after Cain killed Abel. If there is to be spiritual renewal and restoration, it will come through Seth's line, as opposed to Cain's line, which nevertheless materially flourishes with the advancement of civilization. Contrary to the Exodus 3 account of God revealing God's name to Moses for the first time, we are told in this passage that Seth is the first to invoke Yahweh's name; thus with Seth the church, not as institution but as a people who worship God in the midst of a rebellious world, is established. Seth's genealogy serves as a contrast to the previous genealogy of Cain, starting with Seth, the worshiper of Yahweh, and concluding with the righteous Noah. If we accept the span of each ancestor's life to be accurate, then Noah is the first person born after the death of Adam. Noah's name means "rest," because, according to his father, in the midst of toil and laboring hands he will give a consolation derived from the ground that Yahweh cursed. The hope is that Noah will reverse the curse of the once blessed ground of creation levied in 3:17.

The genealogical pattern of stating the years lived by an individual before he dies is altered when it comes to Enoch. We are told that Enoch walked with God, which means he lived a life that was in continuous service to the Creator; and "then he was no more" (5:24). To be "no more" could obviously mean that he died. Even so, some interpret this passage as meaning that Enoch did not taste death, for God took him (rapture?) in the same way Elijah would be taken (2 Kgs. 2:11). Not surprisingly, Enoch became a center point for apocalyptic and gnostic literature, specifically the pseudepigraphic books *1* and *2 Enoch*. If indeed Enoch escapes death and is taken by God, then this is probably the first biblical hint, the first foreshadowing, of the concept of immortality—providing hope that the curse from God on creation might finally come to an end after our physical deaths.

These genealogies bear witness that God continues to reveal Godself to people living in each generation. God's revelation is never absent from the history of humans. In addition, the biblical inclusion of genealogies bears witness to the continuous act of creation. Like God, humans too can participate in bringing forth new life—a process deemed by the Divine as being good. The Hebrew word *yada'*, translated as "know," is used to describe sexual intimacy. Of the 949 times that *yada'* appears in the Hebrew Bible, 22 times are direct references to sexual intercourse, as demonstrated in Genesis 4:17, where Cain "knew" his wife, and 4:25, where Adam again "knew" Eve. It is the same biblical word used to refer to the union of God with the human soul. The intimate sexual union between a loving couple and the possibility of creating and/or nourishing new life becomes an imitation, a foretaste, of the union we are called to have with God. While we recognize that the purpose of sex, in spite of centuries of an anti-body theology, is not solely to be fruitful and multiply, it does become the means by which the next generation enters the world.

Genealogies also establish one's identity as being cast in God's image. Who we are is based on the family we come from, a concept usually dismissed by more hyperindividualist cultures. Yet many communities of color discover that one's ancestors influence and shape who we are and what we can become. Many traditions, specifically in the global South, have recognized the importance of and provided reverence for the ancestors. Yet when Western missionaries invaded their territories, they condemned or forbade this reverence toward ancestors as idolatrous, based on their reading of 1 Corinthians 8. In their minds, reverence and offerings for the ancestors was a form of demon worship. What the Western missionaries missed was that honoring our ancestors forms and

As an Asian American reader, I am struck by the fact that the Torah chooses to tell its history not only through the lens of national events but through the particular struggles and triumphs of ancestors. Early missionaries to Asia discouraged the practice of ancestor worship. . . . The biblical witness, however, while stopping short of the worship of ancestors, emphasizes the important role of ancestral faith and belief. In fact, the Torah tells its story primarily through the vehicle of ancestral faith.

—Frank M. Yamada

"The Pentateuch: Introduction," in *The Peoples' Bible: New Revised Standard Version with the Apocrypha*, ed. Curtiss Paul DeYoung et al. (Minneapolis: Fortress Press, 2009), 130–31.

strengthens our communities and our identities.

Not long ago I spoke to a Euro-American missionary, serving a small rural village in Mexico, who thought that the Day of the Dead festivities were satanic. He told me that he tried hard to dissuade his indigenous converts from participating in such activities after their "conversion" to Christ. He was specifically horrified at the morbid practice of family members spending an entire evening at the cemetery, eating and drinking the deceased's favorite food, at her or his gravesite. His opposition to these rituals ended when the missionary's own father died back in the States. Heartbroken and distraught for not being able to attend the funeral, he accepted the invitation of one of the villagers, who also recently lost his father, to spend the night with him and his family at the graveyard during the Day of the Dead festivities in honor of both fathers. Throughout the night the men shared stories about their fathers, including feelings— at times contradictory—that they held. They shared joys and regrets. With the coming of dawn, the missionary found healing to his grief. More important, for the first time he became part of the community.

Reverence for our ancestors strengthens our families and communities, providing meaning for who we are. The missionary ceased being the outside expert come to "save" them from their theological errors and instead became a fellow sojourner struggling with the community to understand the Divine. Rather than their official teacher, he became their student, learning who God is from the margins of society. Likewise, the genealogies of the Bible, so often overlooked by Sunday school teachers, are the foundation that defines our faith; specifically, it is not an individual faith based on a personal Savior (for those of us who are Christian), but rather a communal faith.

As important as genealogies are, it is crucial that we raise some concerns about them. Probably the most disturbing aspect of biblical genealogies is that the natural order of women birthing children is subverted. In the biblical record, men beget men. Women are seldom mentioned, unless in the rare instance that their inclusion has historical significance, for example, Ruth as King David's great-grandmother (Ruth 4:17). It should be noted that Christian texts also have two genealogies (Matt. 1:1–17 and Luke 3:23–38), both tracing Jesus' King David pedigree, and for the Christian the fulfillment of the messianic hope, although these genealogies do not match. The Matthew passage does contain the inclusion of four women: Tamar (who played the prostitute), Rahab (a prostitute), Ruth (a foreigner), and the wife of Uriah (Bathsheba, who either participated in or was forced into adultery). It is troublesome that when women are mentioned in these genealogies, they are viewed by the male reader in a negative light based on who they are or what they supposedly did.

A second concern with genealogical lists is their tendency toward ethnic purity. While the genealogies in the Genesis section are designed to account for the differences existing between the line of Cain and that of Seth, future genealogies in the biblical text can be and have been used to prove ethnic purity. "Put away your foreign wives!" became a cry during the restoration of Jerusalem after the Babylonian captivity (Ezra 2:59–63; 10:9–44; Neh. 13:23–28). Those who were not "pure" were purged from among the people. Besides purging undesirables because they are "unclean," they are also used to determine who will be privileged with power. Genealogical lists established who belonged to the priesthood (Levi's line), the kingship (David's line), and the nobility.

In the final analysis, the significance of biblical genealogies is ambiguous. While those with more communal ties find comfort in the affirmation of providing reverence to their ancestors, still we must recognize that as they appear they reinforce patriarchy and ethnic exclusion.

6:1–4

Testimonies about the Third Rebellion

Based on a possible fragment of a larger ancient writing or the faded communal memory of mythical proportions concerning the creation of demigods, this short story, comprising just four verses, is reminiscent of other Near Eastern stories that describe the rebellion of younger gods against their progenitors. While initially the story may have existed to explain the origins of a superrace of quasi-deities, the J author included this tale as a prelude to the "flood story" to explain the increasing corruption and wickedness on the face of the earth. Although some ancient mind-set might have been better able to grasp and understand this short mythological yarn of sexual intercourse between gods and humans, we of the modern world, with a more developed theological understanding of Scripture, are puzzled by the inclusion of this curious story within the biblical text, and more importantly, what this tale is trying to convey. Not surprisingly, any proper interpretation of these four verses is fraught with difficulties as disputed meanings of the text arise.

Although similar to other ancient myths, this passage seemed to have served the overall purpose of the J author who chose to include it. This account may not have been part of the original flood story, but it does set the stage for the coming calamity. Maybe the author was less concerned with the elements of the story than the biblical lessons that could be obtained concerning the origins of evil. This passage describes what I call the "third rebellion," the only reference in

Israel's misfortunes were too great to ascribe purely to human sin. Adam and Eve could not bear the weight of all human tragedy. The ancient myth of the fall of the "sons of God" in Gen. 6:1–4 was enlisted to explain the presence of an evil that emanates not from humanity alone, but from something higher as well: not divine, but transcendent, suprahuman, that persists through time, is opposed to God and human faithfulness, and seeks our destruction, damnation, illness, and death.

—Walter Wink

Naming the Powers: The Language of Power in the New Testament (Philadelphia: Fortress Press, 1984), 23.

the biblical text to the historical rebellion of angels. We learn from these four verses that evil is not only within human nature, but it also stands outside it.

Besides the evil humans commit, demonic forces are operating. Rebellion ceases to be limited to a human catastrophe. In this story it also becomes a cosmic catastrophe. All of creation, as Paul will eventually remind us, is affected, groaning to be liberated from the consequences of sin (Rom. 8:20–22). Not only does the story outline the spiritual consequences of a cosmic transgression, but also the more physical consequences, specifically the introduction to the world of a mighty race known as the Nephilim (literally "fallen ones"). The rebellion acted out by these angels with human women provides a rationale and justification for the worldwide cataclysm that is to follow. But God's punishment is not limited to the flood. Human life, which had in the pre-deluge years reached 969 years (in the case of Methuselah, Gen. 5:27) was curtailed to only 120 years (further reduced post-deluge to "seventy years, or perhaps eighty," Ps. 90:10), thus connecting longevity with the eventual falling away from godliness.

The first four verses of chapter 6 become the genesis for what will eventually develop into the Christian concept of Satan, complete with his own host of fallen angels. Although a difficult passage to interpret, many Jewish and Christian leaders came to accept the Hebrew expression *bene 'elohim* (literally "sons of God") to be a reference to angels who married human women and had offspring through these unions.[33] In other places within Scripture where this term is used (i.e., Job 1:6; Dan. 3:25; Pss. 29:1; 89:6; etc.), a direct reference to heavenly beings seems intended. Of course, this interpretation was not unanimously accepted. Others believed that "sons of God" was a reference to the descendants of Seth, Adam's firstborn male after Cain murdered Abel, who married the "daughters of men," a reference to the female descendants of Cain.[34]

---

33. Among those who advocated this view are Philo of Alexandria, Josephus, Justin Martyr, Tertullian, Cyprian, and Ambrose, to name but a few.

34. Among those who advocated this view are Julius Africanus, Theodoret of Cyrus, John Chrysostom, Augustine of Hippo, Jerome, Martin Luther, and John Calvin, to name but a few.

If indeed the two first verses indicate that angels came to earth and had sexual intercourse with human women, it was because they, according to Christians, were seduced by women's long hair (1 Cor. 11:10). Still, the idea of angels engaging in fornication may appear odd to the modern reader, especially for those who have come to believe that there is no sex in heaven, based on a misinterpretation of Matthew 22:23–30, where Jesus teaches that in heaven men and women do not marry because they are like the angels. Centuries of anti-body theology within Christianity have led many to conclude that men and women, in their glorified, resurrected bodies, will be like angels—that is, asexual creatures. If heaven is perfection, and if there is no sex in heaven, then for those who want perfection the conclusion should be obvious: imitate the heavenly model by minimizing, if not eliminating, sex on earth. But such an interpretation is problematic. Angels, according to Genesis 6:1–4, are not asexual, quite the contrary. Jewish tradition has always understood angels to be males, who were circumcised.[35]

Genesis 6:1–4, according to intertestamental Jewish writings, came to be associated with fallen angels. *First Enoch* 6–19 details how angels (referred to as Watchers) took human wives, causing their subsequent expulsion from heaven. Besides "defiling themselves with women,"[36] these fallen angels also taught humanity idolatry, magical medicine, and sorcery. Semihazah, the leader of the angels whose task was to watch over the universe (hence the term "Watchers"), persuaded two hundred fellow angels to engage in sexual intercourse with human women.

Yahweh's pronouncement in Genesis 6:3, where God's sovereignty is reasserted, seems to indicate that the crossing of boundaries between the spiritual and the fleshly was the source of cosmic evil. Throughout, the biblical text appears to mandate maintaining boundaries between the eternal and the mortal, the physical and the divine, the heavenly and the earthly. The supposed union of celestial beings with terrestrial women produced a progeny of a superhuman race of heroes (translated in the Septuagint as "giants") who were spiritually evil. They were called the Nephilim.

---

35. *1 Enoch* 15:7; *2 Enoch* 30:11; *Jubilees* 15:25–27.
36. A phrase used six times in the *Enoch* narrative: *1 Enoch* 7:1; 9:8; 10:11; 12:4; 15:2–7.

When these semidivine titans died, their spirits constituted a race of demons. The flood to come became divine punishment on both humans and demons for their sexual interaction and the evil spirits unleashed as a consequence. The book of *Jubilees* (10:7–11) informs us that when retribution did come, nine-tenths of the demons were bound and punished, while one-tenth were granted freedom. To this day they continue to tempt and torment humanity.

Although all of the Nephilim were supposed to be swept away by the worldwide flood, some seem to have survived, for they reappear in Numbers 13. Moses sends out spies to reconnoiter the land of Canaan. During their reconnaissance, the spies encountered the sons of Anak, descendants of the Nephilim. The spies felt like grasshoppers in comparison to them. The existence of these "giants" is also mentioned in Joshua 15:14; Deuteronomy 1:28; 2:10–11, 21; 9:2; and Amos 2:9.

The legend of heavenly beings fornicating with earthly women helps explain two NT passages that have historically been used to condemn same-gender loving relationships, 2 Peter 2:4–8 and Jude 6–7. God's punishment on Sodom and Gomorrah for their "shameless ways" and "unnatural fornication" (JB) is mentioned in both of these passages and serves as a proof text for an antihomosexual position. If these verses are read with the presupposition that the sin of these ancient cities was intimate same-sex relationships, then the logical conclusion is that these biblical passages condemn homosexuality with warnings of divine punishment. But a closer examination reveals that the authors of these biblical books were not referring to our modern understanding of homosexual orientation. The 2 Peter passage begins with a reference to sinning angels, while in the Jude passage the subjects are angels who traded "supreme authority" for "spiritual chains."

These two biblical passages are not referring to homosexuality, but rather to Genesis 6:1–4, as interpreted by *1 Enoch*, which refers to angels having sex with mortal women, and in doing so disrupting the natural order separating humans from the Divine. The "shameless ways" and "unnatural fornication" that the passages 2 Peter and Jude refer to is sex between celestial and mortal beings. But why then mention Sodom and Gomorrah? Because the men of

Sodom attempted to gang-rape Lot's guests, who were also angels. The townsfolk's unnatural lust for angels, and not homosexuality, is what is being condemned.

> You [woman] are the devil's gateway: you are the unsealer of that (forbidden) tree: you are the first deserter of the divine law: you are she who persuaded him [Adam] whom the devil was not valiant enough to attack. You destroyed so easily God's image, man. On account of your desert that is, death even the Son of God had to die.
> —Tertullian, *The Apparel of Women* 1.1
>
> Translated by the Rev. S. Thelwall, 1867.

The temptation of angels starts the narrative that brings about the flood and the destruction of all humanity, save Noah's family. What these four verses seem to teach us is that we should not engage in sexual relationships with celestial beings. More importantly, they seem to indicate that the boundaries between the secular and sacred should be maintained. But as important as this story might be to understanding why the worldwide deluge was necessary, the story of women tempting angels is problematic. The most troubling aspect is that, once again, women, specifically women's sexuality, are blamed for human rebellion against God.

Not only is Eve blamed for introducing sin to humanity, but now here her daughters are blamed for tempting the angels, and thus introducing sin to the spiritual cosmos. Women, as scapegoats for bringing evil to heaven and earth, must be restrained and contained, thus biblically justifying the establishment of the supposed divine institution of patriarchy.

FURTHER REFLECTIONS
Angels

Early in the Genesis story the reader is introduced to the concepts of angels, celestial beings called *mal'ak*, the Hebrew word for "messenger." Of the 213 occurrences of *mal'ak* in the Hebrew Bible, the vast majority refer to humans, as in the case of the individual who came to King Saul with a message that the Philistines invaded his realm (1

Sam. 23:27). A smaller portion of the time, *mal'ak* refers to heavenly beings or supernatural emissaries, as in the case of the angel summoned to lead and guide Moses to the promised land (Exod. 23:23). Still, in some passages the human or angelic identity *mal'ak* remains in dispute, as in the case of the messenger who traveled to Bethel to proclaim a word from God (Judg. 2:1).

Mel'akim (the plural of *mal'ak*), as heavenly beings, perform a wide variety of functions and tasks. They can bring the word of God to God's prophets (2 Kgs. 1:3), commission a person for a special task (Judg. 6:11–24), announce births (Gen. 18:9–15), guide a person(s) in the correct path (Ezek. 40:1–4), provide salvation from oppression (Num. 20:16), administer punishment (Ps. 35:5), or offer comfort (Gen. 31:11–13). At times, these heavenly beings form the army of God (Josh. 5:13–15), an army that numbers in the thousands (Ps. 68:17). God appoints these warrior angels to guard each nation (Deut. 32:8), and holds them accountable if they fail to maintain justice (Ps. 82). Finally, an ambiguity exists in how these angels relate to God. On several occasions, the "angel of the Lord/Yahweh" at the beginning of a passage morphs into God by the time the passage ends (Gen. 18).

Generally speaking, these angels are faithful to Yahweh. Still, cases exist when angels participate in evil acts. Prior to Noah's flood, women were blamed for sexually seducing angels from God's divine council with their long hair (Gen. 6:1–4; 1 Cor. 11:10). Passages such as these lead the reader of the Hebrew Bible to conclude that there are good angels and bad angels. Still, there appears to be no Hebrew word for these bad angels—no word that can be unquestionably translated as "demon," mainly because the Hebrew Bible lacks a comprehensive understanding of the concept of the demon that developed later in Christianity.

6:5–7:16

Testimony of Noah

Noah is the ninth descendant of Adam, born 126 years after Adam's death. If we accept the longevity of the pre-deluge patriarchs, then Noah is born 1,056 years after the creation of the earth, belonging to the first generation born after Adam's death. A millennium after God created the heavens and the earth, Noah—the new Adam of creation—is destined to become the second father of humanity, for just as all are descendants of Adam, now all will also be descendants of Noah.

The story of Noah is an incongruent product caused by interweaving at least two different sources, J and P. Even a casual reading reveals certain inconsistencies in the story. For example, source P tells us that God instructed Noah "to bring two of every kind" of animal into the ark (6:19–20), while source J states that God instructed Noah to bring "seven of each kind" of clean animals, and two of each kind of unclean animals (7:2–3 JB). Such discrepancies do not take away from the purpose of the story, which is to reveal God's personality. Noah's testimony about God reveals for us a God that is not some ethereal abstract concept, but rather an anthropomorphic Deity.

Noah shows us a God who has form, a physical anthropomorphism. We are told in 6:13 and 7:9 that God spoke to Noah, implying that God has a mouth (Isa. 1:20), lips, and tongue (Isa. 30:27). Throughout the Bible, in numerous places, God is said to have eyes (Ps. 11:4), ears (Isa. 59:1), nose (Exod. 15:8), hands (Isa. 1:15), voice (Ezek. 1:24, 28), wings (Ps. 57:1), and a heart (Gen. 6:6). Noah also shows us a God who has feelings, a psychological anthropomorphism called anthropopathism. God is described in Genesis 6:6–7 as experiencing grief and regret. The Bible also tells us that on several occasions God experienced amazement (Isa. 59:16), jealousy (Exod. 20:5), hatred (Amos 5:21), and anger (Jer. 3:12–13). Finally, Noah depicts God as a God who acts—an active anthropomorphism. The story tells us Noah walked with God (Gen. 6:9), and ends with God closing the door behind Noah's family as they enter the ark (7:16). God is a God who rests (2:2–3), whistles (Isa. 5:26), laughs (Ps. 2:4), sleeps (44:23), grasps (35:2), and stands (35:2). And while Noah does not give us any examples, the Bible also describes God as having intellectual facilities, a cerebral anthropomorphism. The Bible depicts a God who reasons (Isa. 1:18), remembers (Gen. 19:29), understands (Ps. 147:5), and knows (Gen. 18:17–19).

To speak of God using human descriptors is common throughout the biblical text. Such a depiction raises two important issues. First, the stoic philosophical influence on the early Christian church with its proclivity for devaluing the body and contributing to the normative body/spirit dichotomy is foreign to the biblical text. The human body, created by God, has such worth and value that even God is described in anatomical terms.

Second, if God is portrayed in Scripture as having a personality, then more important than the question of whether God exists is the question of what is the personality, the character, of this God whom we say does exist?

Genesis 6:6–7 focuses on two characteristics of God's personality. We are told that God *grieved* in God's heart and *regretted* the act of creation. "To grieve in one's heart" for the Hebrews had less to do with emotions than with the expression it conveys in English. The Hebrew word *leb,* which is usually translated as "heart," was not only the seat of human emotions but also the human will. The Hebrews understood the heart to be equivalent to a combination of the modern concepts of mind and will. A better reading of this verse would portray God as being grieved, pained, over the act of creation, what we today might call "buyer's remorse." What troubled God can be found in 6:5, a summation of the first four verses of this chapter. Humans participated in all forms of evil.

> The view that presents God in a one-sided and formalistic way as an unknowable entity, linked with an equally formalistic and depreciatory view of the littleness of man, and the inevitability of tension between God and man because man is a creature, will be rejected on the grounds that it is dishonouring to God. . . . [T]he idea of the transcendence of God has not been completely freed from its Greek philosophical origin and actually obscures the Christian understanding of God.
>
> —Adrio König
>
> *Here Am I! A Christian Reflection on God* (Grand Rapids: Eerdmans, 1982), 59.

Because God can regret an act, we are left wondering if God ever changes. Can God change God's own mind? Christians have always boasted about the immovability of God. When the author of the book of Hebrews states, "Jesus Christ is the same yesterday and today and forever" (13:8), the author also implies that God is the same yesterday, today, and forever, never changing. Still, Genesis provides us with a portrait of a God who does change, whose action might depend on the situation. If so, this places a greater importance on prayer. This is a God who acts on God's second thoughts concerning the creation process. Upset (another human emotion) over how God's creation chose evil, God resolves to literally wipe humanity, along with all other living creatures, off the face of the earth.

The focus of the story should not be the flood, but rather the consequences of humans who choose evil over the common good. Human moral failings pollute not only the individual and community, but also the earth. Thus not only are humans affected, but so is the planet. To focus solely on the flood and the gathering of zebras, giraffes, elephants, and lions is to relegate this biblical passage to a children's bedtime story. Noah's narratives bear witness to a God who is not angry in search of revenge, but grieves over creation. God grieves because God is emotionally invested in humanity. Yet God's response to his pain is troublesome. In God's pain, God destroys all living things—genocide on a global level. In short, the deluge reverses creation, as if God hit the reset button.

Even though God's participation in global genocide is incongruent with the trait of unconditional love, there is a liberative seed of good news in the story. With condemnation comes salvation. Not all living creatures are destroyed: a remnant exists in the form of a mini-Eden floating above the condemned earth. God instructs Noah to build an ark. No doubt it took faith to build a boat on dry land. We are told by the author of the book of Hebrews that Noah, being warned by God of something that he had never seen before, felt holy fear and built an ark to save his family (Heb. 11:7). Yet we are left wondering if Noah's actions were really a demonstration of such great faith. After all, Noah—unlike us—spoke and walked with God. Is it easier to be obedient to God when one directly walks and converses with God? Regardless, Noah was obedient; but this is a disturbing obedience. If he knew of the coming deluge, why didn't he warn his neighbors? Why didn't he evangelize?

Noah goes about following God's instruction on how to build an ark out of resinous wood. If a biblical cubit equals approximately eighteen inches, then the ark's dimensions were about 450 feet in length by 75 feet in width by 45 feet in height. If these dimensions are accurate, then the ark would have been about half the size of most modern-day large ocean liners, for example, the RMS Queen Elizabeth (1,031 by 118 by 233 feet). The ark that Noah built was not a self-propelling ship, but more like a big wooden box that relied on the currents (or God).

> In Noah's unquestioning obedience to divine commandments and lack of concern for others, lies the destruction of a world.
> —Michael Carden
>
> "Genesis/Bereshit," in *The Queer Bible Commentary*, ed. Deryn Guest, Robert E. Goss, Mona West, and Thomas Bohache (London: SCM Press, 2006), 31.

Like Enoch before him, Noah walked with God. He is chosen for salvation because we are told he was *tsaddiq*, often translated in English as "righteous." He is the first person in the Scriptures to be called righteous. To read the Bible in English can have more influence on the theological ethics we derive from the reading than we are willing to admit. For those who read the Bible in Spanish, they discover a text that provides theological interpretations different from those who read the same passages in English. To read the Bible in Spanish is to find different ways of understanding the Scriptures, ways that expand and challenge the normative interpretations of the dominant English-speaking culture. Genesis 6:9 in English may credit Noah's righteousness as the reason for his salvation, but we get a different interpretation when we read the same passage in Spanish. In Spanish we read, "*Noé, varón justo . . . ,*" literally, "Noah, a just man."

The concept of justice is usually lost in the ambiguous English word "righteous." Where English translations use "righteous," Hispanics would read the words *justo* or *justicia*, "just" or "justice." *Random House Dictionary* defines "righteous" as "morally right or justifiable, acting in an upright, moral way."

Such a definition implies an action that can be performed privately. One can be righteous on a deserted island through appropriate thoughts, acts of prayer, or proper worship of God. To be righteous does not necessarily require others. Justice, on the other hand, can only occur in community, manifesting itself in relation to others. Justice can never be practiced on a deserted island, in isolation; it needs others to whom justice can be administered. Where there is no community, there is no justice. Justice cannot be reduced to a private expression of faith; it is a public action. Communalism rather than individualism is privileged when the Spanish words *justo* and *justicia* are read in the Bible over against "righteous(ness)." To read the passage in Spanish is to discover a Noah who is saved because he did justice. Yet we are left wondering, if God told Noah that God was going to destroy the earth because it was "full of violence," why didn't Noah—like Jonah—warn others? If he would have, would anyone have repented?

Once the ark is completed, in the six hundredth year of Noah's life, God instructs Noah to enter the ark with a remnant of animals. Not only is the fate of animals tied to the fate of humans, but vice versa. As they enter the ark, it is God who closes the door behind them. One can imagine that as the door closed, humanity continued in its folly. "My people are destroyed," according to the prophet Hosea, "for lack of knowledge" (Hos. 4:6). The masses ignored the signs of the time. Jesus warned, "For as in those days before the flood they were eating and drinking, marrying and giving in marriage, until the day Noah entered the ark, and they knew nothing until the flood came and swept them all away" (Matt. 24:38–39).

To read today's newspapers is to read about violence that dwarfs any violence that might have existed in Noah's time. Wars, rumors of wars, terrorist acts, child abuse, senseless murders, narcotics abuse, and continued economic and physical conquest fill the lives of humanity. While we may take comfort in the rainbow, still the consequences of our actions—either actively or through our complicit participation in this violence—place us in the same peril as Noah's contemporaries. We too will be swept away, not by floodwaters, but by anger, hatred, and self-serving individualism that surround us as we continue to drink and be merry.

7:17–8:14
Testimony about the Flood

Legends concerning worldwide floods can be found throughout the ancient world, from the indigenous people of the Americas, to Africa, through the Mesopotamian region, toward the northernmost expanses of Europe and Asia, and out to the Pacific Islands. The prevalence of stories from diverse cultures concerning a catastrophic global deluge have led some to conclude that these stories are recollections of some distant event that was so stupendous that it has continued to be passed from generation to generation, even though time has blurred the details. While stories exist throughout diverse cultures concerning a single cataclysmic event, no archaeological evidence has thus far been uncovered that can prove or disprove the flood story.

The version of the flood story that appears in the biblical text is a correlation of at least two different flood stories. For example, source J tells us that the flood lasted forty days (7:17) and was caused by rain, while source P insists that the flood lasted one hundred fifty days (7:24) and was caused by the release of waters above the sky and beneath the earth. Regardless, the final flood story as it appears in our Bibles is no doubt influenced by two older Near Eastern stories: the Gilgamesh Epic and the Atrahasis Myth. The Babylonian Gilgamesh Epic goes back to 3000 BCE. Similar to the later Genesis story, the gods decide to inundate the entire planet. One of the gods, Ea (lord of wisdom), decides to save Utnapishtim of Shuruppak

> The Himalayan mountains soar to 28,028 feet in Mount Everest. For the flood story to be literally true, water more than five miles deep would have had to cover the earth. Since the earth is round, not flat, the water could not simply fall off the edges so that dry land could appear. . . . [A] five-mile depth of water covering the entire earth is more water than any of us could imagine. It is also a quantity that could not ever be absorbed by the earth.
>
> —John Shelby Spong
>
> *Rescuing the Bible from Fundamentalism: A Bishop Rethinks the Meaning of Scripture* (New York: HarperCollins, 1991), 30.

from the impending calamity. Ea provides his favorite servant with directions on how to construct the boat:

> O man of Shuruppak, son of Ubara-Tutu, tear down your house and build a boat, abandon possessions and look for life, despise worldly goods and save your soul alive. Tear down your house, I say, and build a boat. These are the measures of the barque as you shall build her: her beam equal her length, let her deck be roofed like the vault that covers the abyss; then take up into the boat the seed of all living creatures.[37]

Utnapishtim enters the ark with his family and animals. After six days of rain, the entire earth is underwater and all of humanity is destroyed. Before leaving the ark, Utnapishtim sends out three birds to see if the waters have receded. One of the birds, the raven, does not return; but the others, the dove and the swallow, return. At this point, Utnapishtim leaves the ark, releases the animals, and offers sacrifice. While similar to the Noah story, an important difference in the conclusion exists. The myth ends with Utnapishtim and his wife being given immortality. Noah, on the other hand, gets drunk, and his wife remains nameless.

> The Church, like the Ark of Noah, is worth saving; not for the sake of the unclean beasts and vermin that almost filled it, and probably made most noise and clamour in it, but for the little corner of rationality, that was as much distressed by the stink within, as by the tempest without.
> —William Warburton, bishop of Gloucester
>
> *Letters from a Late Eminent Prelate* (New York: E. Sargeant, 1809), 84.

Did a worldwide flood actually occur? Or was it a local flood that appeared global? Or was a popular local legend simply incorporated by the authors of the biblical text? Such questions are irrelevant to the reasons why a flood story appears in the Bible. The literal or symbolic acceptance of the global deluge is unimportant to the teaching goals of the biblical writer or writers. The story appears to make a theological statement concerning the character of God, a God who

---

37. *The Epic of Gilgamesh*, trans. N. K. Sanders (Baltimore: Penguin Books, 1960), 108.

can create and destroy an entire world. This is a God who judges human rebellion while showing mercy to the remnant that remains faithful to God's justice.

A little over a year elapsed from the moment Noah walked onto the ark until the day he left. While death and destruction reigned outside, a miniature Eden existed within the confines of the boat, with Noah playing the role of a second Adam. Outside the ark, God's act of creation was reversed. On the second day of creation (the first creation story), God divided the waters in two—a "vault" above the earth, and another below (1:6–8). By the time of Noah, God undid creation by allowing the springs of the deep and the sluices of the heavens to flow freely so that the waters could come together again (8:2).

As the days dragged into months, it must have been difficult to remember in the damp and dark ark what God made so clear in the light of day. Living in accordance with our faith may be difficult, but, at least to some degree, it is clear. Obedience to God may create chaos as fierce as the tempest raging outside the ark. How many of the faithful have at one time or another cried out to heaven, *Eli, Eli, lema sabachthani*—"My God, my God, why have you forsaken me?" (Ps. 22:1, quoted by Jesus in Matt. 27:46; Mark 15:34). When no hope was in sight, when all seemed lost, we are told that God remembered Noah and all the beasts and cattle that were with him in the ark. Even if, unlike Noah, there is no happy ending, God still remembers. Even when crucifixion ends with death—God still remembers. Even when we shake our fist at what seems to be an empty heaven— God still remembers. Again, whether the flood occurred as written in the biblical text is of little importance. What is important is that in the midst of our own floods, when we are hanging on for dear life to a piece of wood lest we drown—God still remembers. We are never alone. Because God remembers, we are provided with the courage and strength to either endure until the treacherous currents ebb, or face death with dignity, knowing that no matter what eventually happens, there is resurrection.

As the waters began to subside and the mountaintops began to be visible, Noah opened the porthole and sent out a raven, an unclean fowl. We are told that the raven flew back and forth, but are not told if it ever returned. Next, Noah sent out a dove, a clean fowl. Finding nowhere to perch, the dove returned. Noah waited seven days before again sending out the dove. This time it returned holding an olive leaf in its beak. The dove, and the modern term "offering an olive branch," have come to symbolize peace. God's regret for creating humans, like the waters surrounding the ark, had subsided. The olive leaf represented God suing for peace. For Christians, the water, according to the author of 1 Peter, symbolizes baptism, the new Christian initiation ritual. As Noah and his family were saved "by water," so too are Christians saved by a water that does not simply wash off physical dirt, but confirms a pledge made to God to follow Christ (1 Pet. 3:20–22).

The story of the flood tells us several important things about God. God creates, God destroys, God judges, God saves, and God remembers. The story also teaches us that God changes. The flood story ends where it began. We are told that all living creatures that roamed the earth were destroyed because of humans' evil imagination. The story starts with the depravity of people and ends with continuing human depravity. Even though evil is washed from the earth's face, rebellion remains. When the story concludes, we discover a Noah who falls short of the glory of God, a man who becomes drunk, an act frowned on by the prophets. "Woe to him who gives drink to his neighbors, pouring it from the wineskin till they are drunk" (Hab. 2:15 NIV). Noah's narrative ends with the start of human rebellion manifested as the tower of Babel. Universal rebellion against God and God's ways continues. Humans do not change, but thankfully God does. The God who brought the flood promises never again to destroy the earth in like fashion. Rebellion, wired into the human condition, will never again be washed away.

8:15–9:17

Testimony Concerning a New World Order

With God, even global catastrophes are followed with saving grace and hope for a renewed creation. The earth was now dry and it was time for the only surviving family, the remnant, to disembark from the ark that brought them to safety. Following God's instructions, Noah set loose all the animals that were under his care. As it was in the beginning, God commanded that all creatures be fruitful and multiply so as to fill the earth.

Upon setting foot on dry ground, Noah built an altar and there sacrificed several clean animals to God. The whole animal was presented as a burnt offering. And as the sweet savory fragrance of Noah's gratitude rose into the heavens, God was pleased, so pleased that God swore never again to curse the earth because of the evil imaginations contrived in the hearts of humans. The evil tendencies of humans remain in a post-deluge world. Even though the story ends where it began, never again will God strike down every living creature due to human wickedness. Scaring humans into obedience with threats of worldwide calamity and devastation did not and will not work. Humans did not change, but the unchangeable God did. Humans will hopelessly continue to imagine evil in their hearts; nevertheless, God's resolve to wipe them out will not be part of this new world order, for a more intimate relationship is established between God and humans. God transforms God's self into a God of long-suffering patience and endless mercies.

As a manifestation of God's supremacy, the earth, for as long as it lasts, will move in an orderly manner through the different seasons. God's power can bring about the destructive force of a worldwide deluge, but this is also a power that can regulate the productive force by which the earth bountifully feeds all living creatures, including humans. The rhythms of the earth—night and day, winter and summer, cold and heat—all work together so that sowing and reaping can occur. With each new season of reaping comes the renewal of salvation, similar to that experienced by Noah, as the earth produces the basic needs of humanity. God becomes a God of harmony whose hand is not limited to cataclysmic death-dealing events. Because God is a God of life, cosmic harmony is required. Along with Noah we discover that regardless of the flood of worries swirling around us, and currents threatening to pull us under at any moment, we all can take comfort in the faithfulness of a God of life who promises not to abandon us because of the evil imaginations contrived in our hearts.

Starting with chapter 9, the disembarking is again told, but this time pulling solely from the P source, as opposed to 8:15–22, which was a product of J and P. In this version, the theme of creation's renewal begins with God blessing Noah, instructing his family to be fruitful and multiply. God's original will for the first humans, Adam and Eve, has not changed. Noah will now become the obedient progenitor of a new humanity within a new world order.

But this new world order has a dark side. Fear becomes normative on the earth. While animals, prior to the flood, were subjected to humans, now they exist in mortal terror of humans. In the new world order that is to follow the chaos of the deluge, humans are to become the dread of all animals. Like plants and foliage, animals will now provide humans with food. Along with the earlier 1:29–30, 9:3 has led many to conclude that up to this point humans were vegetarians. It is after the flood that humans become carnivorous, no longer living in perfect harmony with the animals. Not until some messianic future will the lamb again lie down with the lion.

Even though humans can now kill animals for food, all life, even the life of animals, remains sacred to God. Because blood contains the source of life, the soul of the living creature, one requirement is given to carnivorous humans. They cannot eat flesh that still has blood. Eventually, with the codification of the law, the prohibition of eating blood will be included (Lev. 7:27). This becomes a core principle in following God, so important that when the early Christian church concludes that believers need not be circumcised, they still held on to the requirement prohibiting eating blood (Acts 15:20).

Not only do humans kill animals for substance, some humans resort to killing other humans, at times for profit. Still, God prohibits the shedding of human life, because humans are created in the image of God, the *imago Dei*. Whosoever sheds the blood of humans shall have his or her own blood spilled by humans, blood for blood. Originally this was the responsibility of the victim's next of kin; with time, the responsibility was assumed by the sociopolitical governing body. Unfortunately, whenever we discuss biblical passages dealing with murder, we limit the concept of shedding human life to a particular violent act that brings immediate death. No doubt taking a knife and plunging it into another, or taking a gun and pulling the trigger while aiming at another, brings death—relatively fast and relatively efficiently.

But the shedding of human life can never be limited to such immediate violent acts. Just as deadly, just as efficient, but not necessarily as fast is when we allow our political and economic systems to murder for us so that we may benefit from the prevailing social structures. Institutional violence moves ethics from the individual to the collective realm, recognizing that the unfair global distribution of the earth's resources also causes the shedding of human life through poverty. When tens of thousands of human beings die each and every day of hunger and preventable diseases so that an elite few can amass the vast majority of all the earth's wealth, and we remain silent, then we too become complicit with the shedding of life. We become complicit with institutional violence.

Institutional violence is the by-product of powerful groups and institutions determined to maintain an unequal and unjust political and economic order so that their amassed power and privilege can be maintained and increased at the expense of society's most vulnerable members. Murder, the spilling of blood, can no longer be limited to an act perpetrated by one individual against another individual. Even more devastating are the countless faceless (no)bodies in the eyes of the world who live short and brutal lives so that the few can enjoy life and life abundantly. Yet these so-called nobodies are endowed with the very image of God, making their death a cosmic outrage. They, the victims of institutional violence, like any other human beings, deserve to be valued and treated with dignity.

> [Several Christian movements contend] that the daily experience of violence in many societies, which affects their most vulnerable members, is closely related to the reality of socioeconomic injustice, ecological destruction, militarization of society, uneven distribution of wealth, poor access to education and health, poverty, unemployment, racism, gender inequality, and global economic policies that benefit only a small portion of the world's population.
> —Salvador A. Leavitt-Alcántara
>
> "Institutionalized Violence," in *Hispanic American Religious Cultures,* ed. Miguel A. De La Torre, 2 vols. (Santa Barbara: ABC CLIO, 2009), 1:301–2.

In this new world order, God establishes an unconditional covenant with Noah, with his descendants, and with every living creature. This is the first covenant, the first legal agreement made between God and humans. Unlike the other covenant in Genesis made with Abraham, or the covenant made in Exodus at Mount Sinai, the covenant made with Noah is not made exclusively with the people of Israel; it is a covenant made with all of humanity. But it is not just with humans; it is a covenant made with all of creation. The well-being of humans will from now on be intertwined with the well-being of the entire planet and all forms of life it contains.

The sign of the covenant shall be God's weapon, the bow, set on the clouds, what today we call the rainbow. Whenever it rains, God will see the rainbow and remember the covenant made, and thus will not destroy the earth by flood. We too will see God's bow and take comfort in God's promise; for even though the bow is an instrument of war, the unstrung bow in the sky will testify to God's pledge to never again make war on humans.

Although God promises to never sweep away all creatures through the waters of a flood, some, including the author of Peter (2 Pet. 3:5–7), insist that the promise is only limited to a watery destruction, leaving open the possibility of a fiery apocalypse on the day of judgment.

> Noah was found perfectly virtuous,
> in the time of wrath he became the scion:
> because of him a remnant was preserved for the earth
> at the coming of the Flood.
> Everlasting covenants were made with him
> that never again should every living creature perish by flood.
> —Sirach 44:17–18 (JB)

9:20–29

Testimonies of Ham

The story of Noah's flood begins with an account of sexual irregularities, the union of mortal women with heavenly beings (Gen. 6:1–4), and ends with the sexual irregularity between Ham and his father, Noah. According to the story, Noah, shortly after the flood, became a tiller of soil, following in the footsteps of the first man, Adam, who also was responsible for tending the garden to bring forth the earth's fruits and produce. We are also told that Noah is the first person to plant a vineyard, and thus make wine, fulfilling his father Lamech's prophecy. Lamech named his son Noah (meaning "rest") because "Out of the ground that the LORD has cursed this one shall bring us relief from our work and from the toil of our hands" (5:29). One night, after drinking too much of the consolation derived from the ground, he passed out drunk and naked in his tent. He probably did not know the potency of his new discovery; consequently he is not blamed or condemned by the biblical writer.

Caution should be taken in demonizing the drinking of alcohol. Among several Christian denominations, drinking has been equated with sinful behavior. Yet the biblical text does not condemn the drinking of wine or "strong drink." According to Deuteronomy, a tithe of all that the land produces is to be collected each year and enjoyed in the presence of God. But if where God chooses to give his name a home is too far away, then the tithe is to be converted to cash and spent "for whatever you wish—oxen, sheep, wine, strong drink, or whatever you desire. And you shall eat there in the presence of the LORD your God, you and your household rejoicing together" (Deut. 14:22–27). And for those who are Christians, let us not forget that Jesus' first miracle was to make wine out of water for a party! (John 2:1–12). What the biblical text condemns is drunkenness (Isa. 5:11), not drinking.

Even so, the purpose of this biblical story is not to espouse moderation in drinking, but to relate what occurs after Noah gets drunk. We are told that his son Ham entered his father's tent and "saw" or "gazed" on his father's nakedness, and for this his posterity was cursed. Surely seeing one's father naked should not cause divine retribution, or else most of us who saw our father without clothes (e.g., in the bathroom or changing clothes at a gymnasium's locker room) would be in trouble. To gaze on nakedness meant more than simply seeing. Gazing can be a euphemism for sexual intercourse (see the Babylonian Talmud, *Sanhedrin* 70a quote below). However, we should exercise caution in asserting that Ham participated in some homosexual act, even though by gazing on his father's nakedness it is implied that he sexually took advantage of him. According to some, Ham either raped Noah or castrated him, a point reiterated in rabbinical writings:

> Rab and Samuel [differ,] one maintaining that [Ham] castrated [Noah], whilst the other says that he sexually abused him. He who maintains that he castrated him, [reasons thus:] Since he cursed him by his fourth son, he must have injured him with respect to a fourth son. But he who says that he sexually abused him, draws an analogy between "and he saw" written twice. (Babylonian Talmud, *Sanhedrin* 70a)

Another possibility is that Ham slept with Noah's wife, his mother. Leviticus 18:8 identifies "uncovering the nakedness of one's father" and "the nakedness of one's mother," which is prohibited, since the expression is thought to refer to engaging in a sexual relationship with the woman of one's father.

Although ambiguous as to which act Ham engaged in, it is clear that the passage illustrates how he asserted his power over his father by subjugating and humiliating him. Placing Noah in a sexually subjugated position was, in effect, an assertion of Ham's power. The act of sexual domination by a son over against the father is a grasp for power. This might explain why Ham, the ancestor of the Canaanites, after "gazing" on his father's nakedness, told his two brothers. Sharing this news, which one would expect to be kept hidden, becomes a public announcement that Ham is now "the man."

By telling his two brothers what he has done, he positions his dominance within the new post-deluge world. But ironically, rather than ascending to new heights of power, Ham is cast down, through a curse, to a position of servitude. It is interesting to note that among Ham's descendants are the Egyptians (who enslaved the Hebrews) and Canaanites (who stood in the Hebrews' way of possessing the promised land). Was the curse of Canaan divine justification for the future Israelites' prejudices and distain for the Canaanites? Could it be that the writer of Genesis wanted to reveal that it was sinful and wicked for Ham (and through him, his descendants the Egyptians and Canaanites) to subjugate or humiliate the Hebrews by setting themselves up as the rulers of the land? If so, then Noah's prophecy finds fulfillment with the conquest of the promised land and the subjugation of the Canaanites.

Upon hearing Ham's account of what transpired, Ham's two older brothers, Shem and Japheth, took a cloak, walked into Noah's tent, and covered him, keeping their faces turned away so as not to gaze on him. When Noah arose from his drunken stupor and realized what had occurred, he exclaimed in horror for what Ham "had done to him." Subsequently, he cursed Canaan, saying that he would be a slave to his brothers. Here is where the text becomes problematic. Verse 24 clearly states that Noah saw what "his youngest son" had done to him, but he cursed Canaan. Is Canaan a fourth son? This might explain the part of the curse that makes Canaan a slave to his *brothers*, Shem and Japheth (vv. 25–26). If he was instead Ham's son, then he would have been Shem and Japheth's nephew, not brother. Or maybe Canaan and Ham are the same person? The J narrative may have listed Noah's sons as Shem, Japheth, and Canaan, while the P source named them as Shem, Ham, and Japheth, Japheth being the middle child for J and the youngest for P.

But if Canaan is indeed Ham's son, why is he, and not the other sons of Ham, cursed? Why Canaan, and not Cush, Egypt, or Put? Why does Noah curse his grandson Canaan for the offense of his son Ham? Introducing Canaan as Ham's son into the story might have coalesced the two different sources; but it created the troublesome theological concept that children are held responsible for the sins of the father—a proposition repudiated by most, but not all (e.g., Deut. 5:9) Jews and Christians. The prophet Jeremiah will eventually ask if the fathers eat unripe grapes, will their children's teeth be set on edge? He answers no. Each will die due to his own sin (a dismissal of the concept of

> R. Huna also said in R. Joseph's name: "You have prevented me from doing something in the dark [sc. cohabitation], therefore your seed will be ugly and dark-skinned." R. Ḥiyya said: "Ham and the dog copulated in the Ark, therefore Ham came forth black-skinned while the dog publicly exposes its copulation."
> —*Midrash Genesis Rabbah* 36:7

original sin). Every person who eats unripe grapes will have his own teeth set on edge (Jer. 31:29–30). If Ham sinned, then it is he, not Canaan, who should have been cursed.

The curse of Ham (although literally it was the curse of Canaan) was believed to be, since early rabbinical writings, the turning of his skin black.

It is this curse that led Europeans to religiously justify the enslavement of Ham's children, Africans. In nineteenth-century America, Southerners who advocated the consignment of Ham's descendants to perpetual servitude believed and advocated this interpretation of Noah's curse. The curse of Ham has played a crucial role within American history since its origins by providing biblical justification for both slavery and segregation. No biblical story has been so consistently used as proof text for the enslavement and oppression of those from African descent. Apologists for the institution of slavery argued that Ham was born black and hence his sin brought down on him and his descendants the curse of being slaves.

Other apologists would argue that blacks constituted "another species of man" from Adam. They believed that Adam and all of his descendants were of the white race.[38] Some believed blacks to be humans without souls, while others simply saw them as "two-footed beasts" who entered Noah's ark as animals.[39]

> Ham was born black; hence his descendants are the black race. A curse was placed upon Ham because of his wickedness; the curse involved the servitude of Ham's son Canaan to the descendants of Shem and Japheth. Thus all blacks are to be understood as under the curse of God, and slavery is justified because God intended it.
> —Thornton Stringfellow
>
> *Slavery: Its Origin, Nature, and History Considered in the Light of Bible Teaching, Moral Justice, and Political Wisdom* (New York: J. F. Trow, 1861), 35.

38. William Sumner Jenkins, *Pro-Slavery Thought in the Old South* (Chapel Hill: University of North Carolina Press, 1935), 272.
39. For the former see Josiah Priest, *Bible Defense of Slavery: Origins, Fortunes and History of the Negro Race*, 5th ed. (Glasgow, KY: W. S. Brown, 1853), 33; for the latter see Ariel (Bucker H. Payne), *The Negro: What Is His Ethnological Status?* 2nd ed. (Cincinnati: Self-Published, 1867), 45–46.

Noah may have cursed Canaan, but he goes on to bless Shem and Japheth, probably because they covered his shame. He blesses Yahweh, the God of Shem, and predicts that God will enlarge Japheth, who will live in the tents of Shem. The story ends with a postscript, reminding us that Noah lived an additional three hundred fifty years after the flood, dying when he was nine hundred fifty years old (Gen. 9:29).

9:18–19; 10:1–32; 11:10–25
Testimonies of Shem, Ham, and Japheth

Noah left the ark with his family, including his three sons, Shem, Ham, and Japheth. From this trinity of Noah's boys, Scripture tells us that the entire world would be repopulated. Of course, women must have helped them, although they remain silent and invisible in the begetting story. Still, those who left the ark were faithful to God's command to be fruitful and multiply, as evidenced by the genealogy that is presented. The genealogies of Noah's sons are given to help the reader understand certain theological propositions: (1) that all the people of the earth are related, derived from one man (Noah) and one God; (2) because of this unity of humanity, God embraces all nations, even those that fail to recognize God; and (3) why, in spite of human unity, there still exist different types of people—not just physical differences, but more importantly differences in cultures and fortunes. If the theological lesson gleaned from the genealogy is that all of humanity has one source, then the ethical response is that strangers are more than just my neighbors—they are my family.

Genesis proceeds in chapter 10 to provide what has come to be called the Table of Nations, a conflation of at least two sources, J and P, plus later interpolations, which are separated by centuries and arranged according to some historical or political relationships. This might explain the inconsistency as to who exactly was Noah's cursed son, Ham or Canaan. A possible solution might have been making Ham the father of Canaan. The genealogy may present different people groups, but for the author they are all under the authority, whether they realize it or not, of one God—Yahweh.

The Table of Nations attempts to present a list of seventy individuals (clans) who were historically and politically related to one another. Chapter 10 is not an attempt to tie these people to a particular race or language; nevertheless, for centuries scholarly attempts have been made to connect the descendants of Noah with modern-day ethnicities, races, and nations. Attempts have been made to connect the Japhethites with those of the north and west, the Hamites with those from the south, and the Shemites with those of the east (not too far east because no mention is made of Chinese, Mongols, or American native tribes). But even if the Table of Nations was at one time accurate concerning the migration of people from where Noah settled toward the lands of Europe, Africa, and Asia, it would still be inaccurate because it fails to consider subsequent migrations of peoples, historical miscegenation, or the original physical and racial characteristics of the people listed. For this reason, the so-called Table of Nations provides little value when modern ethnological methodologies are employed. What the Table of Nations does expose is how ambiguous and unreliable the biblical text is in revealing any racial origins of people. It is pure speculation on the part of anyone to assign Noah, or any of his sons, to any particular race.

Yet absurd biblical interpretations have been proposed, making such connections to advance certain ideologies. For example, among Japheth's sons are Magog, Tubal, and Meshech. The prophet Ezekiel will one day be instructed by God to address Gog and the country of Magog, the prince of Rosh, Meshech, and Tubal (Ezek. 38:2–3). Using a great deal of imagination, Hal Lindsey, of the 1970 apocalyptic best seller *The Late Great Planet Earth*, concluded that Magog, Tubal, and Meshech represent what was during Lindsey's time the Soviet Union. While many believed that the tribes of Magog, Meshech, and Tubal might have settled in the Black Sea region, it takes a leap of faith to connect these ancient people with the Soviet Union prior to its collapse. Nevertheless, by linking Genesis 10 to Ezekiel 38, Lindsey predicted that sometime during the 1980s the Soviet Union would invade Israel and trigger Armageddon.[40]

---

40. Hal Lindsey, *The Late Great Planet Earth* (Grand Rapids: Zondervan, 1970), 48–60.

Although not all interpretations take such fanciful turns, many do provide a perilous foundation on which oppressive structures can be built.

More insidious than predicting that the Soviet Union would attack Israel is interpreting Scripture to justify the supremacy of one particular race. Biblical scholarship once relegated the ability to reason to the Japhethites, physical labor to the Hamites, and the things of the spirit to the Shemites—a dangerous interpretation responsible for providing spiritual cover in the rise of European imperialism. Lacking any archaeological, historical, or ethnographical evidence, some simply believe that the descendants of Japheth were whites who would populate European lands. For example, Finis Jennings Dake, in his annotated reference Bible, elucidates that there is a "prophecy that Japheth would be the father of the great and enlarged races. Government, Science and Art are mainly Japhethic. . . . His descendants constitute the leading nations of civilization."[41] It becomes problematic to connect the ancient children of Japheth with modern-day Europeans and then imply that it is God's ordained purpose for these people to take their exalted place in world history. Such interpretations have led to the dispossession and disenfranchisement of the vast majority of the world's nonwhite population. While Ham was to be cursed as a servant race, and Seth was to be blessed as a chosen race with a particular relationship with God, Japheth, in the minds of such scholars, was to be blessed as an enlarged and superior race.

> In world politics, . . . in medicine, in the field of education, child care, the status of women, social welfare, the rights of the individual, freedom of speech and religion—in all these areas the Western branch of Japhethic civilization has been the leader and teacher of the rest of the world. In the last 25 centuries world leadership has remained in the hands of the Japhetic peoples. "God enlarge Japheth," said Noah, and God certainly did.
>
> —Arthur W. Kac
>
> *The Messianic Hope: A Divine Solution for the Human Problem* (Grand Rapids: Baker Book House, 1975), 16.

41. Finis Jennings Dake, *Dake's Annotated Reference Bible* (1963; repr. Lawrenceville, GA: Dake Bible Sales, 1981), 36.

The children of Ham, on the other hand, were believed to be destined for physical labor. Again, lacking any archaeological, historical, or ethnographical evidence, some simply assumed that the descendants of Ham, due to whatever occurred during Noah's drunken stupor, would be blacks who would populate Africa. But not just blacks. According to Arthur Custance, "all the so-called colored races—the yellow, red, brown, and black—the Mongoloid and the Negroid," were derived from Ham.[42] Hence we now have the biblical justification for a superior race, the Japhethites, and an inferior race, the Hamites.

Although Ham is destined to servitude, ironically, among the most famous to come from this line is the mighty hunter Nimrod, son of Cush. He is one of two figures listed who appears to be an individual rather than clans or people. Not much is said about Nimrod, except that he is reckoned as the world's first potentate. Although we are not told anything about his relationship with God except that he was a mighty hunter in Yahweh's eyes, his name might betray his character. The Hebrew word "to rebel" (*marad*) may be the root of the Hebrew word Nimrod. But what was it about Nimrod that was rebellious? Nimrod is credited with building an empire that included Babel (Babylon), Erech, and Accad. From there he continued to Assyria and built Nineveh, the capital city of the Assyrian Empire. If there is any connection with the word "rebellion" and Nimrod's name, Walter Brueggemann suggests it might be that empire building is a rebellion against Yahweh.[43]

Another son of Ham was Canaan, who is cursed for whatever happened during Noah's drunken stupor. Making Canaan the son of Ham is problematic, because as a people the Canaanites are ethnically closer to Shem, father of the Semites, even to the point of speaking a Semitic language. Maybe the Canaanites' inclusion within the ancestral line of Ham has to do with the political and economical domination of the Canaanites by the Hamite people, the Egyptians. Or maybe Canaan's placement in Ham's ancestral line has more to do with politics than with history. After all, the Canaanites

---

42. Arthur C. Custance, *The Doorway Papers*, vol. 1: *Noah's Three Sons: Human History in Three Dimensions* (Grand Rapids: Zondervan, 1975), 12–14.
43. Walter Brueggemann, *Genesis*, Interpretation (Atlanta: John Knox Press, 1982), 92.

inhabited the land that the children of Abraham felt, via divine will, belonged to them. For propaganda purposes, it made sense to keep the Canaanites separate from the Hebrews by placing them in the Hamite tribe. Furthermore, cursing Canaan provided spiritual and moral justification for their decimation, thus facilitating their conquest. The Hebrews can express kinship with the surrounding Arabs, yet they maintain a distance from the Canaanites, who ironically are probably closer.

Finally, in chapter 11 we are given the descendants of Noah's son Shem who are blessed with a special relationship with God. They are the line by which God becomes known to the world. The term "Semites" derives from Shem and in modern times refers to those who speak Semitic languages. Ironically, some from Shem's ancestral line were non-Semitic people (e.g., the Elamites). It is from Shem that the future nation of Israel will arise, ten generations from Noah's son Shem to Abram, just as in chapter 5 there were ten generations from Adam to Noah. Among Shem's descendants is Eber, who becomes the eponymous ancestor of the Hebrews and through whom this chosen people came to be known.

The biblical narrative of all the people of the world begins to narrow its focus toward the narrative of one man, Abram, and the clan he would lead. This is why Shem's genealogy, even though he was the eldest son, comes last. With this last genealogy, the text moves away from a primeval history toward the birth of a particular family and the saga of its existence. It is from a singular descendant of Shem's ancestral line that, according to the text, God will reveal Godself, blessing all nations who bless this particular clan that will arise from Abram's loins.

11:1–9

Testimony about the Fourth Rebellion

The first rebellion against God was by humanity (3:1–12). The second rebellion came from the family (4:1–16). The third rebellion consisted of celestial beings (6:1–4). Now we come to the fourth and last major rebellion of the biblical primeval period, the rebellion of nations. Although some may argue that Genesis is a book demonstrating the steady decline of humanity toward greater depravity and sin, it would probably be more helpful to view the text as illustrating how humanity consistently falls short of the glory of God, with no single act being more depraved or a less offensive rebellion against God's ethical standards. If these primeval rebellions are to be connected, we should focus on the way the consequences of rebellion are rooted in how social systems, specifically political structures that are constituted by God and/or humans to safeguard life, usually end by rebelling against their assigned tasks by disenfranchising and dispossessing the very people they were supposed to protect.

This passage of Scripture attempts to answer important questions in the mind of the ancient reader: Why do many different nations and languages exists? Why are these different ethnic/racial groups alienated from each other? Why are there ruins consisting of towers in some areas of Babylon? How did these towers come to be ruins?

Sometime after the flood, Noah's family, the sole survivors of the deluge, began to be fruitful and multiply. They had a common language and vocabulary. Does this mean that only one ethnicity or one race, rooted in Noah, existed on the earth? Is the differentiation of languages brought about by God's response to the tower of Babel the start of ethnicities? The story starts with all the people of the earth gathered in one location speaking one language and ends with them being scattered to the four corners of the earth speaking different languages, thus contradicting the previous chapter (10:5, 20, 31), which provides the reader with a table of nations, explaining how different groups moved to various territories and established their own states. In any case, this passage begins with the people moving eastward and settling in the plain of Shinar, probably the Tigris-Euphrates Valley, which comprised the territories anciently known as Sumer and Akkad. This area, which included Babylonia (known to the Hebrews as Babel), was ruled by the mighty hunter Nimrod (Gen. 10:10). It was at Babel that humans attempted to return to God—to paradise—via a tower.

The rebellion committed at Babel was rooted in an arrogance of power, where political and economic order become ends in themselves. The nation said: Let us make a name for ourselves, a name that rivals that of God. This is the same arrogance of more recent imperial powers, whether it is the boast that the sun never sets on the British Empire, the declaration of a Third Reich that would last a thousand years, or a self-image of the United States as a beacon on a hill for all other nations. No doubt the J author's own ambiguity toward the building of the Jerusalem temple during J's times can be read into the building project at Babel. This story serves as a warning against the threat of imperial power during the writer's own time, as well as for those of us today who read the text and struggle with our own colonial appetites. All empires attempt to survive through their own resources, and like Babylon of old, through the labor and resources of surrounding people groups.

Babel's arrogance, like that of the previous rebellions, was to become Godlike with access to the realm of God. More than likely the tower was a ziggurat, or patterned after one, consisting of a seven-story stepped temple where gods were believed to make appearances. Usually, the temple had a sanctuary on the first level matched with another on the highest level. The ziggurat-type tower that was built at Babel signified human vanity contrasted with human insignificance. The story's humor is that humanity's attempt to build a structure that scrapes the sky is so inconsequential that God misses its importance and must come down to earth to be able to better see the town and tower that the children of humans built.

This biblical text maintains a separation between the celestial and the terrestrial. Heaven is God's dwelling place, the private domain of God and God's host. For the author of the story, human rebellion is rooted in the attempt to breach the established boundaries between the sacred and the secular. To trespass these

> Their man-made environment—the city with its ziggurat or artificial mountain—will replicate the structure of the cosmos, but here they will rule, not God. It is a supreme act of hubris, committed time and again in history—from the Sumerian city-states, to Plato's *Republic*, to empires, ancient and modern, to the Soviet Union. It is *the attempt to impose a man-made unity on divinely created diversity.*
> —Jonathan Sacks
>
> *The Dignity of Difference: How to Avoid the Clash of Civilizations* (New York: Continuum, 2002), 52.

boundaries is to invite divine retribution and its consequences. Through a play of Hebrew words, the story of the tower of Babel teaches that humans build with bricks (*lbn*), while God confuses (*nbl*). Even the Hebrew word *babel* is a play on the word *balal*, which means "to mix." From the word *babel* we get our English word "babble," though etymological roots indicate the term originally meant "entrance of God."

Not only has this story been used to maintain a separation between the sacred and the secular, but during the time of Jim and Jane Crow in the U.S. South, it was used to advocate God's divine will to maintain segregation among the races and ethnicities.

Everett Tilson, writing in the days of segregation, shows how some in his time maintained that the confusion of languages at Babel was God's "penalty for their attempt at racial integration"; but, as he insists, God's punishment was for the attempt of integrating God and humans.[44]

> [The confusion of languages] was an act of special Divine Providence to frustrate the mistaken efforts of godless men to assume the permanent integration of the peoples of the earth.
>
> —G. T. Gillespie
>
> *A Christian View on Segregation* (Winona, MS: Association of Citizen's Councils, 1954), 9.

In verse 7 the Hebrew words *lo' shema'* are used, which literally mean "not hear." God confuses their language so that they can no longer hear one another. It is not so much that people could not hear and understand one another's language, but rather that they stopped hearing or listening. Even though today we have the ability to understand one another's languages, the consequences of the tower of Babel remain; we still are unable to hear or listen to one another, making conversation across cultural lines fraught with difficulties and perils—even when the same language is spoken. However, for one brief moment, we were shown how it is possible to hear one another, regardless of our different languages, cultures, ethnicities, and races.

---

44. Everett Tilson, *Segregation and the Bible* (New York: Abingdon Press, 1958), 27.

For those who are Christians, the Pentecost event that started the Christian movement reverses the consequences of the tower of Babel. According to Acts 2:4–11, Peter, full of the Holy Spirit, addressed the crowd gathered "from every nation under heaven" outside the house where the disciples were meeting. When Peter began to preach the gospel, each person heard the message in his or her own language. It is important to note that the miracle of Pentecost is not that the crowd representing various nations understood the language spoken by Peter, but rather they each heard the message in their own tongue. Again, the emphasis is not on speech, but on hearing. At the tower of Babel diverse languages were used to separate people. Now, the ushering in of God's Spirit unified God's people, transcending this earlier separation. As a result, three thousand were converted, representing Parthians, Medes, Elamites, Mesopotamians, Judeans, Cappadocians, Pontusians, Asians, Phrygians, Pamphylians, Egyptians, Libyans, Cyrenes, Romans, Cretans, and Arabs, all of whom represented the first Christian church, probably the very first multicultural church—a paragon to be emulated by all future Christian churches. From Acts to Revelation, from the alpha to the omega, the ideal Christian church, as the body of Christ, is one that is multicultural.

FURTHER REFLECTIONS
Grace

The issue facing humanity is not if God exists, but rather what is the character of this God whom the faithful claim exists. God's existence will never be proven through reason, science, or experimentation. God's existence is, in the final analysis, an article of faith. Any attempt to validate God's existence is futile. But for those who do believe, the real question requiring exploration is the character of this God whose existence is accepted. The biblical text, starting with Genesis, is an effort of believers seeking to understand this God responsible for creating the heavens and the earth.

A salient characteristic of this God can be determined by how God responds to human rebellion. The early biblical writers attempted to show God's grace in the midst of God's wrath. After the first rebellion, when the first man and woman disobeyed God's instruction concerning the tree of the knowledge of good and evil, both were cast out of the garden of Eden. Yet in the midst of casting them out, God weaves clothes made of animal skins for the humans to wear. God's grace provides protection against the elements of nature and the harshness of human existence.

During the second rebellion, when Cain slew his brother Abel and was cursed to wander across the face of the earth, God again shows grace. God places a mark on Cain to serve as divine protection. Because of God's grace Cain is sheltered from being killed. During the third human rebellion, while the earth's inhabitants did what seemed right in their own hearts, God unleashed the waters above and below the earth to wash away every last remnant of life. Yet with the destruction of all life, God provides grace by preserving the family of Noah and a remnant of all the animals. Through them, humanity is saved from oblivion. Finally, while humans build towers so as to reach into the heavens and invade the domain of God, God confuses their languages so that they are unable to communicate with one another. Grace is again explicit in the consequences of dispersing humanity. Cultures and diversities, along with all the richness variety brings forth, are established.

No doubt, concerns can be raised about some of the actions in which God engaged. It is difficult to reconcile a loving and forgiving God with the God that wiped out all living things with a worldwide deluge. Still, while it may be difficult at times to understand God's acts, at least, no matter how severe and unjust those acts may seem to be, there is grace. We may still need to wrestle with God, demanding to see God's face; but we wrestle in confidence with a God of grace.

11:27–19:38

The Story of Abraham and Sarah

11:27–12:4
Testimony of Abram

Abram was an immigrant. If he was living today, we would probably call him an undocumented immigrant, or the more pejorative term, an illegal alien. Abram left the familiarity of home and extended kinship relationships to venture into a new land and live among a people who were not his own. In a time when most lived and died close to where they were born, the call or need to migrate was pregnant with hardships and difficulties. Within closed societies, xenophobia—then and now—made life difficult for the one who could never belong, no matter how much the immigrant tried to assimilate. To be an alien like Abram is to live in the absence of societal and familial structures that can provide protection and security. To be an alien is to live radically vulnerable to those who are deemed as belonging.

The story of God's people is the story of aliens. All the patriarchs of Genesis were sojourners. The narratives of Isaac, Jacob, and Joseph are the stories of aliens trying to survive among unfamiliar people in a land that belonged to others. The people who will come to be called Jews are formed in the foreign land of Egypt. They become a nation while traversing the desert, having no land to claim as their own. They will experience exile in a far-off place called Babylon and disenfranchisement on their own terrain due to military occupation by foreign empires (e.g., Rome). Is it any wonder that the second most common phrase throughout the biblical text exhorts the reader to take care of the alien among you, along with the widows and orphans? About forty verses appear in the Hebrew Bible instructing the Israelites not to mistreat or oppress the alien. The common theme of these verses can be summed up in Leviticus

19:33–34: "When an alien resides with you in your land, you shall not oppress the alien. The alien who resides with you shall be to you as the citizen [or native-born] among you; you shall love the alien as yourself, for you were aliens in the land of Egypt." Obviously, the experience of the Hebrews dwelling in a foreign land without rights profoundly shaped their self-awareness, so they designed specific laws on how to care for the "undocumented" among them.

Because Abram was an alien, all who came from his loins are descendants of aliens. God constantly reminds them not to forget this history, and thus be just to the stranger who resides among them. The biblical term "stranger" or "sojourner" (KJV) best captures the predicament of the modern U.S. alien. This is a person who exists in the in-between space of being neither native-born nor a foreigner. As such, the alien lacks the benefits and protection ordinarily provided to those tied to their birthplace. Vulnerable to those who profit from their labor, the alien derives security from the biblical mandate of hospitality. Treatment of the sojourner is based on three biblical presuppositions: (1) the Israelites were once aliens who were oppressed by the natives of the land (Exod. 22:21); (2) God takes sides and intervenes to liberate the disenfranchised (Exod. 23:9); and (3) God's covenant with Israel is contingent on all members of the community benefiting (Deut. 26:11).

> What we'll do is randomly pick one night every week where we will kill whoever crosses the border . . . step over there and you die. You get to decide whether it's your lucky night or not. I think that would be more fun . . . [I would be] happy to sit there with my high-powered rifle and my night scope.
> —Brian James, anti-immigrant talk radio host with KFYI-AM in Phoenix
>
> "Officials: Radio Host's Call to Kill Border Crossers Dangerous," *Mohave Daily News*, April 8, 2006.

Those who claim to be Christians soon discover that the authors of the Gospels connect the alien with the hope of salvation. For those of us who have been undocumented, comfort can be found in Matthew 2:13–14: "an angel of the Lord appeared to Joseph in a dream and said, 'Get up, take the child and his mother, and flee to Egypt, and remain there until I tell you; for Herod is about to search for the child, to destroy him.' Then Joseph got up, took the child and his mother by night, and went to Egypt." While most who read this scriptural passage from the privilege of citizenship may not find it necessarily foundational to their faith, those of us who are not native-born read God's hope actively connecting with our despair of being uprooted. Responsibility toward aliens is so paramount that God incarnated God's self as an alien. The radicalism of the incarnation is not so much that the Creator of the universe became a frail human, but rather that God chose to become an alien, fleeing the oppressive consequences of the empire of the time. In so doing, Jesus willingly assumed the role of the ultra-disenfranchised. Over two thousand years ago the Holy Family arrived in Egypt as political refugees, migrants fleeing the tyrannical regime of Herod. Jesus too was undocumented, a victim of circumstances beyond his comprehension or control. Jesus understood what it means to be seen as inferior because he was from a culture different from the dominant one. I have no doubt that Jesus wept as a child for the same reasons many aliens weep today. Those of us who are or have been undocumented aliens discover a savior who knows our fears and frustrations.

Basing our ethics on Abram's and Jesus' experiences of being aliens has led religious institutions, like the Catholic Church, to provide guidelines on how to treat the alien within our midst. The encyclical *Gaudium et Spes* declares:

> Justice and equity likewise require that the mobility which is necessary in a developing economy be regulated in such a way as to keep the life of individuals and their families from becoming insecure and precarious. Hence, when workers come from another country or district and contribute by their labor to the economic advancement of a nation or region, all discrimination with respect to wages and working conditions must be carefully avoided.[1]

Theologian Jon Sobrino insists that God chooses those who are oppressed in history—the hungry, the thirsty, the naked, the alien,

---

1. Second Vatican Council, *Gaudium et Spes: Pastoral Constitution on the Church in the Modern World*, 1965: I, 66.

the sick, the prisoner—and makes them the principal means of salvation.[2] God does not appear to the pharaohs or Caesars of history. Leaders of empires whose policies cause death to God's people are more aligned with the satanic than with the Divine. For this reason God appears to their slaves, their vassals, and those disenfranchised by the empire. Because God's ways never change, we can expect that God will appear not to U.S. presidents or members of Congress, regardless of their professions of faith, but to those most marginalized in the land because of these politicians' policies. And without a doubt, among the disenfranchised of the land are the undocumented, be they Abram and Jesus in the past or the undocumented alien today.

We are first introduced to Abram at the conclusion of Shem's genealogy, where the primeval history of the world concludes with the start of Hebrew "history." The past story of humanity makes way for the story of one particular family. Even though God chooses one people, the promise made to God's chosen exhibits caring for all of humanity, for they too can partake in the blessing. The God of Abram is not limited to this one family, this one clan, this one tribe. Abram's God is the God through which all nations can find a blessing because Abram's God is the God of all nations. This biblical passage does more than merely serve as a bridge between primeval and Hebrew history; it also bridges the story of human rebellion with the story of human promise, the story of God's judgment with the story of God's salvation.

The text begins with the story of Terah, Abram's father. We discover he had three sons: Abram, Nahor, and Haran, possibly triplets as 11:26 suggests, but Haran dies before Terah. Besides Terah outliving Haran, the biblical narrative provides scant information about him. According to *Midrash Genesis Rabbah* (38:13):

> Rabbi Hiyya the son of the son of Rav Adda of Jaffa: "Terah sold idols. . . . One time a certain woman came with a plate filled with fine flour. She said to [Abram], 'Here, offer this

---

2. Jon Sobrino, *Jesus the Liberator: A Historical-Theological Reading of Jesus of Nazareth*, trans. P. Burns and F. McDonagh (Maryknoll, NY: Orbis, 1993), 259–60.

before them.' He took the stick in his hand, broke all the idols, and put the stick into the hand of the biggest [idol]. When [Terah] returned, he said to [Abram], 'Who did this to them?' [Abram] said to him, 'I can't hide it from you: A woman came with a plate of fine flour and told me, "Offer this before them." I brought it to them, when one said, "I'll eat first!" and another said, "I'll eat first." The biggest of them took the stick and broke them.' [Terah] said to [Abram], 'Don't try to fool me! Do they know what's going on?' [Abram] said to him, 'Won't your ears hear what your own mouth says?'"

Although we usually credit Abram for being the one who left his kinfolk for a new land, in reality it was Terah who began the journey. Maybe he was part of the great dispersal resulting from the events that occurred during the construction of the tower at Babel; or he might have also heard God's call to head toward the promised land; or maybe, like so many older parents who are forced to cross borders, he simply followed his younger children on the trek. Whatever the reason, we are told that he took his son Abram, Haran's son Lot, and his daughter-in-law Sarai, who we will later discover is also Terah's daughter (20:12), and left Ur of the Chaldeans for the land of Canaan (11:31).

Why does the author introduce Sarai as Terah's daughter-in-law rather than his daughter? Either the author fails to mention this fact because it was considered a scandal for a brother to sleep with the daughter of his father (Deut. 27:22), or because once married to Abram, Sarai ceased to be her father's possession and instead belonged to Abram, thus she was only recognized as his wife. The first thing we are told about Sarai is that she is barren, making Abram's name, which means "exalted father," ironic. Sarai's barrenness becomes a threat to the continuation of the story, for if she is unable to have children, then Shem's genealogy comes to an abrupt end. We are left wondering how the childless exalted father will continue begetting children so that he can live up to his name. But Sarai's barrenness is more than just a physiological statement. Walter Brueggemann reminds us that her barrenness symbolizes a people without promise. As Brueggemann states, barrenness is the way of human history, an effective metaphor for hopelessness; but in the arena of barrenness, God's life-giving action takes place.[3]

The passage tells us that Terah left Ur of the Chaldeans to go to the land of Canaan, but upon arriving at Haran, he settled there. Although some scholars debate the location of Ur, others identify it as one of the oldest cities in southern Mesopotamia (in present-day southern Iraq), located about 125 miles north of the mouth of the Euphrates. Ur is part of Sumer, archaeologically considered the first great civilization of the ancient world. It is also considered to be a black civilization, raising the question, Was Abram black?

If Terah was going from Ur to Canaan, he must have gotten lost, for he did not choose the most direct route. He traveled 550 miles northwest to Haran, located in northwestern Mesopotamia (present-day Turkey). The entire route taken from Ur to Canaan places Haran at about the halfway point, with Canaan lying 500 miles to the southwest. At Haran the family stopped and settled. Haran was linked to Ur through commerce and religion. Both locations were centers of the worship of the moon god, and Abram's family members were apparently devotees—at least Joshua seemed to think so. At the great assembly at Shechem, once the Hebrews possessed the promised land, Joshua addressed the people by first reminding them their ancestor, Terah, the father of Abraham and Nahor, served other gods (Josh. 24:2). This might explain Terah's name, which has been associated with the Aramaic word (*yerak*) for "moon"; or the name of Laban, Nahor's grandson, which means "white" or "pale," a

> According to one tradition the original home of Abraham was Ur of the Chaldeans—a land whose earliest inhabitants included blacks. . . . In view of the black presence in the region of Abraham's origins, then, there is reason to believe that black blood flowed in the veins of at least some of the original Hebrew inhabitants, who, many scholars have argued, were very mixed from the beginning.
>
> —Charles B. Copher
>
> "The Black Presence in the Old Testament," in *Stony the Road We Trod: African American Biblical Interpretation*, ed. Cain Hope Felder (Minneapolis: Fortress Press, 1991), 154.

---

3. Walter Brueggemann, *Genesis*, Interpretation (Atlanta: John Knox Press, 1982), 16.

possible reference to the moon; or even Sarai, whose name means "princess," another possible reference to the moon (the princess of the sky).

Terah died at Haran when he was two hundred five years old (Gen. 11:32). If Abram was born in the seventieth year of Terah's life and left Haran when he was seventy-five years old, then Abram left Haran when Terah was one hundred forty-five years old, sixty years before Terah died. He left his father's home because God commanded it: "Go from your country and from your kindred and your father's house to the land that I will show you" (12:1). It should be noted that centuries later, a deacon named Stephen (Acts 7:4) has Abram leaving Haran after his father dies.

The call of Abram becomes the call of all who choose to follow God. All who are to follow the Divine must leave their old life behind and follow toward a new creation. When Jesus roamed the earth some wanted to follow him, but they insisted on first waiting for their fathers to die so that they could bury them. Abram did not wait, and neither should we. Jesus responded, "Let the dead bury their own dead; but as for you, go and proclaim the kingdom of God" (Luke 9:60). Abram's hand was on the plow, and he did not look back. He obeyed and left, breaking with tradition and the past. There were no preconditions before God called or chose Abram. Unlike Noah, we are not told that God chose Abram because he was righteous or just. Indeed, as Abram's life unfolds, we discover a very flawed man. Nevertheless, God chose him.

Abram did not need to first change his life or become more acceptable to God before being chosen. All he did to make himself worthy of God was obey. Abram's obedience becomes the foundation of faith. His experience, and by extension the experience of the people of Israel, is given universal value. Like them, we all become sojourners on this earth, resident aliens wandering toward the promised land. The author of the book of Hebrews will lift up Abram's exemplary obedience as a demonstration of faith that guarantees the blessings hoped for and proves the existence of the realities that presently remain unseen (Heb. 11:1, 8).

Because Abram obeys, God promises to make him (not Sarai) a great nation, blessing him and making his name so famous that future generations will use it as a blessing. Unlike those who solely rely on their own abilities, set out to make a name for themselves (Babel), and fail (11:4), Abram discovers that obedience to God is what makes one famous. Those who bless Abram will be blessed, and those who curse Abram will be cursed. All the people, all the nations of the earth, will be blessed through him. Abram, like Noah before him, becomes a new sort of Adam who is also given a new Eden (the promised land). He becomes a transmitter of blessings, a hope for the world wishing to return to Eden. God's purposes for the world will rely on this one man and his descendants, a difficult task since he and Sarai are advanced in years and she is barren. Any hope of fulfilling the promise will only be attributed to a miracle from God.

God's promise to bless Abram, his descendants, and all people who choose to find their blessings in him reinforces the doctrine that there is only one God, the God of Abram, who rules over all other gods, and by extension, the entire earth. Foreigners are welcome to accept the rule of God, and just as important, the rule of God's chosen—the real foreigner in the story. To choose Abram and his descendants by which the world will be blessed becomes dangerously close to a choice based on ethnicity that stands over and at times against the rest of the world. But if the world submits to the spiritual superiority of this one ethnic group, they too can be blessed. Such a submission, if based solely on ethnicity, would become highly problematic.

Thus we must ask how non-Jewish nations will be blessed. Is it by submitting to God's chosen, or by submitting to God's ways that God's chosen demonstrates for us? God says to Abram, "I will bless those who bless you" (12:3). How do we who are non-Jewish bless Abram, or for that matter, bless God? Paul, the future apostle to the Gentiles, writes, "the promise that he would inherit the world did not come to Abraham or to his descendants through the law but through the righteousness of faith" (Rom. 4:13). We bless Abram, and God, by doing what God requires of us. And what does God require of us? He requires us to do justice, to love mercy, and to walk humbly with our God (Mic. 6:8). Justice cannot take place on an individual basis. Community is needed if justice is to occur, if loving mercy is to happen. Hence the call of God for Abram to be an example of God's justice requires the establishment of a people, of a nation; thus Abram must have descendants. If God is a God of justice, then all who are committed to justice are a blessing to the one who God chooses to exemplify justice, even if at times they fall short. Only when we practice justice can we call Abram our spiritual father and be grafted onto the vine.

12:5–9

Testimony Concerning the Promise

Abram is made a promise that hints at a covenant. The patriarch is promised possession of property plus a prolific progeny. But for God's promise to be fulfilled, two obstacles must be overcome: first, Sarai is barren and advanced in age, and second, the land that is promised is already occupied. Regardless of these impediments, Abram continues to hope against all hope. Because of his act of faith, NT writers will deem him justified before God (Heb. 11:8–10).

God tells Abram to leave his country, his family, and his father's house for a land he does not know; nevertheless, Abram will trust God to show it to him.

Genesis 12 tells us that Abram took his wife Sarai, his nephew Lot, all the possessions they amassed, and the people they acquired and left Haran. It is interesting that after mentioning the amassed possessions they brought with them is a side note of other possessions—acquired people. Although slavery surely existed before the Abram narrative, this is the first place in Scripture where it is mentioned. What is disturbing is how nonchalant

> By faith Abraham emigrated from the land of his fathers and became a foreigner in the promised land. He left one thing behind and took one thing with him. He left his worldly understanding behind and took faith with him; otherwise he undoubtedly would not have emigrated but surely would have thought it preposterous.
> —Søren Kierkegaard
>
> *Fear and Trembling*, ed. C. Stephen Evans and Sylvia Walsh, trans. Sylvia Walsh (New York: Cambridge University Press, 2006), 14.

the statement of humans owning other humans is, with no moral, social, or cultural judgment. For the writer of Genesis, slavery is so normalized and legitimized that there appears nothing strange about this peculiar institution. Hence it is simply mentioned without any regard to the slaves who also had to travel to a foreign land without their consultation or permission. What family did they leave behind for a promised land that would offer them no promise?

Abram and company first arrive at Shechem, one of the oldest Canaanite cities, located in the hill county of Canaan, on the pass between Mount Ebal and Mount Gerizim. The word Shechem in Hebrew means "slope," most likely derived from the geographic location of the city on the side of a mountain. At the oak of Moreh (lit. "oak of teaching"), Abram builds God an altar. The oak of Moreh was probably a Canaanite sacred site where it was believed the tree was the source from which oracles were offered. From Shechem he moves to Bethel (lit. "house of El," the high god of the Canaanite pantheon). There too he builds Yahweh an altar. Yahweh, at this point, is perceived more as the deity of a tribal religion connected to one family rather than the one and only God of a monotheistic faith. By building an altar, the first within the promised land where Yahweh is to be worshiped, Abram is replacing the local deities with his. What better place for this cosmic paradigm shift or switch to occur than on the former sacred site of the previous gods—a strategy that will eventually be employed by Christians spreading the good news among indigenous people. As the cross entered new lands, the holy structures of the native people were either converted to churches or torn down so a church could be built on its ruins.

But more than just establishing one's deity over others is occurring in this passage. At Shechem God reveals to Abram for the first time that *this* is the land Abram and his descendants will eventually possess. Liberation theologian and philosopher José Porfirio Miranda explains that to inherit and possess the whole world will mean that Abram's descendants will teach all nations to achieve justice on earth. It is to this goal that all the promises made to Abram were directed, beginning naturally with that of having descendants.[4] But God's promise has a dark side. Does God give

---

4. José Porfirio Miranda, *Marx and the Bible*, trans. John Eagleson (1971; repr. Maryknoll, NY: Orbis, 1974), 218.

through taking? Liberation theologian Gustavo Gutiérrez might be correct in reminding us that Abram is the father of all believers because the promise made to him was a gift accepted in faith;[5] but the gift came at the expense of others. What do you do with those already living on the land? Moses instructs the people wandering through the desert that "when the LORD your God gives [the land inhabitants] over to you and you defeat them, then you must utterly destroy them. Make no covenant with them and show them no mercy" (Deut. 7:2). The future general who would lead God's people into the land of the promised, Joshua, tells us that God calls for genocide: "Then they devoted to destruction by the edge of the sword all in the city, both men and women, young and old, oxen, sheep, and donkeys" (Josh. 6:21).

Some may argue that God's judgment expressed in Genesis 15:16 against the original inhabitants of the land really demonstrates God's patience with a "wicked" people. In effect, God gives the indigenous people over four hundred years to repent. Unfortunately, such an argument coming from those who benefited from the conquest sounds a bit self-serving. Besides, what possible act by a nation deserves the genocide of its people? No matter how apologists may want or try to justify the genocide that is to come, the flip side of promise for some remains death and destruction for others.

12:10–20
Testimony of Sarai

Our first introduction to Sarai reveals the problematic status of women in the Bible, even when the woman happens to be the matriarch of the faith. Sarai's name in Hebrew may

> It is the Canaanite side of the story that has been overlooked by those seeking to articulate theologies of liberation. Especially ignored are those parts of the story that describe Yahweh's command to mercilessly annihilate the indigenous population. . . . The covenant, in other words, has two parts: deliverance and conquest.
> —Robert Allen Warrior
>
> "Canaanites, Cowboys, and Indians," in *Ethics in the Present Tense: Readings from Christianity and Crisis, 1966–1991*, ed. Leon Howell and Vivian Lindermayer (New York: Friendship Press, 1991), 47–48.

---

5. Gustavo Gutiérrez, *A Theology of Liberation: History, Politics, and Salvation*, trans. Sister Caridad Inda and John Eagleson (New York: Orbis, 1988 [1973]), 92.

mean "princess, queen, woman of noble or royal birth"; but in reality she is seen and treated as an object. Sarai, like all other women in Genesis, is understood to be property—a possession of the man who owns her. Rather than basing familial relationships on the pre-rebellion verse where "the man and his wife were both naked, and were not ashamed" (2:25), male-female relationships were based on the first consequence of human rebellion—patriarchy—where the woman's desire would be for her husband, and he would rule over her (3:16). The biblical text takes for granted that women are the possession of men—they are property. Their identities are constructed through their sexual relationships to men, either as a married woman, virgin daughter, barren wife, widow, concubine, or sex slave. A woman's status as man's property is best illustrated in the last of the Ten Commandments, "You shall not covet your neighbor's house, . . . wife, . . . slave, or ox, or donkey" (Exod. 20:17). Like a house, slave, ox, or donkey, the wife is reduced to another owned object that should not be coveted by other men. Any woman, including Sarai, can be offered up as ransom in order to save the lives of men. This is a pattern we will again witness when Abram's nephew Lot offers up his two virgin daughters for rape by the townsfolk in order to save the lives of two male strangers taking refuge under the shadow of his roof.

Genesis 12 opens with a famine occurring in the land that God promised to Abram. As a result, Abram travels to Egypt; but as he approaches the border he grows frightened that Pharaoh will kill him to take his beautiful wife. So he instructs Sarai to claim they are siblings. He literally offers up his wife as a ransom to save his own life, a profitable transaction because in the exchange for his "property" Abram is offered sheep, cattle, donkeys, slaves, and camels. Pharaoh takes Sarai as his wife, probably meaning that they had a sexual relationship. When a man offers up a woman for sex and is paid for the transaction, that man today is usually called a pimp.

There is no indication in the text that Abram's life was in danger. Indeed, when Pharaoh discovers that Sarai is Abram's wife, not his sister, he is shocked Abram played such a deceitful trick on him. He immediately returns Abram's human possession and provides a military escort to the empire's frontier. The reader is left wondering if Abram's actions were motivated by an unsubstantiated racial bias against the Egyptians. Like Abram, many today from the dominant culture construct marginalized communities of color as dangerous places, fearing to drive through "certain" neighborhoods. This fear is best manifested by quickly locking car doors when driving through barrios or ghettos. Fear of the other, who like Pharaoh is constructed as oversexed and violent, has led many white men to protect their women and property from the "colored" menace. A history of lynching dark male bodies for simply looking at or talking to white men's human possessions illustrates the extent of constructing the other as a threat to white women.

Abram's actions may indeed have been motivated by a bias toward the Egyptians. Or maybe it had less to do with fear of the other than with a desire to turn a profit by turning a trick. Abram comes to Egypt because there is a famine in the land promised to him by God. In the previous verses God may have promised Canaan to Abram and his descendants, but when the land fails to provide sustenance, the so-called man of faith takes matters into his own hands and heads south, crossing the border into the empire where resources abound. There he is given flocks, oxen, donkeys, men and women slaves, she-donkeys, and camels for his wife. The riches poured on Abram by Pharaoh are so great that Abram eventually leaves Egypt a very wealthy man—so wealthy that when offered a reward by the king of Sodom for saving him and four other kings, Abram refuses lest it be said he was enriched by these kings (14:22–24). It was selling his wife to Pharaoh that enriched Abram.

Yet we are left wondering if Abram thought the transaction was final. After all, he sold his wife for a profit. Pharaoh, we are told, made her his wife—his possession. Maybe Abram no longer had a need for Sarai. In the previous verses we are told that God promised to bless Abram and make his name famous and give the promised land to his descendants. Nothing is said about Sarai or her part, if any, in this promise. Indeed, one could argue that she stood in the way of God's promise being fulfilled. She was barren and beyond the age of childbearing. If Abram sold his wife, he probably did not expect to get her back. He would return to the promised land without her, richer, thanks to the profitable transaction he made with Pharaoh, and probably with a younger and more fertile wife—one who was not barren. Maybe he would return with the young slave girl Hagar, who he probably acquired in Egypt. With the older and barren Sarai disposed of, God could now fulfill the promise of descendants.

Sarai may be objectified; still, we must ask who this woman named Sarai is who is reduced to a possession to be sold. Yes, she was Abram's wife, but she was also his half sister. Although they had different mothers, they shared the same father, Terah (20:12). She was barren and elderly. The irony is that the new Eve, mother of a nation, is unable to bear children. She is the first of a line of barren women whose appearances in the text only occur in relationship to her sexuality or fecundity (or lack thereof). Ten years Abram's junior (17:17), she is at least sixty-five years old (12:4). While many elderly women are attractive, we are left wondering if her beauty was such to inspire praise from all of Pharaoh's officials. Maybe the real issue has nothing to do with physical attractiveness, but rather with blaming the woman for her beauty, making it her fault for attracting unwanted attention. Or maybe in a perverse form of logic Abram's status is increased by having his woman, his possession, accepted by the empire's leader, thus making Abram an equal to Pharaoh.

In any case, while men discuss the terms of the transaction, Sarai remains silent. She has no voice, no say in a business deal that will impact her remaining years. She, like any other object, has no input as to who owns and possesses her. Her recourse is obedience.

If there exists any good news in this narrative, it is that God

> The husband is the chief of the family and the head of the wife. The woman, because she is flesh of his flesh and bone of his bone, must be subject to her husband and obey him; not, indeed, as a servant, but as a companion, so that her obedience shall be wanting in neither honor nor dignity.
>
> —Pope Leo XIII
>
> *Arcanum Divinae*, February 10, 1880.
>
> Since women are becoming ever more conscious of their human dignity, they will not tolerate being treated as mere material instruments, but demand rights befitting a human person both in domestic and in public life.
>
> —Pope John XXIII
>
> *Pacem in Terris*, §41, April 11, 1963.

hears the silent Sarai. Men may be satisfied with the sales arrangements that were made, but God was not. God inflicts Pharaoh
and his household with severe plagues, thus foreshadowing future
descendants who will also go down into Egypt due to famine, face
the mistreatment of becoming possessions (slaves), and have God
intervene through plagues to bring about their liberation.

Sarai is a silent woman betrayed by her husband, Abram. When
his nephew Lot is captured in war as booty (14:12), Abram risks all,
even his life, to save him. But when his own wife becomes Pharaoh's
booty, Abram hides behind a lie. Not only does he betray his wife,
he is revealed for lacking integrity. The future writer of the book of
Hebrews may sing praises to Abram's faith, but this passage presents
a faithless man. He leaves the promised land because of famine, not
believing God will provide. He fearfully lies concerning his wife,
lacking faith in a God who will safeguard him so that the promise
given can be fulfilled. He sells his wife for riches rather than rely on
God to provide for his needs. At every turn, Abram demonstrates
his lack of faith, undermining God's divine plan; and in so doing
he jeopardizes the divine promise. Biblical scholar Gerhard von
Rad probably says it best: "the bearer of promise himself [is] the
greatest enemy of the promise; for its greatest threat comes from
him."[6] Finally, the holder of God's promise is shamed by the worldly
pharaoh, who demonstrates greater obedience to and fear of the
God of Abram than Abram does.

Why then does God tolerate such unfaithfulness? Rather than
presenting a narrative where Abram, the patriarch of the faith, is
portrayed as pure, faithful, and heroic, the biblical text shows us
a very human Abram, warts and all. The biblical narrative is less
concerned with whitewashing the leaders of the faith than presenting
us with a God who accepts the unworthy as instruments of God's
new creation. Because all fall short of the glory of God, no one is
deserving, no one is perfect. Genesis is not a book that presents us
with bigger-than-life heroes; rather it shows us ordinary folk who
like us fail at times to rise to our better selves. Faithless people like

---

6. Gerhard von Rad, *Genesis: A Commentary,* trans. John Marks, rev. ed., OTL (Philadelphia:
Westminster Press, 1972), 169.

Abram provide hope for the rest of us that we too could be used by the Creator.

Abram may have lacked faith, but Pharaoh did not. Unfortunately for him, God's promise did not materialize. Contrary to the promise given in the previous verses that God would bless those who bless Abram and curse those who curse Abram (12:3), Pharaoh was cursed after blessing Abram. Pharaoh blessed Abram with riches. Unbeknownst to him, Abram sold him property with unclear title. Even though it was Abram who was faithless, it was Pharaoh who God cursed with severe plagues. Abram's acts complicate, if not bring into question, the divine promise. One may bless Abram and yet be cursed.

It would be great if the narrative ends with learned lessons. Unfortunately, this is not the case. Later on, Abram perpetuates a similar stunt on the unsuspecting king of Gerar, Abimelech (20:1–18). If Genesis 20 is a variant of the same story, then it indicates how different stories are woven together to give us Genesis. But if it is a different story, then Abram learned nothing about faithfulness while in Egypt. To make matters worse, the father's sin is later repeated by his son Isaac, who following in Abram's footsteps also offers Rebekah, his wife, to King Abimelech (26:1–11), unless this too is a variant account of the same story (which some scholars assert). In any case, women, as property, fare poorly in all these accounts.

13:1–18

Testimony of Lot

We are told that Abram was a very rich man, possessing great numbers of livestock and large quantities of silver and gold. How did this itinerant migrant acquire such great wealth? The answer to this question is found in the previous chapter. Abram's wealth is connected to the dishonesty he exhibited while in Egypt. Pawning off his wife proved to be a profitable venture (12:16). Wealth was more a result of Abram's deceit than God's favor. Yet this great fortune evaporated by the third generation. His grandson Jacob would have to work in order to earn a dowry for his wives (29:14–15, 18). The wealth accumulated by one generation is at times squandered by the next.

After being escorted to Egypt's borders by Pharaoh's soldiers, Abram heads for the Negeb, the southern part of Canaan. This hot, dry region receives less than eight inches of annual rainfall, though portions of the region can still sustain the pasturing of flocks. While the land is capable of supporting the indigenous population, its natural resources were more than likely strained by the presence of wandering bedouin.

The clan of Abram and the clan of Lot moved from place to place throughout Canaan depending on where pasture and water for their flocks were found. They made their way to Bethel, literally "house of God," where Abram had first pitched his tent and erected an altar. There he again invoked the name of Yahweh. It is interesting to note that while in Egypt, Abram built no altar to his God, nor did he call on the name of the Lord. After wandering in Egypt, away from the promise, away from the responsibility of walking in the ways of God, he returned to his original commitments to God. Bethel became the place where he could rededicate himself to God's ways.

We at times imagine in the Abram narrative that Abram, his wife Sarai, his nephew Lot, and a few servants are trekking through Canaan. But in reality each clan consisted of many individuals, enough for Abram to raise an army of 318 fighters from among his own clan (14:14). Hence two large clans with numerous livestock were competing with local inhabitants for scarce natural resources. Is it any wonder that disputes broke out between those living on the land (the Canaanites and the Perizzites), Lot's herdsmen, and Abram's

> It is only a small step from Abraham and Lot's world of 3500 or so years ago into our own day and age. In so many areas of our world—for example, Brazil, Guatemala, India, and other places—similar questions of the vital access to cultivable land and control of the fruits of its cultivation continue to be concerns, more often than not involving the question of life and death itself.
>
> **—Anthony R. Ceresko**
>
> *Introduction to the Old Testament: A Liberation Perspective* (Maryknoll, NY: Orbis, 1998), 306.

herdsmen? But this story is more than simply the bickering between the people of Abram and Lot. This is part of the age-old story concerning property rights and access to water and fertile land.

Wishing to avoid conflict, Abram suggests that he and Lot part company. If Lot goes in one direction, Abram commits to go in the other. Looking around, Lot notices that the Jordan plain is well irrigated. It is lush and appealing, like the garden of Eden or the land of Egypt. Based on appearance, Lot chooses what seems to be the best; but he will end up with the worst. That the people of Sodom, according to the text, were vicious and great sinners against Yahweh should have raised concerns, leading Lot to move more cautiously; but instead he pitches his tents on the town's outskirts. With time, the lure of the city wears away at his resolve and he and his family soon make their home within the wicked city's midst. As Lot moves eastward, Abram moves westward, toward Canaan and God's promise. This story of parting ways also serves to show how the different people, linked by similar culture and language, came to occupy the land, with Moab and Ammon, Lot's descendants, east of the Jordan River, and Israel, Abram's descendants, west of the river.

It is easy, as many have done, to celebrate Abram's magnanimity. Giving his nephew first pick of the land risked he would be left with the least desirable portion. Although Abram may not have known how this narrative would unfold, he believed in God's promise. He knew that in the end, the promise made all the land his. Lot may have chosen the best land, but Abram trusted in a God who would give him all the land. Maybe it is easier to be magnanimous when you live by God's promise. Those who know and believe in the God of life can be generous and fair toward others because they know how the story ends, even if they remain uninformed on how the story unfolds.

If Lot had been as faithful as Abram, he might have responded to Abram's munificence by dividing the land so that both clans would benefit from the best the land had to offer. Maybe the land could have been divided north and south rather than east and west. But Lot saw an opportunity and snatched it. Jesus recounts the parable of the rich landowner who had a great harvest, yet nowhere to store his excess. In response to this dilemma, the landlord built bigger and greater barns to store more produce, thus ensuring sufficient time and resources would exist to enjoy food, wine, and merrymaking. Today, we would call entrepreneurs who expand their industry shrewd capitalists, taking advantage of a bullish economy. Such persons, due to their business acumen, quickly become pillars of our community. They become ideal candidates to head the local Chamber of Commerce. We might even be tempted to nominate such productive go-getters to be the head deacon or elder of our congregation. Yet Jesus calls this person a fool, for that very night the landlord's soul was demanded (Luke 12:13–21). The community leaders we normally praise are usually condemned by Jesus. There appears to be an inconsistency between those who, like Lot, place profit first, and those who instead place the needs of others first. We might applaud Lot for being a good businessman; still, we should question the foundation of his moral character—a character that focused on himself rather than consider Abram and how to fairly treat him.

Even though Abram failed to demonstrate the ways of God while in Egypt, God still renewed the promise first made when he entered Canaan. God's promise was unconditional. Look toward the north and south, the west and east (the direction Lot took); all these lands, God promises, will be Abram's and his descendants'— descendants who will outnumber the dust on the ground. Believing in the promise, Abram settled by the oaks of Mamre, near Hebron, and there built God an altar. After Egypt, he found restoration.

14:1–16

Testimony on War

Genesis 14 is an oddity, appearing more as a war chronicle than a story. The chapter recounts an international war where four kings from a far-off eastern empire are pitted against five local kings who, after thirteen years as vassals, are now refusing to pay tribute. In an attempt for one sovereign power to dominate others, superior military power is employed to maintain or protect imperial rights. War, whether conducted by empires of old or empires today, has the same offensive goal. Although efforts have been made to connect the kings mentioned to historical persons, no archaeological evidence pinpoints this conflict or its participants. The events of this chapter may very well have been connected to some distant and faded memory. We are left with a mixture of historical and nonverifiable names and places. Even the route taken by the eastern empires to subdue the local sovereigns is unusual, looping far south of the military objective. Further complicating this story is the difficulty of placing it within the standard documents or sources (J, E, and P). The source of this story is unknown, and its presence in the text is puzzling.

Unlike the rest of the Abram/Abraham narrative, the story opens with international events. Halfway through the story we are told that when Sodom is sacked, one of the casualties is Abram's nephew Lot, who is carted off along with all of his possessions. Abram is notified of these events by a survivor of the battle who makes his way to the patriarch. At this point in the story Abram is called a "Hebrew," the first time this term is used in the biblical text. "Hebrew" as a descriptor appears five other times in the book of Genesis: in chapter 39 (twice) when Potiphar's wife accuses the Hebrew slave boy Joseph of attempted rape; once in chapter 40 and and again in chapter 41 to describe the Hebrew dream interpreter within Pharaoh's court; and once in chapter 43 to describe Egyptian discriminatory practices against Hebrews. The term "Hebrew" is seldom used in the biblical text, but when it is, it usually appears in the mouths of non-Hebrews to describe Hebrews or is used by Hebrews to describe themselves to foreigners.

The term "Hebrew" is not used to describe ethnic or religious identification, but rather is a descriptive term. "Hebrew" may be connected to the Akkadian term *habiru,* which means "wanderer," thus describing Abram's clan and descendants as wanderers. Or it might be based on the word's root (minus the suffix) *'eber,* which can refer to the personal name Eber, an ancestor of the Semitic people from which Abram comes (10:24–25). But *'eber* has also been rendered (by, e.g., the Greek translation, the Septuagint) as "one who passed over," as in pass over a river. Thus Abram the Hebrew is Abram the one who passed over the Euphrates; or the Israelites as Hebrews are those who passed over the Red Sea or the Jordan River.

In a real sense, all who place their trust in Abram's God are Hebrews, grafted onto the vine. To trust and follow God is to pass over into a new life of walking, by faith, in God's way. Such ontological Hebrews are wanderers in this life, passing over and through a world where injustice reigns. They become the salt that reminds an unbelieving world, structured where the few exploit the many, of God's liberation and salvation from disenfranchisement, dispossession, and displacement.

Upon hearing the news of Lot's predicament, Abram is transformed into an action hero, a warlord who sets out to save his nephew through military conquest. He gathers 318 "trained men, born in his house," for the campaign. In this chapter war is glorified, and this is the first place in the biblical text where war is celebrated. For Abram to participate in violence, the biblical narrative must be reinterpreted, usually to the disadvantage of those who will become the victims of war. Abram's initiation of a military campaign must be reconstructed as defending virtue and appear to have no ulterior motive for gaining from the military conflict. Here Abram enters the conflict to save his nephew Lot; but when his own wife was in the clutches of Egypt's pharaoh, Abram sat on his hands and profited (12:10–20). In 14:23 we are told that he refuses to participate in the spoils of war; and yet in verse 20 he has enough spoils to offer Melchizedek a tithe.

Abram, God's chosen one to demonstrate God's justice to the world, rushes to war, raising ethical concerns about war in general. Can violence ever be harnessed for good or declared just? Can those who claim to follow the Prince of Peace engage in violence? Violence is not a political tool that can be picked up and used, then put down later, never to be used again. The use of violence forever changes a person and a society. Generally, those engaged in violence and the hate it unleashes become unfit for the process of creating a new and just social order. The biblical text attributes the prohibition on King David's building a temple for God in Jerusalem to his use of violence: "you have shed much blood and have waged great wars" (1 Chr. 22:8).

This story of Abram engaging in the violence of war raises the complexity of the issue; specifically, is violence at times the only option available for the followers of the God of peace? Ethicist Thomas Schubeck provides the illustration of a homeowner who confronts a burglar in the act of robbing his home. The homeowner has two options: he can either recognize the humanity of the burglar as a troubled person, beginning a dialogue based on a genuine interest in the burglar's well-being; or he can see the burglar as a thief who needs to be physically expelled from the premises by whatever means necessary. While the former may be closer to the gospel call to turn the other cheek, or forgo the spare cloak, the latter takes into account other considerations, specifically protecting one's family or oneself from the possible violence the burglar may inflict.[7]

Nevertheless, while those of the dominant culture continue to struggle with the issue of whether violence can be ethically employed, for those who are marginalized throughout the world violence remains a constant reality. Internationally, violence continues to be used to secure gains in financial markets. Abram's "trained men, born in his house" (i.e., house-born slaves), were not consulted before Abram decided to wage war, even though they were the ones who more than likely would die on the battlefield. Those relegated to the margins of society are never consulted in the decision process about going to war. To go or not to go to war is determined in the halls of power, with an eye toward the geopolitical gains of such an encounter. It is not the Native American living on a reservation, the African American relegated to the urban ghetto, or the Latina/o relegated to the country's borderlands who is calling for more guns, missiles, or the latest fighter jet.

Ethical debates concerning what makes a war just may have validity among ethicists of the dominant culture, but for the masses living under the strain of racism and classism, such debates rapidly become irrelevant. The marginalized are the ones who are primarily disenfranchised by war. High military spending in advanced industrial economies diverts capital to non-growth-producing sectors, crowding out investments, reducing productivity, and increasing unemployment. Additionally, the increase in the defense

---

7. Thomas L. Schubeck, *Liberating Ethics: Sources, Models, and Norms* (Minneapolis: Fortress Press, 1993), 70.

budget, financed through deficit spending, creates an inflationary impact on the economy that disproportionately harms the poor, contributing to an increase in income inequality.[8] In short, while war financially benefits the nation's elite class, the preparation for war further devastates the poor.

Yet in some cases Abram's God commands war, while at other times God forbids it. In the Hebrew Bible the violence caused by war is condoned some of the time and condemned at other times. Within the New Testament, Jesus abhors violence; still, he warns of the violence that will be committed against those who follow him to the cross. All too often, the commitment of the believer to follow Jesus' example leads to violence. However, violence should never be accepted as a necessary evil, nor rejected as antithetical to Jesus (he clearly used violence to cleanse the temple and prophesied the violence of the day of judgment). Violence and war are realities that often arise due to the dominant culture's grip on power. Such violence can be immediate or drawn out, as in the case of institutional violence, such as the economic forces that foster ghettos and barrios. Governments, during Abram's time as well as today, act violently when they maintain social structures that inflict prolonged harm or injury on a segment of the population, and that segment today is usually disenfranchised due to race or economic standing.

The decision facing those who choose to follow Abram's God today is whether to participate in the use of violence or to advocate nonviolent resistance to oppressive structures. As Gustavo Gutiérrez reminds us, it is important to contrast "the unjust violence of the oppressors (who maintain . . . despicable system[s]) with the just violence of the oppressed (who feel obligated to use it to achieve their liberation)."[9] Not only does Gutiérrez distinguish between the two types of violence, but he also questions the prevailing double standards that exist: "We cannot say that the violence is all right

---

8. John D. Abell, "Defence Spending and Unemployment Rates: An Empirical Analysis Disaggregated by Race," *Cambridge Journal of Economics* 14 (1990): 405–19; idem, "Military Spending and Income Inequality," *Journal of Peace Research* 31, no. 1 (1994): 35–43; and Errol Anthony Henderson, "Military Spending and Poverty," *Journal of Politics* 60, no. 2 (1998): 503–20.

9. Gustavo Gutiérrez, *A Theology of Liberation*, trans. and ed. Sister Caridad Inda and John Eagleson, 15th anniversary ed. (Maryknoll, NY: Orbis, 1988), 64.

when the oppressor uses it to maintain or preserve 'order,' but wrong when the oppressed use it to overthrow this same 'order.'"[10] To remain silent or to do nothing in the face of violence is to be complicit in it.

To ask if counterviolence is ever an option for the followers of Abram's God is to ignore that violence already exists in the hands of the oppressor. Thus the question is not if followers of God's ways should utilize violence, but rather, do they have a right to defend themselves from the already existing violence?

For example, biblical scholar Jorge Pixley notes Moses' violent act of killing an Egyptian, a member of the dominant culture, for striking a Hebrew slave, a member of a marginalized group (Exod. 2:11–22). This act appeared justified even though a future commandment received by Moses would state, "Thou shalt not kill" (Exod. 20:13 KJV). Pixley suggests that certain exceptions to this commandment exist, such as capital punishment or the killing of enemies in times of war. Pixley also implies that the preferential option for the oppressed may lead to the act of taking life. Moses' killing of the Egyptian could be seen as a defensive act to protect the life of the marginalized. That God (the ultimate defender of the oppressed) seems to accept Moses in later years justifies Moses' earlier use of violence for the sake of defending the oppressed.[11]

> I am not a nonviolent man. I am a violent man who is trying to be nonviolent.
>
> —César Chávez
>
> Frederick John Dalton, *The Moral Vision of César Chávez* (Maryknoll, NY: Orbis, 2003), 120.

If the oppression of the marginalized is maintained through institutionalized violence, that is, through social structures designed to privilege the few at the expense of the many, then any hope of finding salvation or liberation from the status quo will inevitably

---

10. Idem, *The Power of the Poor in History*, trans. Robert R. Barr (Maryknoll, NY: Orbis, 1984), 28.

11. Jorge V. Pixley, *On Exodus: A Liberation Perspective*, trans. Robert R. Barr (Maryknoll, NY: Orbis, 1987), 8–9.

confront those same social structures. While all violence may be evil, not all decisions to use violence are unethical. History has demonstrated that denouncing unjust social structures is simply not enough, for those accustomed to power and privilege will never willingly abdicate what they consider to be a birthright. It seems that those who usually call for nonviolence are those who wish to maintain the unjust status quo. Some ethicists from the margins maintain that violence, when employed by the marginalized to overcome their own oppression, is in reality self-defense and can never be confused with the continuing violence employed by those in power. *Agape* (unconditional love) for the very least among us might lead a person, in an unselfish act, to stand in solidarity with the oppressed in their battle for self-preservation.

Yet the early Christian community (pre-Constantine) maintained a prohibition on violence, even though we know some early Christians were among the ranks of Roman legions. When Jerusalem was burned and sacked in 70 CE, the Christians living there refused to fight the Roman armies. Warfare was understood to be a denial of Jesus' message to love one's enemies and a rejection of the life he asked his disciples to follow. For the early church, Jesus Christ was leading a revolution to be won through his crucifixion. Not until 313 CE, when Christianity became the state religion and took on political power under Constantine, was it necessary to develop concepts for conducting "just" war to maintain the empire.

For Martin Luther King Jr. the aim of nonviolence was the creation of a relationship with the oppressors in the hope that they too could be redeemed by God's grace. King did not advocate passivity; rather he called for an active confrontation with injustice. Nonviolence was the embodiment of the Christian ideal of *agape*, an unconditional love that confronts the aggressor so that he or she can also learn the gospel demand for *agape*. Pragmatically, King insisted that the use of violence by the marginalized only encourages the oppressor (who controls the tools of torture) to unleash even greater violence, leading to a never-ending spiral of hatred. He maintained that violence only provokes greater retribution, and those without arms will find themselves at a greater disadvantage. Rather than continuing the cycle of violence, King looked toward the radical

Returning hate for hate multiplies hate, adding deeper darkness to a night already devoid of stars. Darkness cannot drive out darkness; only light can do that. Hate cannot drive out hate; only love can do that. Hate multiplies hate, violence multiples violence, and toughness multiplies toughness in a descending spiral of destruction.

—Martin Luther King Jr.

Strength to Love (Philadelphia: Fortress Press, 1963), 37.

love advocated by Christ as the solution to oppression.

Abram, with his house-born slaves, pursued the enemy "as far as Dan." But there was no Dan during the time of Abram— Dan was the name given to the region where the postexodus tribe named for Abram's great-grandson settled. Dan, during the time of Abram, was known as Laish (Judg.18:29). Calling Laish "Dan" reveals that this text must have been written (or edited) after the exodus. At Dan Abram's forces launched a night attack, defeating the forces of the four eastern kings and pursuing the fleeing armies to Hobah, north of Damascus. He recaptured all the goods of Sodom, Gomorrah, Admah, Zeboiim, and Zoar, freeing the captives, including his nephew Lot. Still, it remains difficult for the reader of this tale to reconcile the routing of the imperial armies of four kings by a nomadic wanderer.

14:17–24
Testimony of Melchizedek

Abram the warrior is victorious in battle. On his return from battle, at the Valley of Shaveh, which is in the vicinity of Jerusalem, the warlord meets the king of peace. An obscure figure named Melchizedek (meaning "king of justice"), who reigns in Salem (the word for "peace"), brings Abram bread and water.

Besides being the king of Salem, he is also a priest of El Elyon, translated as "God Most High," who Melchizedek claims is the creator of heaven and earth. El Elyon is a Canaanite god, more specifically the god of the Jebusites, who lived in Salem, the ancient pre-Israelite Jerusalem. The inclusion of this story might have been an attempt to legitimize Jerusalem as a sacred site. Even though El Elyon is the head of the Canaanite pantheon and Melchizedek is his priest, Abram accepts his blessing and offers him a tithe. It is odd that a Canaanite cult is presented in such a positive light within the biblical text, especially when we recognize that superiors blessed subordinates, who in turn provided tithes to those who are of a higher status. The giving of tithes was not a goodwill offering but recognition of one's superiors. This leaves us with the question: is this Canaanite cult superior to Yahwism? Or maybe this text shows us how syncretism operates.

> There is absolutely no concept in the Old Testament with so central a significance for all the relationships of human life as that of *tsedaqah* [justice]. It is the standard not only for man's relationship to God, but also for his relationships to his fellows, reaching right down to the most petty wranglings—indeed, it is even the standard for man's relationship to the animals and to his natural environment.
> —**Gerhard von Rad**
>
> *Old Testament Theology*, vol. 1: *A Theology of Israel's Historical Traditions*, trans. D. M. G. Stalker (New York: Harper & Row, 1962), 370.

Abram seems to fuse or confuse this Canaanite God called El Elyon with Yahweh. While Melchizedek worships the Canaanite deity who created both heaven and earth, in Abram's mind Melchizedek is really worshiping Yahweh, who is the one and only creator of heaven and earth. Eventually, El Elyon will become one of the names for Abram's God. We should not be surprised that at the genesis of what would become the Judeo-Christian faith we find syncretism. In a sense, all faiths are syncretistic, that is, all religions are transformed as they pass through different cultures. As new faith traditions interact with new social environments, both the culture and the religion are transformed so both forces can coexist. At times, the changes to the religion and the culture are dramatic. At other times, these changes are modest, even unnoticeable, as in the case of adopting the descriptive name of another's god. Regardless as to the degree of change that occurs, one thing is certain: both the religion and culture never remain the same—both become new expressions.

Disguising his God in the clothes of a Canaanite deity could very well have been a shrewd maneuver on Abram's part. After all, the land he resides on, although promised, does not belong to him. And even though he may be returning from winning an improbable military campaign, he still resides on this land at the pleasure of the original inhabitants. He and his clan exist with the threat of being annihilated. By adopting the name of a Canaanite god whose title corresponds, no matter how superficially, with Abram's God, Abram creates a nonthreatening presence (regardless of the promise) with those who actually possess the land. All the power, praise, and due devotion that belong to El Elyon are now transferred to Yahweh. Outwardly, to the satisfaction of Melchizedek, Abram is now worshiping a Canaanite deity; but in reality Abram recognizes that he is truly worshiping the God of the promise. Abram might have even thought his supposed superior, Melchizedek, to be naive, if not ignorant, about the true essence of El Elyon; only Abram, who has spoken with Yahweh, has the fuller knowledge of the spiritual world.

Although Abram's encounter with Melchizedek at first brush may appear unimportant, it develops significant meaning for future readers, especially Christians. In Psalm 110 the psalmist describes the Messiah, that is, the anointed of God. The description provides us with the ideal priestly king who would sit at the right hand of God. This anointed Davidic king would be "a priest forever according to the order of Melchizedek" (Ps. 110:4). Future gospel writers would connect the concept of the anointed priestly king with Jesus, having Christ quote Psalm 110 as a reference to himself (Mark 12:36). Nevertheless, it is the author of the book of Hebrews who makes the case most clearly that Jesus is from the order of Melchizedek (Heb. 5:6). In Hebrews 5–7 the author argues that the Melchizedek who met Abram on his way back after defeating the kings from the east was a type of Christ, a king of justice and peace who had no mother or ancestry and whose life has no beginning or end (7:3). Because Levi's descendants are accepted into the priesthood and are obligated to collect tithes, and Levi was figuratively in the loins of Abram, who paid tithes to his superior, then the Jewish Levitical priesthood also paid tithes to Melchizedek, recognizing the latter's superiority as a priestly order (7:4–10). Although the author of Hebrews may have concluded that Jesus is a second Melchizedek

(7:15), others, reading their Christian biases into the Genesis text, have erroneously deduced that the Melchizedek who met Abram was in reality the preexistent Christ.

15:1–21
Testimony Concerning the Covenant—Version 1

What follows God's promise and Abram's entrance into the land his descendants will eventually possess is the establishment of a covenant. Because the concept of God's special relationship with God's chosen people is foundational to the biblical narratives, several versions of the story are provided. Chapter 15 is usually attributed to J or E, or more likely a combination of both. The merging of these two traditions might explain the apparent contradictions between verse 5, which takes place in the evening, and verse 17, which takes place at sundown.

Chapter 15 starts with Abram having a vision. God tells Abram not to be afraid, for God is his shield and great will be his reward. Here we are presented with a God who is a protector. Like a shield, God encompasses Abram, a reassuring characteristic for those who face life's disappointments. Abram was originally given a promise of land and descendants. But life marched on, and he grew older, remaining childless on a land that was not his own. He was resigned to having a stranger, one of his servants, Eliezer, be heir to his possessions. John Bright reminds us that such arrangements were in accordance with the slave adoption practices of the time. According to the Nuzi texts of the fifteenth century BCE,[12] childless couples would adopt a son who would serve faithfully until the couple died, at which time the adopted son would inherit the couple's possessions. In the event a natural son was born, the adopted son would yield all rights to the inheritance.[13] In the midst of hopelessness, of

12. Nuzi is an ancient city located in present-day northeastern Iraq where several thousand tablets provide insight to the Hurrian culture, helping scholars gain a better understand of early biblical times.
13. John Bright, *A History of Israel*, 3rd ed. (Philadelphia: Westminster Press, 1981), 79.

unfulfilled promises, God reassures him that he is still shielded. He is told to look up at the sky and try counting the stars; his descendants will outnumber them. The promise will be fulfilled by a child that would come forth from Abram's own body, thus promising and providing a man with a womb on which religious and political privilege is to be centered.

To that end, God cuts a covenant with Abram. To "cut a covenant," according to Bright, was a widespread ancient practice found among Semitic nomads that usually occurred between the clan's deity and the clan's founder.[14] It involved cutting animals in two and literally passing between the carcasses. The prophet Jeremiah records a similar ritual of passing through animals that occurred among the people (Jer. 34:18–19). The one walking through the halves of the dead animal(s) was symbolically calling down on him- or herself the same fate faced by the sacrifice if he or she failed to live up to the agreement or covenant being made. In the case of Abram, this is a unilateral, unconditional ritual/agreement solely obligating one party—God. Through this nocturnal ritual, God answers Abram's concern as to how he would know the promise would be kept. So Abram gathers a three-year-old heifer, goat, and ram; cutting their bodies in half, he arranges the remains opposite each other, creating a path between them. He also offers up a turtledove and young pigeon, but these he does not sever. As can be imagined, birds of prey soon swoop down on the carcasses, but Abram drives them off. Some have thought these birds of prey to symbolize evil or an evil omen. If so, Abram demonstrates the importance of vigilance when waiting on God's faithfulness.

As the sun sets, Abram falls into a deep sleep. He is seized with terror, for God comes and tells him that his descendants would be exiled in a land not their own where they would be enslaved for four hundred years, after which they would leave with many possessions. By this time, the sun has set and it is dark. Whether Abram is still dreaming or fully awake we are not sure, but what the text tells us is that "a smoking fire pot and a flaming torch" cross between the animal halves. God, who is a consuming fire, passes through

14. Ibid., 99.

these animals, thus making a covenant with Abram and his descendants that that which was promised will come to pass. The promised land would stretch from the river or wadi (northeastern border) of Egypt to the Great River (Euphrates), encompassing what will be the furthest extent of King David's empire at the time of his death.

> [Born-again Christian evangelicals] are filled with ideas that this is the Promised Land and their duty is to help the Jews. It is not the Promised Land. It is our land.
> —Izdat Said Qadoos, Palestinian villager
>
> Jim Rutenberg, Mike McIntire, and Ethan Bronner, "Tax-Exempt Funds Aiding Settlements in West Bank," *The New York Times*, July 6, 2010.

The promise made to Abram finds fulfillment about a thousand years later by King Solomon (1 Kgs. 4:21, 24), and then only for a very brief moment in time. We are left wondering if the author writing during Solomon's time justified the establishment of the Davidic kingdom by reading it into the covenant made at the start of the people's existence. Borders are justified as God ordained, hence also justifying the means by which the land is to be obtained and held.

FURTHER REFLECTIONS
Names of God

What is God's name? Much later, prior to the exodus, Moses will demand from the burning bush to know by what name is God to be called. It is at that point that humanity discovers from God's own lips that God's name is Yahweh. Although the definition of the word "Yahweh" is somewhat uncertain, it appears to derive from the Hebrew word *hayah*, "to be." Hence the closest translation for Yahweh is: "I AM WHO I AM." God's holy name is so sacred that pious Jews to this day refuse to utter it, often simply referring to God as *ha-shem*, "the Name." Some even spell God as G-d. But prior to the revelation of God's holy name in Exodus, Genesis referred to God by many different names.

What is in a name? To the ancient reader of the text: much. Names were believed to manifest the nature of what was being named. For this reason, careful scrutiny is given to the names of the different individuals in Scripture, specifically in Genesis. If indeed we can discover something concerning the essence of a person based on his or her name, what can we discover about God based on the different names that are used throughout Genesis?

In Genesis most of God's names are derived from the Hebrew word *'el* (Semitic *il*), which means "strength, might, force." El is also the name of many gods throughout the Semitic world and denotes powerful and strong deities. For the Canaanites, El was the chief deity among their pantheon, later displaced by the storm-god Baal or Hadad. As the Genesis story developed, names that were probably attributed to local Canaanite deities were used to describe Yahweh. For example, Yahweh takes the names El Elyon, who is associated with the ancient prepatriarchal shrine at Jerusalem (Gen. 14:17–24), and El Olam, who is associated with the shrine in Beersheba. The patriarchs basically worshiped Yahweh under different names, some names having pre-Israelite origins and probably connected to foreign gods.

As we read through Genesis, Yahweh is referred to as (1) *El Elyon*, which simply means "God Most High" or "God, the Exalted One," a reference to the highest god of the Canaanite pantheon of which Melchizedek served as priest (Gen. 14); (2) *El Roi*, which means "God who sees," but it can also mean "God of divining" and can be the name of the deity of the spring Beer-lahai-roi that Hagar encountered (Gen. 16); (3) *El Shaddai*, which probably means "God of the mountain," a possible reference to a mountain deity (Gen. 17); (4) *El Olam*, which means the "God of eternity," a local Canaanite deity whose name was applied to God when the Israelites took possession of the god's shrine (Gen. 21); (5) and *El Bethel*, literally "God of the house of God," a possible reference to the local deity of the town of Bethel (Gen. 31).

To further complicate the issue, the monotheistic God of the Israelites is at times referred to in the plural. Although *El* is singular, Yahweh is also referred to as *Elohim*, the plural form of *El*, even though the latter term in the majority of occurrences has a singular sense. This could be a possible reference to the plurality of God's majesty, which includes the host of heaven. God as plural raises questions concerning the monotheism of the people who would become the Israelites. Other questions we are forced to consider deal with whom exactly were the patriarchs worshiping. We must also ask if the early people who would eventually become the Israelites also worshiped the Canaanite god El, who stood distinct from Yahweh. Or were they worshiping Yahweh, who they saw manifested as El? Either way, there seems to be some fusing and confusing of Yahweh's name with those of the local deities.

16:1–16

Testimony of Hagar

Sandwiched between the two versions of God's covenant with Abram is the testimony of Hagar. God promised that Abram's descendants would outnumber the dust of the earth (13:16) and made a covenant that his offspring would be more numerous than the stars in the heavens (15:5). But did God mean that all these descendants would come from Sarai's womb? After all, the promise and covenant were not made with her. Abram may be eighty-five years old, but Sarai is seventy-five, well beyond the age of childbearing. A decade has gone by since the promise was first made to Abram, and still no children. Maybe Abram is not being proactive enough? In this narrative, Abram and Sarai take matters into their own hands and "help" God keep God's promise. But in so doing the patriarch and matriarch of the faith become the oppressors of the story. When we read this narrative, the focus is usually on Abram and Sarai, not on their "uppity" slave girl Hagar. Such readings either minimize or silence Hagar's testimony. What would happen if we reread the story and made Hagar the center of the narrative?

Sarai is unable to conceive and blames (curses?) God for

> Hagar's predicament involved slavery, poverty, ethnicity, sexual and economic exploitation, surrogacy, rape, domestic violence, homelessness, motherhood, single-parenting and radical encounters with God.
> —Delores S. Williams
>
> *Sisters in the Wilderness: The Challenge of Womanist God-Talk* (Maryknoll, NY: Orbis Books, 1993), 4

her predicament. Taking matters into her own hands, she offers up her slave girl's body to Abram. Within biblical patriarchy, children define a woman's status. The one who was silent when her own body was offered up to be appropriated by Pharaoh now becomes the protagonist and gives up the body of her Egyptian slave to be appropriated by her husband. Claiming motherhood through the birth of a child by one's slave girl, fathered by one's husband, was an acceptable practice in eliminating the barren wife's culturally imposed shame. It was better to endure the humiliation of having one's husband produce a son by means of another woman than to remain barren. Sarai does not seem to be motivated by seeing God's promise to Abram fulfilled, nor by the desire of her husband for a son, but rather by her own standing, which is diminished by her barrenness. Hence Sarai accomplishes what God prevents through the object, not the person, of Hagar. Sarai's power over Hagar is not due to a power she might possess, but rather flows from her station as wife within the biblical patriarchal hierarchy of the family. Sarai, herself a subordinate, participates in the plight of all subordinates—to compete against each other.

Since her time, others have suffered from what ethicist Katie Geneva Cannon calls "the Sarah syndrome."

> Again, others of us, as Black women and Black men in the church, suffer from the Sarah syndrome and try to be little false gods to those around us. Far too many Black women spend their whole lives in the church and never get religion, never experience an active faith or a loving God because they are so busy controlling the Spirit that gives them meaning.... But whenever we get caught in the Sarah syndrome, we snatch back our lives and our wills from God and we try by hook or by crook to make people do what we want them to do. When we are suffering from this syndrome, we pray that our will be done instead of humbly surrendering ourselves before God and asking that God's will be done.[15]

15. Katie G. Cannon, "On Remembering Who We Are," in *Those Preachin' Women*, vol. 1: *Sermons by Black Women Preachers*, ed. Ella P. Mitchell (Valley Forge, PA: Judson, 1985), 46.

Upon being given Hagar, Abram "takes" her. If we are not careful, in order to justify the faith's patriarch, we might excuse his actions as simply acceptable for his time. Still, the Hebrew word used to describe Hagar is *shiphah*, which originally connoted "virgin slave girl." Hagar was a younger woman who was forced to have sex with Abram, an eighty-five-year-old man. Picture a young maiden, more than likely a teenager, being forced to have sex with a very senior man. Most of us would be, and should be, repulsed by such abuse.

Poor women, who are disproportionately of color, seldom have the luxury of controlling their own bodies. To feed their family and ensure their survival, some of these women find few options other than to use their bodies as commodities. Still, anyone who becomes vulnerable to sexual exploitation, whether consciously as a means for survival or against one's will, is a victim of injustice.

This is a testimony of the woman Hagar, who lost her personhood and instead became a womb to be used by Sarai, who owned her body,

> Sarai tells Abram to have sex with her Egyptian slave, Hagar, so that Sarai can take Hagar's baby as a way of fulfilling God's promise to Abram. . . . We readily recognize that this is about raping a slave, as we would see it in our own time. Yet we seek to explain it away. . . . In other words, we have been trained to read the Bible as though there isn't much difference between the culture of our time and place and that of the text—*except* when it becomes so obviously problematic that we assert, rightly or wrongly, that the culture behind the biblical text must have been dramatically different from our own!
>
> —Randall C. Bailey
>
> "The Bible as a Text of Cultures," in *Peoples' Bible*, ed. DeYoung et al., 13–14.

to accomplish her personal agenda. But how could Sarai, herself a victim of abuse when pawned off to Pharaoh during her visit to Egypt, participate in the abuse of the woman who was under her care? Did she not learn anything from her own experiences? All too often, those who are oppressed become future oppressors, repeating the oppressive structures originally imposed on them. As Paulo

Freire reminds us, "the oppressed find in the oppressor their model of 'manhood.'"[16]

Once Hagar conceived, she looked "with contempt" on her mistress Sarai. The Hebrew expression connotes that Sarai became a "lighter weight." Yet when most of us read this passage, we usually accuse Hagar of putting on airs, of not knowing her place, of being subversive. Many biblical interpreters have portrayed Hagar as sassy or haughty. Once she was with child, and Sarai was not, we assume Hagar rubbed Sarai's nose in her barrenness. But could it be that Hagar was simply traumatized and resentful that her mistress offered her up for rape? Coupled with Sarai's low self-esteem due to infertility, the tension between these two women might have little to do with the uppity domestic help. Losing face, Sarai demanded that her husband Abram resolve the situation. But Abram was satisfied, getting what he wanted. Rather than protecting Hagar from his first wife, he simply turned her over to Sarai, so that his wife could treat Hagar as she saw fit.

Sarai proceeded to treat Hagar badly. The Hebrew word 'innah connotes harshness and excessive severity. Although Sarai, like many U.S. white women, lived under the oppressive structures of patriarchy, she had enough privilege to be able to abuse other women of color (e.g., domestic help). Rather than women, regardless of race or ethnicity, working together against the forces of patriarchy, white and economic privilege proves a space within disenfranchisement groups where those further from the white ideal can be exploited. According to womanist Renita Weems, Hagar's story reminds women of color "that *women, although they share in the experience of gender oppression, are not* natural *allies in the struggles against patriarchy and exploitation.*"[17]

Hagar reacts by fleeing (her name is probably related to a Semitic word that means "flee," from the same root as Arabic *hegira*). She

16. Paulo Freire, *Pedagogy of the Oppressed,* trans. Myra Bergman Ramos (New York: Continuum, 1993 [1970]), 28.
17. Renita J. Weems, "Reading *Her Way* through the Struggle: African American Women and the Bible," in *Stony the Road We Trod: African American Biblical Interpretations,* ed. Cain Hope Felder (Minneapolis: Fortress Press, 1991), 76.

flees from the house of bondage toward the desert, just as a future generation of Israelites will flee Egypt and also wander in the desert. Her flight denies Sarai's claim of Hagar's child as hers, heir to Abram. From the oaks of Mamre at Hebron, where Abram settled, Hagar makes her way toward her homeland, Egypt. She makes it to Shur, some seventy-five miles south from Hebron, probably somewhere on the frontier between Egypt and Canaan. There the unexpected happens. A divine messenger appears, the first annunciation scene recorded in the Bible, and Hagar is instructed to return to Sarai and suffer affliction under her hand. Yet no assurance is given that Hagar would be protected if she does return to Sarai's authority. Furthermore, the celestial messenger addresses Hagar as Sarai's property in verse 8, thus providing a divine denial of her personhood.

Imagine if a runaway slave is told to return to oppression. Just as Paul's letter to Philemon, delivered by Onesimus, a runaway slave (Phlm. 10–11), is problematic for anyone who has experienced the chains and whips of overseers, so too is Hagar's instruction to return to slavery and sexual abuse. As disturbing as God's instructions are, the reader assumes that returning leads to her unborn son's physical survival. Born in the house of Abraham, her future son, Ishmael, also becomes an heir to the promise of God, and as such an interloper to the covenant as understood by Jews and Christians.

At this point the truly unexpected occurs. Hagar, the lowly marginalized woman, gives God a name, a privilege extended to no other person throughout Scripture. Only a superior, according to ancient custom, was able to name those who are lower in status. But here we have the first biblical record of a person giving God a name. Her actions become an overt strike against the predominant patriarchal structures of her time. And what name does this slave girl choose for God? She chooses *El Roi*, literally "God who sees," a name that unites the Divine with her human experience of suffering—for God sees the suffering of this marginalized woman. Yet if God truly sees, then it becomes troubling that God is seeing Hagar's sexual abuse and still is calling her to return to slavery.

Before God sends her back, God makes Hagar a promise comparable to the one made to Abram, minus the land: Hagar's descendants will be too numerous to count. God instructs her to name the child Ishmael, which means "God hears," because God heard Hagar's cries of distress. Ishmael will be "a wild ass of a man," no doubt a stereotypical dig at the surrounding Arabs (Ishmaelites) with whom the Israelites have always been in conflict. But more importantly, God's promise to Hagar indicates that God is not limited to Hebrews. In this passage God promises to create another people who will also be numerous. Indeed, just as Jews see Abram as the founder of their faith and Isaac the promised child from which they descend, today's Muslims also see Abram as the founder of their faith, but Ishmael as the promised child from which they descend. Hence Islam, according to Muslims, is the first Abrahamic faith because Ishmael was born before Isaac.

What is interesting to also note is that God makes this promise to a woman—and not just any woman, but an oppressed woman. Such a promise was not even made to Sarai, the matriarch of the faith, who only hears of God's plans for her secondhand. Doesn't speaking to God and receiving a promise from God make Hagar, not Sarai, the true matriarch of the Hebrew Bible?

Hagar suffered from classism (a slave), racism (an Egyptian foreigner), and sexism (a woman raped by Abram). This story of the used and abused woman is a motif that resonates with many women of color. For some it would be easy to claim that Hagar's encounter with the Divine points to a God who liberates. Those seeking a liberationist God can claim good news in a God who is found in the wilderness, in the midst of the struggle of those on the margins of economic power and white privilege. For followers of liberation theology, God is a God who accompanies the disenfranchised. Yet those of us who constantly seek liberationist motifs within the biblical text need to guard from imposing neat theological resolutions to oppressive and problematic narratives. Is the God who appears before Hagar really interested in liberation for her and oppressed women in general? After all, God sends her back to oppression. Although most men who engage in the liberationist movement rely heavily on a Marxist understanding of economics to understand the plight of the poor and their need for salvation,

Latin American biblical scholar Elsa Tamez reminds us that Hagar complicates the history of salvation. God may send Hagar back to oppression so that her child can be born in Abram's house, thus ensuring that the child can participate in the history of salvation and claim the rights of inheritance; nevertheless, she reminds those struggling with the poor for liberation and salvation that because the poor are gender differentiated and culturally located, sexism must be seriously considered prior to the implementation of praxis.[18]

Many women of color, specifically womanists, have pointed out that Hagar's relationship with Sarai reflects the historical U.S. relationship between white and black women. Hagar, who was an Egyptian and African, had no say as to who could enter her body. She, like so many of her African descendants, existed to serve the needs of those who owned her. For this reason, womanist theologian Delores Williams, in her book *Sisters in the Wilderness*, finds in Genesis 16 a rape narrative that resonates with the African American experience, specifically the experience of black women. As slaves, black women, like Hagar, were required to offer up their bodies at the whim of their owners. Not only were black female slaves required to satisfy their master's desires, but they also faced the humiliation and degradation of being "rented out" to other white men as concubines. Like her future descendants, Hagar was marginalized by gender, ethnicity, and class. Yet Williams reminds us that Sarai's property, as a surrogate mother, experienced consciousness-raising. She becomes a model for all oppressed women, being the first woman in the Bible to seek her own liberation by fleeing Sarai's cruelty. Even though she is carrying Abram's child, she chooses possible death in the desert, thus denying those who own her any right to the fruits of her body. Even though we need to be cautious about imposing liberationist motifs on the biblical text, for Williams it is in the wilderness that God's presence is manifested. Although God is found in the desert, Hagar obeys and, against her best interests, returns to slavery and abuse. There she gives birth to the promised child, whom Abram

18. Elsa Tamez, "The Woman Who Complicated the History of Salvation," in *New Eyes for Reading: Biblical and Theological Reflections by Women from the Third World,* ed. John S. Pobee and Barbel von Wartenberg-Potter (Oak Park, IL: Meyer-Stone Books, 1986), 14.

names Ishmael; even though a few verses earlier we are told that it was God who named Hagar's child.

17:1–27

Testimony Concerning the Covenant—Version 2

Does God make two covenants with Abram? Unlike chapter 15, which is attributed to J or E or some combination thereof, chapter 17 seems to be a product of P. Like chapter 15, chapter 17 seems to follow a similar pattern: the promise is repeated, renewed, and sealed with a covenant. We are left wondering if chapter 17 provides a different narrative concerning the establishment of the covenant, or just a continuation that occurred sometime after the events of chapter 15. In this version God appears to Abram stating that God's name is El Shaddai, probably best translated as "God, the one of the mountains," a possible reference to Sinai. Regardless of the name's original meaning, it has been eclipsed by the definition "God Almighty." This God called Shaddai instructs Abram to "walk before me, and be blameless." To walk before God is to walk in the ways of God: to act justly, love tenderly, and walk humbly with one's God (Mic. 6:8). Thus Abram is instructed not only to do justice but to teach the world justice. Unfortunately, he falls short, as we saw in Egypt and will see again in Gerar and in his treatment of Hagar.

In this version of the covenant narrative, Abram, who is now ninety-nine years old, already has a son, Ishmael. But while Ishmael came from his loins, he is not the child of Sarai, but rather her slave girl, Hagar. God will soon inform Abram that the promise will not be fulfilled through Ishmael, but rather through a child to be born to Sarai. It is interesting to note that the promise is really to Sarai, not Abram. After all, he already has a child and after Sarai's death will have six more with Keturah. It is not his seed that carries the promise, but Sarai's womb. To signify Sarai's role in birthing a nation, her name is changed to Sarah, a variant spelling. All this occurs without God bothering to directly speak to her. She and her body are acted on without her needing to be present. Abram's name is also changed to Abraham, again a variant spelling of the same name.

These name changes signify a special destiny to which both Sarah and Abraham are called. Ishmael is to be rejected for the promised child, planting the seed of enmity between the children of Ishmael and the children of the not-yet-born Isaac—an antagonism that still exists today. Upon hearing that a promised child will soon arrive and the absurdity of an elderly couple having a child, Abram laughs. No doubt, God must have also laughed, explaining why this future child is to be called Isaac, which in Hebrew means "he laughs."

This new covenant is to be sealed through the ritual of circumcision, a mark on the body—specifically the male body—that would serve as a perpetual outward expression of the establishment of the "chosen people," their special relationship with God, and the promises made to them, especially the promise of land. This is not a new practice, but was customary among Western Semites and Egyptians (either as an initiation ritual or purely for hygienic reasons). Among the Semites, the Philistines, Babylonians, and Assyrians did not participate in this ritual. Not only were God's people called to be circumcised, but according to tradition, the angels in heaven were all born circumcised,[19] leaving one to wonder if there is any such thing as a female angel.

Circumcision, although commanded by God, could provide a false guarantee of salvation. Moses called the people to circumcise their hearts (Deut. 10:16). The prophet Jeremiah railed against those who were circumcised only in flesh but still housed uncircumcised hearts (Jer. 9:25–26). For those who are Christians, Jesus makes a similar argument against individuals who believed that claiming Abraham as father was sufficient for salvation. He warns them that God can raise children for Abraham from the stones by their feet (Matt. 3:9). Yet, with all this talk about circumcision, we are forced to ask how women, as part of the people chosen by God, also enter into a covenant with God if there is nothing to circumcise.

Abraham sets out to obey God by circumcising himself, his son Ishmael, and his entire household. We are told that he circumcised all the men who were born into his household and those who had been bought. Once again, the normalization of slavery appears.

---

19. *Jubilees* 15:25–27.

To circumcise men who were bought indicates that they were not like today's notion of employees. The power to mutilate someone else's body indicates that these persons did not possess ownership of themselves. Abraham, the founder of the faith, the one relegated with the task of teaching the world justice, was a slaveholder, a problematic paradox.

Although circumcision became the norm for the patriarchs, the practice was either forgotten or ignored by the time of Moses. In a strange passage, God tries to kill Moses because of this ritual's lapse. God is finally appeased when Moses' quick-thinking wife, Zipporah, circumcises her son and touches Moses' genitals with their son's foreskin (Exod. 4:24–26). Once the practice is reintroduced (Josh. 5:2–3), it becomes an everlasting covenant. Even when facing death, it is important that the sign of the people's bond to God not be broken.

> According to the decree, they put to death the women who had their children circumcised, and their families and those who circumcised them; and they hung the infants from their mothers' necks.
>
> —1 Maccabees 1:60–61

What makes circumcision crucial in the life of the people is that it binds them together, even though the promise of land ceased to exist during the Babylonian captivity and from the temple destruction in 70 until 1948. God ceases to be tied to a piece of property or one specific geographical location. Instead, wherever Abraham's children live in the world, their God is present with them.

Although circumcision became the sign of Jewish identity, it also became the focal point of the early Christian church. One of the first challenges faced by the early church dealt with the inclusion of non-Jews. Must Gentiles convert to Judaism before they could become Christians? More specifically, do they first need to be circumcised? Acts 15 records the controversy that took place at Antioch. Several church elders from Judea disrupted Paul's missionary ventures, exclaiming that "unless you are circumcised according to the custom of Moses, you cannot be saved." Even those who have proven their faithfulness can still expose the prejudices lurking in their hearts.

Take the example of Peter, who, while at Galatia, refused to eat with the Gentiles (Gal. 2:11–14). Ironically, this is the same Peter who faced criticism for visiting the home of the uncircumcised Gentile Cornelius, a Roman centurion (Acts 10–11). Still, while in Antioch, when men of Jerusalem arrived to insist that Gentiles must first be circumcised before being saved, Peter avoided eating with the uncircumcised.

In an age of political correctness, many churches are scrambling to erase centuries of exclusion by now appearing to be multicultural, making "diversity" the church buzzword of our time. For example, three-hundred-year-old German hymns are quickly translated into Spanish and flashed on the overhead screen. Sermons are preached instructing Euro-Americans why it is their Christian duty to reach out to the less fortunate Latino/as with the gospel message of salvation understood as assimilation. Attempts are made to appear culturally sensitive by offering taco dinners at the congregational fellowship meal. For many of these churches, their approach attempts to include Hispanics without necessarily changing the cultural milieu of the congregation. All too often, when the predominately white middle-class congregation wrestles with issues of inclusiveness, they unwillingly revert to a multicultural façade for the sake of political correctness. All are welcomed, as long as the church power structures that privilege the predominant Euro-American congregation remain intact. The underlying meaning of politically correct congregations is that Hispanics can join, as long as they first convert to Euro-Americanism and respond appreciatively to whichever way their culture gets "translated." In other words, they must circumcise their identity to take on the supposed superior religious identity of the dominant culture.

The circumcision controversy plaguing the early Christian church was eventually settled in Jerusalem in favor of the Gentiles. They could become Christians without first having to become Jews. Nevertheless, the circumcision controversy still exists today. The debate no longer centers on cutting off one's foreskin. Instead, what Hispanics are often called to do is cut off their identity, their culture, the symbols by which they perceive the Divine. In many cases, Latina/os (as well as all other people of color) must first become Euro-American before becoming Christians. They must adopt Euro-American theology, hermeneutics, philosophy, liturgy, politics, and, most importantly, church structures. They must prove their Christianity by describing their faith in the cultural symbols of the dominant culture. To insist on believing in one's own Hispanic symbols only proves (like the uncircumcised Gentiles of old) that they are not really believers, and even if they are, it is a more primitive and backward form of faith than that of their Euro-American superiors.

Unfortunately, the Christ presented to these uncircumcised Hispanics is wrapped within Euro-American cultural structures. Christian theology assumes the superiority of Euro-American paradigms and methodologies, even when they directly contradict Hispanic culture and identity.

However, any understanding of faith based on the individualistic characteristic of Euro-Americans will be destined to fail among people who place greater emphasis on the communal. Latino/as are insisting in perceiving the Divine through their own Hispanic eyes. To do otherwise becomes blasphemous.

18:1–33

Testimonies from the Visitors at Mamre

During the hottest part of the day, the Lord visits Abraham by the holy tree at Mamre, although at first Abraham does not recognize Yahweh. Instead, Abraham notices three men approaching his tent. Upon seeing the strangers, Abraham leaps into action, bent on transforming strangers into guests. Rather than just offering bread and water, Abraham prepares a bedouin feast. Choosing a young ox, fat and tender, Abraham orders his servants to slaughter the beast and cook a meal. He asks Sarah to make cakes, and along with butter and milk, he lays out a banquet before them as they rest in the shade of the holy tree. For Abraham, the alien in a foreign land that is not his own, the virtue of hospitality, a tradition marked by mutual aid and generosity, was not a philosophy needing acceptance, but a praxis— an action—that was taken on behalf of the stranger.

Hospitality is an action to be implemented by those who claim allegiance to Scripture. While it is desirable for all to participate in this virtue, one needs to be cautious that the practice of hospitality does not mask deep injustices. Consider, for example, the biblical call to show hospitality to the alien within our midst. For some U.S. Christians and Jews, the proper response toward the Latin American undocumented aliens is to show them hospitality. Yet the virtue of hospitality is probably not the best way to approach the U.S. immigration situation, especially since the 1994 implementation of the North American Free Trade Agreement (NAFTA). To insist on hospitality as the virtuous response to immigration ignores the nineteenth-century policy of Manifest Destiny that deprived Mexico of half its northern territory—land that included gold deposits that would be discovered in California in 1849, silver deposits in Nevada, oil in Texas, and all of the natural harbors (except Veracruz) necessary for commerce. The pseudoreligious ideology of Manifest Destiny is responsible for enriching the United States while depriving Mexico of its future ability to create wealth. Additionally, the twentieth-century policy of gunboat diplomacy unleashed a colonial venture that deprived Latin American countries of the natural resources while providing the United States with an unlimited supply of cheap labor.

When the U.S. military provided the freedom for U.S. corporations (e.g., the United Fruit Company) to build roads into developing Latin American countries to extract, by brute force if necessary, their natural resources, why should we be surprised that some of the inhabitants of these same countries, deprived of a livelihood, take those same roads following their resources? The United States has a Latin American immigration crisis, yet the United States fails to recognize that the reason Latin Americans come is because they are following what has been stolen from them. They come to escape the violence and terrorism the United States has historically unleashed on them in an effort to protect "American interests." An immigration problem exists because, for more than a century, the United States has exploited—and continues to exploit via NAFTA—their neighbors to the south. To practice the virtue of hospitality assumes the "house" belongs to the one practicing this virtue who, out of the generosity of their heart, is sharing her or his resources with the other, who has no claim to the possession. But it was because of Latin American natural resources and cheap labor that the U.S. house was built. The virtue of hospitality masks the complexity caused by the consequences of empire. Due to U.S.–sponsored "banana republics" throughout the twentieth century, Latin Americans hold a claim to this U.S. house. Rather than speaking about the virtue of hospitality, it would historically be more accurate to speak about the responsibility of restitution.[20]

While Latin Americans may hold a claim, the "strangers" visiting Abraham held no claim, thus providing Abraham with the opportunity to show hospitality. While we can celebrate Abraham's generosity, we are disturbed by the obvious patriarchy in which said generosity is rooted. While men ate, women remained invisible. Sarah, who helped prepare the meal, does not join the strangers, but sits hidden in her tent within earshot. Women are not invited to the feast, where we will soon discover God presides. Yet the stranger does ask for Sarah, revealing for the first time that these strangers might be divine. With the announcement of Sarah's impending pregnancy, it becomes clear that one of the strangers is God. This episode must have been what the author of the book of Hebrews had in mind when the writer encouraged his or her readers to always show hospitality to strangers, for some have entertained angels without knowing it (Heb. 13:2). When the stranger asks for Sarah, is he requesting that she join them? The text is not clear. What is clear is that an opportunity is missed that would have testified that all, even women, are welcomed to the Lord's banquet table!

Throughout Scripture we encounter the term "angel of the Lord" or "angel of God." Usually, this angel turns out to be God, but just as often it refers to some celestial being who is not God. There are also occasions where the identity seems to shift between God and God's spokesperson. If indeed one of the strangers is God incognito, it shows us a God who exists in the mundane tasks of life (e.g., eating). God is present in the everyday along with all of its particularities, or what Hispanics call *lo cotidiano.*

20. Miguel A. De La Torre, *Trails of Hope and Terror: Testimonies on Immigration* (Maryknoll, NY: Orbis, 2009), 9–14.

The primary source by which Latina/os participate in the doing of theology or ethics is their lived everyday experience of marginality. To focus on daily existence is to critically analyze the good and bad that shapes and forms the daily human life. More than just analysis, *lo cotidiano* has the potential to become the catalyst for structural changes, serving as the foundation on which all liberative ethical praxis is determined and implemented. For theological and ethical discourse to be relevant, ethics must be contextualized in *lo cotidiano*. There is recognition among Latino/as that the God they worship became human, enfleshing Godself, then and now, in the everyday lives and experiences of the dispossessed. For Hispanics, the salvific nature of God is experienced in the daily struggles of humanity. God's presence and accompaniment in the everyday makes whatever occurs in daily life the subject and source for all ethical and theological reflection. A God who participates in *lo cotidiano* collapses the dichotomy between theory and praxis. The inclusion of everyday struggles provides a heart to the Eurocentric tendency of overemphasizing the rational. Grounding ethical and theological reasoning in *lo cotidiano* subverts the normalized direction of the discourse from the center toward the periphery. The everyday brings the margins to the center and, in the process, challenges those accustomed to setting the parameters of the discourse.

The text reveals that not only are humans changed when they encounter the Divine, but the Divine also changes when encountering humans. After all, the crucified people of today, who suffer under structures of oppression so the privileged and powerful can have an abundant life, have a God who fully understands what

> Daily relationships become the basis and image of all social relations. This is why analysts stress that daily life permeates the public as well as the private spheres, because the activities carried out in both spheres "imply a level of dailyness, daily actions that confer upon this oppression, day after day, an air of naturalness." This is why women stress the need to change the way things are done in daily life in order to construct equal models of interhuman relationships.
> —María Pilar Aquino
>
> *Our Cry for Life: Feminist Theology from Latin America*, trans. Dinah Livingstone (Maryknoll, NY: Orbis, 1993), 40.

it means to suffer at the hands of political and religious authorities because their God has wounds on God's hands, feet, and side. For Christians, God's encounter with humans through the incarnation means God carries on God's flesh the stigmata caused by the everyday.

Unfortunately for Sarah, the divine stranger was participating in the everyday of patriarchy. Still, she rebels against the patriarchy set up by the men sitting under the tree, and from the margins she laughs. She laughs at the news that when the strangers return next spring, she will be with child. And who would not laugh? After all, Sarah was almost ninety years old and her husband Abraham was ninety-nine. All her life she has been barren, a condition considered by Scripture to be a disgrace. Twenty-five years earlier she heard this same promise, secondhand. Even then she was past the age of childbearing and, taking matters in her own hands, offered her servant Hagar to be raped so that through her she could produce an heir for Abraham. Sarah recalls her youth when her husband was able to pleasure her and wonders if she could again experience ecstasy. No wonder she laughs incredulously. Indeed, Abraham had also laughed when he heard the announcement of her impending impregnation (17:17). Imagine how your congregation would react to the news that a childless couple in their nineties were with child. Would they respond any differently? Would not joyous laughter fill the sanctuary?

Although Abraham is not rebuked for laughing, it appears as if Sarah is, for she expresses fear when caught by God. Yet we can wonder if the absurdity of this elderly couple producing a child was so outrageous that everyone present could not help but also laugh, not in disbelief, for as we are reminded nothing is impossible for God, but in the ludicrousness of the prophecy. What a healthy image: God, God's angels, and the faith's matriarch and patriarch, rolling around on the ground in uncontrollable laughter. Hence Sarah is able to conclude, "God has brought laughter for me; everyone who hears will laugh with me" (21:6). Indeed, all who are able to hear this good news can join in the laughter with her and her God. To ensure we never forget this humorous occasion, she names her promised child Isaac (*yitshaq*), a play on the Hebrew word for laughter (*tsahaq*).

After the meal, the strangers head in the direction of the city of Sodom, and Abraham—being a proper host—accompanies them a portion of the way. Yahweh is going to Sodom because God has heard the outcry of the city's oppressed. Still, God wonders whether to share God's intentions with Abraham. Sodom's call to justice is not a theological call limited to the prophets. We discover in this narrative, for the first time, that the very purpose and reason God intervenes in human history is to take sides against the oppressors (Sodom) by siding with the oppressed (those who suffer the injustices of the Sodomites). In short: God takes sides.

Although this narrative is concerned with the particularity of Sodom and Gomorrah, it also represents people everywhere and what could await them if they uncritically amass power and privilege at the marginalization of the disenfranchised. The determination as to who will be blessed or cursed, which originally depended on how people interacted with the nation to arise from Abraham's descendants, is now extended to include all of humanity depending on which nations establish justice and righteousness. This shift as to why nations are blessed or cursed moves God from a desert deity of a particular tribe to sovereign judge of all the earth.

As two of the visitors make their way to Sodom to extract God's retribution, God remains behind with Abraham, who, according to verse 22, stood before God (those of lower status stand before those of higher status), although earlier versions of the text apparently stated that it was the Lord who stood before Abraham. This is an unfortunate variant textual tradition (if not correction?) used by the early scribes. Before employing the text that conforms Scripture to God's majesty (God stands before no one), the original text provided an interesting glimpse into God's character worthy for humans to emulate. If the Almighty is willing to stand before the powerless, counting all power as if nothing, then so too should those among us who possess privilege or power. We who are Christians should follow the example provided in Philippians by Jesus, who, though himself in the form of God, made himself as nothing, taking the form of a servant, assuming the lowest station (Phil. 2:6–8). In the earlier version of this text, God is willing to be counted among the least of these by the Creator's willingness to stand before the created.

As God stands before Abraham, God is portrayed as a Deity in the process of thinking if God should share God's thoughts with a human. The text continues by contrasting Abraham's faithfulness with Sodom's unfaithfulness. Yet it is the faithful who plead for the unfaithful. Abraham understands that salvation, redemption, and grace are as much for the oppressor as they are for the oppressed. In his attempt to bring salvation to wicked Sodom, Abraham questions God's sense of justice. Walter Brueggemann observes:

> It is as though Yahweh rather simplistically accepts popular practice [that good people prosper and evil people suffer and die] until Abraham raises the question. . . . A very early text note shows that the text before any translation originally said, "Yahweh stood before Abraham. . . ." [This] earlier version suggests with remarkable candor what a bold posture Abraham assumes and how presumptuous is the issue he raises. Whether the textual change is accepted or not, this text reports that Yahweh must think a quite new theological thought. God is pressed by Abraham to consider an alternative.[21]

"Will not the Judge of all the earth do what is just?" (18:25) is a question Abraham audaciously raises concerning Yahweh's character, not necessarily a declaration of established truth. Abraham's query is more a question challenging God to live up to God's own rhetoric. We must ask if through Abraham's questions God learns something about judgment. If we read our theology of God's perfection into the text, then such a question is heretical; yet the text shows God moving to consider a more humane course of action thanks to Abraham's intercession. Hence maybe the original text, before corrected by the scribes, was correct. It is God who should have stood before Abraham, learning.

21. Walter Brueggemann, *Genesis*, Interpretation (Atlanta: John Knox Press, 1982), 168.

Abraham asks if God would truly destroy the righteous along with the wicked. Is judgment communal? Is guilt collective? These are theological questions that move beyond the particularity of Sodom. Was Ulysses S. Grant, when writing his memoirs toward the end of his life, correct about the Mexican-American War when he wrote: "The Southern rebellion was largely the outgrowth of the Mexican War. Nations, like individuals, are punished for their transgressions. We got punished in the most sanguinary and expensive war of modern times."[22]

Or does God really notice the fall of an individual and insignificant sparrow? In short, how significant is the minority?

Although Abraham is but "dust and ashes" with no right or power to question God, he does so anyway, and God is neither frightened nor angered by his or our inquiring. Abraham demonstrates how to stretch God's capacity to offer grace. He discovers a different God than the pre-flood Deity who destroyed the entire world, including innocent babies and children, due to the people's wickedness. This is a God willing to save a city from destruction due to a very small number of innocent persons. The remnant of the few righteous is more important in the sight of God than the majority of sinners—a theme to be repeated throughout Scripture (e.g., Jer. 5:1; Ezek. 14:12–20). God's prefers to save rather than to punish!

> Here we have the oldest discussion known to us of the subject of the righteousness of God in the sphere of the Old Testament . . . for this Judge even a very few "righteous" carry so much weight that for their sake the great mass of the "wicked" go unpunished, instead of the reverse, namely, that isolated "righteous" people also would be drawn along into a judgment inflicted upon the "wicked." Here again we are faced with the God whose purpose finally is not judgment and curse, but salvation and blessing.
> —Martin Noth
>
> *A History of Pentateuchal Traditions*, trans. Bernhard W. Anderson (Englewood Cliffs, NJ: Prentice-Hall, 1972), 238–39.

---

22. Ulysses S. Grant, *Personal Memoirs,* 2 vols. (New York: Charles L. Webster, 1885–1886), 1:54–56.

But why stop at ten, as does Abraham? Is not one enough to save all the wicked in the city and prevent the raining of fire and brimstone? Christians claim to believe so, naming that one as Jesus Christ. But while God promises to spare the city if only ten righteous persons are found, the destruction of Sodom goes as planned, as if this exchange never took place. Although textual experts would insist Genesis 19 is an older narrative grafted onto Genesis 18, still—ethically speaking—the narrative must conclude that none was found righteous in order to justify the city's destruction.

Abraham teaches us that prayer can change God's heart from a planned chastisement for human transgression toward mercy. We also learn that the individual actions of justice by the faithful matter, even saving the entire city. But unfortunately, while Abraham in faith pleads for wicked Sodom, he is silent when his innocent son is called to be the sacrificial lamb.

19:1–7, 9–25, 27–29

Testimonies from Sodom and Gomorrah

Sodom's sin is an abomination before God—a perverse and prevalent sin that undermines the very foundations of faith. Its constant practice contributes to the downfall of civilization and leads nations toward barbarism. It is a lifestyle practiced among the highest echelons of government. Almost all who ever served as U.S. president, in the U.S. Congress, or on the Supreme Court bench have been guilty of the sin of Sodom. Many of today's religious leaders, specifically those who we frequently find on our television screens pleading for contributions, have also engaged in the lifestyle accented by Sodom's sin. God's destruction of Sodom and Gomorrah served as a warning that society holds a sacred responsibility in rooting out this sin, seeking always to abolish this defiled praxis from within their midst. Because of the deadly consequences caused by tolerance toward Sodom's sin, it is important to correctly define what the sin of Sodom actually is.

Genesis 19 depicts how Lot is rescued a second time. Earlier he was saved through the intercession of human hands (Abram); this time he is to be saved through heavenly hands (the two angels). The story opens with the two angels who are sent to Sodom to bring about its destruction and find lodging in the house of Lot. Although no physical evidence exists, archaeological research suggests that the cities of Sodom and Gomorrah were located somewhere in what are now the shallow waters (18 feet deep) of the southern end of the Dead Sea. Like his uncle Abraham in the previous chapter, Lot shows hospitality to his guests. But similarities with Abraham's encounter with the angels ends with verse 4 when a frightening and terrifying scene unfolds before Lot's guests settle down for the evening. The young and old men of the town surround the house, bang on the door, and demand the strangers be handed over to them so that they could *know* them ("to know" being a euphemism for having a sexual relationship).

As we envision all of the town's men before Lot's house we are forced to ask: Where are the women of the city? We know by verse 4 that the men were wicked, but what about the women? When Abraham asked God in the previous chapter if ten righteous men could be found would the city be spared, we wonder what would have happened if Abraham would simply have asked for ten righteous *persons*? Patriarchy blinds us to women's presence in the story. All the men may have been wicked, but what about their wives? Their daughters? Is the city's salvation or destruction based solely on the faithfulness, or lack thereof, of men? Do women who may have been righteous remain invisible?

Women are absent as men demand that the foreigners be turned over to them. A similar scenario is recorded in Judges 19, which appears to be a repetition of Genesis 19. Even some identical phrases are found in both stories. In Judges 19 a Levite, journeying home along with his concubine, stopped in the town of Gibeah. An old man of the town offered hospitality, but when night fell the men of the city came banging at his door, demanding that the Levite be sent out so that the townsmen could rape him. Like Lot, the old man went out to meet them, offering his virgin daughter and the Levite's concubine as ransom. Yet unlike the account in Genesis, a rape does take place—not of the virgin daughter, nor of the Levite stranger, but of his nameless concubine. Missing, however, is the same intense level of condemnation among modern readers for men who actually raped a woman to death as there is with the attempted yet never completed rape of men (angels?) by men. One is left asking: Why? Is the rape of a woman by a mob of townsfolk less grievous for God and God's followers than a similar story about the potential rape of men by a mob?

The demand from Sodom's men to rape the two strangers has led many interpreters of this text, over the centuries, to associate homosexuality with Sodom's sin. So ingrained is this interpretation that we have come to accept it as true. This passage has been consistently used to justify the condemnation of same-sex relationships. Yet to claim that homosexuality is the sin of Sodom is problematic. Linking this biblical passage to homosexuality is complicated if we recognize that no specific equivalent exists in the Hebrew (or Greek) text for the word "homosexual." No biblical word exists whose meaning remotely defines the essence of how the contemporary word "homosexuality" is used. The Hebrew text, as well as the Greek, uses idioms making any interpretation of the passage difficult. The term "homosexual" did not even come into existence in English until 1892. The word "sodomy," derived from the town's name and associated with its supposed sin, did not enter the English language until the thirteenth century, and even then was not always connected with anal intercourse, as it is today. In different historical periods, sodomy has meant everything from anal copulation, to acts of heterosexual oral sex, to bestiality. Hence a danger exists in juxtaposing ancient biblical prohibitions with contemporary sexual milieus without considering the historical and cultural social location from which these prohibitions arose.

Relying on the biblical text to determine what Sodom's sin was makes homosexuality an even more unlikely candidate. While it is true that in several places throughout Scripture Sodom has come to signify evil and rebellion, nowhere does the Bible refer to or link homosexuality to Sodom. What then is the sin of Sodom that societies must protect themselves from, lest the wrath of God be unleashed? Commenting on Sodom's sin, the prophet Ezekiel (16:49) wrote that Sodom's iniquity was the city residents' unwillingness, due to their pride and haughtiness, to share their abundance with those who were poor and marginalized. It is this haughtiness that becomes the root cause of the abomination they participated in before the eyes of God. Amos (4:1, 11) prophesied the destruction of Israel for following Sodom's example of "oppressing the needy and crushing the poor." For the prophet Isaiah, Israel is referred to as Sodom and Gomorrah because it was committing the same acts that led to the destruction of those cities: "Hear the word of the LORD, you rulers of Sodom! Listen to the teaching of our God, you people of Gomorrah! . . . Your hands are full of blood. Wash yourselves; make yourselves clean; remove the evil of your doings from before my eyes; cease to do evil, learn to do good; seek justice, rescue the oppressed, defend the orphan, plead for the widow" (Isa. 1:10–17). Israel's sin, like that of Sodom and Gomorrah, is a lack of justice done in the name of the orphans and widows. Within patriarchal societies, the most vulnerable members are those who are not under the care of a man, specifically the orphan who has lost her or his father and the widow who has lost her husband. Deprived of a male protector, they cease to hold any standing in a male-centered society. For this reason the Bible makes their care the responsibility of all.

Early rabbinical writings attested that throughout early Judaism, a link did not exist between Sodom's sin and homosexuality.

Others [the Sodomites, like the Egyptians] had refused to receive strangers when they came to them, but these made slaves of guests who were their benefactors. And not only so—but, while punishment of some sort will come upon the former for having received strangers with hostility, the latter, having first received them with festal celebrations, afterward afflicted with terrible sufferings those who had already shared the same rights. They were stricken also with loss of sight—just as were those at the door of the righteous man—when, surrounded by yawning darkness, all of them tried to find the way through their own doors.

—Wisdom of Solomon 19:14–17

Our Rabbis taught: The men of Sodom waxed haughty only on account of the good which the Holy One, blessed be He, had lavished upon them. . . . They said: Since there cometh forth bread out of [our] earth, and it hath the dust of gold, why should we suffer wayfarers, who come to us only to deplete our wealth. Come, let us abolish the practice of travelling in our land.

—Babylonian Talmud, *Sanhedrin* 109a

The first persons who actually defined Sodom's sin as a homosexual act lived centuries later. The Jewish philosopher Philo of Alexandria (c. 25 BCE to 50 CE) wrote: "But God, having taken pity on mankind, as being a Savior and full of love for mankind, increased, as far as possible, the natural desire of men and women for a connection together, for the sake of producing children, and detesting the unnatural and unlawful commerce of the people of Sodom, he extinguished it, and destroyed those who were inclined to these things."[23] Likewise, Josephus (c. 37–100 CE), who was commissioned by Roman authorities to write the history of the Jews, wrote: "[When the] Sodomites saw the young men to be of beautiful countenances, and this to an extraordinary degree . . . they resolved themselves to enjoy these beautiful boys by force and violence."[24]

The sin of Sodom, as defined by the biblical text and the early rabbinical writings, does not refer to a loving relationship between two individuals of the same sex. What then is the sin of Sodom and Gomorrah? What is the sin in which many political and religious leaders today participate? According to every passage found throughout the biblical text in which Sodom's wickedness is mentioned, homosexuality is never listed as the cause for God's wrath. Such an interpretation came centuries later. The sin of Sodom and Gomorrah, according to the Bible, was a lack of justice done in the name of the society's dispossessed. God's anger consumes Sodom and Gomorrah because of the dominant culture's refusal to show hospitality to those residing on their margins.

In the biblical world, hospitality meant more than simply being neighborly; it was a carefully orchestrated social practice to receive strangers and make them guests. Strangers, lacking legal standing, were at the mercy of established community leaders who were willing to serve as their host. Their very survival would depend on falling under the protection of a member of the town. Throughout the biblical text, prophets reminded believers of these ancient traditions, warning them that hospitality was to be extended to the marginalized. Dishonoring the orphan, the widow, the alien—in

23. Philo of Alexandria, *On Abraham* 27.137, trans. C. D. Yonge, 1854.
24. Josephus, *Antiquities of the Jews* 1.11.3, trans. William Whiston, 1998.

short, those who were disenfranchised—signified a godless nation liable to God's wrath. This is why Jesus, when giving instructions to his disciples preparing to embark on a missionary journey, stated that those cities that refused them hospitality would face a worse fate than Sodom (Luke 10:1–12).

Rather than using this passage to condemn homosexuality, we would be more biblically sound to use this story to condemn how first-world nations economically treat the peoples of third-world nations, which is not so different from what the Sodomites hoped to do to the aliens in their own midst. Today, inhabitants of first-world nations exhibit the same xenophobia demonstrated by the Sodomites. Like the residents of Sodom who sought to physically rape the foreigners in their midst, we today economically rape the poor and the undocumented alien. In ancient Sodom as in the modern United States, those in power desire to subordinate the stranger, the undocumented, and the alien in their midst.

If a strong desire among today's readers insists that Sodom's sin was a sexual act, then the only argument that could feasibly be made is that same-gender gang rape perpetrated by heterosexual men is wrong. Even then, rape is not a sexual act, though it is violence involving sexual organs. Rape is foremost an act of domination in which pleasure is achieved through the humiliation and subjugation of the victim. Lot's daughters became unsatisfactory substitutes for the purpose of sexual abuse because the goal of the townsfolk of Sodom was not to quench sexual appetites but to dominate and domesticate the strangers within their midst. The desire of mortal men to rape "heavenly messengers" was an attempt to subjugate the things of heaven to the will of humans. It was an assault on God's authority! The sin of Sodom is not homosexuality, but unchecked heterosexuality in its attempt to dominate everything, even the things of God, to the male.

If we remember that the two strangers were not humans but angels, then sexual intercourse with heavenly beings by humans would be a transgression of the natural order. Passages in the New Testament that refers to Sodom's sin and God's punishment for their "shameless ways" and "unnatural fornication" (2 Pet. 2:4–8 and Jude 6–7 JB) begin to make sense. When read with the presupposition that the sin of these ancient cities was intimate same-sex relationships, then the logical conclusion is that the passages condemn homosexuality, with warnings of divine punishment. But a closer examination reveals that the authors of these NT books were not referring to our modern understanding of homosexual orientation. The 2 Peter passage begins with a reference to sinning angels, and in Jude the subjects are angels who traded "supreme authority" for "spiritual chains." These biblical passages refer to the Genesis 6:1–4 account of angels having sex with mortal women and, in doing so, disrupting the natural order separating humans from the Divine. The "shameless ways" and "unnatural fornication" in the passages in 2 Peter and Jude are sexual intercourse between celestial and mortal beings. Sodom and Gomorrah are mentioned because the men of Sodom attempted to gang-rape Lot's guests, who were angels. Their lust for heavenly creatures reverses the earlier lust heavenly creatures held for humans. Their unnatural lust for angels is being condemned, not homosexuality.

Lot bravely stands before the rabble pleading they desist, that they do not commit the abomination of taking unjust advantage of the foreigners who have taken shelter under his roof. But the mob's anger quickly turns toward Lot, himself a resident alien in their town. From behind the door, the angels reach out and take hold of him, dragging him back into the house. The irony of the story is that the one who set out to protect the heavenly beings now falls under their protection. The two angels strike the mob with momentary blindness (a feat to be repeated in 2 Kgs. 6:18 when a similar fate strikes the invading Aramean army). They warn Lot of the coming doom and instruct him to gather his family for an immediate escape. The text then tells us that Lot went out to recruit his prospective sons-in-law, leaving the reader to wonder if they were among the mob, also blinded. After all, the text does state that all of the town's men were at Lot's door. If so, then the sons-in-law's response to Lot is all the more puzzling. For whatever reason, either disbelief in Lot's message or preference for Sodom's ways of life, they laugh in his face, refusing to escape with him. Some will always prefer allegiance to their town, state, or nation rather than to God, regardless as to how poorly their government treats foreigners, aliens, and immigrants. They choose solidarity with the dominant culture rather than with those forced to live on the underside of history.

But before we commend Lot for quickly renouncing Sodom, the text reminds us that he delayed leaving. One would think that Lot and his family would be eager to flee such a wicked and corrupt city, but instead he seems to linger. The angels must prod him to escape the coming doom. Even when told to head for the hills, Lot pleads to be allowed to escape to the small village of Zoar. His request is granted and Zoar is spared the coming retribution, a feat Abraham was unable to accomplish. As they make their way to Zoar, God rains fire and brimstone on Sodom and Gomorrah. The cities' destruction could have been caused by a volcanic eruption or a tectonic shift causing an earthquake that released either natural gases (e.g., hydrogen sulfide) or asphalt and petroleum—a likely scenario considering the Dead Sea coastal area is rich in sulfur and asphalt deposits. If these natural products ignited, it would explain Abraham seeing smoke rising as if from a furnace while looking in the direction of Sodom and Gomorrah.

The text reminds us that God remembered God's promise to Abraham and saved Lot and his family. God did say God would spare Sodom if ten just men were to be found. Its destruction indicates that none was deemed righteous. This leads us to wonder, were Lot and his family spared because they were just? Lot's willingness to offer up his daughters for rape to the mob gathered at his house, his wife's punishment for looking back, and his daughters' future incestuous plots seem to indicate a lack of righteousness. Was it Abraham's faithfulness that saved Lot? It seems that there was not much that Lot did to save himself. "God remembered Abraham" (19:29), hence indicating that "the prayer of the righteous is powerful and effective" (Jas. 5:16).

The theological and ethical claim made by this story is that God, as a consuming fire, intervenes in human history so as to punish evil. Wickedness may prevail, but it can never endure. The wages of sin is still death. God will not forever tolerate injustice toward the poor and alien, with whom God stands in solidarity—not because they are holier, but because they are dispossessed. If indeed God takes sides with those living on the underside of history, then either God brings ruin to nations and empires that continue to grind the disenfranchised, the alien, the undocumented under the millstone of oppression, or, in the final analysis, God owes Sodom and Gomorrah an apology.

19:26

Testimony of Lot's Wife

The Sodom and Gomorrah story reaches its climax when Lot's nameless wife is turned into a pillar of salt. Although nameless in the Bible, the questionable midrash *Sefer ha-Yashar*, also known as the *Book of Jasher*, which is accepted to be, by the Latter-Day Saints, of authentic ancient Hebrew origins, calls her Ado (19:52). This nameless biblical woman has been dismissed throughout history as a vain and materialistic woman who, because of her character, deserved her punishment. The rabbinical text Wisdom of Solomon blames the destruction of Sodom on their wickedness, and the transformation of Lot's wife on her unbelief. "Evidence of their wickedness still remains: a continually smoking wasteland, plants bearing fruit that does not ripen, and a pillar of salt standing as a monument to an unbelieving soul" (Wis. 10:7). When people leave wickedness behind, some still pine for their previous evil ways, symbolized by glancing reminiscently toward the past. As Jesus would eventually warn: "No one who puts a hand to the plow and looks back is fit for the kingdom of God" (Luke 9:62).

Her sinfulness has become normative in modern biblical hermeneutics. Walter Russell Bowie notes that Lot's wife was "the woman caught in the whirlwind of fire from doomed Sodom because she was still too reluctant to leave the wicked city. . . . [S]he was representative of all those in every time who are caught in the consequences of the evil they cannot quite let go."[25] W. Sibley

---

25. Walter Russell Bowie, "Exposition of the Book of Genesis," in *The Interpreter's Bible*, ed. George Arthur Buttrick (New York: Abingdon Press, 1952), 1:630.

Towner describes the moment of transformation into salt as follows: "Then Lot's wife—she of imperfect righteousness, she who will have no future role in the history of salvation—looked back."[26] And in Edith Deen's account, "Lot's wife was a worldly, selfish woman, one who spent lavishly and entertained elaborately."[27]

Lot's wife's condemnation even comes from the mouth of Jesus, the only other place in the Bible where she is mentioned. When discussing the urgency by which the last days approach those accustomed to luxurious living, Jesus provides us with a warning: "Remember Lot's wife" (Luke 17:32). The assumption is that Lot's wife was narcissistic, seeking the pleasures of this world. This theology is read back into the text, even though the Genesis account is silent about the character of Lot's wife.

All that the text tells us about Lot's wife is summed up in six Hebrew words, which translate literally: "And his wife looked back from behind him and she became a pillar of salt." Based on this solitary mention, elaborate character portraits of Lot's wife are constructed. Why? To justify her demise. If she is not portrayed as a foolish woman with a self-indulging heart, then her punishment would appear capricious, especially if because she was a woman

Lot did not bother discussing the options facing them as he did with his prospective sons-in-law. The text fails to note any discussion with Lot's wife concerning what could befall them. Verse 15 simply has the angels stating, "Take your wife and your two daughters, . . . or else you [masculine singular] will be consumed." For most of us, our sense of justice is offended that the God of

> Who will weep for this woman?
> Isn't her death the least
>   significant?
> But my heart will never forget
>   the one
> Who gave her life for a single
>   glance.
>   —Anna Akhmatova
>
> "Lot's Wife" (1924), in *The Complete Poems of Anna Akhmatova*, ed. Roberta Reeder, trans. Judith Hemschemeyer, 2nd ed. (Boston: Zephyr, 1992), 273–74.

---

26. W. Sibley Towner, *Genesis,* Westminster Bible Companion (Louisville: Westminster John Knox Press, 2001), 173.

27. Edith Deen, *All of the Women of the Bible* (New York: Harper & Brothers, 1955), 17.

second chances, the God of love, mercy, and forgiveness, would act so harshly, especially when we consider that the text is ambiguous about who was informed concerning the danger of looking back. In order to justify Lot's wife's punishment she must either be vilified or simply ignored.

Even though her presence is implied throughout the Sodom and Gomorrah story, she remains invisible. For example, when we are told that Lot prepared the two angels a meal of unleavened bread, more than likely it was his wife, under a patriarchal rule, who did the preparing, serving, and cleaning up afterward. Yet, for a brief moment, Lot's wife takes center stage in the story. She becomes visible when she looks back and is turned into a pillar of salt. Maybe her transformation is simply a folktale explaining the natural formations that resemble human figures found in the region—a myth based on the configuration of a weird rock. Josephus and his contemporary Clement of Rome claimed to have seen the pillar of salt that was once Lot's wife and was still standing during the first century CE. A century later, Irenaeus would also attest to seeing the pillar.[28] Even modern-day tourists are usually pointed to a pillar and told that it was once Lot's wife. Regardless as to the validity of the story, it remains a disturbing tale of a person who is punished for attempting to see the destruction of the city. Yet when Abraham also looks toward Sodom's demise, he is not turned into a pillar of salt (19:27–28).

Rather than depicting Lot's wife as either the totality of worldliness, or the other extreme, of virtuousness, maybe we should see her as we see the rest of us, a human who falls short of the glory of God. As an invisible member within a patriarchal society, she probably did the wash with her neighbors—also nameless women. They might have been present when she twice gave birth, as she might have been when they gave birth to their own children. She shared gossip and stories with them as she tended her garden, prepared meals, or simply rested under the stars after a long day of heavy menial work. The men of the city may all have been wicked,

---

28. Josephus, *Antiquities* 1.11.4; Irenaeus, *Against Heresies* 31.1.

but these women with whom she shared a similar fate of patriarchal oppression were more than likely her friends.

Sodom, with all its imperfections, was her home—just like many of us have made our homes in the entrails of the empire. She might have looked back to see the life that would no longer follow the well-established rhythms of the everyday. She might have looked back to mourn friends swallowed up in God's wrath who were now no more. She might have looked back to say adieu to all the daily rituals and routines that marked her life and provided meaning to her existence. Who among us would not have also taken a peek, along with Lot's wife and Abraham? Those of us who have known exile, being cast from the land that witnessed our birth, are always in a quest to see the cause of our estrangement. Only then can we hope to find healing and create healthy, well-adjusted lives. We look back lest we forget our identity.

It does not really matter why she looked back. The reality is that we will never ascertain the motives of her heart. The fact is that she looked, and was swiftly punished by God. If she did know of the consequences and still looked back, then she, as Barbara Essex reminds us, committed suicide. But if patriarchal rule meant Lot did not need to inform her of what was occurring, then her looking back was an accident, making her a victim of homicide. What is disturbing is that this would make God guilty of murder.[29] Lot's wife is killed because she is prohibited from remembering. There are no opportunities for absolution or redemption offered to her. This is one of those verses in Scripture that is profoundly

> Edith, the One-Who-Looks-Back (whom the Rabbis named Idit), answers: I looked back to all that I have left behind—my other daughter's grave, my friends and relatives, my home with its cherished mementos, my childhood—and I wept. And so hot was the desert sun and the brimstone torching Sodom that my flowing tears dried instantly, turning me into a pillar of salt.
> —Ellen Frankel
>
> *The Five Books of Miriam: A Woman's Commentary on the Torah* (New York: Putnam, 1996), 26.

29. Barbara J. Essex, *Bad Girls of the Bible: Exploring Women of Questionable Virtue* (Cleveland: United Church Press, 1999), 19.

disturbing, for it seems as if the God of Lot is not the merciful and forgiving God to whom we have become accustomed.

19:8, 30–38

Testimonies from Lot's Daughters

"Look, I have two daughters who have not known a man; let me bring them out to you, and do to them as you please" (Gen. 19:8). With these words Lot was ready to hand over his own daughters for sexual abuse and rape in order to protect the honor of men—men who were strangers. Lot's flesh and blood were offered up as living sacrifices for the sins of Sodom, so that the men who took refuge under the shelter of his roof could continue to have life. Although a reprehensible act on the part of their father Lot, this is not an isolated incident. The episode indicates the relatively low status women held since the foundation of the biblical narrative. But as offended and horrified as we may be by Lot's offer to the men of Sodom, this was the common practice of ancient hospitality, where male guests were to be more protected than household daughters. Women, viewed as property, could serve as ransom whenever the lives or dignity of men, even men who were complete strangers, were jeopardized. It is not solely Lot who should stand condemned, but all men who succumbed to the rationale that normalized and legitimized ancient hospitality customs.

> Lot tried to mediate between males, giving each side what it wanted. No male was to be violated. All males were to be granted their wishes. Conflict among them could be solved by the sacrifice of females. The male protector, indeed the father, became procurer.
>
> —Phyllis Trible
>
> *Texts of Terror: Literary-Feminist Readings of Biblical Narratives*, OBT (Philadelphia: Fortress Press, 1984), 75.

Lot's daughters, as property, were so insignificant in the eyes of the biblical editors that their names are not even important enough to warrant mention for the sake of posterity. What must it have been like to be treated as nameless objects in the hands of one's own father, who stood ready to offer you up to be ravished by the townsfolk?

Probably more troubling for Lot's daughters was trying to reconcile any sense of cosmic justice with their father's action, especially if we accept the rabbinical tradition that Lot might have been the chief justice of Sodom.[30] After all, the angels found Lot by the city gates, the locale usually mentioned throughout the Scriptures as the center where those who dispense justice (and regulate social and economic affairs) sit (Deut. 21:19; Ruth 4:1; 2 Kgs. 7:1). If all this is true, then Lot was not saved for his righteousness. If he sat by the city gates, then he was embedded in Sodom's cultural interaction. Even if he was not a judge at Sodom, a fuller disturbing portrait of Lot emerges in Scripture, one that is not flattering. He is a man who puts his own needs first by choosing the abundant Jordan Valley to the detriment of his uncle Abraham; he is willing to offer his daughters up for sacrifice; his hesitancy in trusting the divine messengers' directive to flee for the hills is demonstrated by his insistence on escaping to Zoar in the valley; and finally his succumbing to drunkenness, which leads to incestuous relationships. He is saved by grace, a promise made by God to Abraham, not by any works.

God's wrath rained fire and brimstone on the towns in the valley where Lot and his daughters took refuge. Fearing that they would not be safe in Zoar, they finally fled for the hills. From that vantage point they saw their whole world swallowed up in God's rage. Unfortunately, witnessing the annihilation of the cities led Lot's daughters to conclude that the devastation was worldwide. After all, hadn't God already destroyed the earth with water? Maybe now God chose to destroy the earth with fire. While living in the cave, the firstborn daughter informed the younger that there was not a man on earth with whom they could have sex, except for their old father. They saw themselves as the earth's sole survivors, and as such became committed in eliminating the perceived shame of not bearing children, specifically sons. No doubt they internalized the patriarchal view that their worth lay in their fecundity. To preserve their honor, and their ancestral line, they hatched a plan. Two nights in a row they served their father wine, getting him drunk. On the first night, while he was in an unconscious stupor, the firstborn

---

30. *Midrash Genesis Rabbah* 50:3.

"knew" him, and on the second night the younger did the same. On both nights he did not realize that they came to his bed or left. This leaves one to wonder how an old, unconscious, drunken man found the stamina to impregnate women two nights in a row.

As they planned, the daughters gave birth to the next generation. Each bore a son whose tribal descendants would be Moab and Ammon. It is these sons who will become fathers of a people, not Lot, who instead fades into history. Lot's older daughter named her child Moab—a play on the Hebrew phrase me-'ab, "from father." Located on the southeastern border of Israel, Moab was intertwined with Israel in its early history. Specifically, Moab participated in multiple military engagements against Israel beginning when the Hebrews entered Canaan until the start of the Babylonian captivity, an era spanning over 630 years. Lot's other daughter named her son Ben-ammi, which can be translated as "son of my people," or "son of my paternal clan." Located east of Israel but north of Moab, Ammon was also engaged in hostile military activities against Israel during the same period of time.

If indeed this biblical section is a product of J—as scholars think it is—written during the early monarchy of Solomon, could it be that the author was using this derogatory narrative as a propaganda tool against the somewhat powerful people that bordered Israel on the east, and with whom King Saul and David fought (1 Sam. 11;14:7; 2 Sam. 8:2; 11:14–21)? We know the Israelites held Moab and Ammon in contempt. "No Ammonite or Moabite shall be admitted to the assembly of the LORD. . . . You shall never promote their welfare or their prosperity as long as you live" (Deut. 23:3, 6). Could the author be engaged in a smear campaign that questions the shameful origins of Israel's enemies and their moral bankruptcy? By extension, could this be a veiled accusation that they remain "bastards" among whom incestuous activities are still the norm? Still, we should not forget that in spite of any existing animosities to which the text testifies, Ruth, the grandmother of King David—the line from which for Christians the Messiah is to come—is a Moabite. And Naamah, wife of King Solomon and mother of Rehoboam— also the line from which the Messiah is to come—is an Ammonite.

No doubt our modern sensitivities are offended by the tale of daughters climbing onto their father's bed in the hope of being impregnated. Nevertheless, the text reflects a certain ambiguity concerning their actions. Remember, in their minds there were no other men living on earth, only them and their father. Should we praise them for their heroic participation in the unsavory act of tricking their father into a sexual relationship for the sake of preserving his ancestral line, or do we instead condemn them for incest? Today many women throughout the world, in order to survive, or to bring salvation to their family or children, must also turn to sexual activities condemned by polite society. They are forced into prostitution in order to live. Others are forced into loveless empty marriages. And like Lot's daughters, they become nameless objects to be used for the gratification and/or advancement of men.

Regardless if we condemn, pity, or celebrate Lot's daughters, the irony of their act is not lost. The Lot of Sodom who demonstrated courage by facing off a mob of men in front of his house ends as a passive old object in the hands of women. The Hebrew word *shakab* (to lie down [with]) usually has a masculine subject and a feminine object. In this section of Scripture, where the word *shakab* is used several times, the norm is reversed. The subject is the daughters, who play an active role during the sexual act, and the object is Lot. Furthermore, it is the daughters, not Lot the man, who exercises authority by naming the sons born to them. Hence the one who offered his daughters to be raped is in turn raped by his daughters.

20:1–26:33

The Story of Ishmael and Isaac

20:1–18; 21:1–7
Testimony of Sarah

Abraham apparently learned nothing from his first earlier encounter with Pharaoh. Once again, he is pawning off his wife by claiming that she is his sister. Even though Sarah may very well be in her nineties, she is supposedly such a gorgeous woman that royalty lust over her, desiring to possess her. Some scholars insist that the events that unfolded at Gerar are simply another version of the earlier events that occurred when Abraham journeyed to Egypt (12:10–20), with the earlier account being a product of the J source, while the Gerar events are a product of E. Although that may be true, both stories can also be viewed separately, even though obvious connections and divergences exist. For example, unlike the earlier version that claimed that Pharaoh took Sarah as his wife, thus implying a sexual relationship, the Gerar version takes great lengths to insist no inappropriate physical activity took place between the king and the matriarch of the faith, possibly because soon after this encounter Sarah is with child. The Gerar account could very well be one event among many where Abraham pimps his wife to secure security and possessions. Telling inhabitants of the towns they encounter that Sarah is his sister appears to be his modus operandi. Abraham specifically instructed Sarah that *everywhere* they travel she is to say that he is but her brother. This might explain why, unlike the earlier Egyptian episode (which could very well be the first time this form of deception was implemented) there is no indication that this time Abraham consulted with his wife. They each simply played the part of siblings. There was no need to remind Sarah of the deception because she already knew her "place."

In the previous chapter, we are told that Abraham has made his home at the oaks of Mamre, near Hebron. The story opens with him traveling south to the land of Negeb, near the border of Egypt, the same region where Hagar had earlier run away from her master and named the God who sees. There Abraham settled between Kadesh and Shur in an area called Gerar, a city whose exact location remains undetermined. When Abraham met the king of Gerar, Abimelech (either a personal name or a title translated as "my father is king"), he told the king that Sarah was his sister. Gazing on this elderly beauty, Abimelech took possession of her.

But that night the king had a dream in which God appeared to Abimelech, warning that he will die for taking another man's wife. Although almost never the case, God can prevent sin from occurring. The king professes his innocence, truthfully claiming he was deceived; nevertheless, God stills hold him accountable for sin he almost committed. Redemption for the king now relies on him going back to his deceiver, the one who placed him in this situation in the first place, to intercede on his behalf. No doubt, for the modern reader, returning to the one who did you harm to intercede on your behalf before God probably appears unfair. But Abraham is called a prophet (20:7), not as the term would come to be used later in the biblical text, but simply as one who is able to communicate between the domain of God and the reality of humans. Abimelech comes off as being more faithful than the father of faith; still Abraham continues to be God's chosen and thus can be used by God to bring about God's will, in spite of Abraham's less than exemplary behavior. The good news of Abraham's usability by God for us today is that all women and men of faith, regardless of whether they constantly fall short of the glory of God, are still crucial to the Almighty, who can, in spite of ourselves, use us to bring about God's will.

When confronted by Abimelech, Abraham finds lame excuses, excuses similar to the ones he earlier voiced to the pharaoh. According to Abraham, he feared for his life, believing that the inhabitants of Gerar had no knowledge of God. Besides, he technically was not lying. Sarah was his sister, half sister to be exact, sharing the same father. But Abraham was wrong; Abimelech did fear God, as demonstrated by his actions. It was Abraham who feared humans more than he feared God, willing to sin by handing over his wife. Or maybe the real issue was not fear but greed. The story ends similarly to the Egyptian account, with Abimelech showering Abraham with sheep, cattle, slaves, and a thousand pieces of silver, along with permission to settle anywhere within his domain that Abraham chooses. Abraham's deception has proven to be very profitable, thus possibly explaining why he continues to reemploy the scam.

While the focus remains on Abraham and Abimelech, this is truly a testimony about Sarah and the many women who have historically found themselves in similar situations. Like the earlier Egyptian narrative, migrant women are the ones who are usually placed in the most vulnerable positions for the sake of their families. All too often, migrant women like Sarah are forced to participate in unwanted sexual activities in order to obtain or keep employment so as to feed their families. Millions of noncitizen women live in a kind of legal no-man's land, at the mercy of employers and federal immigration agents for their livelihoods, increasingly fearful of approaching law enforcement agencies for protection from abuse, specifically sexual blackmail. Take the example of Isaac R. Baichu, a federal immigration officer in New York City, who pleaded guilty in April 2010 for demanding sex from a twenty-two-year-old Colombian wife of an American citizen in December 2007 in exchange for a green card.

> I want sex. One or two times. That's all. You get your green card. You won't have to see me anymore.
> —Isaac R. Baichu, U.S. federal immigration officer
>
> Nina Bernstein, "Immigration Officer Guilty in Sexual Coercion Case," *The New York Times*, April 14, 2010.

It is impossible to tell how widespread sexual blackmail is, but Baichu's case is not an isolated instance. For example, immigration agent Lloyd W. Miner of Hyattsville, Maryland, induced a 21-year-old Mongolian woman to stay in the country illegally, harboring her in his home. A 60-year-old immigration adjudicator in Santa Ana, California, was charged with demanding sex from a 29-year-old Vietnamese woman in exchange for approving her citizenship application. Immigration agent Eddie Romualdo Miranda was acquitted of sexual battery in August 2007, although he did plead guilty to misdemeanor battery and was sentenced to probation. In Atlanta another adjudicator, Kelvin R. Owens, was convicted in 2005 of sexually assaulting a 45-year-old woman during her citizenship interview in the federal building. And in Miami, an agent of Immigration and Customs Enforcement responsible for transporting a Haitian woman to detention instead took her to his home and raped her. According to congressional testimony given in 2006 by Michael Maxwell, former director of Homeland Security's internal investigations, more than three thousand backlogged complaints of employee misconduct had gone uninvestigated for lack of staff, including 528 involving criminal allegations.[1] The New York City Colombian woman, like so many vulnerable migrant women, was forced to engage in oral sex with a representative of the "king" in order to stay in the country with her family. Unfortunately, when her husband found out, he left her. In addition, as of 2010, she still lives in limbo, at the mercy of other unscrupulous Abimelech officials while she waits for her green card.

Although the text reassures the reader that nothing sexual transpired between Abimelech and the migrant woman Sarah, it probably still raised eyebrows to discover a few verses later, at the start of chapter 21, that Sarah is with child. We have no way of knowing if Isaac is born nine months after the Abimelech affair. To complicate the situation, if she was already pregnant when she was at Gerar and entered the king's harem, she surely would have been executed for carrying another man's child once the king found out. While the text assures us that Abimelech is not Isaac's father, we are still left wondering if the father is Abraham. It is after God "did for Sarah as he had promised" (21:1) that she conceives. Did Abraham (as will be the case with a future Joseph, Jesus' supposed father) have anything to do with conception? Is Sarah, like the future Mary, impregnated after God's visit?

Regardless, the biblical lesson is that God is author of all life, with the power to open and close wombs. As the Gerar episode concludes, we are told that God, on account of Sarah, closed the wombs of all

---

1. Nina Bernstein, "An Agent, A Green Card, and a Demand for Sex," *The New York Times*, March 21, 2008.

the women (wife and slave girls) in Abimelech's household. It is only after Abraham intercedes for the king that their wombs are opened. According to Scripture, a healing occurs in verse 17, uncomfortably implying that barrenness is some sort of disease visited on women by God.

God's promise to Abraham comes to fruition. Sarah gives birth. She recognizes the humor of nursing children in her advanced years, and thus laughs in joy with all who hear of her predicament. Having the elusive child is what finally completes her as a woman, a problematic proposition proposed by male church leaders to limit woman's fulfillment solely to the sphere of the family.

After eight days, we are told that Abraham circumcises the child, thus bringing the promised child into the covenant. But while the birth of Isaac indicates God's faithfulness to the covenant made with Abraham, we are left wondering if the covenant should have instead been made with Sarah. After all, none of the other descendants of Abraham (Ishmael by Hagar or the six sons bore to him by Keturah, the woman he married after Sarah dies) is the promised child of the covenant. Not all of the children Abraham sired are of the covenant, but Sarah's only begotten son is.

> Woman's true sphere is within the family circle. He who would substitute anything else, frustrates her true nature, disrupts the providential plan of God and creates serious problems for society at large, which becomes filled with neurotic unhappy, useless and very often, and worst of all, disruptive women!
> —Monsignor James Alberione
>
> *Woman: Her Influence and Zeal as an Aid to the Priesthood*, trans. the Daughters of St. Paul (Boston: St. Paul Editions, 1964), 40.

21:8–21

Testimony of Ishmael

Hagar, who names the Deity *El Roi*, the God who sees, returns to an abusive slavery that the seeing God seems not to notice. She submits to Abraham's dominion, quickly disappearing from the narrative until the moment that the promised child, Isaac, is weaned. Although God promised to also make Hagar's descendants too numerous to count (16:10), the fruit of her womb, in the final analysis, remains divinely rejected because Ishmael's mother is Hagar and not Sarah. The return to the Hagar narrative provides a different perspective than the earlier version in chapter 16. This could be due to the earlier version being mainly a product of the J source, while this text is from the E source. In this version (or continuation) of the story, Hagar again is found in the wilderness, not because she was fleeing Sarah's cruelty, but because she was disposed of by those who owned her. The Hagar of chapter 16 sought her own liberation, her own destiny, by fleeing from Sarah's brutality. But as mentioned, God returned her to slavery. Some seventeen years have elapsed since we first met Hagar. Here we are introduced to a Hagar who seems more broken and trodden on by almost two decades of slavery under a spiteful mistress. For many who are oppressed, the spark of resistance is simply beaten out of them.

Rather than seeking her fate as she did in chapter 16, her fate is determined for her. She is cast out, a victim of circumstances beyond her control. And to make things worse, Hagar and her son are vilified to justify their expulsion.

> Hagar, Egyptian slave woman: She was wounded for our transgression; she was bruised for our iniquities.
>
> —Phyllis Trible
>
> *Texts of Terror: Literary-Feminist Readings of Biblical Narratives*, OBT (Philadelphia: Fortress Press, 1978), 8.

Why must mother and child be sent away? Sarah eventually had her own son, Isaac, but fearing that her son's inheritance could be jeopardized by Abraham's firstborn, Ishmael, Sarah orchestrated Hagar's exile. We are told that Hagar's banishment occurred because of an incident involving her son during a great banquet arranged by Abraham to celebrate the day Isaac was weaned, an event that usually occurred when the child reached his third birthday. It is estimated that at this time Ishmael must have been about seventeen years old. (If Ishmael was thirteen when he was circumcised by his ninety-nine-year-old father [17:24–25], and Abraham was a hundred years old when Isaac was born [21:5], and the feast of Isaac's weaning customarily took place around his third birthday, then Ishmael had to be approximately seventeen years old.) This raises a question. What is a seventeen-year-old doing playing with a three-year-old? Perhaps the older half brother was playing with a younger sibling in the familial way older siblings take care of the younger members of the family. Rather than be upset, one would think Sarah would be comforted that the older sibling took time to entertain the younger child. Nonetheless, the reader concludes that Ishmael was doing more than simply playing with Isaac. It is assumed that the elder Ishmael was mocking Isaac. Although no explicit indication of malicious teasing appears in the text, still a hint of Ishmael's possible behavior is implied in the pun used by the author. The root of the word "playing" (*mitsaheq*) is the same root of Isaac's name (*Yitshaq*), which means "laughter." Was Ishmael mocking the promised child intentionally or was it part of sibling joshing? Regardless of what Ishmael's intentions might have been, Sarah perceived it as a threat.

Sarah does not want her child playing with the son of Hagar the Egyptian. Moreover, there were Ishmael's primogeniture rights to consider. He was a threat to her own son because he was the firstborn; but then again this is the Bible, where the firstborn usually fare poorly. This narrative is no different. Sarah demands that Abraham put Hagar and her son away. Alice Ogden Bellis makes a perceptive analogy:

> Sarah's story is replayed wherever and whenever the oppressed oppress those who have even less power. Sarah is not a hero. She is someone with whom we can empathize if we are honest. . . . Whatever our ethnic group, Americans are privileged far beyond our sisters and brothers in many parts of the world. Maybe Hagar can remind us that even as we seek justice for women, we must be careful not to do it at the expense of others, especially those whose position in society is more marginal than our own.[2]

Abraham hesitates. Maybe he is concerned because the expulsion of a slave wife and her child(ren) was forbidden by the customs of his

---

2. Alice Ogden Bellis, *Helpmates, Harlots, and Heroes: Women's Stories in the Hebrew Bible* (Louisville: Westminster John Knox Press, 1994), 74.

time.[3] Or maybe he has become attached to his firstborn. Regardless of the reasons for his concerns, God instructs him to grant whatever Sarah is requesting. Obeying God, he places the boy on his mother's shoulder (a difficult act if indeed Ishmael is seventeen) and sends them off with barely enough provisions to last for one day. Before we let Abraham off the hook and solely blame Sarah, it is important to remember that Abraham—wealthy Abraham—provides meager provisions for the journey, some bread and a skin of water. Abraham had the means to ensure his son and his slave wife would arrive at a new destination with sufficient provisions to reestablish their lives. He also had enough slaves to accompany them on their journey to ensure that they would not fall into any harm. Instead, Abraham casts out his wife and child with no concern for their future well-being, a trend unfortunately continued to this day by numerous absentee fathers who refuse to provide child support.

Hagar again finds herself in the desert facing death, a familiar scenario for most domestic servants today who, when they cease to be useful, are also discharged. Like poor women today, many of whom are of color, Hagar is robbed of subjectivity. Poor women today, like Hagar, exist as an economic commodity to be used to advance the privilege of those who have power over them. Homeless because of the unwillingness of the father of her child to shoulder his responsibility, Hagar was abandoned. Alone in the desert, facing death, and questioning the promise God previously uttered about the multitude of her descendants, she must have wondered about the blindness of this God whom she named *El Roi*. When reading the story, we need to be cautious about rushing

> [Hagar] and Ishmael together, as family, model many black American families in which a lone woman/mother struggles to hold the family together in spite of the poverty to which ruling class economics consign it. Hagar, like many black women, goes into the wide world to make a living for herself and her child, with only God by her side.
>
> —Delores S. Williams
>
> *Sisters in the Wilderness: The Challenge of Womanist God-Talk* (Maryknoll, NY: Orbis, 1993), 33.

3. John Bright, *A History of Israel*, 3rd ed. (Philadelphia: Westminster Press, 1981), 79.

to the conclusion that God saved the day. It is important to note that Ishmael is never referred to by name in this story. Indeed, Phyllis Trible reminds us that God, in verse 12, refers to him as "the lad" instead of Abraham's "son," and Hagar as the "slave woman" rather than Abraham's "wife." Hagar is debased by Sarah, rejected by Abraham, and now belittled by God.[4]

Alone, out of provisions, and lost in the wilderness of Beersheba, it is only a matter of time before the inevitable happens. The young adolescent reverts to a baby, abandoned under a bush so that his mother can avoid his final hours. Hagar sits a bowshot off, wailing and weeping. God responds, but not to the howling mother. Instead, God appears to Hagar because God heard the crying of the lad. Ishmael becomes the center of the story as Hagar moves to the margins. Hagar's testimony is replaced by Ishmael's. In chapter 16 the nation promised to Hagar is now, through Ishmael, to come forth as a great nation. It is because of him that God saves, opening her eyes so that she could see a nearby well. According to Islamic tradition, this is the well of Zamzam, which is located in Mecca, where Abraham and Isaac will eventually build a sanctuary (Qur'an 2:125–29), called the Kaaba, to which all observant Muslims face five times a day to pray. Today millions of Muslim pilgrims participating in the hajj stop at the well of Zamzam where Ishmael first drank to also drink its waters. Ishmael is saved and makes the wilderness of Paran his home, becoming an expert bowman. He becomes the ancestor of the bedouin Arabs.

Again, before rushing to praise God for saving the outcast, we are left with some very disturbing questions requiring our consideration. Why send Hagar and Ishmael into the wilderness in the first place? Was it to pacify an ungrateful and ungenerous Sarah? We can rejoice that God saves mother and child in the desert, but how many other mothers and children (as well as fathers and brothers) who are of Hispanic descent are presently dying in the U.S. Sonoran Desert (on the southern border) due to unjust immigration laws? Are they any less worthy than Hagar and Ishmael? Does the God who sees not "see" them?

4. Trible, *Texts of Terror*, 21.

22:1–24

Testimony of Young Isaac

"You want me to do what?" We can only imagine that Abraham's response to God's monstrous command to sacrifice his beloved son would be one of shock and puzzlement, even though the very first verse of the narrative that has come to be known within Judaism as the *Akedah* (the binding) reassures the reader that God does not really want Abraham to kill his boy. Although the New Testament maintains that God does not tempt anyone (Jas. 1:13), in the Isaac story God is obviously tempting Abraham. Although scholars assert a difference in nuance between tempting (an enticement to deliberately sin against God and/or neighbor) and testing (an enticement to ascertain the depths of one's commitment to God), for the one going through the trial such differences seem to be more aligned with an academic debate based on semantics. If it comes from God, we call it a test; but if it comes from anywhere else (i.e., Satan, demons, other humans, society), we call it a temptation. Regardless of the term we choose, for the one going through the anguish of having to decide whether to kill one's child, the command from God must seem both capricious and sadistic. Nevertheless, the reader knows, from the start of the story, that God is testing (tempting?) Abraham to determine to what extreme he is willing to go in order to be obedient. But this is a test where no one truly wins—neither Abraham, nor Isaac, nor God—certainly not the ram!

Abraham is being asked more than to kill his son. He is being asked to give up the promised future for God's sake, in the same way he already gave up the past when he left country and family for a land he had yet to see (12:1–2). Abraham is asked to live in the space where the promise of life represented in the form of Isaac and his descendants conflicts with the command of death represented in the assassination of the promised child. So God instructs Abraham to go to the land of Moriah, which has traditionally been identified with Mount Moriah, on which the temple of Jerusalem was later built (2 Chr. 3:1). If so, then this is the first sacrifice God requests be made at what would become the holy site at Jerusalem. Accompanied by two servants, Abraham travels three days to the appointed location.

The text is silent concerning any communication Abraham may have had with his wife Sarah. Did she know what was going on? Patriarchy meant that the head of the household could slaughter his children without the knowledge of the children's mother. One can only imagine how Sarah, who has lived all her life with the societal stigma of barrenness, would have responded to the possible loss of the gift God gave her. Some time has passed since the birth and weaning of Isaac. Isaac is old enough to walk for three days beside Abraham, ask questions concerning what exactly they will be doing, and carry the load of wood on his back that will be used to build the altar.

When Abraham sees the site where the sacrifice will occur, he leaves behind his two servants and finishes the trek alone with his son. He probably does not want them to witness the act that he is about to commit. As they approach the spot, Isaac notices that the sacrificial lamb is missing, prompting him to ask his father where they will obtain one. Abraham responds by both naming and providing insight into the character of God: 'elohim yir'eh, "God will provide," for Abraham's God is a God who provides. The reassurance to the boy that God will provide teaches the reader something new about God, while providing Abraham with a way of prolonging Isaac's deception until the very last moment.

In *Fear and Trembling*, Søren Kierkegaard, writing under the pseudonym Johannes de Silentio, attempts to understand Abraham's sacrifice of his son Isaac. Hard as he tries to interpret this strange account, Johannes fails in every attempt to grasp the narrative's meaning, even though it seems as if everyone else perfectly understands the story. Rather than conceive of Abraham being some mystical hero of the faith, Johannes sees the patriarch as a man of flesh and blood, and thus interprets the passage literally. Johannes wonders how Abraham could be sure he understood his mission correctly. Did God really instruct him to kill his son? Or maybe he was experiencing a delusional vision? What if, Johannes imagines, a preacher eloquently preaches on this passage stressing Abraham's radical obedience, only to have one of his congregants, moved by Abraham's act of faith, go home and execute his child? How ironic if the next Sunday the same preacher asks what demon possessed the congregant to murder his son. After all, how many throughout history have slaughtered family members because they heard voices instructing them to do so? Usually we conclude that people who murder members of their family because some voices told them to do so are criminally insane. Why then don't we also declare Abraham to be criminally insane?

Johannes wonders if faith can make the murder of one's son a holy act. Can Abraham theologically suspend the ethical for what he believes to be a higher purpose? In despair of trying to figure out Abraham's horrifying deed, an act that everyone else claims to comprehend, Johannes cries out, "Abraham, I cannot understand!" The shock of this incomprehensible narrative leaves Johannes, a nonbeliever who is interested in faith, in a state of "fear and trembling," for Abraham, in a movement of infinite resignation, sacrifices Isaac and thus renounces the world and his position in it as a moral agent. But simultaneously Abraham makes a movement of faith and regains everything. The absurd-

> Abraham enjoys honor and glory as the father of faith, whereas he ought to be prosecuted and convicted of murder.
>
> —Søren Kierkegaard
>
> *Fear and Trembling*, ed. C. Stephen Evans and Sylvia Walsh, trans. Sylvia Walsh (New York: Cambridge University Press, 2006), 14.

ity is that in giving Isaac up he knew that he would not need to give him up. Holding these two contradictory beliefs makes Abraham crazy, and it is by virtue of this insanity that he becomes the father of faith. Humans like Johannes may not understand Abraham, but it seems that God does. Only God can judge if madness like that of Abraham is divinely or demonically inspired.

As one can imagine, many scholars have attempted to psychoanalyze Abraham's role in this story. Did he know that even if he was to kill Isaac, God's promise would still be fulfilled? Would God resurrect Isaac, or would Sarah, much older now, give birth to another child? We have traditionally read the text assuming that Abraham was in turmoil over God's command and, in spite of his personal feelings, faithfully obeyed. Yet this man of faith seems to have shown no qualms in sacrificing the other members of his family, giving the bodies of his wives and other son over to certain suffering.

> The fact that Abraham has sacrificed his first wife Sarah to strangers on two occasions, has sacrificed his second wife Hagar first to affliction and then to ostracism, and has sacrificed his firstborn son Ishmael to the savagery of the wilderness, casts an ambiguous shadow on the testing of Abraham in Genesis 22.
>   —Danna Nolan Fewell and David M. Gunn
>
> *Gender, Power, and Promise: The Subject of the Bible's First Story* (Nashville: Abingdon Press, 1993), 52.

Why then do we assume he would hesitate now?

We are left wondering why Abraham silently obeyed. After all, when it came to strangers in Sodom and Gomorrah, he pleaded with God for their rescue (18:25). Why then does he not raise his voice to save his own flesh and blood, his own son?

Although Abraham passed the test by demonstrating his willingness to sacrifice his son, in effect he failed. If he chose not to kill his son and disobey God, what would have been the consequence? Would he have been punished by God—or worse, eternally cut off from God? If so, is he willingly sacrificing another member of his family to protect his own skin, as he has done before? I wonder how many of us would fail to pass any test or temptation because of our unwillingness to sacrifice our own child. Many of us who would refuse, thus proving our faithlessness, would rather choose to be punished by God—that is, to sacrifice ourselves, rather than let harm touch a hair on the head of one of our children. It seems that by obeying, Abraham saves himself at the cost of his child. Although he passes the test and is called a man of faith, most would view such an act as cowardly. Which fathers or mothers, regardless as to how sinful they may be, would not joyfully sacrifice themselves in order to save their child? Some might argue that no one, not even immediate family, should come before God. We must reject even them for the sake of God. Yet the major biblical Jewish figure, Moses (Exod. 32:32), and the major biblical Christian figure, Paul (Rom. 9:2–3), were each willing to be cut off from God for the sake of their people. Their love for their people was so great they willingly sought to be blotted out of God's presence if it meant the salvation of others. And in reality, isn't laying down one's life for another the heart of the Christian gospel as emulated by Jesus (John 15:13)?

When Abraham and Isaac arrived at the spot God pointed out, they constructed an altar on top of the wood. When finished, Abraham bound his son Isaac and placed him on the altar. The Qur'an also recounts this story, only it remains ambiguous as to whether the text is referring to Isaac or Ishmael. While the Bible gives no voice to Isaac, portraying him as a silent agent on whom Abraham and God act, the Qur'an gives voice to the lad to be sacrificed. When Abraham tells the lad what God commanded, the lad responds, "O my father! Do that which thou art commanded. Allah willing, thou shalt find me of the steadfast" (Surah 37:102, trans. Muhammad Marmaduke Pickthall). While the Qur'anic version portrays a courageous lad who fearlessly chooses and faces his fate, the biblical text shows us a silent lamb being led to the slaughter.

Just as Abraham failed the test he passed, Isaac fares no better. If this had happened in our modern times, there is no way of calculating the cost of professional therapy that would have been needed so that he could work through the image of seeing his father lift up a knife ready to slit his throat. As horrible as killing one child is, in today's society many parents cause similar harm to their children, convinced that they are following the voice of God. How many Christians who believe that faith can cure their sick child have suspended all medication only to witness that child succumb to a preventable disease? Similarly, how many stories have we heard of children who become dead to their parents for marrying someone outside their race or ethnicity, or by revealing a sexual orientation different from what their parents think is God's norm? Many Isaacs have been laid on the altar of intolerance and sacrificed because their parents, like Abraham, thought they were being faithful and obedient to God. Yet if God is a God of life, how can killing our children, physically or figuratively, satisfy God?

As Abraham lifts the knife to slaughter Isaac, God's angel calls out from heaven and stops him. Satisfied that Abraham holds God in awe, there remains no need to carry out the earlier instructions. No doubt God already knew the outcome; therefore the test or temptation was not conducted for God's sake, but for the sake of the one being tested. It was Abraham, and not God, who discovered how far he was willing to go to obey his God. The supposed happy ending leads us to conclude that God does not will death; rather, God wills life. This becomes a tale that distinguishes the Israelites from their neighbors. Other cultures may sacrifice their children to bloodthirsty gods, but our God requires no such human offerings.

Nevertheless, just as Abraham and Isaac did not fare well in light of the test that was passed, if we are honest with the biblical text, neither did God. The God of this passage is not that different from the God of Job. Job was a healthy, wealthy man greatly blessed by God. Then one day God, prompted by Satan, decimates Job's family and takes away his wealth and health. The entire book becomes an attempt to figure out the theodicy question, why bad things happen to good people. We are left with the troubling answer from God as to why evil befell such a faithful person like Job. "Because I wanted to," is the heavenly response we hear. God's response leaves us unsatisfied. Bad things happen because they do, and humans are in no position to question God. In Job, as in this passage on Isaac's sacrifice, God comes off as capricious. Like the Greek Olympian gods, Abraham's God, to the terror of humans, afflicts them with tests.

The same God who spares Isaac is silent when another father offers his daughter as a human sacrifice. God provides a ram and saves Abraham's beloved son, but what about Jephthah's unnamed daughter (Judg. 11:29–40)? When her father lays the faithful innocent virgin of Gilead on the sacrificial altar to fulfill a foolish vow that he made, there is no angel dispatched to save the young woman. There is no ram to take her place. Where then is the God of life? Is she dispensable because she is not a son? To read the story of Jephthah's unnamed daughter in the light of Isaac's salvation leaves us with very uncomfortable questions.

To read stories such as these forces us to read our theology into the text, specifically God's commitment to life, in a feeble attempt to save God from appearing as the source of not only life but also death, and not only good but also evil. These passages lead to the troubling conclusion that God is the cause and author of all that is good—*and all that is evil*. As the prophet Amos reminds us, "Does evil befall a city, unless the LORD has done it?" (Amos 3:6 RSV). The prophet Isaiah understands God to say, "I form the light, and create darkness:

I make peace, and create evil. I the LORD do all these things" (45:7 KJV). This is a God who sends evil spirits to torment, as in the case of Saul (1 Sam. 18:10) or Jeroboam (1 Kgs. 14:10). Before the Jews and Christians develop the idea of Satan, God brings evil to humans.

Because Abraham was faithful, God reiterates the promise that his descendants will be as numerous as the stars of heaven and the grains of sand by the seashore. All nations of the earth will bless themselves by his descendants as a reward for his obedience. Well, not all nations. A new caveat is added to the promise. For the first time we are told in verse 17 that Abraham's descendants will come into possession of the land through conquest. The salvation of a child will lead to the slaughter, decimation, and genocide of the land's indigenous people. The dark side of the promise of life is the curse of death.

Abraham, Isaac, and God do not fare well with the test that was passed, but neither does the ram that Abraham saw that was caught by its horns in a bush. The ram was sacrificed in place of the patriarch's son. In a sermon preached by Daniel García, during the Hispanic Instructors Program held at the Perkins School of Theology, the focus fell on the convenient ram that cost the powerful nothing, yet provided them with life abundant. According to García:

> The poor and improverished of the land are sacrificed. Those who are caught in life's situations and circumstances are sacrificed. They are, so to speak, the convenient rams for the sacrifice, in order to spare the children of power. We know that those who exploit others always find someone for the sacrifice. That way, they avoid sacrificing themselves. They always find a convenient ram. But let us also remember that part of the teaching of this text about the intended sacrifice of Isaac is that human beings ought not to be sacrificed. The ram is an animal, and may be sacrificed. But when our farm-worker brothers and sisters are sacrificed, and so are so many other workers, sacrificed on the altar of capitalism, that is not right. That is sinful idolatry.[5]

5. Quoted in Justo L. González, *Santa Biblia: The Bible Through Hispanic Eyes* (Nashville: Abingdon Press, 1996), 58.

21:22–34; 23:1–20
Testimony Concerning Land

With a few keystrokes on a personal computer, a New Yorker sipping a cappuccino at a Starbucks in India can transfer a fortune from Germany to Brazil within microseconds. Any (no)body can be hired to make any object, any place on earth, to be sold to anybody anywhere so that somebody can profit. The globalization of the economy has made wealth less dependent on the land under our feet. As important as land has been for creating, sustaining, and maintaining wealth, the global neoliberal economy constructed a "new world order" in which wealth can be created apart from land. Nevertheless, in the ancient biblical world, possession of land served as a source of power; it is from land that all that sustains life has sprung.

These two passages are loose ends in the overall narrative, one dealing with obtaining substance from the land, while the other focuses on taking possession of land.

The biblical text seems to be calling for Abraham to be a member of a landed community, rather than conquering the land needed. At the end of chapter 21, King Abimelech is reintroduced. This was the king of Gerar to whom Abraham tried to pass off his wife as his sister, an exchange, as in Egypt, that concluded with Abraham's enrichment. Having been tricked once, Abimelech now comes to Abraham, along with his military might in the form of Phicol, the commander of his army, and demands that Abraham swear by his God that he would not trick him again. He returns the same kindness he has shown Abraham as a guest within his domain.

> For a colonized people the most essential value, because the most concrete, is first and foremost the land: the land which will bring them bread and, above all, dignity.
> —Frantz Fanon
>
> *The Wretched of the Earth* (New York: Grove Press, 1963), 44.

While Abraham agrees, he still reproaches Abimelech about a well that his servants seized. Battles and wars in this region of the world, past and future, are associated with obtaining the scarce resource of water. The land is valuable because it contains water. Access to water was and still is today vital for survival. Although Abimelech feigns ignorance, he is still willing to work out an agreement. In exchange for use of the land, Abraham offers sheep and cattle, but he sets aside seven lambs to symbolize the covenant they are about to cut. These seven lambs signify the well Abraham dug, hence the name of this location, Beer-sheba, which also served as a pun: *be'er* (well) *sheba'* (seven or oath), with the emphasis on the word "seven." This location, which lies in a gap in the Judean hills, became the chief city of the Negeb.

After cutting the covenant, and with the departure of Abimelech and Phicol, Abraham participated in a curious act. He planted a tamarisk tree and worshiped El Olam (the everlasting God). This is problematic because the tamarisk could be considered a sacred tree where the local deities dwell. Additionally, the term El Olam, even though Abraham is using it to refer to Yahweh, was more than likely the name of the local deity. Yet the father of faith seems to be participating in these acts that will be forbidden by later Israelite law. The passage ends by revealing that Abraham dwelled in this land, "the land of the Philistines," for a long time. This is an anachronism, for the Philistines do not show up on the scene until several centuries after Abraham's time.

While the latter part of chapter 21 was concerned with obtaining the land's resources, chapter 23 focuses on obtaining the land itself. The story begins with Sarah's end. She dies at 127 years of age. Some of the rabbinical traditions believe she had a heart attack when she heard that Abraham took off with Isaac in order to sacrifice the child to God. Others traditions have her dying as she heard Isaac recount what occurred to him during the father-son outing—the shock of almost losing him led to her death. Regardless of whether these events are connected, the fact remains that she died. According to the text, Abraham mourned and grieved for her. As touching as his spilled tears may be, Sarah might have better appreciated a display of such emotions if they were to occur before he pimped her to the Egyptian pharaoh or the king of Gerar. All too often we express emotions at the loss of persons we ignored and mistreated while they lived.

Abraham desires a place to rest Sarah's bones, but he is a stranger to the land, a sojourner with no rights to property. Besides, as a seminomadic breeder of small animals, he lives on the margins of towns and villages. Although he approaches the sons of Heth (the eponym of the Hittites) to acquire some land, these are probably not the Hittites from the Asia Minor group that were established later in history and did not settle this far south. More than likely, the "sons of Heth" refers to some indigenous Canaanite people.

What takes place between Abraham and Ephron, owner of the cave that Abraham wants, is a negotiation, a dance. Ephron offers to give Abraham the cave with the adjacent property. Of course, he is really not offering to "give" away the property. Abraham graciously refuses the "gift" offered and insists on paying for it. Ephron says sure, after all, what is a little thing like four hundred shekels of silver among friends. Obviously, it is a lot, a small fortune. Abraham does not blink or try to negotiate the price; instead he pays it and buries his wife. Eventually, he would join her (25:9–10), as will their son Isaac (35:29), Isaac's wife Rebekah (49:31), their grandson Jacob (50:13), and his first wife, Leah (49:31). Except for this modest plot, Abraham, who was promised all the land, owns nothing. But the little that they do own in the end ties the family to the land that is promised.

> Did the patriarchs who forsook everything for the sake of the promise go unrewarded? No, answers our narrative. In death they were heirs and no longer "strangers."
>
> —Gerhard von Rad
>
> *Genesis: A Commentary*, trans. John Marks, rev. ed., OTL (Philadelphia: Westminster Press, 1972), 250.

Today, on the supposed spot where the patriarchs and their wives are buried, sits a Muslim mosque, Haram el-Khalil, built above a cave.

Even though these two passages deal with land use prior to the promise of Abraham's descendants acquiring all the land, the use and possession of land was not considered to be the exclusive right of the titleholder. It was God, the creator of the earth and all that it holds, who ultimately owned the land, thus making exclusive personal possession of the land impossible. "The land shall not be sold in perpetuity, for the land is [God's]; . . . you are but aliens and tenants" (Lev. 25:23). Land was not produced or created by humans; rather, it preexisted as a gift of the Creator. The land is held in stewardship for God so that the owner and her or his neighbors can obtain the basic necessities of life. Hence Abraham had a right to the resources, water, and a plot in which to bury his loved one. Property serves the livelihood of all in the community rather than becoming the form of their subjugation. To live on the land required obedience to God, who is in fact the true land (Lord). Any improper land stewardship was deemed to desecrate the land. Hence safeguards provided by the biblical texts attempted to establish justice and prevent landownership from unjustly stratifying the population.

Two types of claims could be made on property. The biblical text champions inclusiveness. The land is held in stewardship for God so that humans, along with their neighbors, can obtain the basic necessities of life. This paradigm of landownership was extended to the early Christian church, in which all believers shared their possessions (including their real property), according to each person's needs (Acts 2:44–45). This NT concept has its roots in the wilderness experience of Israel when the bread provided by God, manna, was sufficient to meet each person's daily needs (Exod. 16:18). When accumulated in excess, the manna spoiled.

Diametrically opposed to this inclusive claim on property is our modern Western form of landownership, whose roots are in Roman law. One of Rome's enduring contributions to Western civilization is the exclusive construction of land. Title on property is exclusive, to be used, enjoyed, and disposed of unconditionally by the owner in a "fee simple estate." The function of the state and the backbone of Roman law were to protect such private property rights.[6] These property rights appropriate all of the property's resources to the privileged few who can amass large tracts of land at the expense of those who are unable to secure any. The accumulation of resources unneeded for subsistence—excess commodities—becomes a form of domination over those who must barter to obtain bare necessities.

The mercantile exclusive view of land as a commodity to be

---

6. Justo Gonzáles, *Faith and Wealth: A History of Early Christian Ideas on the Origin, Significance, and Use of Money* (San Francisco: Harper & Row, 1990), 14–19.

acquired by whatever means necessary to increase personal wealth at the expense of others is what produces injustices. Many biblical prophets frequently condemned their own community for its avarice for land. During times of economic crises, the biblical distribution of land rights was ignored as some purchased the "inheritance" of their weaker neighbors, creating an urban elite profiting from the conversion of subsistence farming to exportable cash crops. About this practice, Jeremiah wrote: "Woe to him who builds his house without righteousness and his upper rooms without justice; his neighbor serves for nothing, and he does not give him his pay. Who says, I will build myself a spacious house with large upper rooms" (Jer. 22:13–14, my trans.). According to the prophet Isaiah, "Woe to those touching house to house, bringing near field to field until no end of space, and you are made to dwell alone in the middle of the land" (Isa. 5:8, my trans.). Also Micah 2:1–2: "Woe to those plotting wickedness . . . they covet fields and seize them and houses, and carry them off. And they oppress a man and his inheritance" (my trans.).

24:1–67
Testimony of Rebekah

Death is knocking on Abraham's door. He just buried his wife and is faced with one last task—marry off Isaac—for only through him can the promise made by God be fulfilled. If Isaac does not find a wife from among his own people, Abraham's descendants might never get to outnumber the stars of heaven. Chapter 24, the longest chapter in the book of Genesis, tells us how Isaac obtains a wife, and how the promise and hope are kept alive.

The chapter opens with the elderly Abraham entrusting his faithful servant with the task of finding Isaac a suitable wife. Although the text does not name the servant, most scholars assume it is Eliezer, probably based on him being mentioned by name in the *Targum of Pseudo-Jonathan* version of the narrative. Eliezer of Damascus was the servant named by Abraham to inherit his estate before God made clear that Abraham's heir was to come from his loins (Gen. 15:2). With Isaac's birth Eliezer's claim came to an end;

yet he demonstrates a faithfulness that places the other before his own opportunities.

The faithful servant is instructed to return to Abraham's kinfolk, and from among them find a wife for his son. Isaac is not permitted to find for himself a wife from the daughters of the Canaanites among whom they live. Not to marry a Canaanite woman could be based on the fear of diluting the purity of Abraham's stock or the purity of his religious practices. With these instructions, Abraham sets in motion the norm of endogamous marriages, that is, marriages that occur within the same extended family or clan. Abraham's instruction concerning marriage eventually takes form as law. According to Exodus 34:14–16, Jewish men are not to marry foreign women because "their daughters who prostitute themselves to their gods will make [Israel's] sons also prostitute themselves to their gods."

This tension to marry from within is to plague the Israelites, best illustrated in the book of Ezra. Ezra, returning from the Babylonian exile with instructions from the Persian emperor to rebuild the temple in Jerusalem, was appalled to discover marriages between Jewish men and non-Jewish women, specifically the intermingling by the community's leaders, although nothing is said about Jewish women marrying non-Jewish men. To marry non-Jewish women was a clear violation of the Pentateuch law that forbids the union of Canaanites with Jews as first established by father Abraham. Ezra's solution was simple: men were to put away their foreign wives (Ezra 10:3), with no regard to these women or to the children produced by these unions.

Ignoring any egalitarian call of welcoming the foreigner, the postexilic community established by Ezra soon found itself weakened by internal economic abuses. Returning Jews benefited from the economic misfortunes of the Jews who did not go into exile, while concealing their profiteering in piety (Isa. 58:1–12; 59:1–8). The Jews who remained found themselves enslaved as they lost their lands to the returning Jews (Neh. 5:1–5), and were cheated of their wages by these same returning Jews, who set up new businesses (Mal. 3:5). The book of Ruth, written during this period, becomes an alternative voice to the imposition of Ezra's social structures. Here

God uses a "foreign wife," a Moabite, similar to the ones put away by Ezra, to represent society's most vulnerable members. Ruth is saved by the egalitarian laws that the returning exilic leaders aborted.

The book of Ruth provides a radical alternative to the societal construction advocated by Ezra the scribe. If the Pentateuch laws had been rigidly followed during the time of Ruth, then the story of Ruth would not have occurred. To begin with, the marriage of Ruth the Moabite to the Jewish son of Naomi was contrary to Exodus 34:14–16, which, based on Abraham's instructions to his faithful servant, forbade mixed marriages. Yet once this foreign woman entered the religious community through marriage, she could not be denied the right and protection to remain within the community. Boaz, her husband, can become a model for us today on how to demonstrate compassion and justice to aliens like Ruth. Although this later biblical text will present us with a non-Jewish woman who marries into Israel and from whose womb the future King David (and for Christians, the Messiah) will come forth, for now Abraham refuses to consider any of the local women for his son.

Abraham's faithful servant swears an oath to fulfill his master's instructions by placing his hand under Abraham's "thigh"—a euphemism for genitalia. It is important to note that because the male genitals signified human potency, patriarchs of the faith like Abraham and Israel (47:29–31) would swear oaths by them. Its elevated status is best illustrated by the sign of the covenant between God and humans—circumcision (17:10–14)—thus raising the question of how women enter the covenant with God if they lack male genitals to circumcise. This emphasis on male genitalia is troubling, especially when we come across bizarre passages like David winning Michal to be his wife through the gift of one hundred Philistine foreskins (2 Sam.

> The sacredness of the patriarch's genitals was such that, in an early time, one even swore oaths on them (Gen. 24:2–3, Abraham; 47:29–31, Israel), suggesting that any failure of respect toward one's physical progenitor or the head of one's household was sure to be visited with swift retribution.
> —L. William Countryman
>
> *Dirt, Greed, and Sex: Sexual Ethics in the New Testament and Their Implications for Today* (Philadelphia: Fortress Press, 1988), 35.

3:14), or the penalty imposed of having the hand of any woman severed from the body if she, while participating in a brawl, lays hold of a man's genitals (Deut. 25:11–12).

With the faithful servant's hand on Abraham's genitals, an oath is sworn to bring back a wife for Isaac from his own people and not take him to his kinfolk's home lest he does not return and thus forfeits the promise made by God to Abraham. We can notice the conflation of different narratives concerning the instructions given to the servant. One source (J) has Abraham asking for *any* woman of his kindred (vv. 4, 40), while the other source (E) has a particular woman in mind who may choose not to return with the servant (vv. 5, 8). We can also notice different narratives coming together in the giving of an expensive gift to the maiden twice (vv. 22, 53). Still, such disconnects remain unimportant to the overall story.

Trusting that God will send an angel or messenger before him to prepare the way in faith, the servant goes about his task of fulfilling his oath, confident that God will bless his venture. When the servant reaches Nahor he "puts out a fleece" that allows God to act (cf. Judg. 6:37–40). He would stand by the spring outside the town where the young women come to draw water. Springs, along with wells, are locations where the possibility for marriage usually begins (Gen. 16:7–14; 21:8–21; 29:1–12; Exod. 2; John 4). No doubt the earth's water is associated with the possibility of fertility. While standing by the spring, the servant decides to ask one of the girls to tilt her pitcher so that he can drink. If she does so, and offers to also water his camels, then she would be the one God has chosen for Isaac.

He has not finished setting the parameters for the test when Rebekah comes out of the town to draw water. Verse 16 tells us that she is beautiful and a virgin untouched by any man. It is interesting to note that the text tells us nothing about Isaac's virginity, or lack thereof. When the servant asks her for some water, she replies by calling him "my lord" and offers to also water his camels, a laborious task; to provide drink for ten thirsty camels that just crossed a desert is an arduous undertaking, requiring multiple trips to the spring to obtain sufficient water for them to drink. Camels can drink from twenty to thirty gallons of water in ten minutes. That comes to two to three hundred gallons of water she is offering to fetch!

After Rebekah passes the servant's test, he places a gold ring weighing a shekel through her nostrils, and on her arm places two bracelets weighing ten gold shekels. When he asks her who she is, Rebekah responds by stating that she is the daughter of Bethuel, son of Milcah, wife of Abraham's brother Nahor. In most biblical genealogies, only men beget other males. The names of women are mostly absent. Yet here, when it comes to Rebekah's genealogy, her grandmother Milcah, not her grandfather Nahor for whom the town is named, is highlighted. Milcah (Hebrew for "queen") is the family matriarch, who along with Nahor's concubine Reumah (22:20–24) gave birth to the original twelve tribes that became part of the Aramean people. Rebekah's origins are matriarchal, countering the prevalent Abrahamic patriarchy. This self-understanding affects her child rearing, as we shall later note, culminating with her son Jacob identifying himself as the son of his mother rather than his father, Isaac (29:12).

The tension between patriarchy and matriarchy is evident in Rebekah's testimony. She strongly identifies herself through her grandmother and brings the stranger to her mother's, not her father's, house. She does not wait for her father or brother to extend hospitality to the stranger, customarily the responsibility for men to offer, but invites the stranger to stay at her house. It is interesting to note that her father, Bethuel, is mainly invisible throughout the narrative. She is portrayed as an independent woman, speaking to male strangers, an act prohibited in patriarchal social order. Yet while we celebrate her independence, her marriage is still arranged for her.

When Rebekah runs home to recount what had happened to her, her brother Laban runs out to meet the man at the spring, probably motivated by the extravagant gold pieces lavished on his sister. After Laban guides Abraham's servant to his mother's house, the servant retells the story, emphasizing how the God of his master Abraham brought all things to fruition. Until now, God's interactions in the affairs of humans were quite obvious. God spoke to, walked among, and dined with humans. This physically present God now becomes less visible. Rather than God physically stating what God is about to do, humans are to look retroactively toward what occurred and discern the hand of God. God does not tell us God is present; it is up to us to "see" God's presence in the turn of events, to read God into life's trials and tribulation.

God need not physically be present to act in human affairs as God did in the past. We are introduced to a mature faith that discerns the hand of God in human life. The servant credits God for finding a spouse for Isaac, while the skeptic (or pragmatist) might claim that going to the town of Abraham's kinfolk improved the odds of him finding her. The servant states that Rebekah passed God's test, while the cynic might insist that it was really the servant's test that Rebekah had to pass, and by claiming it was God's, justified his final decision to propose she return with him and marry Isaac.

Although Rebekah is portrayed as an independent woman, she is not so liberated as to determine who she would marry. The servant arranges her marriage with her father and brother without her consent. Even when she agrees to leave with the servant, she is not providing consent to the marriage; she is just agreeing to leave quickly rather than wait ten days. We are left wondering if her rush to depart is based on wanting to leave the family that "sold" her for the lavish gifts bestowed on them, or her eagerness to meet her unknown new husband.

The servant declines staying ten additional days when asked to do so, no doubt wishing to return quickly due to Abraham's imminent death. Rebekah leaves with her nurse, who we later discover is named Deborah. In a way, her journey to Canaan parallels that of Abraham (12:1), who also voyaged to a foreign land leaving behind kinfolk, home, and the familiar. It is Rebekah, not her intended husband Isaac, who truly walks in Abraham's steps—following in his life experience of alienation.

After a long journey back to Canaan, Isaac finally sees his "mail-order" bride. We are told by the text that Isaac immediately fell in love with Rebekah. Not surprisingly, Rebekah's feelings toward Isaac are unknown, and remain unknown throughout the rest of the book of Genesis. We are not told if she is happy with her new husband, or if she is homesick for what was left behind. All we know is that she comforts her new husband, who was distressed over his mother's death.

In modern terms, Rebekah and Isaac's family puts the "funk" in dysfunctional! . . . We know that Isaac is a mama's boy. . . . He watched his father expel his older brother and stepmother into the wilderness. He witnessed his mother's anger, jealousy, and resentment toward Hagar and Ishmael. He had heard the story of how his father almost forced his mother into adultery because he was afraid to be honest about being her husband. Isaac grew up in a dysfunctional family filled with tension, deception, and violence. . . . His hopes for a happy and healthy family are doomed from the start.

Barbara J. Essex

Bad Girls of the Bible: Exploring Women of Questionable Virtue (Cleveland: United Church Press, 1999), 24–25.

The chapter ends with Isaac bringing Rebekah into his mother's tent to consummate the marriage. Once consummated, Isaac is finally consoled over the loss of his mother. An ambiguous space is created in this tent where one woman (mother) is replaced by another (wife) through sexual union. It may be true, as we shall soon discover, that Rebekah will remain barren for the next two decades, but that does not stop her from having to take up the task of mothering—physically taking Sarah's place in her tent as Isaac's mommy. The reader is left wondering if Isaac obtained a wife or a replacement (with benefits) for his mother. Rebekah becomes the wife-mother expected to continue doting and spoiling what appears to be a man-child.

25:1–18

Testimony of Abraham's Sons

When Sarah died at one hundred twenty-seven years of age, Abraham was about one hundred thirty-seven. Even at this advanced age, he marries, though we have no information about the woman, except that her name is Keturah, which might mean "incense" or "perfumed one." Who is this mystery woman? Was she young or old? Was she one of Abraham's slaves, like Hagar? Did Abraham look for his wife among his kindred as he did for Isaac's wife? Or is she a local woman, the type he would not let his son marry? Was she purchased from a traveling caravan of merchants who specialized in spices, hence her name? Any attempt to give personhood to Abraham's wife is pure speculation; yet unfortunately, for many women in the book of Genesis, as well as in the entire biblical text, speculation is all that is available. What we do know is that she bore Abraham six boys. She may have also given birth to girls, but they are seldom counted. Each of the six sons, like the future twelve sons of Israel, will represent tribes. It is possible that these six sons/tribes, like the twelve tribes of Israel, formed a confederation of nations.

Among the six sons/tribes listed, the nation that makes the most appearances in the Hebrew Bible is the Midianites. In one version of the Joseph story, he is sold into slavery to traveling Midianite merchants. It is interesting to note that within one generation the Midianites grow so that they fill a caravan of merchants, while Israel is limited to just twelve sons. Some four hundred years later, Moses flees to the land of the Midianites, where he is befriended by one of their priests, Jethro (Exod. 2:15). Tradition has it that he takes a wife from these people. Later, toward the end of the book of Exodus, the elders of Midian, together with the Moabites, attempt to expel the invading Israelites (Num. 22:4–7). Eventually, many Midianites are the victims of genocide (Num. 31:1–12) at the hands of the Israelites.

Listing these tribes/nations as descendants of Abraham reminds the reader that Israel is related to its neighbors— not just the six sons/tribes of Keturah, but also the twelve sons/tribes of Ishmael that are later mentioned in the chapter, and the twelve sons/tribes/ villages of Esau mentioned later in Genesis (36:10–14). Even though they may be related, they do not share in the divine promise. They too,

> For the children of Keturah are not of the promised line, so it seems that they can flourish. Any threat to Isaac's status as heir of the promise is negated by the overt statement that everything of Abraham's was given to Isaac (although even this is undermined by the mention of gifts to the other sons), and that the sons of his concubines (note the plural; Gen 25:6) were sent east, away from Isaac.
>
> —Roland Boer
>
> *Marxist Criticism of the Bible* (New York: T & T Clark International, 2003), 30.

like Ishmael, are ultimately rejected by God. It is Isaac who receives all of Abraham's possessions. By verse 6 the woman who began as Abraham's wife is now referred to as his concubine; and, as sons of Abraham's concubine, they receive a present and are shipped eastward, away from God's promise.

Like Ishmael before them, because they do not share in the inheritance they are eliminated, lest they threaten the promised child. What a horrible thing to be the son of Abraham, unless, of course, you happen to be Isaac. Even then, you might end up on the sacrificial altar.

It seems that God should have made God's covenant with Sarah rather than with Abraham. It is not Abraham's seed that is blessed; instead it was Sarah's womb. Abraham fathered eight boys that we know of (not counting any possible girls), but only the one born of Sarah was the promised child. The other child who received a lesser promise from God, Ishmael, received God's blessing because of a promise made to Hagar, not Abraham, concerning her child.

When Abraham reaches one hundred seventy-five years of age, "a good old age, an old man and full of years," he dies. In 25:8 the author adds an odd comment concerning his burial: Abraham "was gathered to his people." His people are in Ur, hundreds of miles away. Does this mean that they all joined him in Canaan and were also buried in the cave of Machpelah? Although, throughout the book of Genesis, there is an absence of the concept of an afterlife, we are left wondering if this verse could be a glimmer of hope that something more than a temporal life might exist. Maybe there is some place where we are gathered along with the people who preceded us into the unknown?

Ishmael, the son sent into exile, returns, and he and Isaac bury their father. It is interesting to note that Ishmael seems to show no bitterness toward Abraham or Isaac concerning being sent away. Maybe Ishmael made peace with his situation. Maybe he has prospered and considers the early hardships, although painful, a thing of the past. Or maybe the source, P, from which this passage is taken, was not familiar with the earlier ejection stories (chap. 16, which was mostly J; and chap. 21, which was E). Even though Ishmael did not show bitterness toward his younger half brother Isaac, it would not have been surprising if he had. After all, Ishmael's line has become foreign. He is not part of God's chosen people. A promise was made that he would bring forth nations, and for all practical purposes the promise was fulfilled. His twelve sons, like the future twelve sons of Israel, will represent a nomadic people inhabiting the Syro-Arabian desert. Ironically, although the promise of Isaac has yet to be fulfilled (he had no land and his wife was barren), all of the other boys born to Abraham were fruitful and multiplying. The reader is left wondering if God's promise was preempted.

The biblical text has the Ishmaelites make a few appearances before they disappear from the pages of history. For example, the other story of Joseph being sold into slavery has the passing caravan of Ishmaelites purchase him. Again, like the Midianites in the one version of the story, it is interesting to note how within one generation the Ishmaelites grew in comparison to Isaac's descendants. But with time the term "Ishmaelites" became a term for any nomadic group dwelling in the northern desert regions of north Arabia. We can note how the term "Ishmaelites" becomes a synonymous term with nomadic traders, as in the case with the Midianites (Judg. 8:24). With time, they became associated or merged with the bedouin who lived in northeast Arabia, only to be resurrected later with the emergence of Islam. Even though Ishmael may have shown no bitterness when he accompanied Isaac in burying their father, still the chapter ends noting that he set himself to defy his brothers. The plural "brothers" must refer not only to Isaac but also to Keturah's sons.

26:1–33

Testimony of Isaac

Maybe in some distant past, Isaac was an important figure from southern Canaan who might have even rivaled the northern figure of Abraham in importance. But by the time Isaac's story makes its way into the biblical text, little information about him survives. With the exception of the sacrifice story told earlier (which is really part of the Abraham narrative) and the later tale when he is older and easily tricked out of a blessing (which is really part of the Jacob narrative),

Isaac's story, in which we capture a glimpse of the man, is mainly limited to this one chapter. Even then, what we see is not necessarily flattering. For all practical purposes, Isaac is reduced to a transitional figure guiding the reader from Abraham to Jacob. With the exception of the last two verses dealing with Esau's wives, the chapter is made up of several short episodes in which Isaac is the principal figure.

Chapter 26 opens with another famine gripping the land, no doubt brought about by a drought. From his settlement in Beer-lahai-roi (25:11), Isaac decides to move to Egypt where there is greener pasture. Although he is a seminomad, he must still gather his family and belongings to cross hazardous areas in order to enter a country with different customs, traditions, and language that will more than likely misappropriate his labor and simultaneously blame him for all the woes the host country is undergoing. They may even kill him so that members of the host country can steal his "possessions," specifically his wife. Isaac, like many immigrants today, will discover xenophobia, manifested in ways that make living oppressive. In his time, that difficulty was manifested by quarrels over wells, while members of the dominant culture, out of spite, would fill his wells with stones and dirt. In our time, the same hostility for the stranger is expressed through repressive laws, as in the case of Arizona Senate Bill 1070, which in 2010 legalized racial profiling, empowering state law enforcement agencies to detain anyone who looks "suspicious," which often means looking like economically marginalized Hispanics. As difficult as it may be for most of us to imagine leaving behind the land that witnessed our birth for a new life in strange territory, in 2008 more than two hundred million migrants throughout the world (almost half of which were women) made the same decision Isaac made. There is famine in the land, and if Isaac does not migrate, he and his family might die.

Isaac moved due to famine. Today's migrants move for a multitude of reasons. The most common reasons for individuals to risk all, even their lives, to cross borders are: (1) disparity in income between their country and the potential host countries; (2) increasing demographic imbalances where populations of low-income countries grow significantly compared to high-income countries; (3) the globalization of the economy where the liberalization of flow of goods, capital, and services creates pressure for labor mobility; (4) the need in economically advanced countries for low-skilled and service-based workers; (5) the decrease for the need of migrants within economically advanced countries that creates pressure for outward migration; (6) advances in technology in the form of affordable travel and real-time global communication systems that make the sharing of opportunities possible; (7) the consequences of foreign policies of economically advanced nations, especially when they lead to political upheaval; and (8) armed conflicts in less economically advanced nations manifested as civil wars, revolutions, ethnic cleansing, or any other type of war.[7]

Isaac had planned to move to Egypt, but God erects a roadblock. Why? Maybe because Isaac would have been seduced by the same fate faced by nearly all migrants today—being absorbed into the more dominant culture. If Isaac is the sole person through whom God's promise of land is to be fulfilled, then it is perilous for him, and more importantly his descendants, to settle in prosperous Egypt, where foreign gods might be venerated. But if he does not go down to Egypt, how will Isaac survive?

The unequivocal biblical answer is that survival depends on the Lord! Isaac will stay in the land God promised to his father. God directly speaks to Isaac, just as God earlier spoke to Abraham. Abraham may be dead, and Isaac may not be like his father; nevertheless, God's voice continues to speak to each new generation. For the first time, the covenant made with Abraham concerning multiple descendants and a land to possess is made to Isaac, the heir apparent to the promise. God will fulfill the terms of the covenant for Abraham's sake, because Abraham listens to God's voice. Now it is Isaac's turn to follow in his father's footsteps.

Isaac obeys. Rather than making it all the way to Egypt, he stops at Gerar. The text tells us that the king of Gerar is a Philistine, an anachronism since the Philistines settled on the coastal lands of Canaan (later named Palestine after the Philistines) shortly after being repulsed from Egypt by Rameses III around 1180 BCE, some

---

7. Gervais Appave and Ryszard Cholewinski, eds., *World Migration 2008: Managing Labour Mobility in the Evolving Global Economy* (Geneva: International Organization for Migration, 2008), 2.

five hundred years after Isaac. The reader of chapter 26 cannot help but notice similarities with earlier chapters, specifically chapters 12 and 20. As in chapter 12, a famine rages in the land. As in chapter 20, King Abimelech is reintroduced. If Abimelech is a personal name, then he must have been very old; but more than likely this is a title used by the sovereign (which translates as "my father is king") or a successor/son using the same name. All three chapters share a similar theme: the patriarch, fearful that he would be killed so that the townsmen can take possession of his wife, states that his wife is his sister. At least with the two stories in the Abraham narrative, Sarah was a half sister, thus technically not a falsehood; but with Isaac, this claim that Rebekah is his sister is a bald-faced lie. Of the three "wife is my sister" stories found in Genesis, this is the one that is less scandalous because Rebekah is never taken into the king's (Pharaoh's) harem. Or is it less scandalous?

Isaac's deception, unlike that of Abraham, is not uncovered through divine revelation, but instead through human observation. Abimelech looks out the window and sees Isaac fondling his wife. This raises an interesting question as to where exactly was Isaac fondling his wife. In public? Such intimate behavior, both in the ancient world as well as in our own time, is reserved for the private sphere of the household. Was Abimelech looking *out* the window, or *in* the window? Also, the Hebrew word used for fondling is *tsahaq*, the same word translated as "playing with," which originally upset Sarah when she observed Ishmael playing with Isaac (21:9), making us wonder how exactly was Ishmael, who was at least fifteen years older, "playing" with the young toddler Isaac.

There seems to be something cowardly about Isaac's (and Abraham before him) act of self-preservation. Yet the "fathers" of the faith seem to excuse, if not praise, Isaac's deception. Martin Luther argues that Isaac had every right to be afraid; indeed, rather than acting rashly, throwing himself into danger by telling the truth, he avoided danger. Isaac may be fearful and thus appear weak, but "he is excused, for he is a fearful and a steadfast man."[8]

Others excuse Isaac by reading into the text the proposition

8. Martin Luther, *Lectures on Genesis*, 5:41–50.

that his wife was never in any real danger. Instead, the main purpose of this "wife is my sister" story is to demonstrate Isaac's cleverness and the surrounding people as gullible. Yet the psalmist reminds us: "No one who practices deceit shall remain in [God's] house; no one who utters lies shall continue in [God's] presence" (Ps. 101:7). How do we recognize God's call to a higher moral standard based on honesty with Isaac's (and Abraham before him) character of telling falsehoods?

When the passage is read through the eyes of women,

> Accordingly, one asks whether what Isaac does is a sin. I answer that it is not a sin. No, it is an obliging lie by which he guarded against being killed by those among whom he was staying if he said that Rebecca was his wife. Yet it is a weakness of faith. . . . But God wanted him to be weak, in order that there might be an example which teaches the church that God is not offended . . . for He overlooks this and leaves it unnoticed.
>
> —Martin Luther
>
> *Luther's Works*, vol. 5: *Lectures on Genesis: Chapters 26–30*, ed. Jaroslav Pelikan, trans. George V. Schick and Paul D. Pahl (St. Louis: Concordia Publishing House, 1968), 41.

it becomes even more problematic. Why? Because women, as personal property, could be offered up to save the lives of the men who owned them. Like his father, Isaac appears willing to offer up his wife, who, like Christ, pays the price for the sin of *man* so that Isaac can be saved and live. Indeed, the king who has not spoken with or heard God's voice appears more faithful, recognizing the guilt that would be incurred if he took the patriarch's wife. The episode ends very differently than the two versions dealing with Abraham. While Abraham turned a profit on his deception, Isaac is simply given a royal guarantee that no one, on pain of death, can touch his wife.

The next mini-episode informs us that God blessed Isaac and he became rich, connecting the acquisition of riches as a manifestation of God's blessing. We are told that he sowed his crops in the land and he reaped a hundredfold. But finding plentiful water, fruitful breeding, and bountiful crops are simplistic indicators of divine blessings. All too often, especially within our modern capitalist society, blessings are equated with wealth and health. We should therefore not be surprised when our capitalist culture develops prosperity theology—a theology that maintains because we are "kids of the King" all we need to do is claim and believe the blessings God wants to bestow on us. True believers, according to this doctrine, are those who are financially wealthy. But such a theology proves problematic for many, especially communities of color. Within the United States (as well as throughout the world), those who are disproportionately displaced, dispossessed, and disenfranchised belong to communities of color. Because those lacking financial resources also lack proper health coverage, they more than likely also lack health. Hence it is only a small portion of communities of color that possess health or wealth. If being chosen means material blessings, then God must hate communities of color, evidenced by how many of them exist in poverty.

Isaac follows his father's lifestyle. The patriarchs are portrayed as seminomads living at the edges, if not margins, of towns and cities. Since Abraham first entered the land, they have wandered throughout Canaan, the land God promised. Their wandering was a result of their occupation as herdsmen, constantly needing to seek fertile ground and water sources for their flocks, consisting mainly of sheep and other small beasts. They stayed away from deserts; hence they were not true bedouin. Occasionally, especially during times of famine, they ventured down into Egypt. Other times they settled for long periods, Abraham by the oaks of Mamre near Hebron and Isaac at Beer-sheba. Settling at a certain location provided the opportunity to engage in some minimum farming, as indicated in verse 12. Only Lot settled in the city, and that did not turn out well for him.

We are told by the passage that the neighboring Philistines began to envy him. They seal the wells dug by Isaac's father, filling them with dirt and stones. But Isaac goes to great lengths to avoid conflict or friction with his neighbors. Even King Abimelech approaches him and insists that Isaac leave Gerar, for he has become more powerful than the townsfolk. At this point in the narrative, it would be more prudent and safer to simply move on to where their presence would not raise the quarrelsome ire of the land's original inhabitants.

They left, but everywhere they dug up a well that contained water, the local shepherds would adamantly insist that the water found was theirs. The first place this occurred, he called the well Esek, a Hebrew word for "contention." It happened again when he dug a second well, so he called the place Sitnah, a word for "enmity." Finally, when he dug a third well, no one molested them, so Isaac named the well Rehoboth, meaning "enlargement," for God "has made room for us, and we shall be fruitful in the land" (v. 22).

Those who are sojourners today, trying to avoid the envy, or more likely fear causing quarrels with neighbors from the dominant culture, also seek Rehoboth, a place where God also made room for them so that they too can thrive in the land. For many who crossed borders and cultures, they find that with time they can begin to assimilate into the dominant culture. Within a generation or two, even the mother tongue is lost. Yet their lingering traditions, customs, or phenotype features continue to make them outsiders no matter how many generations they have dwelt among those of the dominant culture. A hyphenated identity is created (i.e., African-American, Asian-American, or Hispanic-American) attempting to reconcile two distinct and separate cultures into one person. This locution erects within their very being a schizophrenic (Latin for "split mind") existence. They soon realize that hyphenated identities mean they are too African, too Asian, or too Hispanic to be accepted by the dominant culture, and too Americanized to be accepted by their native compatriots. As multicultural people, belonging to two or more cultural inheritances, yet fully accepted by none of them, makes them simultaneously "outsiders" and "insiders" on all sides.

From Rehoboth Isaac travels to Beer-sheba, where God appears to him during the night. For the first time, God introduces Godself as the "God of your father Abraham." Abraham's God is not the god of a particular place, neither like the gods of Egypt nor the gods of Gerar; rather, the God of Abraham is the God of a family, a clan, a people. When foreigners come to a new land, they more than likely adopt the indigenous gods associated with the new location. This occurred at the close of the exodus when the chosen entered the promised land and adopted the local gods (e.g., Baal). But the God of Abraham does not exist in just one locale; rather, wherever the children of Abraham find themselves, God is already there. The God of all the universe is also the local God of a particular clan; and it is for Abraham's sake that Isaac, and by extension his descendants, are blessed. This is also the first and only time in Genesis where God refers to Abraham as "my servant."

After his encounter with the Almighty, Isaac builds an altar. Then he pitches his tent and instructs his servants to dig a well. Before any venture is undertaken, God must come first, for as the psalmist reminds us, "Unless the Lord builds the house, those who build it labor in vain" (Ps. 127:1). The biblical order of priorities seems to be: first God (altar), then family (tent), and finally work (digging the well). Only by first seeking the reign of God and God's justice will all other things be added.

The last mini-episode concerning Isaac's adventures involves the reappearance of Abimelech, king of Gerar. The king visits Isaac with his adviser Ahuzzath and the commander of his army, Phicol. This episode is eerily similar to when Abimelech, king of Gerar, visited Abraham with Phicol, the commander of his army, many decades earlier, before Isaac was offered up to God as a lad on the sacrificial altar. Like the earlier story in chapter 21, the patriarch begins by rebuking Abimelech for being treated wrongly. Also, like the earlier version of the story, Abimelech, realizing God is with the patriarch, sues for a treaty of mutual nonaggression. The place was thus named Beer-sheba by Isaac, forgetting (if one assumes this is a different story) that his father already named that place with the same name—a name that also served as a pun: *be'er* (well) *sheba'* (seven or oath), with the emphasis this time being on the word "oath."

25:19–35:22

The Story of Esau and Jacob

25:19–34
Testimony of Isaac's Family

The start of the Esau and Jacob narrative begins with a troublesome proclamation. Verse 19 exclaims, "These *are* the generations of Isaac, Abraham's son: Abraham begat Isaac" (KJV). Until now, the biblical text focused on Sarah's barrenness and how this condition threatened God's promise of a multitude of descendants. Hence it seems odd that Sarah is written out of the story at the start of this new cycle of the narrative. We return to the formula of men begetting men. Equally troubling is the next verse, which describes Rebekah, Isaac's wife, as the daughter of Bethuel and the sister of Laban. When we are first introduced to Rebekah, she describes herself as the daughter of Bethuel, son of Milcah, wife of Abraham's brother Nahor (24:24). Although in most genealogies, as we have seen, only men beget other males, in Rebekah's genealogy her grandmother Milcah, not her grandfather Nahor, was highlighted. But by the time we get to this new segment of the narrative, we notice a turn toward greater patriarchy as the women begin to fade from the story.

Isaac married Rebekah when he was forty. For twenty years, Rebekah was barren. So Isaac prayed to God and God answered Isaac's prayer. As with Abraham and Sarah before them, the fulfillment of God's promise depends on the God of life who is able to open wombs. But unlike Abraham and Sarah, the text implies that Isaac prayed and God immediately answered his prayer with Rebekah's conception. If this is so, why did Isaac wait twenty years to pray for children?

It is also interesting to note that even though it is Rebekah who is barren, Isaac is the one who has his prayers answered. Why doesn't

Rebekah pray to God, demanding that her "shame" be taken away, as did Hannah, the future mother of the prophet Samuel (1 Sam. 1)? Missing is the drama that we saw during Sarah's barrenness and will see with Rachel's future barrenness. It is as if Rebekah is not in any hurry to have children, nor is the lack of birthing men humiliating for her. Rebekah's lack of supposed interest in the cradle goes against the historical norm of what women should desire.

Unlike her mother-in-law and her future daughter-in-law, there is no offering of slave girls to her husband. In fact, this is the only recorded instance of a monogamous marriage among the patriarchs. But before we celebrate this only example of monogamy, we must recognize, as we shall soon see, that this was a failed marriage based on lies and deceit.

> A cradle consecrates the mother of the family; and more cradles sanctify and glorify her before her husband and children, before Church and homeland. The mother who complains because a new child presses against her bosom seeking nourishment at her breast is foolish, ignorant of herself, and unhappy.
>
> —Pope Pius XII
>
> *Address to Women of Catholic Action,* October 26, 1941.

So, why wait twenty years to ask for children? Why delay being fruitful, and thus also delay God's promise as made to Abraham? Maybe, based on the disturbing way in which Rebekah, for Isaac, replaced Sarah (24:67), Rebekah already had a full-time occupation—mothering Isaac. And maybe Isaac waited twenty years because he enjoyed being the center of Rebekah's attention and did not want to share her with others. Such an explanation is plausible based on how Isaac, for the rest of the narrative, is portrayed as an old, feeble, passive figure within his own story. Maybe the traumatic experience of a young Isaac being laid on the altar to be sacrificed by his father continues to haunt him into adulthood, contributing to his passive depiction in Scripture.

Regardless of the reason for delaying the prayer that led God to open Rebekah's womb, the prayer was eventually uttered and Rebekah did conceive. But something was wrong; Rebekah felt turmoil in her womb, making this the first time that Scripture records a difficult pregnancy. Probably not knowing that she was carrying twins, she must have wondered what caused the violent movements she continued to feel. Her frustration, and probably pain, led her to cry out: "Why is this happening to me? Why go on living?" The assertive Rebekah to whom we were introduced in chapter 24 reappears. She becomes the first woman in the biblical text recorded as directly appealing to God for answers to her circumstances. She goes to a recognized holy site to consult Yahweh, asking for an oracle. Although the text is clear that Rebekah is seeking the God of her husband, we are left wondering if there was a sanctuary to Yahweh already in existence at this time, or if she simply went to some holy site used by the surrounding people and there, among the idols, prayed to Yahweh.

Rebekah prays and God answers in poetic form. Does Rebekah share God's answer with her husband, or does she keep the revelation to herself? We do not know. Even so, not only does God reveal to Rebekah the cause for the war waging in her womb, but God also reveals to the reader that the youngest, not the eldest, is chosen to fulfill God's promise to Abraham. Hence Rebekah discovers that she is carrying twins. Each will become its own nation. Before they are even born, sibling strife that will eventually tear apart the family begins. The rabbis believed that Jacob was trying to kill Esau while they shared their mother's womb, hence Rebekah's difficult pregnancy.[1]

These two boys, like the nations they represent, will become bitter rivals; but the youngest, the chosen, the elect, will have mastery over the oldest. Reading this, we are left asking why. Why is the youngest (again) chosen instead of the oldest? Why must one be chosen and another divinely rejected? What is disturbing is that before either child sees the light of day, one is already rejected by God. Would God have been more merciful if the rejected child was never formed in the womb? Why bring into existence one who is already rejected? And if rejected from the start of existence, before any act can ever be committed to justify divine dismissal, should we be surprised if this heavenly denunciation manifests itself negatively? Can anything be done to earn God's favor once rejected? And if not, can one blame the discarded seed for how it develops?

1. *Midrash Genesis Rabbah* 34; Babylonian Talmud, *Sanhedrin* 91b.

Theologians may argue over double predestination,[2] and surely this passage may provide a proof text; still, for the disenfranchised, double predestination can become a dangerous theology that can justify oppression. The elect are chosen by God not because of anything they may do, but because God, in God's ultimate wisdom and mercy, chose them. But how will the elect know they have been chosen? It matters not if they make a commitment to follow and serve God, because it is God who does the choosing, not humans. God chose Jacob and not Esau. It matters not if they choose or fail to choose God. So, do the elect know they are chosen due to their good works? No. Jacob is not necessarily the paragon of holiness. Indeed, toward the end of the narrative it is the reprobate Esau who demonstrates greater love, imitating the gospel message of reconciliation by offering forgiveness for the wrongs Jacob perpetrated on him. Are the elect then chosen due to God's foreknowledge? Again, no. According to John Calvin, an advocate of double predestination, election is not due to God foreknowing a person's future actions and attitudes. God's choosing some and rejecting others is not due to any human action, whether that act be committed in the past or in the future. God's choosing is an independent act of God not contingent on any human action, or lack thereof.[3] So how then do the elect know they are chosen?

Jacob is destined for greatness because a sovereign God said so, regardless of any actions he may take or whatever circumstances in which he might find himself. Why? Because the elect are those who are blessed by God. Jacob's blessing means he will become a great nation whose descendants will take possession of the land on

> As the Lord by the efficacy of his calling accomplishes towards his elect the salvation to which he had by his eternal counsel destined them, so he has judgments against the reprobate, by which he executes his counsel concerning them.
>
> —John Calvin
>
> *Institutes* 3.24.12.

---

2. Double predestination argues that God freely chooses some to be saved (the elect) and others to be damned (the reprobate). Predestination is double because it recognizes that the divine decree consists of election and reprobation.

3. John Calvin, *Institutes of the Christian Religion* 3.22.1–7.

which they are but sojourners. Esau is not blessed because Jacob will have mastery over him. If to be elected is to be blessed, specifically manifested in the form of wealth, and if the elect fail to explore the causes of poverty, then a theology is constructed that justifies why some are rich and most are poor. After all, is not the road to heaven long and narrow and few are those who traverse it? Such a spiritual epistemology concludes that the poverty experienced by the majority of communities of color within the United States, and the majority of the world's population, is not due to economic structures that benefit the few (disproportionately of European descent) at the expense of the majority; but rather, because like Esau, God rejected them while they were still in their mothers' wombs. They are inherited reprobates. Poverty, and the lack of opportunities (blessings?) associated with it, become divinely sanctioned, a necessity that provides the elect with the opportunity to demonstrate paternal generosity. Double predestination may be a theology that resonates with those whom the dominant culture privileges, but for the majority of humanity relegated to the underside of power and privilege, it is a devastating theology that traps the marginalized to their lower station in life as God ordained.

With their lives already predestined, Rebekah gives birth to two boys. The first to emerge is called Esau because he was ruddy (*'admoni*) in color, a pun with the nation the child will eventually represent, Edom (*'edom*). Furthermore, he emerged hairy (*se'ar*), as if completely wrapped in a shaggy mantle. Esau's hairiness provides the etymology for "Seir," the mountain range southeast of the Dead Sea where the Edomites will eventually dwell. Following Esau was his twin brother, with his hand grasping Esau's heel (*'aqeb*); thus he is named Jacob (*ya'aqob*), another pun. To seize by the heel denotes an overreaching, a supplanting. While these similarities in sound may explain Jacob's name, his name actually means "may God protect," a meaning for which the text does not account.

As the twins mature to adulthood, Esau becomes a skilled hunter, a man of the open country. By contrast, Jacob becomes a homebody, a quiet man preferring the motherly security of the tents while attending to the sheep. Each boy chose a different way of life. The oldest was a hunter, a much older profession than a shepherd;

nevertheless, both existed on the edge of "civilization," defined as the settled village, town, or city. It is interesting that Isaac favored Esau, his opposite. Maybe it was because Isaac saw, or was attracted to, a certain manliness demonstrated by his son, a manliness that Isaac seemed to lack. Jacob, on the other hand, was favored by Rebekah. She loved Jacob with a blind disregard for the rest of her family, a love that eventually led to the disintegration of her home, including the loss of her son.

One day Esau returned hungry and exhausted from the countryside. The hunt must not have gone well. He notices Jacob making some reddish soup. Esau says, "Let me eat some of that red stuff, for I am famished." The same word to describe Esau at birth as "ruddy" is used to describe the boiling "red" stuff Jacob was cooking, a continuous play on words. The text says that it was because of this that the name given to him was Edom. Jacob agreed to sell him the pottage (more than likely Egyptian lentils, which are red) in exchange for Esau's birthright. The birthright belonged to the eldest son, even if born seconds before his brother. Usually the birthright consisted of a double portion (two-thirds) of the inheritance and, on the death of the father, leadership of the family. But in this case the birthright meant more. The promise and covenant made with Abraham, passed on to Isaac, was now the birthright for one of Isaac's children. As the eldest, it belonged to Esau. But Esau had such low regard for his birthright that he sold it for a kettle of pottage. Many biblical commentators have taken this passage as proof of Esau's more carnal nature. Immediate gratification of his appetites overshadowed any concerns about the weightier aspects of life. Esau simply lived for the moment. Yet, before we condemn Esau, we might remember that the selling of birthrights was not simply a private transaction between two individuals. Maybe Esau was trying to trick his younger brother. Surely Isaac would not consent to such an arrangement.

The selling of Esau's birthright also does not bode well for Jacob. Rather than meet the needs of his brother, Jacob, looking out for his own betterment, strikes a deal with his brother, who is under duress. Although rabbinical thought maintained that transactions made while under duress are not binding, still it is troublesome that God's promise, as part of the birthright, is obtained in such an unsavory manner. Can God's promises be obtained through iniquitous negotiations? Yes, God chose Jacob over against Esau; but did Jacob need to make his chosenness a reality by manipulating Esau's momentary weakness? We would expect a nobler Jacob, one worth emulating when waiting for God's will to unfold. Still, maybe Jacob's shadowy shenanigans are what make the text so realistic. Maybe Jacob demonstrates the ambiguity of clear-cut right and wrong responses to situations. Maybe for those who are in situations where the social structures (religious and cultural) are stacked against them, the ethical response is to undermine those very structures because they are unfair constructs designed to maintain oppression. Maybe when all the rules and traditions are aligned to separate the oppressed from sharing in the resources enjoyed by the few, the proper ethical response is to upset the system, even if it means taking advantage of the privileged by selling them a pottage of lentil soup for some of the resources they simply take for granted by showing it such a low regard.

Isaac's family, on the outside, seemed like the perfect nuclear family, a monogamous relationship with two sons, each successfully engaged in his own profession. But like the façade worn by many families today that appear a bit too perfect and ideal, dysfunctional relationships are undermining family stability, leading all to an eventual breakup. Parents pick their own favorite child, loving them at the expense of other family members. Rather than seeking the good of one another, brothers take advantage of the situation to advance their personal interests. One leaves the testimony of Isaac's family troubled, hoping and praying that our own families fail to emulate Isaac's.

27:1–45

Testimony of a Dysfunctional Family

In an earlier chapter, Jacob obtained Esau's birthright through direct negotiation, regardless of how exploitative such negotiations may have been. In this chapter, Jacob obtains Esau's blessing through fraud, taking advantage of his father Isaac's feeble condition. Isaac, by this time, has grown old. His eyesight is dim, unable to distinguish between his sons or to see the destinies God had planned for them. Death is also knocking at Isaac's door, but before he dies he has one last important task to accomplish. He must bless his favorite and oldest son, Esau. It was customary to place great emphasis and prophetic importance on the words of a dying man, especially a patriarch. Summoning his eldest, he instructs Esau to fetch his quiver and bow and hunt for deer. With it, Esau should make the kind of savory venison dish Isaac likes and bring it to him. After Isaac has had his fill and is strengthened by the food, he would dispense his blessing on his favorite son.

Like Sarah before her at the oaks of Mamre (18:10), Rebekah situates herself outside Isaac's tent and eavesdrops. Once Esau sets off to the countryside to track a meal for his father, Rebekah beckons her favorite son, Jacob, and repeats to him what had transpired between his father and his brother. She puts into motion a scheme that would bring to fruition the oracle she received while pregnant, that the elder would serve the younger (25:23). She instructs Jacob to go to their flock and bring two good kids to her. With them, she would prepare her husband a meal (as if domesticated kids can substitute for the taste of wild game). With meal in hand, Jacob could take it to Isaac's tent and obtain the blessing in Esau's stead. But Jacob protests—a possible attempt by the author to make Jacob's role in the deception less objectionable by making sure the reader knows that Rebekah is the author of the trickery. After all, she is a woman and the prevailing sexism would expect such tempting behavior (as it did with Eve) to come from a woman. Yet, before we let Jacob off the hook, it is important to note that his protests are not because he thought Rebekah's scheme is morally questionable, but rather it is too risky. He is concerned that Isaac might touch his smooth skin and realize it was not the hairy arm of his brother. If that were to happen, Isaac might curse rather than bless Jacob.

Rebekah assures Jacob that if that were to occur she would take responsibility, having the curse instead fall on her. So Jacob does as Rebekah instructs. While he fetches the kids from the flock, Rebekah retrieves Esau's clothing. She dresses Jacob in his brother's best outfit and, with the skins of the two kids slaughtered for the meal, covers Jacob's smooth parts, specifically his arms and neck. Hair feels somewhat different than the fur of animals, but it does not matter; the author is more interested in characterizing Esau, and the future Edomites, as some sort of brute beast. Disguised as his brother, Jacob enters Isaac's tent ready to defraud his blind father. When Isaac asks who is there, Jacob answers that it is Esau with a meal prepared to Isaac's liking. But Isaac is suspicious. He recognizes Jacob's presence. So he quizzes his son about the curious speed with which he concluded the hunt. Jacob, pretending to be Esau, praises Isaac's God for placing the animal so quickly in his path. Still not convinced, Isaac asks his son to come closer. Upon feeling his arms, he concludes that it has to be Esau, although he hears the voice of Jacob. So he again asks if he is really his son Esau, to which Jacob answers in the affirmative. Isaac again asks his son to come closer so that he can kiss him. As Jacob kisses his father, Isaac smells Esau's scent, which must have been so odoriferous that it clings to the clothing Jacob is wearing. No doubt, the writer is again insulting Esau, and by extension the Edomites. Esau's strong body odor on Jacob finally convinces Isaac that this truly is his eldest son.

Or does it? Scholars have argued that Isaac was never really convinced, that he knew it was Jacob all along. What father, regardless as to how blind he may be, would not recognize the presence of his own son? Still, some believe Isaac went along with the charade because he recognized God's will. Even though he wanted to bless the older, he realized that God wanted him to bless the younger. Jacob did not trick Isaac, according to this interpretation; it was the other way around. Isaac took advantage of the opportunity presented to him to avoid responsibility for hurting his favorite son by denying his blessing.

After eating the meal prepared for him, Isaac gives his blessing to Jacob. Regardless of whether Isaac was tricked or simply played along, he confers on Jacob the riches of the earth with its abundance of grain and wine (fertility). Nations would serve him, bowing down before him (domination). He would be master of his brothers. It is interesting to note that the plural form, "brothers," might suggest more than just Esau. Those who curse him would be cursed, while those who bless him would be blessed.

In Genesis 27, the woman herself is the trickster who formulates the plan and succeeds, moving the men around like chess pieces. Lest the reader think that here one finally encounters a more liberated woman, beware that again success is gained through the symbolic counterpart of sex—food.

—Susan Niditch

"Genesis," in *Women's Bible Commentary*, ed. Carol A. Newsom and Sharon H. Ringe, expanded ed. (Louisville: Westminster John Knox Press, 1998), 22.

Jacob receives his father's, and by extension his God's, blessing by playing the trickster. But the real trickster in this story is Rebekah. She is not the first, nor will she be the last, trickster portrayed in Genesis.

She follows the path of other tricksters, such as Abraham and Isaac claiming before sovereign leaders that their wives are their sisters, and will be followed by many more tricksters, like Laban switching wives on Jacob, Joseph's brothers showing Jacob the bloody coat to prove Joseph's demise, Rachel sitting on her father's idol while stating she is menstruating, or Tamar playing the prostitute with Judah. At first glance, deception seems morally questionable. How can a blessing conferring a divine preferential option be obtained through trickery? Such a proposition offends the moral sensitivities of many Euro-American Christians who normally discount deceit as a sin.

Yet for the marginalized the trickster can very well provide an ethical methodology for those within oppressive social structures who have no other option for obtaining liberation from disenfranchisement.

People who are truly on the margins do not expect to receive benefits legitimately. Accustomed to being rejected by the powerful, they learn to survive by hook or by crook. If Scripture is to be relevant to today's "damned," it must be freed from the dominant theological paradigm, which assumes that blessing in this world is a reward for good behavior and exclusion a punishment for bad.

—Bob Ekblad

Reading the Bible with the Damned (Louisville: Westminster John Knox Press, 2005), 76.

What option is available when the structures are designed to prevent one from sharing in blessings and riches? Rebekah, as a woman within a patriarchal order, could not approach her husband and demand justice; nor could the youngest reason with a father who already favored the manlier Esau. The patriarchal social structures provided no room for dissent.

Moral reasoning normatively operates along a good-evil binary structure. Either you are with the forces of good, or you are aligned with the forces of evil. But we live in a world where the good is defined through the reasoning and/or experience of those with power to legitimize and normalize how they define the good. Such definitions more often justify the prevailing social structures that cause disenfranchisement while mitigating the power and privilege of the elite few. Any moral framework (e.g., patriarchy) that causes harm, if not death, through institutional violence to a dispossessed portion of the community must be declared immoral. Unfortunately, a prevalent theme within moral thought is an either/ or Western rationalism that clearly demarcates good from bad. How then can one incorporate the both/and ambiguity common in the messiness of life? If this good-evil dualism proves ineffective in analyzing moral agency, then what paradigm is available for the marginalized?

One biblical image that can provide a methodology toward a more just and liberative social structure is the figure of the trickster. Tricksters allow us to suspend strict paradigms and definitions of morality, what is right and what is wrong, to provide the opportunity to study and comprehend how social structures are constructed to the detriment of the marginalized by those same structures. Trickster figures radically subvert established norms that attempt to preserve the traditional moral values and virtues. Rebekah as trickster allows us to look beyond the deception she was advocating and comprehend how the patriarchal structures under which she must operate provide few if any alternatives. The biblical trickster figure provides a moral justification for the employment of deception as a means of self-preservation for those who face overwhelming odds against surviving. How? By being rule breakers, a needed praxis if the marginalized wish to break free from the rules that hold them in a subordinated space. Tricksters relish disrupting the norm, causing chaos to outwit those who view themselves as superior and, in so doing, reveal their hypocrisy. Not as powerful as the oppressors bent on domination, the trickster is forced to rely on deception to exploit the oppressor's false sense of self-righteousness, which usually masks greed for power, privilege, possessions, or any combination thereof.[4]

Divine will concerning the inheritance of God's promise made to Abraham and then to Isaac comes to fruition through trickery. With his blessing obtained, and the transition of God's promise transmitted to the next generation, Jacob leaves his father's presence. As he leaves, Esau returns from the hunt. Esau enters Isaac's tent with the prepared meal and asks for his father's blessing. At this point Isaac is seized with a great trembling, realizing he was tricked. Or maybe his trembling is due to the frightful realization that even though he is the patriarch, he is not really the ruler of his domain. He explains to Esau that he already gave away his blessing and what was given could not be taken back. Loudly and bitterly Esau cries out, asking that he too be blessed, for his brother, rightly named, has supplanted him twice, first taking his birthright (*bekorah*) and now his blessing (*berakah*).

Even though the blessing was taken through trickery, it will stand; Jacob would be master over Esau. The moment of discovery of what occurred, of how the unsuspecting Esau learned he had lost everything, is extremely poignant. The pain is unbearable for him, being rejected by God, mother, brother, and now his father. Esau bursts into tears. Because Jacob is the chosen one, it is easy to demonize Esau in this narrative; yet, as tears roll down Esau's face, one can feel pity, confused as to a divine will that chooses one and not another. The book of Hebrews goes so far as to call Esau "an immoral and godless person" (12:16). But why? How is Jacob any less immoral? Isaac responds to Esau's pleads for a blessing with silence, an indication of his helplessness in the situation. Eventually he does answer, but with an opposite blessing, even using the same words of the blessing given to the disguised Jacob. Only this time the riches of the earth would be far from him. Esau would live by the sword, a possible reference to the Edomite custom of plundering caravans traversing through their region and raiding neighboring territories. Furthermore, and more importantly, Esau will serve

4. Miguel A. De La Torre, *Latina/o Social Ethics: Moving Beyond Eurocentric Moral Thinking* (Waco, TX: Baylor University Press, 2010), 105–6.

his brother. But even in servitude the hope of liberation still exists. Eventually he would win his freedom, shaking off his brother's yoke from his neck, according to verse 40. This last verse seems to have been added much later, sometime after the Edomities regained their freedom from Israel (2 Kgs. 8:20–22).

Esau hates Jacob, and can you blame him? He resolves to kill his brother as soon as his father dies. When Rebekah finds out, she fears losing her favorite son, as well as Esau, who would have to flee for committing fratricide. She sends Jacob away for a few days to her brother Laban's house in Haran. Ironically, the one blessed becomes a refugee. There he would be safe, waiting for Esau's temper to cool. There is a naive hope that Rebekah would send for him once it is safe to return. But what she thought would be a short duration stretches over two decades. In a way, the curse she was willing to assume if her plans failed in verse 13 did fall on her. Sadly, she is never able to send word, dying without seeing her favorite son again.

It is not just this family that is dysfunctional, but also their descendants, even to this day. When we read today's newspapers and see the continuous conflicts in the Middle East among people who are kin, according to the biblical text, we are struck with how dysfunctional their relationships remains.

FURTHER REFLECTIONS
Trickster Images

Tricksters are not easily described or defined. Tricksters can play a noble role; but they can also be cruel and vengeful. Regardless as to how tricksters are portrayed, they are survivors who outwit those who view themselves as the tricksters' superiors by revealing what most wish to keep hidden. Their methods in exposing the injustices under which they must toil occur in a moral realm that can be found beyond good and evil, beyond the framework of what society, culture, or religion defines as right or wrong. Not surprisingly, tricksters seldom recognize rules or regulations of either society or religion.

Tricksters' survival acumen provides the disenfranchised with paradigms on how to overcome oppressive situations. Or, more than likely, they become the surrogate figures on whom the survival tactics of the marginalized are projected. These trickster figures are usually portrayed as relying on their cunningness and deception to exploit the greed, weakness, or false sense of self-righteousness possessed by those who are dominant within society. Tricksters' folklore, at times humorous, resonates with survival strategies. Not surprisingly, most disenfranchised groups have stories concerning a trickster figure.

Most see Jacob as a trickster figure, but we find many tricksters throughout the book of Genesis. Among them are the serpent in the garden of Eden whose seductive suggestions lead the first couple toward their humanization (Gen. 3); Abram, who on several occasions tricks rulers into believing Sarai is his sister, and in the process obtains much wealth (Gen. 12, 20); Lot's daughters, who trick their father so that the race (in their minds) could be preserved (Gen. 19); Rebekah, who has little standing in a patriarchal order, encouraging her son Jacob to fool his father out of the blessing (Gen. 27); Laban, who switches his daughters and fools Jacob into marrying the older one first (Gen. 29); Rachel, who steals her father Laban's gods and feigns a menstrual cycle so as not to reveal her thievery (Gen. 31); Jacob, who reconciles with his brother Esau and agrees to follow him to Esau's homeland, only to go in the opposite direction out of fear of a trap (Gen. 33); Simeon and Levi, who trick the more powerful Shechemites into thinking they will form an alliance only to decimate their town to avenge the rape of their sister (Gen. 34); Joseph's brothers, who trick Jacob into thinking his favorite privileged son is dead (Gen. 37); Tamar, who plays the prostitute to trick Judah into fulfilling his obligations (Gen. 38); and Joseph, who hides his identity from his brothers to see if indeed they are remorseful for their earlier treachery (Gen. 42–45). It is difficult to read the book of Genesis and not see the recurring motif of the trickster.

Tricksters usually undo the established order, designed to benefit those who hold power, by outwitting and subverting the status quo that more often than not is oppressive to marginalized communities. The function of the trickster is to place humans and gods in compromising positions so as to raise their consciousness in considering the consequences (physical and spiritual) of their actions. Ideally, the one being tricked is forced to seek solutions to their dilemmas by exploring possible alternatives previously unexplored. For these reasons, many faiths that possess a trickster figure neither fear nor villainize the trickster, but usually express admiration.

For the oppressed to directly challenge the more powerful might lead to their demise. But through deceptive and cunning resistance, the chances for success can be greatly enhanced. But is playing the trickster moral? We can never evaluate the trickster by moral codes, even though the trickster is usually ethical. The trickster may deal in lies and deceit, but only to reveal a deeper truth obscured by moralists. Through tricks, tricksters create situations that force humans to imagine new possibilities that realism and conventional wisdom have ruled out. What the tricksters throughout the book of Genesis reveal is their refusal to remain passive participants in social or religious structures that relegate them to the margins. Those who are usually marginalized, living in fear of the loss of their very existence, develop tactics and strategies to cope and survive. The trickster figures can provide oppressed groups a survival mind-set to emulate.

26:34–35; 28:6–9; 36:1–43
Testimony of Esau's Wives

When Esau turned forty, he married two women, Judith and Basemath, both foreigners, both Hittites. Scripture tells us that these marriages deeply disappointed Esau's parents, Isaac and Rebekah. This might be the reason Esau did not inherit God's promise. To avoid a similar displeasure with their other son, Jacob, they instructed him to go to Paddan-aram, the land from which Rebekah came, and there choose a wife from among their own people (28:1–5). This is a different reason given for Jacob's departure than where he is said to be escaping the murderous rage of his brother Esau (27:41–45). Seeing that his parents sent Jacob away to find a wife from among their own kind, Esau surmised that his parents held the indigenous women of Canaan in low esteem. In an attempt to compensate, he approached his uncle Ishmael to receive permission to marry his cousin Mahalath. When the story concerning the women Esau married is recounted in chapter 36, different names are used for his wives. Instead of the Hittities Judith and Basemath, and the Ishmaelite Mahalath, the text indicates that he married a Hittite named Adah, a Hivite named Oholibamah, and an Ishmaelite named Basemath. Some may attempt to smooth out this apparent contradiction by insisting that Esau married a total of five women, or that he married three women who had two names, or that the three women changed their names after marriage. Others might simply accept the contradiction.

Regardless of the correct names of Esau's wives, the text reveals the difficulty of defining modern marriages along biblical paradigms. Many today are convinced of their sacred responsibility to protect the biblical definition of a traditional marriage. But what we have come to call the traditional marriage has absolutely nothing to do with the Bible. What we call a traditional marriage is more of a societal construct that evolved over time. A biblical marriage is one where a woman's property and her body became the possession of her new husband. As the head of the household, men had nearly unlimited rights over wives and children. A woman became available for a man's possession soon after she reached puberty (usually eleven to thirteen years old), that is, when she became physically able to produce children. Men could have as many sexual partners as they could afford, as was the case with Esau and Jacob. Polygamy and concubinage were the norm, and no explicit prohibition of these practices exists in the Bible.

Although one can find many examples of how the Bible cannot be a guide for modern-day marriages, the example provided by Esau's marriage has to do with the question of who one can marry. It seldom matters how the couple felt about each other; wives were chosen from good families not only to secure the legitimacy of a man's children, but to strengthen political and economic alliances between families, clans, tribes, and kingdoms. Most marriages were endogamous, that is, they occurred within the same extended family or clan, unlike the modern Western concept of exogamy, where unions occur between outsiders.

Unfortunately, the text advocates xenophobia, an abhorrence of the mixing of blood among different ethnic groups who worship foreign gods. Specifically, the biblical text has always been suspicious of foreign wives (of course, no mention is made of foreign husbands). In their minds, maintaining ethnic integrity assured the continuation of the faith and the hope that God would fulfill God's promise to God's chosen. The chief concern was how to maintain an ethnic identity rooted in their God Yahweh while surrounded by neighbors who worshiped other gods. Nevertheless, even though many biblical scholars insist that the concern of taking foreign wives has nothing to do with taking wives from different racial and/or ethnic groups, still, using terms like "chosen" or "elect" is problematic, considering our Western history of racial cleansing. To argue for maintaining the purity of blood assumes the superiority of the blood of one group and the inferiority of another group's blood.

Esau took all that he owned, livestock and wives, and left Canaan for the mountainous region of Seir, which runs north and south. There he became the father of the people known as the Edomites. The Hebrew word "Seir" can be translated as "shaggy," a possible reference to the woodland covering the territory. His move cleared the land promised by God for his brother Jacob.

Chapter 36 ends with a lengthy genealogy concerning the sons born to Esau's clan, followed with a list of chiefs and kings who ruled Edom long before the Israelite monarchy was established. Unlike other genealogies throughout the Bible, this one mentions a number of women. There is Mehetabel, who is identified by her matrilineal line (36:39), thus raising the hope that the reigning patriarchy found throughout the biblical text need not be the norm. Even more encouraging is that two of Esau's clans, Timna and Oholibamah, bear the names of his wife and daughter-in-law (36:40–41). How much richer would the descendants of Jacob have been if they would have allowed their daughters to also leave their mark on their history!

Among some interesting names found in Esau's genealogy are Kenaz (36:11), from whom Caleb will arise, a hero among the Israelites who, along with Joshua, left Egypt and entered the promised land (Num. 32:12); then there is Uz (Gen. 36:28), which is the same as the name of Job's birthplace (Job 1:1), thus indicating a possible Edomite background for Job; and finally there is Bela, son of Beor (Gen. 36:32), who some believe to be Balaam, son of Beor, the prophet hired to curse the Israelites (Num. 22:5–6). One future king who will arise from among the Edomites is Herod the Great.

Throughout the centuries, Edomites and Israelites will struggle against one another in the same way Esau and Jacob struggled in their mother's womb. The prophecy given to Rebekah that the elder shall serve the younger (Gen. 25:23) comes to fruition with King David's victory over Edom (2 Sam. 8:13–14). Nonetheless, the future Israelites are instructed not to abhor the Edomites, for after all they are siblings (Deut. 23:7). And even though Esau may not have been the "chosen" through whom the promise made to Abraham was to be passed, still, as Abraham's grandson, he does somehow share in the promise made by God. To that end, Esau did acquire land that his descendants possessed, and they became a nation in their own right before Israel or Judah.

> It can be said . . . that the Pentateuchal writers took Esau seriously, sometimes portrayed him tenderly, and in the end, felt constrained to preserve a detailed account of the history of his family that would reserve him a permanent place on the margin of the elect line. Small comfort, perhaps, but better than silence.
> —W. Sibley Towner
>
> *Genesis*, Westminster Bible Companion (Louisville: Westminster John Knox Press, 2001), 240.

27:46–28:5; 28:10–22

Testimony on the Staircase to Heaven

When we last left Jacob, he had to hastily leave Beer-sheba to avoid the murderous wrath of his brother after tricking his father out of the blessing meant for Esau. The story concerning the consequences of Jacob's deception was part of the J and E material. A shift is now made to the P material, which usually does not record any of the unfavorable stories concerning the patriarchs, and thus does not consider Jacob's deception of Isaac. Consequently, in this section

Jacob is leaving town not as a refugee but as a migrant, so as not to repeat the error made by his brother of marrying local foreign women.

The narrative opens with Rebekah horrified that her eldest son married Canaanites. Mixed marriages were feared, for they led to assimilation and the worship of other gods, specifically the gods of the foreign wives. If indeed this passage was the work of the P source, then the author, writing around the time of the Babylonian captivity, is interested in providing a theological lesson to those in P's own time who were also marrying foreign wives, and thus prone to apostasy. Assimilation in the form of mixed marriages usually signifies a moving away from one's own family and religious identity. Like his uncle Ishmael and the Ishmaelites before him, Esau and the Edomites became foreign to the chosen people; no doubt they still remained related, but they became a different people with a different identity than the children of Israel. In the mind of the P writer, choosing foreign wives and their gods can mean death to Jewish identity and community. Thus Esau symbolizes what the children of Israel must never do. Instead, they must walk in Jacob's path and "not marry one of the Canaanite women" (28:1).

The fear of losing one's identity through marriage to foreign women is not limited to the ancient Jewish community; it is also a fear and reality for many immigrants who come to the United States. While some migrants seek assimilation, even forbidding their mother tongue to be spoken in the home, many other migrants fear that their descendants will be absorbed into the dominant culture in which they find themselves. Sons of immigrants, known as the 1.5 generation, who arrived in the United States as children, are usually forced to simultaneously navigate both sexual maturation and cultural adaptation. Both of these processes, as author and scholar Gustavo Pérez Firmat points out, became interwoven so that gender and cultural identity became integrated. Thus cultural preference merged with sexual preference. To marry the foreign women of the dominant culture is to move away from the cultural identity to which one was born. In trying to become a man in a foreign country, Firmat argues, both regression and assimilation remain constant temptations as one attempts to construct his identity on the hyphen of being a Hispanic-American, Asian-American, or any other type of hyphenated American.[5]

Since Rebekah is worried to death that Jacob might follow in his brother's footsteps and marry Hethites, Isaac sends him to the home of his maternal uncle, Laban, to find a wife from among his own people. Instead of sending a servant to procure a wife for their son, as Abraham did for Isaac, Jacob is sent off to find his own wife. While in the previous chapter Jacob tricked his father out of Esau's blessing, here Isaac, on his own initiative, blesses Jacob, bestowing the divine promise and designating him as heir to the covenant made with God. Isaac asks El Shaddai (God Almighty) to make Jacob fruitful so that he can multiply, becoming a group of nations that take possession of the land originally given to Grandfather Abraham. Rather than a picture of a dysfunctional family reeling from the consequences of deception, we are shown a well-adjusted family where the father willingly blesses his child before sending him off on a journey to find a wife.

On his way to Haran the sun begins to set, so Jacob stops for the night at a well-known place, more than likely a place that housed a local sanctuary. Taking one of the stones, probably one of the sacred stones through which dream oracles are sought, he places it under his pillow or uses it as a pillow and falls asleep. He dreams of a ladder planted in the ground reaching into heaven. Probably the stairway or ramp resembled a ziggurat, which for a temple provides the steps to traverse between earth and the heavens. The summit of the temple is where the gods reside. On these steps, he sees the angels of God descending and ascending. Heaven ceases to be some remote ethereal place detached from the things of earth and humans. Rather, heaven and earth are connected, each affecting and impacting the other. And for those attuned to the spiritual, the lines separating the two blur. Indeed, the kingdom of God is among us.

Then Jacob sees Yahweh standing over him, entering into the dream to create a new reality. The biblical text provides the reader a glimpse of heaven on earth, of a metaphysical existence beyond and within the present. The angels serve as a backdrop for the

5. Gustavo Pérez Firmat, *Life on the Hyphen: The Cuban-American Way* (Austin: University of Texas Press, 1994), 41–45.

presence of the Almighty. And God says, "I am the LORD, the God of Abraham your father and the God of Isaac" (28:13). For the first time God repeats the promise originally made to Abraham and Isaac. Jacob may have tricked his father out of a blessing, but here God willingly transfers the promise to Jacob. The oracle received years earlier by his mother (25:23) becomes the expressed divine will. The refugee, the foreigner, the alien, and the sojourner are the recipients of God's promise. God promises to stand in solidarity with the outsider, the one who is dispossessed. His descendants will be like the specks of

> We are climbing Jacob's ladder
> We are climbing Jacob's ladder
> We are climbing Jacob's ladder
> Sisters, brothers, all.
>
> Every round goes higher, higher
> Every round goes higher, higher
> Every round goes higher, higher
> Sisters, brothers, all.
>
> Sinner, do you love my Jesus?
> Sinner, do you love my Jesus?
> Sinner, do you love my Jesus?
> Sisters, brothers, all.
>
> If you love Him, why not serve Him?
> If you love Him, why not serve Him?
> If you love Him, why not serve Him?
> Sisters, brothers, all.
>
> —A black spiritual

dust on the ground, spreading to the west and east, to the north and south. Through Jacob, all the tribes will be blessed. As Jacob journeys through foreign lands and lives far from the promised land that witnessed his birth, God will not abandon him, nor will God abandon any present-day migrant who, like Jacob, is the recipient of undeserved grace.

When Jacob wakes he is awestruck. Without any hesitation, he embraces the reality of the dream. Surely, without knowing it, he has stumbled on the house of God, the very gateway to heaven. Until now, God chose Jacob. Here Jacob is willing to make his father's God his own. Using the stone pillow on which he slept, Jacob converts it into a sacred monolith to symbolize the Lord's presence, and then pours oil on it. Such pillars were common in almost every Canaanite sanctuary, which is why God eventually orders their destruction (Deut. 12:3). Jacob also changes the name of that place, which was known as Luz, to Bethel (Hebrew for "house of God"). Bethel would become a Canaanite sanctuary city dedicated to El, a major Canaanite deity. But with the establishment of the northern kingdom of Israel, King Jeroboam I would make the more ancient Bethel an important cultic center to rival Judah's sacred site in Jerusalem. Still, the house of God is not limited to Bethel or Jerusalem. It is wherever the seeker of God's face happens to be. Any home can become a Bethel, not just Luz. The question we all must wrestle with is the proper response to the question: Is our present home Bethel—the house of God?

Jacob then does the unexpected. After seeing the Almighty, and hearing the Creator of all confer the original promise made to Abraham and Isaac on him, Jacob negotiates. Most humans who experience God's presence, even in a dream, might humbly fall to their knees and worship the Creator, but not Jacob. He will serve God only if God meets certain expectations. If God accompanies him on his journey, provides food and clothing, and returns him to his father's home, then he will call Yahweh his God and pay a tithe (probably a one-time offering to maintain the sacred pillar). Jacob's prayer is a perfect example of how not to pray, where God is seen as some sort of barterer. "O God, if you give me X, I'll promise to do Y." "Bless me with health and wealth and then I'll serve you for the rest of my life." Nonetheless, maturity in faith can only be achieved when we commit ourselves to serving God, even when we remain in sickness and poverty. It is interesting to note that God does not respond to Jacob. While Jacob makes his foolish stipulations, God's will proceeds unabated.

29:1–30a

Testimony of Rachel

Jacob is on a mission. He arrives at the land of the sons of the east looking for a wife from among his own people, lest he marries one of the Canaanite women closer to home. From Canaan he journeys about 400 miles north to the city of Haran in the Paddan-aram area, homeland of the Arameans, consisting of those from the patriarchal family who did not journey to the promised land of Canaan along with Abraham. Paddan-aram is located in upper Mesopotamia (modern-day Turkey), in the northern region between the Tigris and the Euphrates rivers. Jacob is headed to the house of Laban, his uncle, to find a wife from among his daughters. Nahor, Abraham's brother, was Laban's grandfather. Laban was also brother to Rebekah, Jacob's mother, responsible for her betrothal, a transaction that proved profitable for him (24:53).

As he approaches Haran, he comes across a bucolic setting where three flocks of sheep lie beside a well. Whenever the biblical reader comes across a tale staged at a well, more than likely a love story is about to unfold, for the well is the Bible's favorite place for betrothal scenes. At the mouth of the well is a large stone, no doubt to protect the precious water from pollution. Jacob inquires on the *shalom*, the overall well-being, wholeness, and completeness of his uncle Laban. As the shepherds reply all is well with him, they notice and point out his daughter Rachel approaching the well with her sheep. It seems that among the Arameans, during this time period, women were given a greater degree of freedom than found in other parts of the biblical text. Here she is, walking among men and even speaking to Jacob, at this point a stranger.

Jacob is immediately smitten by Rachel, although we are not told if the feelings are mutual. Maybe hoping for a moment alone with her, he asks why the shepherds have not yet moved away the stone to water their sheep and return them to pasture. Here Jacob discovers that the stone cannot be moved until all the flocks have been gathered, either because the stone was too heavy, requiring several men to move it, or because it was a prearranged agreement to prevent any one shepherd from taking more than his or her fair share. As soon as Rachel joins Jacob and the other shepherds, Jacob, who until now has been portrayed as weak and pale in comparison to his brother Esau, moves the stone single-handedly in her presence, an act of Herculean bravado in an attempt to catch the beautiful young maiden's eye.

After Jacob waters Rachel's sheep, he kisses her and bursts into tears, revealing his identity as kinsman. Upon hearing this, Rachel runs to her father and informs him of all that has transpired. Hearing the news of Jacob's arrival, Laban runs to greet the young lad, embracing him warmly while proclaiming that Jacob is "surely my bone and my flesh" (v. 14). Echoes of an earlier encounter, when

Abraham's servants meet Rebekah by the well, can be detected (24:1–67); however, there are some subtle differences. In the Rebekah narrative, the woman fetches water for the man's animals. Here Jacob, the man, fetches water for the woman's animals. Rather than introducing himself as the son of Isaac, he introduces himself as his mother's child. Michael Carden points out that Rebekah may have raised her son not to conform to normative patriarchal roles; nevertheless, his encounter with Laban would soon provide Jacob with "a crash course in patriarchy."[6]

Another difference with the earlier narrative is the economic status of the would-be suitors. Abraham sent a servant who lavished rich presents on Laban. No wonder Laban rushes out to greet Jacob, maybe hoping this newest encounter would be as profitable as the last. But alas, while the wealthy Abraham sent servants to do his bidding, Jacob appears with no gifts or funds; instead he is in need of work. Indeed, he takes advantage of Laban's hospitality and stays as his guest for a month.

When Laban embraces his nephew, he proclaims that Jacob is truly of his bone and flesh, either a reference that they are related or, more symbolically, they are both cut from the same cloth; that is, both men are tricksters. The question for the reader is which trickster will outfox the other. It would seem that Laban will outwit young Jacob; but in the end, it is Jacob who leaves as a wealthy man, even though he is without funds when he begins working for Laban.

After a month passes, Jacob moves from being Laban's guest to being his employee. The question is what wages to pay him. Jacob, infatuated with Rachel, offers a solution. He would work seven years

> **Wily Rebecca explains:** By keeping Jacob home by my tent, schooling him in the traditional ways of woman, I raised my smooth-skinned, sweet-smelling boy as my *daughter*, shielding him from the harsher ways of men. In this way, I set Jacob up to play the woman's role in the family drama.
> —Ellen Frankel
>
> *The Five Books of Miriam: A Woman's Commentary on the Torah* (New York: Putnam, 1996), 50.

---

6. Michael Carden, *The Queer Bible Commentary*, ed. Deryn Guest, Robert E. Goss, Mona West, and Thomas Bohache (London: SCM Press, 2006), 48.

as a bride-price payment for Rachel, an exaggerated period of time considering that the price of a virgin is fifty silver shekels (Deut. 22:28–29). In the earlier Rebekah narrative, the decision to marry rested with her (Gen. 24:58); but here it is Laban who decides. Again, we know Jacob loves Rachel, for the seven years pass as if they were but a few days; but again, are the feelings reciprocal? It really does not matter what Rachel's feelings are, for property that is purchased with seven years of labor has no input in such a transaction.

There is one problem with the agreed transaction: Leah, the older spinster sister. Biblical readers have consistently attempted to make Leah unattractive to justify Jacob's desire for Rachel. The text tells us that Leah's eyes were *rakkot*, while Rachel was shapely and beautiful. The Hebrew word *rak* can be translated as "tender," meaning that Leah's eyes could be "lovely" (so KJV and Living Bible), or they could be "sore, weak, lacking sparkle" (so NIV, RSV, and JB). Some scholars have used the meaning of Leah's name ("cow") to indicate that she had cow eyes or was bug-eyed. By comparison, Rachel's name is Hebrew for "ewe." Their names could be references to physical traits, or more likely they could refer to their trades: Rachel, as the text tells us, is a shepherdess, while Leah could be assumed to be a cattlewoman—a popular trade in that region of the world. Regardless of the reason for their names, one thing is certain: Rachel shares Jacob's fate of being the second-born attempting to surmount the privileged status of an older sibling. We may not know if Jacob and Rachel shared a similar love for each other, but we do know they shared a similar life experience.

Seven years pass in the length of one verse (v. 20). It is time for Jacob to claim his possession. Laban responds by throwing a wedding feast. The Hebrew word used to depict this banquet is *mishteh*, which best describes a drinking party. Heavy drinking, a veiled bride, and the darkness of the bedchamber contribute to Jacob meeting his match. Not Rachel. Not even Leah. Jacob's match is Laban. Leah's father orchestrates a deception similar to the one perpetrated by his sister Rebekah. Just as the young trickster fooled Isaac, blinded by age, out of a blessing intended for an older sibling, so too does an older trickster fool Jacob, blinded by love, out of a lovemaking intended for a younger sibling. Although it was Leah who had "weak" eyes, it was Jacob who failed to see the switch, similar to how his father, whose eyes were also weak, failed to distinguish between him and his brother Esau. The question left unanswered for the reader is if the sisters were in on the deception, or were they simply pawns in their father's scheme.

As the fog of alcohol wears off, and the light of day breaks through, it becomes apparent that it is Leah, not Rachel, by his side. Of course, this immediately raises questions for readers: How could Jacob consummate his marriage and not know it was not his beloved? Did Jacob go along with the trick to get both women and the riches that came with the oldest? By going along with the charade does he not injure the apple of his eye, Rachel? Who is tricking whom? In any case, Jacob is incensed. "What have you done to me?" he demands of Laban. But the response received is that what is done is done due to the customs of the land. Thus the story comes full circle. Laban's response must have sounded like a stinging rebuke, for after all what brought Jacob to Laban's house in the first place was going against custom and usurping his brother's birthright and blessing.

Laban offers Rachel to Jacob once the marriage week celebrating his union with Leah comes to an end. This offer is in exchange for seven more years of labor, and even in violation of what will eventually be considered a prohibition of the same man marrying two sisters (Lev. 18:18). Laban disposes of both his properties for a handsome profit, even if it means Leah, the eldest, is consigned to a loveless union facing the resentment of her sister every day. Jacob will finally get his possession, but it costs him fourteen years. In addition, Rachel now comes with baggage: her sister and the slave girls of each, Zilpah and Bilhah.

29:31–30:24

Testimony on Sibling Rivalry and the Sons They Birth

Until now, women have partaken in the promise of birthing nations. Sarah is to give birth to the promised child from whom all nations will be blessed (17:15–17). Hagar, the slave girl, will also birth a great nation, the Ishmaelites. And Rebekah will be the mother of two nations (Israel and Edom). But after Rebekah, women cease birthing nations and become instruments by which the house of Israel comes into being. The third generation of matriarchs, Rachel, her sister Leah, along with their slave girls, becomes the means by which a nation is established. Israel is birthed from one man, Jacob, with the help of several women. As such, women cease being holders of the promise, and instead become the incubators. The birth of a nation begins with God having compassion on Leah, Jacob's first wife, for Jacob loved Rachel much more than he did Leah. So God opened the womb of the neglected wife while his beloved's remained barren. The motif of blessing the least favorite wife with children seems to repeat itself, especially with the circumstances surrounding the prophet Samuel's mother, Hannah, and her co-wife, Peninnah (1 Sam. 1:2, 4–5).

For the first time, Leah and Rachel are given voice as a battle of wombs breaks out. With the birth of each child, the name given by Leah or Rachel provides insight as to how the peculiar competition between them is progressing. But as we shall see, the meaning of the name given to each son does not always neatly match the gloating speech given by Leah or Rachel. This may be due to difficulties in the translations of puns based on popular etymologies. Although the sisters are struggling with each other for children, it is God, the giver of children, whom they are probably struggling against.

Leah is the first to conceive, giving birth to a son, Reuben. It is uncertain what Reuben's name means, possibly a play on the words "see" (*ra'ah*) and "son" (*ben*). Leah connects the name "*see* a son" with her expression that Yahweh *saw* her misery, so now she will be loved by her husband. She hopes that bearing a child will finally win her husband's love; but unfortunately that is not the case, as evident in the names given to her other sons. She conceives again and calls her son Simeon, a possible reference to the word *shama'*, meaning "heard," for Yahweh *heard* how she has been neglected, so God gave her this one too. Leah again conceives and she names the next boy Levi (*lewiy*), a possible pun with the Hebrew word *lawah*, "to attach": her husband will be *attached* to her because she bore him three sons. She has one last boy, whom she calls Judah, whose meaning is uncertain; nevertheless, according to Leah, the name reflects that this time she would give glory to Yahweh. It is worth noting that it is from the neglected wife, the rejected one, the one who was marginalized, that the future King David will be born. For Christians, the Messiah Jesus, also from the tribe of Judah, comes from the womb of this despised woman. It is the stone rejected that is used by God for God's handiwork. After Judah, the text tells us she has no more children—or did she?

Meanwhile, night after night Rachel hears the sons of Leah crying to be fed. Day after day she hears the babies cooing with joy. Occupying the adjacent tent, she most desires her own children. Rachel grows extremely jealous, seeing her sister give birth to four boys, while she remains barren. Unless she bears Jacob a child, Rachel's status of beloved could be reduced to that of a slave. So she says to her husband, "Give me children, or I shall die!" Her demands anger Jacob, who retorts: "Am I in the place of God, who has withheld from you the fruit of the womb?"

Desperate, she gives Jacob her slave girl, Bilhah, just as Sarah once gave Abraham her slave girl Hagar. Children born from slave girls serving as concubines belonged not to the slave but to her mistress. Jacob takes Bilhah to bed and she conceives, giving birth to a son named Dan, which means "judge" in Hebrew. He is named by Rachel because God was *just* to Rachel, hearing her prayers and giving her a son. The child is "legally" Rachel's because he is born "upon her knees," an expression referring to the adoption of the concubine's child by the mistress.

Bilhah conceives and gives birth to a second son, Naphtali, the meaning of whose name is uncertain. It is probably derived from the northern highland where the tribe eventually set-

> Even more striking—and this point has been continuously overlooked by biblical exegetes—is the fact that Rachel's triumph over her sister is no more than a boast of questionable validity. After all, the son she names is Bilhah's son. Her womb is still closed. This naming-speech is more the delusion of a desperate woman, trying to find comfort in the offspring of her maid.
>
> —Ilana Pardes
>
> *Countertraditions in the Bible: A Feminist Approach* (Cambridge: Harvard University Press, 1992), 65.

tled. Again, Rachel names the son of her slave girl, boastfully crying out that she had fought God's fight with her sister and she had won.

Not to be outdone, Leah gives Jacob her slave girl, Zilpah. Zilpah gives birth to Gad, which is the name of the Phoenician god of fortune, hence explaining why Leah exclaims, "Good *fortune!*" Again Zilpah conceives and gives birth to Asher (*'asher*), a probable pun with the Hebrew word for "happy" (*'ashur*), possibly derived from the name of the fertility goddess Asherah. This may be why Leah connects the name with her comment, "Happy am I! For the women will call me *happy!*"

One day, while harvesting, Leah's oldest son Reuben finds some mandrakes, a Eurasian plant with purplish flowers and branched roots that resemble a human body. Its roots were used to produce a narcotic drug that was believed to relax the womb. The plant was considered to be an aphrodisiac, with supposed fertility-inducing qualities. The mandrake produces a round reddish yellow fruit commonly called the "love apple," about the size of a plum, containing a soft pulp. When Rachel finds out, she demands the mandrake; but Leah snaps that Rachel had already taken her husband, and now she also wants her son's mandrakes. So they make a deal. Leah gets to sleep that night with Jacob in return for the mandrakes. It is interesting to note that this text captures a dialogue solely between two women, a rarity in the biblical text.

As soon as Jacob returns to camp, Leah marches up to him and claims her purchase. Jacob becomes the object of the story, a silent item negotiated for by two women. He obediently follows Leah into the tent and performs the act he was purchased to do. That night she conceives, eventually giving birth to a fifth son, Issachar, which in Hebrew means "man of hire." He was thus named because God paid Leah her wages for giving Jacob her slave girl. She conceives again and gives birth to Zebulun, whose name might derive from the Aramaic word for "gift," *zebed*: Leah believed God gave her a fine *gift*, for now her husband will honor her for bearing him six sons. As an afterthought in the text, Leah gives birth to a final child, a girl. In effect, this is the tenth child of Jacob who, not surprisingly, will not be considered as one of the tribes of Israel. Leah names her

Dinah. Sadly, no reason is given for her name, even though it might be the feminine rendition of Dan (to judge).

Rachel may have taken the mandrake, but it is Leah who gives birth to three more children. With the birth of each child and the bringing of her slave girl to her husband's bed to procure more children, it seems as if poor Leah became further neglected by her husband. Seven pregnancies failed to win his love. Yet ironically, it will be her, and not the beloved Rachel, who will lie beside her husband at the cave of Machpelah (49:31), the family burial plot.

Finally, God remembers poor Rachel and opens her womb, making clear that it was God, not the mandrake, that was responsible for her conceiving. She gives birth to Joseph, whose name can be derived from either 'asaph, "gather, take away," hence explaining Rachel's comment, "God has taken away my reproach" (30:23); or from yasaph, "to add," which would explain why Rachel said, "May the LORD add to me another son!" (30:24). Regardless as to the name's meaning, the text is clear—only God can, be the author of life. It is God who makes women barren or opens their wombs. Feelings of shame and reproach for barrenness are not limited to Rachel. Hannah, the mother of the prophet Samuel, saw herself as worthless until God removed her barrenness (1 Sam. 1). When King David's wife Michal spoke ill of her husband, she was punished with barrenness (2 Sam. 6:23). In the New Testament, Elizabeth, the mother of John the Baptist, lived the life of a barren woman. But in her old age (like Sarah), Elizabeth discovered that God removed the reproach of her barrenness (Luke 1:24–25).

> It is certainly a matter for deep regret that mortals, not knowing what is best for them, and being wholly ignorant of the judgments of God, do not realize what great blessings can come from having daughters or what great harm can come from having sons, and, unwilling, apparently, to leave the matter to him who understands everything and is the creator of us all, worry themselves to death about what ought to make them glad.
>
> —Teresa de Avila
>
> The Complete Works of Saint Teresa of Jesus, trans. and ed. E. Allison Peers, 3 vols. (1946; repr. London: Sheed & Ward, 1950), 3:98.

While today we know the multiple causes for barrenness, to the ancient mind barrenness was the result of disobedience. It was God who was withholding the fruit of the womb. The prophet Isaiah blames the people's unfaithfulness toward God as the reason that their descendants did not outnumber the grains of sand (Isa. 48:18–19). To be barren was to live in a state of humiliation. Yet it is God, according to the text, who closed Rachel's womb and who prevented her from being fruitful and multiplying.

Regardless of Rachel's years of humiliation, Jacob is the one who is biblically blessed. According to the psalmist, "Sons are indeed a heritage from the LORD, the fruit of the womb a reward. Like arrows in the hand of a warrior are the sons of one's youth. Happy is the man who has his quiver full of them" (Ps. 127:3–5). If having many sons is to be blessed, then is choosing to have no children a rejection of God's blessing? R. Albert Mohler Jr., president of Southern Baptist Theological Seminary, seems to think so:

> Christians must recognize that this rebellion against parenthood represents nothing less than an absolute revolt against God's design. . . . The shocking reality is that some Christians have bought into this lifestyle and claim childlessness as a legitimate option. The rise of modern contraceptives has made this technologically possible. . . . Willful barrenness and chosen childlessness must be named as moral rebellion. To demand that marriage means sex—but not children—is to defraud the creator of His joy and pleasure in seeing the saints raising His children.[7]

Children can indeed be the joyous outcome of intimacy; still, we cannot lose sight that the ultimate goal of sex is fulfillment through union with one's beloved, not having children. While reproduction is neither the reason nor the purpose for engaging in sex, it does seem fitting that new life can be a product of two becoming one.

For many, children are among the greatest blessings of life. Nevertheless, it becomes problematic when modern concepts of

---

7. R. Albert Mohler Jr., "Deliberate Childlessness and Moral Rebellion," *Baptist Press*, July 27, 2005.

family are imposed on ancient texts. Viewing children as blessings for their own sake is a relatively new concept. While the psalmist declares that a full quiver of children is a blessing from the Lord, this blessing was primarily an economic blessing. In biblical times children were an asset. Along with women, they were the property of men. If a marriage failed to produce children, a man had the right to put away his wife and choose another. This was in hope that the new woman, the new asset, would produce offspring, preferably boys.

In an agricultural society, the presence of children literally meant extra hands to work the field. It also provided the parent with a form of social security for the future. Children were necessary to ensure financial support in old age. The more children a man fathered, the more financially secure he became. In modern times society has turned toward urbanization. Advances in medicine have contributed to longer lives. Population growth has strained resources, and technology has reduced the number of people needed to work the soil. As a result, large families have become less the norm.

A disturbing story in the book of Job illustrates how children were viewed as property. Today it offends our moral sensitivities, but it made perfect moral sense during biblical times. We are told that all of Job's children—seven sons and three daughters—were killed by Satan on God's authority. This is but one of many calamities to befall Job, but no doubt among the most painful (Job 1:12–19). By the end of the book, God restores all of Job's riches and property, including his children. He fathers seven new sons and three new daughters, replacing those whom he lost earlier in the story (Job 42:10–15). In a world where children are seen as property, the siring of new children to replace the dead ones seemed fair—kind of like the 14,000 sheep, 6,000 camels, 1,000 oxen, and 1,000 she-donkeys that replaced the livestock destroyed earlier in the story. But if children are a product of love, a quite modern concept, then no amount of additional children can ever make up for loss of a particular child or children.

Fortunately, the status of children changes as their identity ceases to be property, and instead becomes a product of love. Jesus makes them the ideal by which entrance into God's reign can occur (Matt. 18:3–4). No longer is the model one male person benefiting from the power and privilege of being the patriarchal head. Instead, seeking the position of the least among us, the child becomes the means toward salvation. Our hope is that the process of returning children (as well as women) to their status as human beings, instead of being seen as property within a patriarchal society, would continue.

30:25–32:3

Testimony of Laban

The biblical text is not kind to Laban, who is depicted as Abraham's nephew, Rebekah's brother, and Leah and Rachel's father. When we first met Laban, we noticed how he responded with lavish hospitality toward Abraham's servant, motivated by the gifts the servant was bearing (24:29–32). Laban is reintroduced a generation later when Jacob, his nephew, comes to his household seeking a wife. This time, there are no gifts; rather, Laban drives a hard bargain, willing to offer Jacob his daughter in exchange for seven years of labor. But on the eve of the seventh year, he switches Rachel for his eldest daughter, Leah. If Jacob still wants Rachel, he must work another seven years (29:1–30). Besides changing wives on Jacob, Laban also changes his wages ten times, always looking for ways to profit more at Jacob's expense. Laban's actions lead to his characterization as a shrewd, deceitful, and greedy person, no doubt a dig intended for his descendants, the Arameans. In contrast, Jacob is portrayed in this section as cunning, skillful, and resourceful when dealing with his father-in-law, outwitting the Aramean.

This section of the biblical text highlights Laban's departure from the biblical narrative with Jacob's departure from his house. Although Laban has always been in a position to take advantage of Jacob, this last episode turns the tables. After the birth of Joseph, Jacob approaches Laban and asks to be released so that he can return to his own home in Canaan. But why ask to be released now? Twenty years have passed since Jacob, as a young lad, set foot in Laban's house. He committed to work a total of fourteen years for both of his wives. So why stay an additional six years? Why not leave as soon as he fulfilled his obligation? Maybe he stayed because of his love for Rachel. He might have been waiting for her to give birth to her first child. After all, tradition would have him divorce her, sending her back to her father's house in disgrace, if she did not bear him a child. Not wanting to exercise that option, Jacob probably had to stay until Rachel gave birth. As soon as Joseph was born, Jacob could start gazing toward Canaan.

But Laban did not want Jacob to leave. This was not out of any familial feelings, but because he learned through divination that God blessed Jacob, and by association he has prospered. This is the first time in the biblical text that perceiving the metaphysical through divination is mentioned. What is interesting is that no negative connotation is expressed concerning the act of divination, even though the law would eventually prohibit it (Deut. 18:9–14). Laban understands that if he wants to continue growing in wealth, he is dependent on Jacob's God, with whom Jacob has found favor. Hoping to continue participating in increasing his riches, Laban insisted that Jacob stay working for him. "Name your price," Laban said.

Jacob agreed to work for Laban, asking for nothing that would deplete Laban's wealth. As payment for continual employment, all future sheep that are born black and all goats that are born speckled or spotted would belong to him. Normally, sheep are white, while goats are black or dark-colored. On the surface it would appear that Jacob bargained for the shorter end of the stick. Those born speckled or spotted from Laban's normally colored flock would belong to Jacob. This is a foolish proposition for anyone having a minimal understanding of animal husbandry. One did not need an advanced degree in genetic engineering to know that the offspring of one-colored animals seldom produce a speckled or spotted litter. To further ensure that this new arrangement would benefit Laban, he separated his flock from all black sheep and speckled or spotted goats, putting three days' journey between them and Laban's main flock. While Jacob attended to Laban's flock, Laban's sons looked after the multicolored flock.

But Jacob had a plan. He took branches (in sap) from poplar, almond, and plane trees; peeling away strips of the bark, he revealed the white (*laban* in Hebrew), milk-like gum in streaks. Jacob then laid them in the watering troughs so that they would be in front of the animals when they came to drink. Jacob knew that when Laban's white sheep and dark goats drank, they also usually mated. It was believed that if the animals looked on the striped branches while mating, it would lead them to produce multicolored offspring. He only did this when the animals drinking water were sturdy, not feeble; hence his flock grew with stronger beasts while Laban's flock shrunk with weaker animals.

Just as Jacob already increased in children, now he was increasing in flocks. Yet he expressed no regret in enriching himself at his father-in-law's expense, attributing the reversal in fortune to God. The text seems to advocate a prosperity theology where God blesses the faithful with material goods at the expense of the unfaithful. Such a doctrine is problematic, for it justifies the present economic social structures that cause, as each year goes by, the rich to get richer and the poor to get poorer. If God indeed blesses with riches, then by definition the poor are outside God's blessing. It is the robber barons who are the true believers because their vast fortunes are in direct proportion to God's favor. Poverty becomes the fault of the poor, who lack spirituality, as opposed to sociopolitical conditions that create poverty.

Laban's sons started blaming Jacob for Laban's declining wealth, a trend that concerned Jacob. Seeing in Laban's face the discord that was brewing, and hearing from God to move on, Jacob prepared to return to the land of his forefathers, to the land of Canaan. He took his two feuding wives aside and explained the situation. Surprisingly they answered in unison, expressing no love lost concerning their father, giving the reader, for the first time, a glimpse of the sisters' thinking and feelings concerning their father's dealings. It appears that the *moher*, the bride-price paid by the groom (in Jacob's case seven years of work for each), was supposed to have been held in trust by the father to provide for the daughters' future security. However, the sisters' claim that they had no inheritance indicates that Laban had probably squandered their bride-price. Like Jacob, they too were victims of Laban's shenanigans. They were upset to be denied any inheritance, treated no better than foreigners.

So Jacob gathered all his flocks and possessions, his wives and children, and left in secrecy the land of Paddan-aram while Laban was away at sheep shearing. But, unknown to Jacob, his wife Rachel stole the household idols belonging to Laban, taking them with her. She steals more than just idols, for the household gods symbolize the authority of the household. The taking of idols by Rachel debunks the assumption that the household of Israel only worshiped one God, Yahweh, known to the patriarchs by many different names and manifestations. Rachel reveals the more common practice of the time; if Yahweh was worshiped, it was but one God above other gods that was also worshiped within a polytheistic environment.

Three days went by before Laban discovered that Jacob left. He gathered his sons and pursued Jacob, overtaking him in seven days at Mount Gilead, apparently an impossible distance from his home to cover in such a short time. He chased after Jacob for seven days to do him harm, but God warned him in a dream the night before their encounter not to molest him. Instead of harming Jacob, Laban indignantly reproached his son-in-law. Hearing Laban's lament, one would think that it is he who was abused. After decades of taking advantage of Jacob, after decades of enriching himself off the sweat of Jacob's brow, he now chose to play the role of the injured party. Unfortunately, many today who have benefited from white privilege also claim that they are the victims of racism. Often, oppressors like to state that they are the real ones who are being oppressed.

Take the example of conservative legal jurist Robert H. Bork, nominated by then-President Ronald Reagan to the U.S. Supreme Court, but whose nomination was defeated in Congress. In his book *Slouching towards Gomorrah: Modern Liberalism and the American Decline,* Bork makes the case that the only group that is truly oppressed in the United States today is white heterosexual males. Like Laban, many today who have benefited from the way the sociopolitical structures were constructed now, with a reversal of fortune, look toward those who have been historically marginalized to blame for their declining power and privilege. Providing a voice for Laban, and many today within the U.S. dominant culture, Bork accuses people on the margins of society of participating in a rhetoric of victimhood to force those whom society has historically privileged to seek absolution from those they have supposedly oppressed. He adds that such actions by people on the margins lead to the vilification of all Euro-Americans. Those college or university professors dealing with issues of race "teach resentment and fear [and their] careers would be diminished or ended by progress in racial reconciliation; [hence it is to these professors' best interest] to preserve and exacerbate racial antagonism."[8]

Playing the victim, Laban went through a litany of questions. Why did Jacob trick him? Why did he take his daughters away as if they were war prisoners? Why didn't Jacob allow him to throw a going-away party with music, dancing, and rejoicing? Why was he denied giving his daughters and grandchildren a departing kiss? Jacob, according to Laban, acted as a fool; and even though it was within Laban's power to harm Jacob, the God of Jacob's father visited him in a dream warning against it. Maybe, Laban reasoned, Jacob left because he longed to return to his father's house; but why steal Laban's household gods?

Jacob confessed his fear that if he tried to leave, his father-in-law might snatch his daughters. Although Jacob was no slave, his legal status was similar. Having no standing in his father-in-law's house, Jacob had little if any rights under Laban's roof. According to tradition, which eventually would become law, if a slave was acquired unmarried and was given a wife by the master and had children, the wife and children were still considered the property of the master. If the slave was released, the wife and children could be forced, at the master's discretion, to stay behind (Exod. 21:4–6). This might explain Laban's curious comment concerning Jacob's wives and

> Forty years ago, as the United States experienced the civil rights movement, the supposed monolith of White Anglo-Saxon Protestant dominance served as the whipping post for almost every debate about power and status in America. After a full generation of such debate, WASP elites have fallen by the wayside and a plethora of government-enforced diversity policies have marginalized many white workers.
> —U.S. Senator James Webb (D-VA)
>
> "Diversity and the Myth of White Privilege," *The Wall Street Journal*, July 22, 2010.

8. Robert H. Bork, *Slouching towards Gomorrah: Modern Liberalism and the American Decline* (New York: Regan Books, 1996), 228–29.

children, "The daughters are my daughters, the children are my children" (31:43). No wonder Jacob left under cover, without saying his good-byes. As to Laban's household gods, Jacob insisted no one took them. Exercising for the first time his power as patriarch of life and death over his household, he declared that whoever was found with them would not live. So Jacob gave Laban permission to search the camp and take whatever belonged to him. Unfortunately, Jacob's word would soon come true when Rachel attempted to give birth to her second son.

After searching Jacob's and Leah's tents, Laban headed toward Rachel's tent. Quickly, she placed the gods in the camel's saddle and then sat on them. When Laban entered the tent, Rachel excused herself from properly greeting him because she had her menstrual period. In effect, she played the trickster as well as her father or husband.

Hastily searching the tent, Laban found nothing and left, looking like a fool. No doubt the author was mocking gods that could be stolen. To make matters worse, a woman made "unclean" in the mind of the ancient reader because she was menstruating could sit on gods with no repercussion. Such a "vulgar" act only demonstrated their impotence.

> Leah: I've always suspected that Rachel masterminded the whole scenario to get back at Father for embarrassing her twenty years before on her wedding day. And so, just as he'd hidden me behind her veil, she hid Laban's idols under her skirt. Our father certainly taught his daughters well.
>
> —Ellen Frankel
>
> *Five Books of Miriam*, 62–63.

When Laban's gods were not found, Jacob went on the offensive. He rebuked his father-in-law, demanding to know what crime he committed. He felt falsely accused because Laban found nothing that was his. Jacob stressed he had been a faithful servant for twenty years, and it was the God of his father that blessed him with possessions.

Laban responded by asking that a covenant between them be established. However, when one carefully reads the account, it seems as if two covenants are being enacted, one dealing with

Jacob's wives, the other with boundaries. Taking a stone, Laban set up a monument. They shared two meals there, and Laban called the place Jegar-sahadutha (Aramaic), while Jacob called it Galeed (Hebrew), both meaning "heap of witness," because a cairn of stones was gathered to witness the agreement. Laban also named the place Mizpah, the Hebrew word for "watchpost," because the monument erected stood watch over Laban and Jacob. They agreed that Jacob was to take no further wives except those from the house of Laban. They also made a nonaggression treaty, each swearing not to cross the monument erected to attack the other.

The next morning Laban arose, kissed his daughters and grandchildren, and returned home. There is no mention of a kiss for Jacob. With the final break from Laban, and as Jacob leaves his exile and returns toward the land God promised, the supernatural starts to become more real. Jacob notices angels, so he names the place Mahanaim, the Hebrew word for "two camps," because "this is God's camp." What does a camp of angels mean? Why is it manifested now? The answer might be found in Psalm 34:7 (my trans.): "The angels of Yahweh pitch their camp surrounding those who fear God, and God delivers them." Jacob will soon encounter his greatest threat, his brother Esau, who swore to kill him. If Jacob and his sons are slain by his brother, the promise God originally made to Abraham comes to an end, unfulfilled. More now than ever, as he enters the promised land, Jacob needs divine protection.

32:4–33:17

Testimony of Esau

Before Jacob resettles in the promised land, he first needs to make peace with Esau, his brother, whom he has cheated out of a birthright and tricked out of a blessing. The last time Jacob was in his company, Esau threatened to kill him (27:41). But twenty years have elapsed. Maybe time has pacified Esau's rage. Or maybe his brother has become more intent on making good on his earlier threat. Either way, the issue between the two brothers needs resolution. So Jacob sends messengers ahead of his caravan to the land of

Seir to inform Esau of his imminent arrival and that he has done well at the house of Laban. But the messengers return to Jacob, informing him that as soon as Esau heard the news, he immediately rode off with four hundred men to intercept Jacob. Upon hearing this news, Jacob becomes distressed, growing greatly afraid. Unfortunately, the emotions not mentioned are regret and remorse. No doubt Jacob imagines these four hundred men approaching with swords drawn. Would his brother finally take his vengeance and decimate Jacob and his caravan?

Jacob divides his caravan into two camps, reasoning that if his brother attacks one, the other could escape. Then he offers up a heartfelt prayer. He cries out to the God of his father Abraham and the God of his father Isaac, the one who promised that he would prosper and that his descendants would outnumber the sand by the sea once he returned home. Although Jacob humbles himself in a prayer that recognizes his unworthiness, he still implores God to snatch him from his brother's clutches, insisting that God keep God's promise.

The next day Jacob prepares a substantial gift for his brother, consisting of two hundred she-goats, twenty he-goats, two hundred ewes, twenty rams, thirty camels with calves, forty cows, ten bulls, twenty she-asses, and ten donkeys. He separates and carefully spaces them into different droves and sends them ahead with the instruction that as each successive drove encounters his brother, they are to say that all the animals are a gift from Jacob. He reasons that by sending the gifts in advance, his brother might be placated when they finally meet face-to-face.

That night he sends his family across the ford of the Jabbok River. He remains behind, alone, anxiously awaiting his encounter with Esau. But then a man comes and wrestles with Jacob throughout the entire night, a man who is not Esau. The nocturnal battle is so fierce that Jacob's hip is dislocated. The stranger asks to be released before daybreak, but Jacob, with tenacity, refuses until he receives a blessing from the stranger. Could this stranger be some sort of night river spirit, which needs to be released before the sun rises? Or maybe it is a demon? If this was an echo of some ancient interpretation, it becomes ambiguous with the possibility that this stranger might be an angel, as suggested by the prophet Hosea (12:3–4), or even God. Martin Luther believed that it was Jesus Christ.[9] Regardless of who or what this supernatural being is, before Jacob deals with his brother, he must first deal with his God.

The stranger, assumed to be deity, asks for Jacob's name. After Jacob responds, the stranger says that from this day forward he would be known as Israel, Hebrew for "God rules," "God struggles," "God strives," or "God preserves." As the text tells us, he has been strong against God and thus will prevail against men.

Although Jacob enters the battle, it is a new person who leaves, having encountered the Divine. Jacob then asks for the stranger's name. Names in the Bible, especially in Genesis, reveal the essence of the one named. In ancient thought, to know the name of God was to pierce the mystery of heaven. Discovering God's name would have to wait for another day (Exod. 3:14).

> Israel is not formed by success or shrewdness or land, but by an assault from God.
> —Walter Brueggemann
>
> *Genesis*, Interpretation (Atlanta: John Knox Press, 1982), 269.

While the stranger does not provide Jacob with a name, he does provide him with a blessing. But the blessing comes at a cost. Jacob limps away from the encounter, his sciatic nerve damaged, which according to the biblical writer explains why Israelites do not eat this nerve (although no such prohibition makes its way into Jewish dietary regulations). The old Jacob is defeated, losing his ability to ever swagger again; he can now only stagger. Only after the encounter with the stranger is Jacob clear about with whom he has been wrestling all night; thus he names the place Peniel, for there he saw God face-to-face—a mighty, if not impossible, feat considering the belief that to see God meant death (Exod. 33:20). Jacob's encounter reveals a unique characteristic about the faith of the Bible. Surrounding religions unquestionably obey their gods; but the faith of the Bible is one where we can wrestle with our God in the hopes of discovering God's name, God's essence.

9. Martin Luther, *Commentary on Genesis*, trans. J. Theodore Mueller, 2 vols. (Grand Rapids: Zondervan, 1958), 2:197.

Soon after, Jacob sees Esau approaching. The sight of four hundred men accompanying his brother renews Jacob's fear, so he quickly divides his remaining possessions, his women and children. He places the slave girls and their children first, Leah and her children second, and Rachel and her son Joseph last. This is not a move to honor the first group, but expecting the worst, if Esau starts massacring everyone in sight, his family up front would serve as a buffer protecting his beloved wife and child, maybe giving them some time to escape. How Jacob lines up his family shows affection for the son in the rear and disdain for those in the front. Is it any wonder that Joseph will draw his brothers' ire and scorn, even to the point of eventually being manhandled?

> I do not know anything, but it seems to me that this is a man, but also God, like our Lord Jesus Christ. . . . God comes as a man. This is a God who is full of mercy. God could have destroyed Jacob. God lets Jacob beat him. This is just like our Lord Jesus Christ, who lets us crucify him. This is a good God.
>
> —Maria, washerwoman living in Honduras
>
> Bob Ekblad, *Reading the Bible with the Damned*, 90.

Jacob deserves to be beaten by Esau, just as he deserved to be beaten by God. But the unexpected happens. Esau falls on his brother, not to do harm, but to weep on his shoulder. Forgiveness is generously offered regardless of Jacob's failure to ask for forgiveness. God's mercy saves us all from what we deserve. For a brief moment, there is peace between the brothers Esau and Jacob, a lesson and hope for their descendants today that they too can find peace. Esau, the profane and vulgar brother rejected by God in favor of Jacob, magnanimously reveals the face of God more so than any other character in the book of Genesis. Even Jacob has to admit that entering Esau's presence is like coming into the presence of God. Esau refuses the gifts that Jacob offers, for he has plenty, but Jacob insists and Esau relents. Finally, Jacob pays for the deceptions he perpetuated in his youth, although he may not have necessarily learned the lesson well.

Esau suggests they break camp and return to Esau's homeland at Seir. Jacob asks that Esau goes ahead and he will follow, but at a slower pace because he is traveling with a nursing flock and small children; but not to worry, he will shortly follow. So Esau resumes his journey southward toward home and Jacob heads in a different direction, westward—one last trick from an old trickster. A name change failed to signify an immediate change of character. Jacob settles in a land he names Succoth, Hebrew for "booths," because there he built shelter for his livestock.

33:18–34:31

Testimony of Dinah

Sometime after his reunion with Esau, Jacob takes his family to the town of Shechem, the first place his grandfather Abraham camped when he entered Canaan (12:6). It was here that God first promised the land. Jacob encamps outside the town, an important urban center during this time; and there, for a hundred pieces of silver, purchases a piece of land from the sons of King Hamor the Hivite on which to pitch his tents. It is interesting to note that in Hebrew "Hamor" is a male donkey, an ass; this may have been a way of showing contempt for the sons of Hamor, the sons of an ass. In an attempt to assert his claim on the land promised to Abraham, Jacob erected an altar on the land he just purchased, which he called *'el 'elohe yisra'el*, El God of Israel. Centuries later, Joseph's bones will be buried here (Josh. 24:32); and when the David-Solomon kingdom splits, the northern kingdom of Israel will make the town of Shechem its first capital city (1 Kgs. 12:25). Millennia later, Jesus will have a conversation by a well with a Samaritan woman from Sychar (John 4:6).

We know that Jacob was not just the father of boys. After the list of all the sons born to Leah, as an afterthought the birth of Dinah is mentioned (30:21). It is no wonder she goes out seeking the companionship of the other women of the land. An afterthought at home, she must have craved attention and relationships, not wanting to end up like her unloved mother Leah, always desiring the elusive love of her husband. We can only wonder how many other daughters were born to Jacob that have remained invisible, only to be mentioned in passing (46:15). Dinah's birth is barely noticed because she was not male, and even now her appearance in the text is due to the sway it will have on her brothers Simeon and Levi. Throughout the entire story, Dinah remains the object; she is never granted subjectivity. Her voice, her concerns, her pain, her emotions, her frustrations are never voiced. She never says a word! In effect, her testimony remains unheard. All that matters, and all we hear about, is how her abused body as object prompts the men in the story to act.

Dinah transgresses boundaries and ventures outside her father's home to visit the women of the region. This is the tale of a woman who leaves the safety of her domestic domain for the wider public domain of men. From the start, it seems as though Dinah is being set up to share in the blame for what is about to befall her, for venturing outside the home without a proper chaperone.

The victim of rape, then as now, is held somewhat culpable. Death before dishonor becomes part of the acceptable collective consciousness still held by many men. Unescorted, Dinah catches the eye of one of Hamor's sons, Shechem, who carries the same name as the town. We are left wondering if Shechem refers to an individual or an entire clan, a similar concern that will later be raised with Simeon and Levi.

> In moral readings of the text, Dinah represents the curious, wandering soul who brings destruction upon herself by abandoning the safety of the father's house. As exemplum, the fate of Dinah warns nuns and daughters to stay indoors, in the cloister or under their father's protection. Most interpreters tacitly or explicitly accepted cultural stereotypes that assumed that women provoke rape and find pleasure in it.
>
> —Joy A. Schroeder
>
> *Dinah's Lament: The Biblical Legacy of Sexual Violence in Christian Interpretation* (Minneapolis: Fortress Press, 2007), 51.

Regardless, Shechem gazed on Dinah and fell in lust with her, carrying her off and raping her. He saw, he carried off, he raped. In the words of the biblical text, he "defiled" her. If we were to accept the biblical chronology concerning Jacob's life (30:21; 31:41), then

Dinah would be prepubescent, and her older brothers but teenagers during this time. If true, then the crime committed is even graver, the rape of a child. It is interesting to note that several scholars, like Lyn Bechtel,[10] argue that no rape occurred, that this was simply a case of a mutual sexual encounter. Disturbingly, as the story develops, we discover that the one truly dishonored was not Dinah, who was physically abused, but her two brothers, whose reputations were challenged.

Within the ancient social order, a person's ranking within society was determined by either acquiring honor or inducing shame. It was crucial for men (like Simeon and Levi) to maintain or improve the honor of their family, while simultaneously avoiding anything that might bring shame on the family name. Generally speaking, honor is male-centered, for through the man's participation in the public sphere honor can be increased or decreased by his bold and aggressive actions when interacting with other men. While honor is achieved in the public sphere, shame is created within the private sphere. Because of patriarchy, a woman who belonged to one man yet was used by another brought shame to the "owner" of her body. So to protect one's honor, the man must confine the woman to the household, where she can remain secure.

> Some scholars agree that he [Shechem] raped me [Dinah]. Others stand on their learned head in order to prove, to their own satisfaction, that he in fact practiced pre-nuptial kidnapping, nothing more sinister than that, and that the terminology used—within the customs of the ancient Near East, as the sociologists will tell you—supports the notion that no rape was involved.
>
> —Athalya Brenner
>
> *I Am . . . Biblical Women Tell Their Own Stories* (Minneapolis: Fortress Press, 2005), 25.

Even though Dinah was not at fault for the lascivious action of Shechem, she was still guilty of bringing shame to her family. Dinah might have been physically raped by Shechem, but she was emotionally and spiritually raped by the males within her own

---

10. Lyn Bechtel, "What If Dinah Is Not Raped (Genesis 24)," *Journal for the Study of the Old Testament* 62 (June 1994): 19–36.

family, as well as today's scholars and ministers who continue to either ignore her story or perpetuate her as the object of the story.

Shechem's lust soon turns to love as he begins to speak tenderly to his victim's heart. Can the rapist have such a rapid change of heart, from violence to love? We know that a rapist (whether stranger or family[11]) is usually motivated by strong negative emotions like hate, anger, or revenge, not sexual libido. The rapist has a desire to demonstrate power over the victim, a power achieved through the victim's humiliation and domination. When reading this conversion from sexual violence to love, it is important to remember that rape has little to do with sex, even though sex becomes the means by which power is enhanced.

Shechem begged that his father, King Hamor, obtain the girl for him, so the father approached Jacob to barter for Dinah. If a young virgin was seduced (raped), the rapist had but two options: he either married her or paid her father a fixed sum. If the father refused to give his daughter in marriage, the seducer was still liable for three times the original marriage price (Deut. 22:23–29). Rape was not an issue of sexual immorality; rather, it was a violation of property rights. The rapist was guilty of trespassing, sowing his seeds in another man's field. This was a crime punishable by death. If the woman failed to cry out for help, then she too must be put to death, unless the attack occurred in the countryside far from hearing. According to the biblical text, the true victim of rape was not the virgin girl but her father. Her despoiling made her unsuitable for marriage, resulting in a financial hardship for her father (her owner). The importance of marrying off one's daughters was in many cases a political decision, in order to create profitable alliances with other families. Virginity was such a profitable commodity that a father had to be compensated for damages (Exod. 22:16–17).

Hamor thus offered Jacob anything he wanted. He further proposed that they become allies and made all the land available to him to travel through or own. "Give your daughters [Dinah's sisters?]

---

11. Eight out of every ten rape cases involved a perpetrator known by the victim, according to a Department of Justice report. See Patricia Tjaden and Nancy Thoennes, *Full Report of the Prevalence, Incidence, and Consequences of Violence Against Women Survey* (Washington, DC: U.S. Department of Justice, 2000), 1–2.

to us, and take our daughters for yourselves," Hamor proposed. Together, Jacob and Hamor tried to peacefully resolve the situation. From the unpleasant circumstance started by rape, the men saw an opportunity to create an ethnic, political, and economic merger. But try as they might, for Israel miscegenation would continue to undergird the fear of assimilation. Regardless of what agreement would be reached with the men of Shechem, we know that the sons of Israel would never agree to merge with another people.

So when Jacob's sons returned from tending the livestock in the countryside, they were outraged and infuriated, for the rape of Jacob's daughter had insulted Israel. It was not the ordeal Dinah underwent that bothered them; rather, it was the insult to Israel's honor that enraged them. They provided a crafty reply to King Hamor. Because Jacob's family was unable to give their daughters in marriage to uncircumcised men, they would agree to an alliance on one condition: all the men in the town had to be circumcised. Only then, through marriage, would they be able to become one kinfolk. Because Shechem was an important person within the king's household, and he was supposedly madly in love with Dinah, the king agreed to the condition of the alliance. Shechem set out to convince his compatriots to undertake circumcision for the sake of this new alliance. If the townsmen agreed, they would have not only the daughters of Israel at their disposal for marriage, but also their livestock and riches. The townsmen agreed, not knowing that by the end of the story it would be the sons of Israel who would make off with the townsfolk's women and riches.

Until now, all of the patriarchs have been depicted as men of peace, with the possible exception of Abraham's campaign against the four kings (14:1–16). Because they were small in number and vulnerable to their more powerful neighbors, an effort to avoid conflict has permeated the narrative as the patriarchs walked a fine line between being exterminated or assimilated. Here, for the first time, the sons of Israel resort to violent means in dealing with their neighbors. Sexual violence becomes the preamble for war.

On the third day of the process, considered the most painful time, when fever usually rises in the case of adults, the townsmen were still recuperating. At this most critical time for recently circumcised men, Dinah's full brothers, Simeon and Levi, took their swords and marched into the unsuspecting town. There they unleashed an uncontrolled and bloody orgy of vengeance. Taking advantage of the men's incapacitation, the two brothers killed them all. They took back their sister, along with all the flocks, cattle, donkeys, riches, and whatever other goods were in the town. They also carried off all the wives and little children. Vengeance can be profitable.

As sexual property, women could be claimed as war booty. The actions of Simeon and Levi are a common practice in war. The "armies of Yahweh" were to kill all the men (Deut. 20:10–18), disperse the spoils of war, and kidnap the virgin women for servitude or to provide sexual pleasure. If a soldier was captivated by a captured woman, he was allowed to bring her into his home and make her his wife, as long as she was a virgin and was from some distant land so as not to snare her captors into a religious cult (Deut. 21:10–14). She was permitted a month to mourn her parents, but after the time of grief the marriage was to be consummated. But with the passage of time, if he tired of her, he could allow her to leave. However, he could not sell her, for as the Bible states, "he had the use of her" (Deut. 21:14, my trans.). War turned women into spoils of war that, along with other valuable possessions, go to the victors.

If the taking of women is a violation of property rights, then the plunder unleashed by the two brothers had more to do with avenging the property theft by Shechem than any emotions, pain, or feeling experienced by their sister. Not only did the perpetrator and his family pay for the crime committed against Dinah, but so did all the innocent inhabitants of the city. The massacre at Shechem leaves us wondering if it was carried out by just Simeon and Levi, or by the warlike clans of Simeon and Levi. If the latter, then the taking of all the wives and little children of the men they killed becomes mathematically sensible.

When Jacob heard of the sin his two sons had committed, he was upset, but not so much with the vengeful act itself. The text tells us he feared that the other people in the area, the Canaanites and the Perizzites, hearing of what they had done, might join forces to annihilate him and his family. Being fearfully preoccupied with his more powerful neighbors might indicate why no comfort was apparently given to the abused Dinah. But his two sons indignantly responded to Jacob's timid rebuke by retorting, "Should our sister be treated like a whore?" No doubt, in a culture steeped in the tradition of protecting and defending one's women lest shame befalls the family, the brothers are seen by the readers as heroes. It is Jacob who comes off as "not manning up," as appearing weak, passive, and indecisive.

Nevertheless, these actions were not forgotten by Jacob. In his farewell address prior to dying, he angrily recalls the treachery. Reuben, the eldest, who should have been the head of the twelve tribes, lost that position of power when he climbed onto the bed of his father's concubine. Privileges of being the eldest would have passed to the next eldest, Simeon, followed by Levi. However, because of their duplicity and violence, they too lose the privileges of elder due them. That privilege now passed on to Judah, the fourth-born.

So what happens to Dinah? According to some rabbinical writings, Jacob's daughter becomes the unnamed wife of Job, who was possibly non-Hebrew but was converted by his wife. Because the biblical book of Job lacks any indicators to historical setting, some rabbis have made him a contemporary of Jacob.[12] The identification of Dinah as Job's wife is based on the similarity in vocabulary between the description of Dinah's rape as a folly or outrage (*nebalah*) committed in Israel (34:7), and Job's rebuke of his wife as speaking as any foolish (*nabal*) woman might talk (Job 2:10).[13] Dinah, as Job's wife, counsels him, "Curse God, and die" (Job 2:9), a response that is possibly influenced by her own dramatic experiences at the hands of Shechem. Job counters, "Shall we receive the good at the hand of God, and not receive the bad?" This elicited response from Job would then have been referring as much to his own misfortunes as to the traumatic unresolved tragedy Dinah experienced. Yet even such sage advice falls short.

Regardless of whether Dinah was Job's wife, to suggest that the evil she endured came from the hand of God is highly troubling. Such a God is not the father figure that Jesus would eventually

---

12. Babylonian Talmud *Baba Batra* 15b.
13. *Midrash Genesis Rabbah* 19:12.

teach about. But more troubling is not having answers for the questions: Where was God while Dinah and so many others after her were being raped? Why is God silent in the face of such terror? God is quick to lay down the law on what God finds pleasing and not pleasing. What is most troubling about Dinah's testimony, or its silencing, is God's own silence. Nowhere in the text do we find confirmation that God is angered, upset, concerned, or incensed about the violence Dinah faced. Nowhere does God shed a tear over her fate.

The inclusion of Dinah's story in the biblical narrative raises disturbing questions about God. Are the authors of these texts so steeped in patriarchy that their misogynistic views are simply projected on the Deity? Because men do not care about Dinah's ordeal, then God also does not care. To find redemption, one is forced to read into the narrative one's own theology of hope and liberation. But doesn't the reading of one's theology into the text do violence to the text? Maybe so, but it is still necessary in order to save the text from itself. To leave Dinah with no recourse to God, hope, peace, love, and healing undermines the very purpose of faith.

Thus, boldly cognizant that the text itself is silent during the sexual violence faced by Dinah (and by extension millions of women today), we are forced to reread the text with an eye toward solidarity. Even though Dinah predates the Christ event, so that the promise of some future Messiah is fifteen hundred years away, which would have provided little comfort to her in the midst and aftermath of her abuse, still, the message of the gospel is that all the victims of sexual predators—present and future—are Christ crucified. For Christians, Christ's crucifixion is not an act of substitution due to our sins, as per Anselm of Canterbury; rather, it is an act of solidarity during unjust suffering. The victims of sexual abuse are among today's crucified people. They can find solidarity in a Christ who was also abused, beaten, broken, tortured, and humiliated. God was as silent during Christ's abuse, leading him to cry out why God had abandoned him (Mark 15:34), as God was silent during the sexual abuse of Dinah, and as God appears to be silent during the abuse of so many today. The responsibility that is given, as insurmountable as it might appear, is that patriarchal structures that foster sexual abuse must be dismantled. The hope that is given, as fleeting as it might appear, is that there is a resurrection after crucifixion. But even then, we should be patient if this is not enough.

35:1–20, 23–29
Testimonies from Bethel

After what occurred in Shechem, maybe Jacob had to move. Maybe his fears were legitimate, that the other people in the area, the Canaanites and the Perizzites, after hearing what Simeon and Levi did, might join forces to annihilate Jacob and his family. It does not matter if Jacob had to flee the area. "Return to Bethel and settle there" was what Jacob heard. God spoke and Jacob obeyed—a testimony for those of us who cannot hear God's voice because our ears have grown dull due to our constant disobedience. God said to leave, and like Abraham before him, Jacob left. Bethel, the most important shrine in the Jacob tradition, was where he, fleeing as a refugee, first encountered God Almighty—El Shaddai—along with the stairway to heaven. It was there that God appeared and promised to fulfill the covenant made with Abraham. It was also there that Jacob promised to follow this God if he would be materially blessed and kept safe. But years have gone by, and the events of that night grew dim. Familial fidelity to the God of Bethel was compromised with other gods, with foreign idols. Now that he was a wealthy man with many children, it was time for him to fulfill the vow originally made (28:20–21). So God called him back to where he first heard God's voice. Jacob was to put away his foreign gods, wash his clothes and himself, and make a pilgrimage to Bethel, where he was to build God an altar.

He collected all the foreign gods belonging to his clan, along with the earrings and talismans and amulets. There, under the oak tree near Shechem, he buried them. From this day forward, Israel was to have but one God. All other gods were to be forsaken for monotheism. Likewise, we today may not have foreign gods, but we still worship idols. Like Jacob, we are called to enter God's presence; but first we too must forsake our idols—our possessions, power, and privilege. Only by nailing these sins to the cross can we hope for a resurrection, becoming a new creature who can boldly enter the very presence of El Shaddai.

Once ready, they broke camp and set out toward Bethel. Scripture states that a divine terror swept through all the surrounding towns so that no one pursued them. Why would anyone pursue him? Unless, of course, they planned to exact vengeance for the treachery that Simeon and Levi carried out at Shechem. Maybe the divine terror that froze the surrounding towns in fright was the very terror Simeon and Levi unleashed on Shechem. Either way, Jacob's clan left unmolested. Once he arrived at Luz in the land of Canaan, he built God an altar and for a second time renamed the place Bethel. It was at Bethel that Deborah, Rebekah's nurse, died and was buried under an oak tree that came to be known as Allon-bacuth, "oak of tears." The appearance of Deborah as a member of the caravan is odd. She is the only servant in Genesis whose death is recorded, even though we know nothing about her, except that she left Paddan-aram with Rebekah. It is strange that the text tells us about Deborah's death, and yet is silent about the death of her mistress, the matriarch Rebekah. Moreover, how did Deborah find herself in Jacob's caravan? Did Deborah go with Jacob to Laban's house over two decades earlier? If so, why is she not mentioned as accompanying him on the journey? If not, when did she join the caravan?

Just as God appeared to Jacob several decades before on his way to Paddan-aram, now God appears again on his return. Blessing him, God reveals Godself as El Shaddai and renames him Israel. God prophesies that nations and kings will descend from him. His descendants will come to own the land originally promised to Abraham and Isaac. Jacob is told to be fruitful and multiply, an odd command considering he already has twelve children, with another one on the way. It would seem he has been quite successful in multiplying thus far.

After leaving Bethel, still some distance from Ephrath, Rachel goes into labor. Her pains are severe. During the pain of a difficult birth, her midwife attempts to comfort her by announcing that it is a boy. It would be the last thing Rachel would hear. Birth and death, life's realities, become juxtaposed.

With her dying breath Rachel names the child Ben-oni, Hebrew for "son of my sorrow," an ironic twist to her earlier cry that Jacob must give her children lest she die (30:1). Jacob renames the child Benjamin, Hebrew for "son of my right hand," or "child of my south side," possibly indicating the location where the future tribe would settle. We might assume that Jacob's renaming of the child saved the boy from living under the shadow of his father's sorrow.

> Bring that child forth, and do it with all your might! If you die in the process, so pass on over, good for you! For you actually die in a noble work and in obedience to God.
> —Martin Luther
>
> *Vom ehelichen Leben*, Weimarer Ausgabe 10,2, p. 296, trans. Susan C. Karant-Nunn and Merry E. Wiesner-Hanks

Jacob's curse that whoever stole Laban's idols would surely die (31:32) has come to pass. Rachel is buried on the road to Ephrath, at Bethlehem. At her grave Jacob raises a nonsacred monument in her honor. The site becomes a pilgrimage stop for future women who also struggle with infertility and the perils of childbirth. Jacob may not have intended for his monument to become a sacred site, but with time it was credited with magical powers. Even today, this ancient rite continues to be practiced. Women seeking to be fertile circle Rachel's tomb (Kever Rachel) seven times while winding a red string, and then they wear the string around their waist or wrist as a charm, a *segullah*.[14]

> O Merciful King! I have come to pray at the Tomb of Rachel our Matriarch. Let her good acts stand in my stead, especially her heartfelt prayers to You when she was barren which You answered. In her merit please answer my prayers and the prayers of my fellow Jews. Listen to what I utter before You, and fulfill my innermost needs.
> —Prayer recited at Rachel's tomb as per pilgrim brochure

Rachel, unlike Jacob, has no rebirth signified by a name change, nor is there any reconciliation with a sibling. Jacob and Esau may

---

14. Susan Starr Sered, "Rachel's Tomb and the Milk Grotto of the Virgin Mary: Two Women's Shrines in Bethlehem," *Journal of Feminist Studies in Religion* 2, no. 2 (1986): 7–22.

have made peace; but the text is silent concerning Rachel and Leah. Rachel's existence is important because of how it affects the men in the story, Jacob as well as her two boys. Once she accomplishes her task, birthing godly men, she, like most of the women in the Bible, fades from its pages. But Rachel is different. The text spends some time describing her death, even though it ignores her birth. She is the first woman in the biblical text to die during childbirth. But then again maybe the story is included in the text because of the circumstances surrounding her death (birthing Benjamin) and the impact it would have on her husband. This might explain why the text is silent concerning Leah's death.

Jacob's beloved has died. After Rachel's death, he is never the same, mourning her for the rest of his life (48:7). Some believe that he became a new man when God changed his name to Israel. Others maintain that a broken heart is what changed him. Maybe it was a combination of both events. Regardless, the scheming Jacob, fighting to scratch out an existence, gives way to a more passive, somewhat gullible Israel, as demonstrated in the final cycle of stories in the book of Genesis. This might explain why Reuben challenges his authority by having intercourse with his deceased wife's slave girl Bilhah.

The Jacob stories end with the death of his father, Isaac, who lived to be one hundred eighty years old. The mention of Isaac's death at this point is curious. After all, didn't he bless Jacob over two decades ago because he was close to death? In any case, Esau and Jacob are reunited one last time to bury their father.

35:21–22

Testimony of Bilhah and Zilpah

Bilhah's name could be the Hebrew word for either modesty or simplicity, or it could have derived from the Arabic word for being without concern. We know little about this woman, even what her name actually means. What we do know is that she was Rachel's servant. Rachel, who was barren, was unable to compete with her sister Leah, who had borne Jacob four sons. Filled with jealousy, she gave her slave girl Bilhah to Jacob so that any children born of her would be considered Rachel's. Like Sarah before her, Rachel was following the custom of the day as outlined in the Nuzi texts. Two sons were born to Bilhah, Dan and Naphtali (30:1–8). Leah responded by offering Jacob her own slave girl Zilpah, who bore him two more sons, Gad and Asher (30:10–12). Sadly, even though their sons represent four of the tribes of Israel, the women who bore them are not considered to be among Israel's matriarchs. They rapidly disappear from the pages of Scripture. Their very beings were reduced to possessions whose identities depended on birthing male heirs for their mistresses.

Rachel competes with her sister Leah for Jacob's attention—an attention obtained through the birthing of men. Her barrenness was a humiliation, for only through childbearing were women saved, a disturbing understanding of salvation reiterated by the author of the Timothy epistle: "Adam was not deceived, but the woman was deceived and became a transgressor. Yet, she will be saved through childbearing" (1 Tim. 2:14–15). Salvation through childbearing is a concept rooted in patriarchy, a concept that contributed to the Christian belief that the only purpose for a woman's existence was her ability to procreate. Relying on Augustine's writings, the medieval scholar Thomas Aquinas would conclude that insofar as Adam's purpose for existence was an end in and of itself, women's purpose of existence was to procreate.[15]

Women, as human breeders, have an obligation to fulfill God's purpose for them, even if it costs them their lives. Even though women's main purpose is procreation, ironically they were believed to contribute little to the process; hence neither Bilhah nor

> Sexual intercourse does no one any good, except that it harms the beloved. Intercourse performed licitly is an occasion of sin, unless done purely to beget children: A hired wife shall be accounted as a sow, but one already married to a husband shall be a tower of death to those who use her.
>
> —Clement of Alexandria
>
> *Christ the Educator* 2.10.97–98, trans. Simon P. Wood.

---

15. *Summa theologica* 1-1, q.92, a.1.

Zilpah need be considered among Israel's matriarchs. They, along with the legitimate wives of Jacob, are reduced to fertile ground, passive objects that germinated the life source exclusively found in the male seed.

Rachel and Leah had limited standing within society as official wives, but Bilhah and Zilpah had none. Yet as property they all could be trespassed so as to challenge their owner. The text tells us that Israel pitches his tents beyond Migdal-eder, Hebrew for "herd's tower," the stone overlook used by shepherds to watch over their flocks. Such structures were common on land used for grazing. Migdal-eder was located east of the river Jordan, the territory that would eventually be settled by the tribe of Reuben. There Reuben, the eldest son, slept with Jacob's concubine Bilhah. It is easy to assume that Reuben's actions were due to inappropriate sexual desire; but by sleeping with Jacob's property Reuben was challenging his father's authority. The best way to announce a public challenge to a political or social rival was by taking control of his possessions, specifically his women. Women as property become the means by which to gain authority over a rival.

We see this type of challenge repeated by David's son Absalom against his father. Absalom mounted a rebellion against his father that forced the king to leave Jerusalem. Upon entering the city, Absalom pitched a tent on the palace's housetop, in the sight of all Israel, and proceeded to rape all of his father's concubines (2 Sam. 15–16). This was not a sexual act motivated by lust. Women, as sexual property, were the means by which Absalom could wrest authority away from his father. He literally provided public notice that he had taken his father's place and was now in control of his father's possessions.

Reuben, like the future Absalom, was attempting to wrest political power from his father. But this bold move was still considered reprehensible. Women, as men's possessions, became an extension of the men who owned them. To sleep with your father's property was considered an incestuous assault on the father, and thus a grievous challenge to the overall social structure of patriarchy. Reuben was attempting to become the new man of the clan, but his father found out. While it is odd that no reprimand is mentioned (some scholars suggest that it might have been removed by the hand of a redactor), when Israel gives his final blessing Reuben loses his status as eldest (49:3–4). But missing in this political struggle between father and son is the territory where their battle takes place, the body of Bilhah. She remains the object of the story, violated by the patriarchs of the faith, and seemingly forgotten by their God.

37:1–50:26

The Story of the Twelve Sons of Israel

37:1–36

Testimonies of Joseph and His Brothers

The promise that was originally made to Abraham, inherited by Isaac, and passed to Jacob now rests with Joseph. His story becomes a bridge to Exodus, the second book of the Torah, explaining how the Hebrews at one time living in the land of promise find themselves under the yoke of Egyptian slavery and in need of liberation. Before there can be a Moses and an exodus, there must be a Joseph who leads this small clan of Hebrews into Egypt. The story opens with the introduction of Joseph, who will eventually be portrayed as a loyal servant, a man of faith regardless of the adversaries faced, a wise counselor, a successful administrator, a forgiving brother, and the savior of his people. But for now we are introduced to Joseph the teenager, who is at best naive, at worst a spoiled brat.

Joseph is the firstborn of Rachel, Israel's true love, originally barren, while her sister and slave girls were providing her husband with many children, especially sons. After years of childlessness, she finally brings forth a boy. She will eventually die while giving birth to her second child, Benjamin, Israel's twelfth and last son (35:16–20). The text further tells us that Joseph is the son of Israel's old age, and thus Israel loves him more than all of his other sons. He probably saw Joseph as the product of his true love; this would explain why he showered the boy with unhealthy attention.

We are further told that Joseph, the seventeen-year-old lad, shepherded the flocks with his brothers, specifically the sons of the slave women Bilhah and Zilpah. Maybe because these brothers occupy lower stations, being born to slaves and not legitimate wives, or maybe because Joseph is simply a tattletale, Joseph reports to his father the evil spoken by them.

Just as Israel's mother, Rebekah, loved and favored him over and against his brother Esau, now the elder Israel shows partiality toward Joseph. The biblical motif of favoring the youngest becomes a pattern that would eventually benefit the future kings David and Solomon when the story is written during their times.

Israel, the doting father, has a special coat made for Joseph, a coat with long sleeves, although the Septuagint (the Greek translation of the text) will translate this term as "a coat of many colors" (so KJV). In a society where laborers wore shorter garments to free their limbs for manual work, a long-sleeved coat hinted at not having to participate in daily toil. Maybe after the incident with the sons of Bilhah and Zilpah, Israel thought it best not to have Joseph partake in the seminomadic family trade. The situation between Joseph and his brothers has deteriorated so much that his brothers are incapable of even giving him the customary greeting of *shalom*—peace. Besides tattling on his brothers, the outward expression of preference by Israel demonstrated by the gift of the long-sleeved coat, and being excused from participating in hard work, Joseph further contributes to his brothers' ire by having dreams and being foolish enough to share them.

Upon a rock near a bush were an ape and his two sons, of whom he loved the younger and hated the elder. When a watchful leopard descended from his lair the ape trembled for himself and the son he loved. . . . Said the ape: "Of him that I hate I shall know how to be bereft; I shall hide my face from him and he shall be for devouring." And he took him and cast him over his back, intending to present him to the leopard first. But the younger, upon whom he took pity, he carried between his legs and ran. . . . When the ape saw that he could not throw [the hated son on his back to the ground] and the leopard was drawing very nigh, he forsook the one he loved and himself escaped with the one that held sway over his back. . . . The parable: A man should love his sons in equal measures, for him who he loves best and in whom he reposes his hope the wheel will suddenly ravish away; shut thine eye upon him and he is gone. But him that he hated and kept afar will restore his soul and sustain his old age.

Berechiah ben Natronai ha-Nakdan (12th/13th century)

Fables of a Jewish Aesop, trans. from the *Fox Fables of Berechiah ha-Nakdan* by Moses Hadas (Boston: David R. Godine, 2001), 190–91.

Joseph has two dreams. In the first, the brothers are binding sheaves in the countryside. Joseph's sheaves rise upright, while those of his brothers bow to his sheaves. An interpreter is not needed to reveal the dream's meaning. The brothers clearly understand. "So you want to lord it over us," they exclaim, thus hating him even more on account of his dreams. No doubt, Joseph's dream hints at the future with a possible subtle reference to how it will be fulfilled. The agricultural policies Joseph will eventually implement in Egypt will force his brothers (i.e., sheaves) to bow before him. For now, Joseph's dream is perceived as a threat, for if it comes true, the youngest will rule over his elders.

In Joseph's second dream, the sun, moon, and eleven stars bow to him. But in recounting this dream Joseph has gone too far, leading even his father to bark, "A fine dream to have!" The dream's meaning is again clear: father, mother (even though she is dead), and brothers are to bow down before Joseph. Although the father rebukes Joseph for his dream, and probably for the first time aligns himself with the brothers, it is too late. The damage is done and it is beyond repair, as indicated by the brothers' silence and lack of protest to this latest dream. Ignoring a person will prove to be more dangerous than a simple rebuke.

One day, the brothers are off pasturing their father's flock at Shechem. We do not know if Benjamin has joined them; since he is younger than Joseph, he might have stayed home. Israel sends Joseph to check up on his brothers and report back. After wandering around looking for them, he discovers they have moved to Dothan. As he approaches them, the brothers notice him coming at a distance. They conspire to kill the dreams and the one dreaming them. By killing the dreamer, maybe the dreams will not become a reality. Unless they want to bow down before Joseph, he will need to be eliminated.

Dreams are dangerous and those who dream them must be killed, for they point to a reality that does not yet exist. The wish usually held by those who are oppressed and marginalized for a world undergirded by social justice is all too often dismissed as utopian by those benefiting by the present social structures. The idea of a just society is as utopian as Isaiah's dream where "the wolf shall live with the lamb, the leopard shall lie down with the kid" (Isa. 11:6). Yet the utopian dreams of both Isaiah and today's disenfranchised are affirmed with an open-eyed awareness of the present power structures. The dreams of the marginalized are not utopian in the sense of being based on the fantasy world of imagination; rather, these are feet-on-the-ground utopian dreams anchored in the realism of the dispossessed.

The dreams of the oppressed are not flights from present reality to an illusionary world, but a product of a hopelessness that propels toward a praxis that attempts to perfect reality and prevent the status quo from absolutizing itself. The dreams held by the marginalized are not some naive idealism where a future perfect, yet illusionary, social order is established. Utopian dreams, as understood by the disenfranchised, are a rejection of the present social order grounded in structures designed to perpetrate racism, sexism, and classism, designed so that the few can be privileged by all the earth has to offer. In short, it is utopian dreams that protest the way things presently are and imagine, based on the reality of the oppressed, how society can be restructured to create a more just social order. The function of dreams is to guide praxis, even though utopia clashes with the "realism" of those who benefit from the present status quo. For these reasons, dreamers like Martin Luther King Jr., who saw a vision of what could be, must be killed lest they change the realism of their times.

> Today, more than ever, is the time to remember that God has given to all humanity what is necessary for its sustenance. The goods of this earth do not belong exclusively to certain persons or to certain social groups, whatever their knowledge or place in society may be. The goods belong to all. . . . We can call this a utopian perspective, but in a realistic sense of the word, which rejects an inhuman situation and pursues relationships of justice and cooperation between persons.
> —Gustavo Gutiérrez
>
> *A Theology of Liberation*, 15th anniversary ed., trans. and ed. Sister Caridad Inda and John Eagleson (Maryknoll, NY: Orbis, 1988), 121.

No doubt the brothers' decision to kill Joseph harks back to the earlier Cain and Abel story. But one of the brothers, wishing to avoid bloodshed, sets out to rescue Joseph from death, but which one, and how? Chapter 37 probably provides the best example of a conflation of two separate versions of the same story, showing how source analysis operates. The narrative combines the E version, which privileges the northern kingdom of Israel, with the J version, which supports more the southern kingdom of Judah. By dividing the text according to the usage of God's name, Elohim (E) or Yahweh (J), and by the usage of Joseph's father name, Jacob (E) or Israel (J), we can detect the two different narratives that make up chapter 37. The J version makes Judah, the major tribe of the southern kingdom, the better brother, the one who saves Joseph's life. In this version he is sold to a caravan of Ishmaelites (descendants of Isaac's half brother by Hagar), who are passing by, for twenty shekels, the monetary value of a male his age (Lev. 27:5). In the E version, however, Reuben, the progenitor of a major tribe from the northern kingdom, is the hero, the one attempting to save Joseph's life by throwing him in a well, to be rescued later. Meanwhile, Joseph is kidnapped by Midianite traders (descendants of Isaac's half brother by Keturah) while the brothers are eating lunch.

As Joseph leaves the scene, heading toward Egypt, the brothers are left with the problem of explaining his disappearance. They probably did not wish to cause their father great distress; however, more and greater deceit is usually needed to cover up the original lie. They slaughter a goat and dip Joseph's long-sleeved coat in the blood. In one sense they never lie to their father, but they do participate in the sin of omission. They simply show him the bloody coat and ask if it belongs to Joseph. It is Israel who concludes his beloved son was devoured by some wild beast. The one who deceived his father out of a blessing is now deceived by his own sons. The sins of the father now return to him through his sons.

Israel is so distraught over the supposed death of his son that he refuses to be comforted, ending intimate communication with the rest of his family. He tears his clothes as a sign of mourning and puts on a loincloth of sackcloth. Sackcloth was a coarse, dark-colored material made of goat or camel hair that was extremely uncomfortable. His loss is so great he expects to go down mourning to Sheol (mentioned here for the first time in the biblical text), the netherworld located in the depths of the earth where departed spirits go. Thus the chapter ends with Joseph's family surrounded by gloom.

38:1–30
Testimony of Tamar

The Joseph novella is briefly interrupted with an interpolated story concerning Tamar (whose name means "palm tree") and her father-in-law, Judah, one of Joseph's brothers. Judah, the fourth son of Jacob and Leah, leaves his family to stay with Hirah, of whom we know nothing, in a small town called Adullam, located some twelve miles southwest of Bethlehem. While there, he marries an unnamed Canaanite. That he is not condemned for marrying a "foreign" woman (even though it is Judah who is the foreigner) indicates that this text must be a very old story. Judah's unnamed wife bears him three sons: Er, Onan, and Shelah. After some time, Judah chooses a wife from the local people for his eldest son. Her name is Tamar.

The purpose of this story is to ensure the establishment of Judah's male line, told from and for the male's point of view, and connect this bloodline with the land of southern Canaan. Tamar, the foreign woman in the story, even though she is on her own land, becomes the object by which the subject's goal of producing an heir is accomplished. In patriarchy one must dominate (usually the male), while another must submit (usually women, children, and men conquered through war). A careful reading of the Hebrew text reveals few exceptions. For example, Deborah the judge (Judg. 4) and Queen Esther (in the book of Esther) are able to maneuver within the patriarchal structures and carve out a space for themselves from which to exercise leadership. The identities of women are reduced in the biblical text to an extension of their male counterparts, who are presented as the possessors of their female bodies. Tamar is no exception.

A woman's main purpose within the book of Genesis is to produce heirs, specifically male heirs—a theme often repeated throughout the rest of the biblical text. The barren matriarch Sarai offers her slave girl Hagar to Abram for rape so that he can have an heir (16:2). Rachel, Jacob's wife, demands of her husband, "Give me children, or I shall die!" (30:1), as she competes with her sister Leah, also Jacob's wife, for his attention—an attention obtained through the birthing of men. In the minds of these women, barrenness was a humiliation. Yet Johanna W. H. Bos reminds us:

> The story of Tamar points in the direction of a gynocentric bias. The men in the story are wrongheaded irresponsible bunglers, who don't see straight. They are shown up as such by Tamar, who notices correctly and who causes Judah such an "eye-opener" that his view of reality is restored. The tone in which the men are discussed, summarily dispatched by God, or acting as if they were in charge and all the while making fools of themselves, points to a gynocentric bias as well.[1]

According to the story, Tamar married Judah's oldest son, Er; however, Er offended God (we do not know how) and as a result died. The God revealed in this story is disturbing—a God that brings death to those who offend God. Yet when we consider how many of the wicked who made their riches on the sweat and blood of the disenfranchised and yet are able to die peacefully on their satin-sheeted beds, all the while the righteous undergo meaningless if not painful lives and deaths, we are left wondering about the compassion and justice of such a God. Nevertheless, the purpose of the story is not to reveal God's character, but to teach a lesson about human responsibility. To teach this lesson, Er had to die; and what quicker way to eliminate him from the scene than to attribute his demise to God?

Unfortunately, Er died childless. Following ancient tradition, Onan, Er's brother, took Tamar as his wife to perform his duty of impregnating her so that a child could be born in his brother's name. It was considered disastrous for a man to die without an heir to perpetuate his name, hence the development of the custom

---

1. Johanna W. H. Bos, "Out of the Shadows: Genesis 38; Judges 4:17–22; Ruth 3," in *Reasoning with the Foxes: Female Wit in a World of Male Power*, ed. J. Cheryl Exum and Johanna W. H. Bos, *Semeia* 42 (Atlanta: Scholars Press, 1988), 48–49.

of levirate marriage—a custom that eventually was canonized in Deuteronomy 25:5–10. Besides ensuring the deceased man had an heir, the act of marrying one's dead brother's widow kept property within the deceased husband's family, preventing it from going to the household of another man whom the widow might marry.

Onan, for reasons we do not know, refused to impregnate Tamar. Whenever he copulated with Tamar he would pull out before climaxing and spill his seed on the ground. God found this offensive and "put him to death." Christian commentators have historically understood Onan's sin to be masturbation because he "spilled his semen on the ground." Hence a synonym for masturbation is onanism, an eighteenth-century term derived from his name. But the sin of Onan was not masturbation. According to the text, he spilled his seed on the ground because he deliberately abdicated his duty of ensuring that his brother's name would continue. To be specific, his sin was avoiding his levirate obligation to his dead brother by performing coitus interruptus. Maybe he selfishly hoped to split his father's inheritance with his younger surviving brother, leaving out any possible descendants of Tamar.

Although this story has nothing to do with what has come to be known as "the private sin," Genesis 38:1–11 has historically been used to condemn masturbation. For many, either by choice or circumstance, masturbation becomes a way of stimulating sexual gratification and/or reducing sexual tension. Most studies show that for the vast majority masturbation starts around the age of ten and continues until death.[2] Despite the fact that almost every human being has masturbated at some time in his or her life, and even though there is no biblical justification for the prohibition of masturbation, it has long been considered a sin among Christians, even today. The original belief behind this view was that the woman, as an incubator, only provided nutrition to the creation of life. The woman's womb was like a field waiting for the insemination of the male seed, which contained all the necessary substance required for human life. Within the male sperm existed the entire potential child. The womb, by contrast, was neutral, adding nothing to

2. Brian Alexander, "Unleashing Your Wild Side," MSNBC, May 31, 2005.

the child's genetic makeup. Therefore, to waste male sperm, as in the case of masturbation, was to literally destroy the potential for human life. For these same reasons contraceptive devices, while preventing pregnancy, still spilled the male seed, and thus are akin to murder. Religious leaders like Martin Luther saw onanism as a sin more hideous than heterosexual rape, because at least rape was in accordance with nature, while masturbation was considered to be unnatural.[3]

Tamar, twice widowed, found herself with no husband or children, a precarious situation for any woman living within a patriarchal society. Her only hope of maintaining a "good" name for herself and obtaining financial security is to be married to the next brother. But Judah, fearful that his youngest might meet the same fate as his older brothers, tells Tamar to return to her father until Shelah comes of age. Prohibited from marrying any other man but her dead husband's brother, she becomes marginalized, with no way of securing a future. Judah must have thought that there was something wrong with Tamar, who, like the black widow spider, seemed to lose her husbands to death. It never occurred to him that his sons may have been responsible for their own demise. With the passage of time, Tamar realized her father-in-law was not going to honor the tradition that would have required Shelah marrying her. Even though she had custom and the law on her side, she, as a woman, was powerless, relegated to the margins. She lacked the means of holding those with power over her accountable.

> Onan must have been a malicious and incorrigible scoundrel. [Masturbation] is a most disgraceful sin. It is far more atrocious than incest and adultery. We call it unchastity, yes, a Sodomitic sin.
>
> —Martin Luther
>
> *Luther's Works*, vol. 7: *Lectures on Genesis: Chapters 38–44*, ed. Jaroslav Pelikan, trans. Paul D. Pahl (St. Louis: Concordia Publishing House, 1965), 20.

When she hears that her father-in-law will be visiting her town on business (it was the season of sheepshearing), she starts pondering how to force his hand so that he meets his obligations. Unable to

3. Luther, *Lectures on Genesis*, 7:20.

confront Judah directly, Tamar devises a plan, using the power of her sexuality, to force Judah to act "justly" according to tradition. Like so many women throughout history, she uses her body to survive in a patriarchal society. She plays the prostitute and tricks the recently widowed Judah to lay with her. Although Tamar engages in a bold and risky act—risky because she could be killed for becoming pregnant while not being married—she overshadows Judah for a brief moment in time, only to rapidly disappear from the narrative as soon as she accomplishes her assigned task and produces an heir.

The initiative Tamar shows makes her an archetype for all who are marginalized, not just women. Tamar shows how playing the role of the trickster to subvert prevailing oppressive structures is necessary to force those oblivious of their power and privilege to do justice. Tamar removes her widow's garb and puts on a veil commonly used by prostitutes, for a harlot, according to the book of Proverbs, is known by her attire (Prov. 7:10). She sits by the side of the road where she expects Judah will be traversing. Noticing her, Judah is enticed to employ her services. Strange that he does not recognize his daughter-in-law, the wife of his two deceased sons. Surely Judah suffers from a lack of vision.

Tamar plays the prostitute, participating in what has come to be known as the oldest profession. For many, prostitution is immoral, and they are right, but not because it involves sex. Prostitution is immoral because it relies on exploiting the vulnerability of women or men (mostly women) by exchanging their worth and dignity for a few dollars. Regardless that some have attempted to portray prostitutes as fully liberated women in control of their sexuality, the truth remains that it is a system predominantly run by men, at the service of men, for the profit of men. Prostitutes are objects created and condemned by the same male-centered society that benefits from their existence, making prostitution one of the oldest male-dominated and sexually abusive social structures.

Yet the women like Tamar, who are forced into prostitution for economic reasons, are defined by and scorned because of their sexual activities. They become "whores," yet when Solomon takes seven hundred wives of royal birth and three hundred mistresses (concubines), we fail to apply the same term to him. Men are seldom negatively defined by their sexual activities, nor are they held liable for procuring the sexual services of women. Regardless of society's bias toward prostitutes, for Jesus they were the ones entering heaven before the religious leaders of his day who observed God's commands and dictates (Matt. 21:31), perhaps because Jesus understood that these women were the oppressed victims of a so-called victimless crime in which intercourse is reduced to a commercial transaction.

The Bible distinguishes between secular prostitution and prostitution connected with a religious cult. The biblical text appears to treat secular prostitution as natural and necessary. Among the sexual laws appearing in the Hebrew Bible, none forbids a man from visiting a secular prostitute, as illustrated by the Hebrew spies visiting Rahab's brothel in Jericho (Josh. 2:1), or Samson spending the night with a prostitute (Judg. 16:1–3). In these stories the women are not stigmatized. None of these secular prostitutes who serviced these holy men of God is condemned; rather, most of them are portrayed as heroines, with Rahab finding a favorable spot in Jesus' genealogy (Matt. 1:5). Yet if a man was to marry, and discover on his wedding night that his bride was not a virgin, then he had every right to have her stoned for "prostituting herself in her father's house" (Deut. 22:21). What made prostitution wrong in the Hebrew Bible was not the exchange of currency for the chance to copulate, but rather the removal of intercourse from the social system that reduced women to property within a hierarchical male-centered power structure.[4]

The only time the biblical text condemns prostitution is when such action is linked to temple worship. It is important to remember that Yahweh's principal nemeses were the fertility god Baal and the goddess Asherah. Priests of these fertility gods practiced what is called an imitative or homeopathic magic.[5] The rituals practiced by these priests consecrated to fertility gods were based on the law of similarity, which maintained that like produces like. Because they thought that an effect resembled its cause, these priests believed that they could produce any desired effect merely by imitating it. The

4. L. William Countryman, *Dirt, Greed, and Sex: Sexual Ethics in the New Testament and Their Implications for Today* (Philadelphia: Fortress Press, 1988), 164.

5. Sir James George Frazer, *The Golden Bough: A Study in Magic and Religion*, abridged ed. (New York: Macmillan, 1951), 12.

ritual, hoping to create fecundity for crops and livestock, consisted of sexual acts by and with temple prostitutes in the sanctuary to imitate what they hoped to accomplish in the fields. Those who served as temple prostitutes were male and female. For these cultic reasons, these temple prostitutes are banned from God's people as "abhorrent" or a "detestable thing," occupying the lowest levels of social status (Deut. 23:18).

None of Yahweh's priests could marry a prostitute (Lev. 21:7), and if one of the priest's daughters was to become a prostitute, her father was obligated to burn her alive (Lev. 21:9). Yet Jesus' dealings with prostitutes seem to have been influenced by the book of Proverbs. Although the speaker in Proverbs looks down on prostitutes as the antithesis of wisdom (Prov. 7), condemnation is mainly reserved for the man who hires her services. It is he who is the fool, frittering away his wealth (Prov. 29:3). Consequently, Jesus was not afraid to associate with women of so-called bad reputation (Luke 7:36–50), using prostitutes as positive examples for religious leaders to emulate (Matt. 21:31). Why not condemn the prostitute? Because in a patriarchal social order where a woman's primary means of survival is to be under the authority of a father, husband, or son, she who is without a man has little choice for survival than to earn her meals by selling her body. It is not the woman who is to be blamed, but the men who designed the social structures that prevent her from surviving apart from a man. The man is the one who creates the circumstances for a woman to turn to prostitution, and then takes advantage of her situation by paying her.

Prostitution, as a lawful immorality, was tolerated throughout most of Christian history because it protected virtuous Christian wives from the lustful demands of their husbands, and maintained harmony within the political sphere. Its absence, it was believed, would disrupt society, casting it into a debauched chaos. Early Roman moralists, like Cato the Censor, Cicero, and Seneca, regarded prostitution as necessary because it prevented men from breaking up the marriages of others. During the Crusades, prostitution increased. Pious warriors for the Lord were not expected to abstain from intercourse just because they were away from their wives. According to calculations kept by the Templars (the order responsible for keeping records of the Crusades), thirteen thousand prostitutes were required in one year alone just to satisfy the desires of these saintly warriors.[6] Thomas Aquinas, relying on the writings of Augustine, who urged husbands to go to prostitutes rather than commit adultery (with another man's woman),[7] believed that prostitution served a crucial and necessary social function.

Besides relieving the wife from her husband's sexual advances, prostitution was believed to be a safety valve geared to reduce sodomy, adultery, rape, incest, and domestic violence.[8] In Aquinas's mind it appeared better to exchange money for sex than to relieve sexual "lust" within a marriage.

> Thus, Augustine says that a whore acts in the world as the bilge in a ship or the sewer in a palace: "Remove the sewer, and you will fill the place with a stench." Similarly, concerning the bilge, he says: "Take away whores from the world and you will fill it with sodomy."
>
> —Ptolemy of Lucca and Thomas Aquinas
>
> *On the Government of Rules* (De Regimine Principum), trans. James M. Blythe, 4.14.6.

The Curia, the ensemble of ministries responsible for assisting the pope to govern the Catholic Church, partially financed the building of St. Peter's Cathedral in the Vatican through a tax on prostitution. The sum collected was four times more than what Pope Leo X expected to collect from the sales of indulgences in Germany. Yet it is the sale of indulgences that is most remembered as the main means for the construction of St. Peter's,[9] while most ignore that the cathedral was partially built on the backs of women (or more accurately stated, women on their backs). With the coming of the Protestant Reformation, a focus on adultery, which included prostitution, was rethought by men. Martin Luther used harsh comments when referring to both adulterers and prostitutes. He attempted to eradicate prostitution, but eventually

6. Richard Lewinsohn, *A History of Sexual Customs*, trans. Alexander Mayce (New York: Fawcett Premier Book, 1958), 69, 135.

7. *On the Good of Marriage* 8, 12.

8. Ptolemy of Lucca and Thomas Aquinas, *On the Government of Rules* (De Regimine Principum), trans. James M. Blythe, 4.14.6.

9. Lewinsohn, *History of Sexual Customs*, 157.

left the brothels alone, concerned that their closure might create social unrest.

Judah, like so many great religious leaders after him, secures the services of the supposed prostitute; but first he negotiates a price in the form of a goat. To secure that payment would be made at the conclusion of the interaction, he leaves behind some collateral: the insignia that signifies his rank and status, in the form of his signet (the official means of identification), cord (which holds his signet around his neck), and staff (used to control his flock, symbolizing his authority). After meeting his needs and returning to camp, he sends his friend Hirah the Adullamite to deliver payment, but the "temple prostitute," according to the text, has disappeared; and to make matters worse, no one in the village has ever heard of or seen her. That none of the townsmen even thought of Tamar serves as a testimony to her virtue, for none considered her to be promiscuous even while waiting for Judah to act justly. What is damning for Judah is that Hirah is looking for the temple prostitute, not a secular prostitute, thus indicating that Judah's sin may have been religious unfaithfulness to God. Maybe in Judah's mind sexual intercourse with sacred prostitutes would ensure fecundity among his flock through a sympathetic magic that reproduces the act of fertility. Judah, fearful he would become a laughingstock, quickly dismisses the matter.

Three months pass, and Tamar is discovered to be with child. Judah is publicly shamed by a woman under his authority who became pregnant; patriarchy conferred on him the right to restore his honor by finding the man who trespassed on his "property" and have them both stoned. But Judah is impetuous, calling for her and her unborn child to be burned at the stake in accordance with the eventual biblical law concerning daughters of priests who played the harlot (Lev. 21:9). Maybe he is seeking revenge for what he has always believed was the cause of death of his two eldest sons? At the moment of crisis, Tamar acts, producing the symbols identifying the man responsible for her pregnancy so that she, along with the father of her unborn child, could be sentenced to death. Of course, the symbols belong to Judah. To condemn her is to condemn himself. Less an act of magnanimous rectitude and more an attempt at self-preservation, Judah, with his back against the wall, is forced to publicly acknowledge her righteousness, a righteousness that surpasses his own. The subversive act of Tamar as trickster forces Judah to live up to the justice that was always due her.

The story ends with Tamar giving birth to two children, twins by the names Perez and Zerah, echoing the similar birth narrative of Esau and Jacob by Rebekah. And while Tamar disappears from the narrative, accomplishing her assigned task of producing male heirs, we are left questioning if these children are the result of incest. The book of Leviticus prohibits a man from engaging in sex with his daughter-in-law, punishable with both being put to death (Lev. 18:15; 20:12). Nevertheless, Tamar does make one more brief appearance in the biblical text—in Jesus' genealogy (Matt. 1:3).

39:1–23; 41:45, 50–52
Testimony of Potiphar's Wife

What becomes of Joseph, who is sold into slavery by his brothers? How does he fare in the alien land of Egypt? The chapter opens by addressing these questions and concerns. The stage is set to narrate Joseph's rise to power and privilege, his downfall, and his rise to even greater power and privilege. Joseph the slave is sold to an Egyptian named Potiphar. The Hebrew word *saris* is used to describe Potiphar's position within the Egyptian hierarchy. In later contexts *saris* is usually translated as "eunuch," but here and in other early contexts it means "officer" or "official." This position is further described as *sar hattabbahim*, "captain of the guards." While none of the English translations use the word "eunuch" in association with Potiphar, the Babylonian Talmud does. According to rabbinical literature, Potiphar bought Joseph, who was a very beautiful lad, because of his sexual desire for Joseph. In order to protect Joseph, the angel Gabriel was sent to castrate Potiphar, who henceforth was known as Potiphera.[10] If indeed Potiphar was made a eunuch, it might explain why his wife would have felt sexually unfulfilled.

10. Babylonian Talmud, *Sotah* 13a.

The text tells us that God was with Joseph, so all went well with him. Potiphar sees God's hand on Joseph and promotes him to run his household. As the household steward, everything was entrusted to Joseph except the food Potiphar ate. In return, the Lord blessed Potiphar's house for Joseph's sake, thus fulfilling the promise made to Abraham by God that all the tribes of the earth will be blessed through Abraham's seed (12:3). At first glance, the text seems to say that a right relationship with God leads to prosperity for the believer. Similar texts have been used as proof text for a theological belief that has come to be known as "prosperity theology." According to this theology, those who have sufficient faith will always be blessed with wealth and health.

But if one does well and prospers (e.g., the robber barons of the Gilead Age, or even those of this age), does this mean that God is with them? Does prosperity signify being chosen by God? If so, does God then make a preferential option for the rich and wealthy? Yet the Joseph story shows that because of his righteousness, Joseph suffers. True, he may in the future prosper again as Pharaoh's main adviser, but as Job will later remind us, prosperity is not always the end result. Trials and tribulations occur because we lack righteousness, they occur because we are righteous, and they occur for no reason at all. The danger of equating prosperity with God's blessings is that the reverse side of that argument would indicate that dispossession or disenfranchisement is God's curse on the faithless. The good news is not that Joseph prospers because the Lord is with him, but that the Lord is with Joseph. God is present in blessings and through hardships, in feast and in famine. Whether one is sitting on a throne or hanging from a cross, one is never alone. Blessings are not health and wealth; blessings are the presence of the Divine in the everyday.

God's presence does not mean that Joseph will be spared from hardships. Joseph will suffer because he is well built and handsome. This beautiful lad will tempt Potiphar's nameless wife, who will demand that Joseph engage with her in a sexual relationship.

The purpose of the story is to show the reader a faithful hero, faithful to God and to his master. Remember, Joseph is a slave in Potiphar's house, soon to spend years in a prison cell based on a false accusation. Rather than rebel against Potiphar, his enslaver, and seek

And the women in the city said, "[Potiphar's] wife is asking of her slave-boy [Joseph] an ill deed. Indeed he has smitten her to the heart with love. We behold her in plain aberration." And when she heard of their sly talk, she sent for them and prepared for them a cushioned couch (to lie on at the feast) and gave to every one of them a knife and said (to Joseph), "Come out unto them!" And when they saw him they exalted him and cut their hands, exclaiming, "Allah Blameless! This is not a human being. This is no other than some gracious angel!"

—Qur'an 12:30–31, trans. Muhammad Marmaduke Pickthall

liberation from forced servitude, he submits to Potiphar's rule—a troubling text that has been used since then against slaves as a model to emulate on godly submission to masters.

This chapter sets the stage for Joseph's ultimate rise—but first he must sink to the lowest point of his life. The Joseph of the previous chapters who existed in the favoritism of his father, who used bad judgment by revealing his vain and egotistical dreams to his brothers, finally matures. He is here portrayed as a young man of integrity who would not betray his employer (even if that employer is a slave master) or, more importantly, his God. Within this story, Potiphar's nameless wife plays a pivotal role.

The story plot is very similar to, and may be loosely based on, an Egyptian tale probably written for Seti II (1209–1205 BCE) of the Nineteenth Dynasty called the *Tale of Two Brothers*. As in the Joseph story, the younger brother, Bata, works as overseer in his older brother Anubis's house, only to be seduced by Anubis's nameless wife. One major difference is that rather than throwing his brother into prison, Anubis attempts to kill Bata, only to be convinced that his younger brother was innocent; then he proceeds to kill his wife.

In both the *Tale of Two Brothers* and the Genesis story of Joseph, the nameless wife is portrayed as a wanton woman, the quintessence of a salacious cougar. Although Potiphar's wife remains nameless in the biblical text, she is called, according to Jewish medieval tradition, Zuleika. Such licentious women have become a literary one-dimensional caricature who signifies the worn-out theme of the alluring wiles of a seductress. Her predictable role usually leads to the transformation of the man of God, who is able to resist her temptation. Stories such as these elicit a fear of women's sexuality. Such women are deemed dangerous because, like Delilah who tempted Samson the judge, they are the few women in the Bible who engaged in sex without the express goal of procreation. Such women are deemed wicked because they express their sexuality, hence justifying the need to keep such women under control, specifically under the control of men, lest their uncontrolled sexuality bring shame to the husband's or father's honor.

The man's place within the ancient social order was determined by either acquiring honor or inducing shame. Men maintained the honor of their families while simultaneously avoiding anything that might bring shame on their names. Generally speaking, honor was male-centered, for through the man's participation in the public sphere, honor would increase or decrease through interacting with other men. While honor is achieved in the public sphere, shame is created within the private sphere. Because of patriarchy, a woman who belonged to a man, yet was used by someone else, brought shame to the "owner" of her body.

Women who do not remain secure in the household under a man's supervision served as a timeless warning that godly men should fear and must avoid. In such stories, Joseph epitomizes the hero, while Samson will epitomize the failure. Although Potiphar's wife appears as a one-dimensional villain, she is an essential character who moves the story forward, a character that is not developed, but nevertheless demonstrates that God's will triumphs when men of faith remain steadfast. A counternarrative to the vilifying of Potiphar's wife is the story of Susanna, which appears in neither the Hebrew nor Protestant Bible, although it is part of the Catholic canon (as one of the books Protestants call deuterocanonical or apocryphal). Susanna is part of the book of Daniel, appearing as chapter 13. In this story, the theme of Joseph's false accusation is retold, only this time the gender roles are reversed. It is the virtuous Susanna who is accused of adultery by the two elders whose sexual advances she rebuffs. In this recounting, Susanna is the story's innocent victim, saved by the hero Daniel.

It is true that Potiphar's nameless wife is portrayed as the villain of the story. Still, we need to ask if her act of asserting her sexuality can be viewed as an act of rebellion against her relegated role within patriarchy. While not excusing her unfaithfulness to her husband, or her bearing false witness against an innocent lad, we are left to wonder, given her oppression within patriarchy, if her act was an attempt for the nameless wife to find subjectivity. Is she solely responsible in her attempt to seduce Joseph? Can Potiphar, or even Joseph, share in the blame? Is she simply a pawn in some divine game that eventually gets Joseph to be the steward of Pharaoh's court?

No doubt her husband can share in the blame if she is stuck in a sexless relationship in which she probably had no say as to who she would marry. What if her husband trusted his wife, instead of Joseph, to manage the household? Obviously, if she was the overseer, there would be no need for Joseph. Also, if her daily attempts to seduce Joseph were rebuffed, what was Joseph doing alone in the house with her? Joseph is, at the very least, demonstrating poor judgment in allowing himself to be alone with this woman. He may have shown restraint by refusing her advances, but did he allow himself to bask in her attention?

Regardless of her reasons for seducing Joseph, it is important to remember that adultery is considered a sin, not only against the husband but also against God. The marriage bonds were considered sacred and thus protected by the Deity, eventually becoming one of the Ten Commandments. But before we fully condemn Potiphar's wife for her unfaithfulness, we should ask why we failed to show the same indignation in previous chapters of Genesis when the faith's patriarchs (i.e., Abraham and Jacob)—married men—committed adultery by raping (Hagar) or marrying other women beyond their first wife. We excuse them, and not Potiphar's wife, because adultery did not apply to men.

Adultery, as a violation of trust within a marriage, is a modern concept that should not be read into the biblical text. As such, adultery was not regulated under marriage or relationship in biblical categories; rather, adultery was a transgression concerning property rights. Throughout Genesis and the rest of the Hebrew Bible, women (as well as children) are the possessions of men. Man, due to patriarchy, had nearly unlimited rights and power over wives and children. As a possession, women were often equated with other objects, as demonstrated in the last commandment, "Thou shalt not covet thy neighbor's house, wife, slave, ox, or donkey" (Exod. 20:17, my trans.). The woman, like a house, slave, ox, or donkey, is reduced to an object, just another possession—another piece of property that belonged to the man, and thus should not be coveted by another man. To engage in adultery was to trespass another man's rights to his property, not a violation of trust created within marriage. Intercourse with a woman who belonged to another man fell under thievery of the other man's rights to his woman's body and his right to legitimate offspring.

While the unfaithful wife faced harsh punishment (i.e., death), the man reserved for himself the right to engage in intercourse with a multitude of women, even to the point of keeping as possessions as many as his means permitted. The commandment, "Thou shalt not commit adultery" (Exod. 20:14 KJV), could be transgressed only by women. The only time a man could be accused of adultery was if he trespassed on another man's "property," hence violating another man's rights (Lev. 20:10). We can see this understanding of adultery played out in the Gospel of John, where a woman is brought to Jesus, "caught in the very act of committing adultery" (John 8:3–11). It is interesting that only she is brought to Jesus. But if she was caught in the *very act*, wouldn't there have been another person in the room? She alone is brought to Jesus because only she sinned. Her sexual partner's marital status was irrelevant because patriarchy allowed him to engage in multiple sexual relationships. Consequently, no man needed to be brought to Jesus for punishment. It is important to note that Jesus exposed the hypocrisy of patriarchy. When Jesus instructed those who were

> Just when . . . a man needed a bit of peace and privacy in his own home, who should start spouting texts and interpreting God's word in his own home, women. . . . It was well known that with a woman, a dog and a walnut tree, the more you beat 'em the better they be. Equally "natural" was the duplicity of women. According to proverbial wisdom they were saints in the church, angels in the streets, devils in the kitchen and apes in bed.
> —Sheila Rowbotham
>
> Commenting on the prevalent attitudes of colonial Massachusetts. *Women, Resistance and Revolution* (New York: Random House, 1972), 17–18.

without sin to throw the first stone, all the men walked away because they were no different than the one they accused.

More disturbing than Potiphar's wife's attempted tryst with Joseph is the issue of class and ethnic discrimination that privileges this powerless woman of the dominant culture. When her advances fail, she quickly plays on xenophobic sentiments. "See," she says, "my husband has brought among us a Hebrew to insult us." One can hear the disgust with which she pejoratively refers to Joseph as "a Hebrew." One can hear a similar accusatory tone if she would have said, "You brought a black/Latino/Asian/Indian man into our home to insult us," although more than likely an offensive slur would be used. Men of color, historically accused of violating the virtues of white women, can relate to Joseph's predicament.

Men who do not belong to the dominant culture due to race or ethnicity have usually been portrayed as sexually dangerous to civilization, specifically white civilization. Such men are both emasculated in order to keep them at the lowest rungs of society, while simultaneously feared because they might rebel against their relegated place. These male bodies of color are normatively seen and perceived as overly sexualized beings who invoke fascination of and fear for their prowess. We can note the mixing of fear and fascination as portrayed in classical movies by Latino actors like Ricardo Montalban, who was consistently cast as the stereotypical Latin lover, or in the modern popularity of plantation "bodice ripper" novels. Such men of color are dangerous, for at any time they can threaten white civilization, usually symbolized as a white woman. Euro-Americans have historically been taught, through images within popular culture, that the hot Latino Don Juan or the black rapist image signifies aggressiveness and carnality. While black, brown, red, and yellow male bodies are feared; female bodies of color are seen as sensual objects, available for consumption. The most recognized Asian example is the tragic Puccini opera *Madam Butterfly*, while the stereotypical images of Latinas as hip-swinging hussies were epitomized in the movie roles of Carmen Miranda. A false image is created where women of the dominant culture are seen as being aggressively taken, while women of color are viewed as seducers.

Projecting the dominant culture's forbidden desires on darker bodies, whites could engage in sex with these darker bodies absolved of any culpability; for after all it is those conceived of being closer in evolution to the heat of the jungle who are held responsible for compromising the virtues of whites, either through their so-called seductive nature or through their "black magic." To engage in sex with these nonwhite bodies provided whites an opportunity to lose themselves to primitive urges, heightening their momentary sexual experience while reinforcing the subjugation of the darker bodies.

Crying rape by women whose only privilege is belonging to the dominant culture has historically been a concern for men from ethnic or racial marginalized communities. To refer to Joseph as "a Hebrew brought to insult us" is to label him, and all men of color who follow him, as morally deficient, evidenced by their so-called overly sexualized demeanor. This only confirms their preference for matters of the flesh over the rational. In the minds of those in the dominant culture, all bodies that are in the minority are synonymous with unrestrained, primitive, hot sex. Because they are ruled by the flesh and not the mind, their bodies must be controlled to ensure, protect, and advance civilization. And how is this control maintained? In the United States, black men as sexual predators were controlled by lynching or castration. Black women as Jezebels simply got what they deserved and secretly wanted. These sexual acts of terror were justified as effective means of maintaining control over black bodies who were, after all, seen as being ultimately responsible for the violence visited on them.

Accusing an ethnic or racial male minority of a crime, specifically a sexual crime, is easily believed by the overall dominant culture. So Potiphar's nameless wife can lie and Joseph will be thrown into prison. But is deception always wrong? It is acceptable among the marginalized when it leads to a greater good, as in the previous chapter, where Tamar played the prostitute. But Potiphar's wife's dishonesty is negatively portrayed because her deception was self-serving, negatively impacting others. She had to accuse Joseph of rape as an act of self-defense, for within patriarchal society the penalty for her attempted tryst would be death. It really did not matter if her accusation was true or false, for her accusation had already brought shame to Potiphar's household. Still, Joseph's punishment of imprisonment was quite mild. If, under normal circumstances, the death penalty would alleviate some of the shame, we are left wondering why Joseph, a slave after all, was not executed. Maybe the ultimate punishment was not extracted because Potiphar had reservations about his wife's truthfulness? Either way, her honor is not restored, because Joseph gets to live, though confined to jail. But the good news is, as previously discussed, God was with him. Even while in jail, Joseph will soon rise to steward of the penal system, working under the chief jailer.

Finally, one can argue that the God-fearing man should beware of all foreign women, like Potiphar's wife. This was the warning that Ezra would one day voice, commanding that the Israelites "send away all [their foreign] wives and their children" (Ezra 10:3). One might mistakenly conclude that marrying foreign women, especially with a history of returning to one's people to find wives for Isaac and Jacob, is prohibited. But later Joseph is "given" an Egyptian woman named Asenath, daughter of Potiphera, priest of On, to marry (41:45). A counternarrative exists against the future command of putting away foreign wives. Like the story of the Moabite Ruth, marrying outside one's people is not prohibited. Joseph's union to the Egyptian woman produces a *mestisaje*, an ethnic mixture, honored by some sections of the biblical text. Not all foreign wives are evil, needing to be put away. Looking back at the humility he was forced to bear, Joseph named his firstborn *mestizo* child Manasseh, which means "to forget," for God had made Joseph forget his toil and his father's house. Looking forward, Joseph names his second-born *mestizo* Ephraim, which means "to be fruitful," for God made Joseph fruitful in the land of his affliction.

40:1–23

Testimony of the Chief Cupbearer

Pharaoh is angered by two of his officials, the chief cupbearer and the chief baker, imprisoning them for unspecified offenses. Although the text is silent concerning the crimes committed, they had to be serious. Considering the emphasis of Egyptian culture not to mutilate corpses lest the afterlife is negatively affected and the unsavory fate met by the baker, we can assume that the crimes of which these officials were accused must have been grave. We should note that the cupbearer was more than simply a courtier who served wine to the sovereign; he also enjoyed the ruler's confidence. Besides providing wine to the monarch, cupbearers also provided advice, at times heading major projects or initiatives, as was the case with Nehemiah, cupbearer to King Artaxerxes (Neh. 2:1). The chief baker, although also an important official responsible for Pharaoh's meals, may not have enjoyed the privilege of having the sovereign's ear as did the cupbearer.

Both officials are placed in the same prison occupied by Joseph. In the previous chapter, even though Joseph is in jail, we are told that God is with him. His popularity led the chief jailer to appoint him as an administrator (39:21–23). However, with the start of chapter 40, we find the commander of the guard assigning Joseph to attend to the needs of the two new prisoners. The apparent inconsistency as to Joseph's status within the prison system, an assistant warden or a slave to other prisoners, can be attributed to the combination of two separate narratives, J and E.

Both courtiers have similar dreams, but they are sad because no one is present who can interpret the dreams for them. Dreams, as "visions of the night," were believed to be metaphysical messages from supernatural entities. Properly interpreting dreams was considered a scientific endeavor. Professional interpreters consulted dream book compilations to understand the ethereal messages and intentions otherworldly forces wished to reveal. Ancient cultures understood dreams as a way by which gods communicated with mere mortals, a belief shared by Hebrews and their descendants, as was evident with Israel's kings (e.g., the future King Solomon, 1 Kgs. 3:4–15), prophets (Num. 12:6), and individuals (Job 33:15–16). It is through a dream, according to the Gospels, that Joseph, Mary's husband, is encouraged to marry her (Matt. 1:20) and, once the child is born, is warned to flee Herod's coming purge (Matt. 2:13).

The officials of Pharaoh's court had dreams that could reveal the fate awaiting them, but they were nonetheless gloomy, for no professionals were present to interpret their dreams. Joseph asks the officials to tell him the dreams, for, after all, "Do not interpretations belong to God?" Sorcerers and magicians are not needed. Anyone God chooses can interpret a dream, as long as we remember that it is not Joseph who is the interpreter, but God. All Joseph is doing is revealing what God has made clear to him. Yet the biblical text also provides warnings on relying too much on dreams. Elsewhere in the Torah an admonition is given concerning verifiable dream interpreters who lead the people into worshiping other gods (Deut. 13:1–5). The prophet Zechariah also cautions against false interpretations of dreams (Zech. 10:2).

The fact that Joseph can reveal the interpretations of dreams indicates that God is still with him, even in the pit of prison where there exists no hope for liberation. But God's presence here is different than in earlier Genesis narratives. This is not a God who talks with Joseph, as God did with Adam, Noah, Abraham, Isaac, or Jacob. Nevertheless, Joseph "sees" God's presence operating in his life. Most are able to "see" God in their lives when they have a roof over their head, are able to enjoy good health, have plenty of food in the cupboards and wine bottles on the rack. In the light of resurrection Sunday, it is easy to see God's presence. But for many who live in the darkness of Holy Saturday, the day after Friday's crucifixion, and the not yet Easter Sunday of resurrection, all that can be said is *Eli, Eli, lema sabachthani*. For many Christians who are disenfranchised and disposed, the pit of Joseph's prison is located in the space of Holy Saturday, where some faint anticipation of Sunday's good news is easily drowned out by the reality and consequences of Friday's violence and brutality. This is a space where hopelessness becomes the companion of used and abused marginalized communities.

Professions of a hope that everything will work out may temporarily soothe one's anxiety, but are no substitute for bringing about a more just social structure. The hopelessness faced by Joseph and all who are today marginalized is not disabling; rather, it is a methodology that propels toward praxis. Such hopelessness is never an excuse to do nothing. The disenfranchised have no options but to continue their struggle for justice regardless of the odds against them, if not for themselves, then for their progeny. Joseph understood this, and hence hoped against all hope. In the darkness of Holy Saturday, unable yet to see Sunday's light, he continued to seek his own liberation because God, although difficult to see at times, was still present.

Joseph interprets the courtiers' dreams. For the chief cupbearer, the news is good. His head would be lifted up in three days, restored to his position of power and privilege. Joseph professes his innocence and requests that, once restored, the cupbearer does not forget him. For the chief baker, however, the news is grim. His head will also be lifted up, but to the gallows. There his corpse will become food for the birds. Within three days, on Pharaoh's birthday, the dreams' interpretations came true. But unfortunately the chief cupbearer did not remember Joseph. First, Joseph was betrayed by the jealousy of his brothers, then by the lust of Potiphar's wife. Now he is betrayed by the worst sin, the forgetfulness of the chief cupbearer.

The cupbearer saw an injustice in Joseph's wrongful imprisonment and did nothing. To ignore the cry of the oppressed by doing nothing is to become complicit with the causes of their oppression. Whenever amnesia grips a people, forgetting the injustices caused so that they can continue to enjoy their power and privilege, they become complicit with the very structures that brought destruction and death to many. Consider the rhetoric produced when nationalism is fused and confused with Christianity. Take, for example, the mythology that the United States was established as a Christian nation, a new Israel, a city on the hill. Forgotten is how the wealth of North Americans is connected to the genocide of Native Americans so that their lands could be stolen, the enslavement of African Americans so that their bodies could be stolen, and the pauperization of Latino/as so that their labor could be stolen. The sin of forgetting leads to a romanticized Christian America that ignores how this political entity was constructed on ideologies fostering white supremacy, Manifest Destiny, savage capitalism, and colonialism.

One can often hear pundits cry for a return to an America of yesteryear that was supposedly more in line with God's intended will for the country. They usually express real fear about today's America, wanting to return to a simpler time when everyone knew his/her place.

> Normally I'd say "Hello America,"
> but here's The One Thing: This can't
> be the same country I grew up in,
> because in the America I grew up
> in the headlines would be a whole
> lot different today.
> —Glenn Beck
>
> "This Can't Be the Same Country I Grew Up
> In," *Fox News,* July 22, 2009.

When communities of color hear such nostalgia for the "good old days," a cold chill usually runs up their spines, mainly because many are old enough to remember, all too well, the America to which these neoconservative pundits want to return. This was an America where brown bodies throughout the Southwest, like black bodies throughout the South, were often the strange fruit found hanging from trees. This was an America where the killing or the disappearance of nonwhite bodies was a common occurrence, where they learned early, for their own safety and hopes of surviving, to fear—not trust—law enforcement.

To participate in the sin of the chief cupbearer is by far the most injurious that a people can commit. To forget injustices, or worse, to cover them up with some romanticized historical narrative, thwarts addressing the consequences of wrongs that still persist and prevents any hope in establishing a more just social order.

41:1–44, 46–49, 53–57; 47:13–26

Testimonies from the Empire's Underside

Pharaoh's dream of seven sleek and portly cows grazing by the river Nile being eaten by seven repulsive and emaciated cows is more than a warning of approaching economic hardships. The Nile symbolized fertility, the source of Egyptian imperial power, for upon its floods and the fertile land it creates, the fruitfulness of Egypt depended. Any attack on the Nile would be an attack at the heart of Egyptian imperial rule. Hence disturbing dreams by Pharaoh concerning the Nile would be cause for alarm. Pharaoh's second dream, like the first, consisted of seven blighted ears of grain devouring the first set of seven plump ears. These dreams, or better yet, nightmares, deeply troubled his spirit. Yet the might of Pharaoh, his empire, and his gods stood powerless before pending disaster that could eventually overtake them because they could not understand the dreams nor find anyone in the realm that could. Pharaoh, along with all future kings, emperors, prime ministers, and presidents, regardless of the power they claim to possess, must learn that they all stand vulnerable and helpless before a sovereign God.

God may have used Pharaoh's nightmares to remind the negligent chief cupbearer of the young Hebrew with whom he shared a prison cell some time ago who was able to interpret dreams. Still, Joseph's gift, in the hands of Pharaoh, may cause more harm than good. It becomes an opportunity for Pharaoh to consolidate power and maintain his empire. Following a familiar biblical pattern, it would be the least, the rejected and forgotten one languishing in prison, that God chooses as the instrument by which to reveal God's message. But in this case we should be cautious of premature celebration of God always choosing the rejected stone to serve as the cornerstone of God's handiwork. In this narrative, Joseph may reveal to Pharaoh what God is about to do, but his actions may not necessarily be pleasing to the Lord.

Although Pharaoh must have assumed that Joseph was just another magician or wise man, Joseph makes sure Pharaoh recognizes that it is the God who transcends empires who is the source of all dreams, and thus can provide correct interpretations. Such powers are "not in me," Joseph assures the Pharaoh—a statement that does all of us good to remember lest we become too enamored with ourselves. As Joseph reveals, seven years of plenty throughout all the land followed by seven years of famine come to pass. Still, Joseph's counsel to Pharaoh is troublesome for all who have ever lived under the shadow of empire. Joseph advises Pharaoh to choose an overseer who is discerning and wise to take and store one-fifth of the produce of the land of Egypt during the seven years of plenty.

Pharaoh rewards Joseph's sagacity by making him second-in-command, overseeing the collection (taxation?) of a portion of what the land produces. As second only to Pharaoh, Joseph enjoys the splendors of the royal court, countering the thirteen years of misery he endured while a servant in prison. Once stripped of his long-sleeved coat, he is now clothed in the finest garments. When the years of famine finally arrive, Egypt has bread, for Pharaoh's granaries are full and the grain outnumbers the sand of the sea. Regardless of an abundance that is "beyond measure" stored in Pharaoh's silos, the Egyptians soon run out of food and cry out to Pharaoh. Pharaoh responds by sending his people to Joseph, who is in charge of the grain. But rather than meeting the needs of the people, Joseph takes advantage of the situation for Pharaoh's benefit by selling back to the people what they originally produced and handed over to Joseph in the form of taxes. First, Joseph sells the grain until the inhabitants of Egypt and the surrounding area exchange all their money for food. After they run out of money, Joseph takes their livestock in exchange for food. When that runs out, Joseph takes all their land and turns citizens into Pharaoh's slaves. In the final analysis, Joseph may have been more devoted to Pharaoh than to God.

We have grown accustomed to seeing Joseph as the pious and faithful hero of the narrative. Nevertheless, these texts are disturbing, for they provide a portrait of the Most High's servant heartlessly appropriating all of the land's resources for the privileged few at the expense of the many. Imagine if during the midst of the U.S. Great Depression of the 1930s President Roosevelt would have appropriated the land and resources of all Americans in exchange for food, ending with their enslavement to the government. No doubt we would consider it a villainous act. Yet this is what Joseph does, even though the people end by thanking him for saving their lives. As much as we might admire the shrewd Joseph of chapter 41, we are left wondering about the ruthless Joseph that emerges in chapter 47 and the God that made this possible.

This portion of the Joseph narrative raises questions concerning the role land plays in the establishment of oppressive structures. Typically, land is viewed as neutral. Nevertheless, theologian Enrique Dussel reminds us that landownership has but three origins: one either works for it, steals it, or inherits it. If the land is worked for, then more than likely it will be relatively small. But if much land is owned, then undoubtedly it was stolen, usually by impoverishing (as did Joseph) or killing the original inhabitants.[11] Rather than

---

11. Enrique Dussel, *Ethics and the Theology of Liberation*, trans. Bernard F. McWilliams (Maryknoll, NY: Orbis, 1978), 25.

the state meeting the needs of its inhabitants during times of famine, Joseph used their hunger for bread to the state's advantage. The biblical passage shows how the appropriation and consolidation of land lies behind much of the economic, political, and social violence that has plagued humanity. The accumulation of resources unneeded for subsistence becomes exclusive, excess commodities, contributing to domination over those who must barter to obtain bare necessities.

> The land was made to be common to all, the poor and the rich. Why do you, oh rich, claim for yourselves alone the right to the land? . . . When you give to the poor, you give not of your own, but simply return what is his, for you have usurped that which is common and has been given for the common use of all. The land belongs to all, not to the rich; and yet those who are deprived of its use are many more than those who enjoy it. . . . God our Lord willed that this land be the common possession of all and give its fruit to all. But greed distributed the right of possessions.
>
> —Ambrose
>
> *De Nabuthe Iezraelita* 2.53, cited by Justo L. González, *Faith and Wealth: A History of Early Christian Ideas on the Origin, Significance, and Use of Money* (Eugene, OR: Wipf and Stock Publishers, 1990), 191.

Land, once considered the possession of God, became exclusively owned to the detriment of others.[12] Biblical regulations will eventually establish the Sabbatical Year, gleaning, Jubilee, and usury to avoid great disparities in wealth from developing among God's people. These regulations would ensure an equitable distribution of natural resources. Yet Joseph's commodification of Egypt's land turned it into a source of power over others. Whenever these biblical regulations were ignored by the people, biblical prophets arose in the land to condemn this form of avarice as sin. The prophet Isaiah would warn: "Woe to you who add house to house and join field to field till no space is left and you live alone in the land" (Isa. 5:8 NIV). Micah proclaims: "Alas for those who devise wickedness. . . . They covet fields, and seize them; houses, and take them away; they oppress householder and house, people and their inheritance" (Mic. 2:1–2 NRSV).

---

12. The notion landownership is held by God can be found in Exod. 9:29; 19:5; Lev. 25:23; Deut. 10:14; 26:10; Pss. 24:1; 50:12; and 1 Cor. 10:26.

> At first the Europeans had the Bible and we had the land; now the Europeans have the land and we have the Bible.
>
> —Old African proverb

Our modern society, based on Lockean philosophical thought, has championed the importance, if not the sacredness, of property rights—even at the expense of other more important rights (e.g., the right to life). As a society, we have chosen to privilege those rights that continue to sustain the economic dominance of the few. For not all rights are equal. All may agree that humans have a right to receive a daily amount of calories sufficient to sustain life. Nourishment, especially in the richest country the world has ever known, may be a basic human right; yet this right is assaulted by other rights that take precedence, specifically property rights. Regardless of hunger, an individual cannot jump a fence to take an apple from a tree, nor even an abandoned apple that fell off a tree and is in the process of rotting on the ground. To jump the fence and trespass on another's land violates property rights. If arrested, the circumstance of dire hunger and the basic human right to survive is not a legal argument for violating property rights. When it comes to human rights versus property rights, we have chosen to follow Joseph's example and privilege property rights. That protection of property rights, even in the face of human death, is given preference demonstrates how "rights" language is used to maintain the law and order required for the few to continue enriching themselves in spite of the consequences to more disenfranchised communities. Those seeking to create or maintain unjust social structures (e.g., Joseph) have learned that creating their own "rights" or "virtues" to compete with one of the basic human rights of disenfranchised communities provides them the semblance of a moral argument that perpetuates oppression.

42:1–45:28

Testimonies of the Brothers

Egypt, the empire, has what the world needs—grain—thanks to the rich fertile soil resulting from the annual inundations of the Nile.

Throughout ancient history, Egypt was known as the world's bread-basket, a desirable vassal for future conquering empires, be they Persian, Greek, or Roman. But for now, thanks to Joseph's ingenuity, Egypt had stored sufficient grain, at the expense of its people, to feed the surrounding nations at a profit. And with Joseph as vizier, both he and his pharaoh were becoming wealthy and powerful. Meanwhile, back in Canaan, his family, which included his brothers who sold him into slavery, lived on the verge of starvation. With this section of the biblical narrative, the story switches its focus from Joseph's Egyptian adventures to his family, specifically his brothers.

"Why do you keep looking at one another?" said Jacob to his sons. "I have heard that there is grain in Egypt; go down and buy grain for us there, that we may live and not die" (42:1–2). But rather than sending all of his sons, he prevents Benjamin, the youngest and full brother of Joseph, from accompanying the other ten. By favoring Benjamin, is Jacob repeating his earlier mistake when he favored Joseph, or does Jacob simply not trust his sons after what happened to Joseph?

So the ten brothers journey to Egypt to buy grain. Upon arriving, they make their way to Pharaoh's representative to purchase the food they need. When brought into his presence, they fail to recognize their brother Joseph, even though Joseph recognizes them. The brothers bow down before Joseph, their faces touching the ground, unaware that they are bringing into fruition Joseph's childhood dream concerning the bowing sheaves. An elaborate cat-and-mouse game begins that will unfold over three chapters with Joseph playing the role of the cat, while his ten brothers unknowingly play the role of the mice. Although Joseph sets out to deceive his brothers, the text seems ambiguous as to how Joseph treats them. At times he is magnanimous, while at other times he is harsh. Joseph's ambiguity may be due to the conflation of sources, specifically J and E.

We see a harsh Joseph early in the text, when he accuses them of being spies, demanding that the youngest, Benjamin, who remained behind, be brought back to him. In order to evoke fear among his brothers, he imprisons them for three days. On the third day Joseph releases them, and with little concern for his father's pain, demands that they bring back Benjamin. Although Joseph explains that his motives are to test if the ten are spies, the reader knows that Joseph is more concerned with testing their character. Are these the same brothers who sold him into slavery? Have they changed? In other words, can there be reform and redemption? Maybe there is. It seems Joseph believes so. After all, he is forced to leave the room and silently weep when he hears Reuben chastise his siblings for the wrong committed against Joseph many years earlier.

The reader understands Joseph's fascination with Benjamin, who is described as a handsome young lad (*na'ar*), even though he is probably much older. Still, for those who do not know that a familial relationship exists, we are left to wonder what this older powerful man wants with a young beauty like Benjamin. Until the brothers can return and present Benjamin to the vizier, brother Simeon is to remain behind and bound. In an attempt to ease the brothers' trepidation, the Egyptian ruler claims to be a man who fears God. Unfortunately, the brothers miss the first hint concerning the vizier's true identity, for what does an Egyptian pagan know about fearing the true God of the Hebrews?

The royal deceiver plays the trickster, setting out to deceive his brothers, who originally deceived their father Jacob—the ultimate deceiver of Isaac—with news of Joseph's death. Now Joseph as lord of the land instructs his servants to hide each brother's money among the grain stored in their donkeys' panniers. The brothers discover the funds either during their journey home (42:27–28) or after they get home (42:35). In any case, they grow afraid. Returning their money signifies the turning of strangers into guests. The food their donkeys carry is transformed into a gift. But the brothers fail to understand the gift because in their eyes there is no reason to receive such kindness.

The brothers stay in Canaan until they run out of grain and are hard pressed again by the famine. Desperate, they decide to return to Egypt to buy more grain, this time bringing Benjamin, per the royal administrator's decree. We do not know how long the grain lasted or how much time elapsed before their provisions were depleted. What is odd is the disregard the brothers had for one of their own, Simeon, who was still in Egyptian bondage. It seems that Simeon's redemption from prison has more to do with the fact that his brothers ran out of food, grew hungry, and had no choice but to return, rather than any concern the brothers might have expressed for Simeon's welfare. Thank God for the famine or Simeon might have spent the remainder of his life incarcerated.

The brothers return to Egypt, bringing with them their youngest, Benjamin, and double the money that they found in their panniers. In their second encounter, they find a magnanimous Joseph, although they are still afraid that the Egyptian ruler will enslave them and steal their donkeys. Joseph prepares a feast for them at his house and brings the imprisoned Simeon to join them. When Joseph spots Benjamin, his full brother, he is overcome with emotion, having to leave the room. When he returns, he arranges them around the table according to rank, from the eldest to the youngest. The brothers are amazed that he correctly seats them according to age, missing the second hint of the vizier's true identity.

When the meal is served, Joseph and his household eat separately from the brothers, for Egyptians thought it disgusting to eat with Hebrews. Joseph reveals what usually happens when a person of color assimilates to the dominant culture, rather than seeking justice. Unfortunately, members of marginalized racial and ethnic communities often shape themselves in the image of the dominant culture. They learn to mimic the attitudes, beliefs, behaviors, and actions that they have been taught to see as superior. This is a form of colonization of the minds, in which the marginalized learn their "lack of self-worth" and experience self-loathing. Like Joseph, some marginalized persons today in America attempt to become "whiter" than the dominant culture. If salvation requires assimilation, then proof of worthiness lies in being accepted by the dominant culture, even if assimilation leads to acts that are contrary, if not damning, to one's own community of color. Hence the Joseph of old practiced the same type of segregation some persons of color practice today.

Joseph the foreigner, the outsider, is clearly portrayed as being blessed by God. Today we might say he obtained "the American dream." But this does not vindicate assimilation. Class privilege does create opportunities for a few within marginalized groups to participate and benefit from the existing power structures. But there is a danger when Joseph exhibits greater disdain and less patience or compassion than the Egyptian community that is privileging him. We see the same danger today within communities of color. Some who are given a minuscule amount of status become more exacting than their white counterparts with those belonging to their own communities who fall short of the white ideal, usually persons who are darker and poorer. When the marginalized, those who vocally support the many manifestations of white supremacy, are lifted onto pedestals, the message to racial and ethnic communities is clear: If you also want to succeed, then emulate these success stories. You too can become "a credit to your race."

The lure of economic privilege experienced by Joseph has a way of seducing everyone, including those within marginalized groups, to seek benefits for self instead of justice for all. No doubt leaders like Martin Luther King or César Chávez would be greatly disappointed by the lack of radicalism displayed by middle- and upper-class blacks and Hispanics today. They have traded political emancipation for personal advancement. If that can be achieved only by learning to play along with oppressive structures, this is a terribly high price to be paid by those within marginalized communities.

> I think Medgar Evers and Martin Luther King, Jr., would be dismayed by the lack of radicalism in the new black middle class, and discouraged to know that a majority of the black people helped by the Movement of the sixties has abandoned itself to the pursuit of cars, expensive furniture, large houses, and the finest Scotch.
>
> —Alice Walker
>
> In Search of Our Mothers' Gardens: Womanist Prose (London: Women's Press, 1984), 168.

As apologists for systems of injustice, the dominant culture not surprisingly offers lucrative rewards to such spokespersons. Folks today who imitate Joseph remind us that the need for justice goes beyond the dominant culture and historically U.S. marginalized communities. The lure of becoming new oppressors at the expense of other marginalized groups is a reality that finds expression in various forms of oppression within such communities, such as internal racism, sexism, and classism, where proximity to the white male ideal remains the standard for measuring superiority.

The closer one is to the white ideal, the more privilege exists, although still limited within the overall dominant culture. It is easy to detect the sins the dominant culture perpetrates against marginalized communities, and while these oppressive structures should never be minimized, it is also important to be aware of and active in dismantling the ways we emulate, as Joseph did, the dominant culture in oppressing segments within one's own communities. Surely God stands against all oppression, even that perpetuated by the oppressed.

Any decision to find salvation through assimilation is difficult to unpack. Obviously, individual motives are always complex. Exploring human relationships, educator Paulo Freire noted that everyone in some part of his or her being seeks to be a "subject" who is able to act and transform her or his environment. Thus members of marginalized communities who are objects acted on rather than subjects who do the acting have an escape route. While habitually alienated and acted on, they desire acceptance and want to become subjects in their own right. The safe route is to imitate the dominant society whose acceptance they crave. In a very real sense, their consciousness becomes submerged. They become unable, or unwilling, to see how the operating interests and values of the dominant culture are internalized.[13]

Joseph may have acted like an Egyptian, accepting segregation as the legitimate norm; still, he did show hospitality toward all and favoritism toward one, Benjamin, giving him a portion five times larger than any of the others. As the brothers prepared to take their leave, Joseph gave instructions to his steward to fill each man's sack with as much grain as possible and place his silver cup, used for divination, into the sack of the youngest one. The trap leading to the story's climax is set.

Yet we are left wondering what Joseph was doing with a divination cup, paraphernalia of Egyptian religious rituals. The writer of this text must have been familiar with the tradition that eventually found expression in Deuteronomy 18:10, forbidding the use of any divination method or consultation with fortune-tellers. Joseph

---

13. Paulo Freire, *Pedagogy of the Oppressed* (New York: Continuum International, 1994), 25–30.

apparently accepted not only the biases against Hebrews held within Egyptian culture, but also Egyptian religious practices. But does Joseph's participation in Egyptian divination rituals mean a rejection of the Hebrew God? Not necessarily. Joseph demonstrates what many present-day Hispanics call a hybrid spirituality, which means participating in several different religious traditions, even those that may appear on the surface contradictory.

An example of this hybrid spirituality can be found in an account told by Christian minister and scholar Carlos Cardoza-Orlandi. He relates the story of a Dominican family who attended the Protestant church he pastored in New York. Their child was gravely ill. Besides taking the child to the doctor, they also pleaded with the church to pray. The church committed to do so, and with time the child regained health. Unknown to the pastor, the parents also took the child to a santero, a practitioner of an Afro-Cuban religion called Santería, which worships African gods in the form of orishas. When the pastor discovered that the family also visited the santero, he asked the father who cured the child. Was it the prayers of the church or was it the santero's animal sacrifices? But the parents found the question puzzling. They replied that it was God who cured the child. It was the pastor's problem to figure out if God responded to the church's prayers or the santero's rituals.[14] Hybridity brings together different, if not contradictory, religious motifs to create a workable worldview.

Shortly after the brothers leave Egypt, making their way back home, they are overtaken by Joseph's men. The brothers are accused of stealing the divination cup. "Should it be found with any one of your servants, let him die; moreover the rest of us will become [the vizier's] slaves," the brothers exclaim. Each man's sack is searched, beginning with the eldest. When they open the last sack, the one belonging to Benjamin, the cup is found. The brothers tear their clothes in mourning and return to Egypt to face their judge. Joseph offers to set the brothers free to return to their home as long as the "guilty" party, Benjamin, remains as his slave. By framing Benjamin

---

14. Carlos Cardoza-Orlandi, "Drum Beats of Resistance and Liberation: Afro-Caribbean Religions, the Struggle for Life, and the Christian Theologian," *Journal of Hispanic/Latino Theology* 3, no. 1 (1995): 56.

as the thief, Joseph provides the brothers with an opportunity to escape punishment. The brothers could return to their father, justified that Benjamin brought his plight on himself. Will the brothers abandon Benjamin and save their own skins, or will they remain and advocate for him?

Judah intervenes, speaking for all the brothers. Unable to bear the misery, if not death, it will bring to his father, Judah pleads to be a substitute for Benjamin, to take his place; or as Jesus would one day say, "No one has greater love than this, to lay down one's life for one's friends" (John 15:13). Judah, and by extension the brothers, are different men than the ones who sold Joseph into slavery so many years ago. Seeing how much they have changed is more than Joseph can bear. He dismisses all of his attendants. Left alone with his brothers, he reveals his true identity: "I am Joseph"—the dead one is alive!

Joseph could have cursed God for the trials and tribulations he suffered in Egypt. Or, when his brothers showed up to buy grain, he could have taken his revenge, making them slaves. But instead Joseph sees the hand of God. He does not reproach his brothers for selling him into slavery; instead he claims that God sent him ahead to preserve their lives during the famine that has gripped the land. It seems that God uses evil to accomplish God's goals and purposes. Still, we are left with a dilemma: Does God redeem evil and bring good from it, or is God the cause of evil?

When Pharaoh hears about Joseph's brothers, he offers them what is not his, the best land in Goshen. It is not his because more than likely it was obtained during the years of famine when, under Joseph's instructions, Pharaoh acquired lands and riches by selling

> The controlling agenda is the way this family is governed by a dream and the way this family chafes against that dream. What is revealed here is not for the eyes of the empire. The listening community is not asked by the narrator to leave the room with the empire (45:1), but is invited to stay with the family. We are permitted to witness a gospel disclosure: The dead one is alive! The abandoned one has returned in power! The dream has had its way!
>
> —Walter Brueggemann
>
> *Genesis*, Interpretation (Atlanta: John Knox Press, 1982), 343–44.

back to the landowners the grain they originally produced and now needed to survive. In addition, this seeming act of generosity is also a brilliant military tactic. Any threat to Egypt's security would come from the north. Goshen is located in the northeast delta, thus serving as a buffer between any invading army and the Egyptians. If Egypt was to be invaded, the first line of defense would be the Hebrews.

The brothers return home to Canaan with good news. The one who was dead is now alive; and he waits for us in a palace with untold riches. We are saved!

46:1–47:12; 47:27–50:26
Testimony of Israel

Genesis concludes with the testimony of Israel, both the individual and the emerging people who will come to be known by the same name. The twilight of Israel the man coincides with the dawn of Israel the nation. Unfortunately, the narrative fails to provide a concise and cohesive ending. Instead, the reader finds a disjointed and, at times, incongruent story. This may be due to the juxtaposing of different sources (some very ancient) brought together without smooth redacting into a seamless tale. Nevertheless, in these final chapters of the book, which makes a poor attempt to tie together loose ends, certain concluding themes emerge that are worth exploring.

Israel the man again finds himself a migrant. Genesis, more so than any other book in the Bible, is a book of migrants and refugees: from the first migrants of the book, Adam and Eve, who are expelled from their home; to the faith's patriarch, Abraham, who leaves home and family based on a promise from God; to Jacob, who escapes the wrath of his brother Esau. Genesis is the story of displacement. To engage in present-day immigration debates is to remember that the genesis of the Judeo-Christian faith is based on the story of immigrants. In a way, to reject immigrants today is to reject the founders of our faith.

On his way to Egypt, Israel stops at Beer-sheba to offer sacrifices to the God of his father Isaac. Almost a lifetime ago, a young refugee named Jacob, at the start of his life, left Beer-sheba to go to the home of Laban, fleeing the wrath of his brother. Now, as a grown man, he again finds himself as a migrant, this time rushing to see the son he thought was dead. At Beer-sheba Israel has a vision. God reiterates the promise that, from his descendants, a great nation will emerge. Then God makes a startling statement: God too will go down to Egypt with him. In an age when gods were tied to geographical locations, Israel's God is beyond tribal identities. The God of Israel can also be found in the land of Egypt, or in any other land where humans are present. As the psalmist reminds us:

> If I ascend to heaven, you are there;
> if I make my bed in Sheol, you are there.
> If I take the wings of the morning
> and settle at the farthest limits of the sea,
> even there your hand shall lead me,
> and your right hand shall hold me fast
> (Ps. 139:8–10)

Israel's God, unlike all others, is everywhere; hence a migrant people need not fear ever moving beyond the reach of their God. They will never be alone or abandoned.

Israel the man, in this passage, becomes the last patriarch to converse face-to-face with God. Israel knew God; but neither Joseph nor any of his brothers would ever experience their father's intimacy with the Deity. Yet they too can come to know God.

For Joseph and the rest of us, we are left with seeing and interpreting God's presence in our lives, even when we do not physically see or hear God. Israel the man may have conversed face-to-face with God, but what greater faith is it to still be able to converse with a God one can neither see nor hear.

Israel journeys to Egypt with his family, livestock, and

> To know Yahweh, which in biblical language is equivalent to saying to love Yahweh, is to establish just relationships among persons, it is to recognize the rights of the poor. The God of biblical revelation is known through interhuman justice. When justice does not exist, God is not known; God is absent.
>
> —Gustavo Gutiérrez
>
> *Theology of Liberation*, 110–11.

possessions. We are told, according to the P source, that a total of seventy family members made the trek. Still, some inconsistencies exist in the official count. For example, the dead sons of Judah (Er and Onan) and the sons born to Joseph in Egypt, Manasseh and Ephraim, are counted among those who went with Israel to Egypt. Maybe the author is less concerned with who went to Egypt than the number seventy, which becomes a symbolic number because it is a multiple of seven, which signifies completeness and perfection (e.g., seven days of creation). Seventy will eventually become the number of the community elders (Exod. 24:1, 9). But what is missing from the count, hence revealing the misogyny of the text, are the women, the wives and daughters. Only men are counted; women remain invisible, even though they too must make the journey as aliens.

Once Israel and his family arrive at Goshen, a fertile region in the hinterland of Egyptian society, Joseph mounts a speedy chariot to meet his father. They embrace and weep. The son thought dead is alive! After the tearful reunion, Joseph instructs the brothers on how to use the Egyptians' loathing of shepherds to gain access to this land far from the network of the Nile's irrigation canals. The horror urban Egyptians hold for rural Hebrews is probably rooted in the ancient animosity among competitors for water, to irrigate either fields or flocks. This unease can be traced to the first pair of brothers, Cain and Abel, who ended badly. Joseph's instructions to his family are odd when we consider that Pharaoh already pledged to Joseph's migrating family the best the land of Egypt offers (45:18). Regardless, Joseph, along with five of his brothers, petitions Pharaoh to stay and pasture their flocks at Goshen. Another version of the same story appears immediately after the first. In this version, Pharaoh first provides land to Joseph's family (in the land of Rameses, an obvious anachronism since Rameses makes his appearance in history centuries later), after which the family is formally presented to Pharaoh. During this exchange, Pharaoh asks Israel his age, to which he responds one hundred and thirty years. He characterizes his years as few (less than his grandfather Abraham, 175, or his father Isaac, 180) and unhappy (maybe because of the loss of his beloved Rachel and the loss—albeit now found to be only temporary—of his favorite son Joseph). Once again, the unexpected happens: Israel the man blesses Pharaoh the king. Simultaneously, Israel the nation blesses Egypt.

This may be Pharaoh's palace, but it is Israel that is holding court. If blessings are given by superiors to inferiors, then Israel is superior to both Egypt and Pharaoh. By having Israel bless Pharaoh, and by extension his nation, God's promise originally made to Abraham that through his descendants all the nations would be blessed (Gen. 12:3) starts to come true. Because God is also in Egypt with Israel, God continues to operate through individuals who might not even know, let alone recognize, the God of Israel. In both versions of the same story, Pharaoh may be the one who is offering the land. However, in reality, the offer Pharaoh is making remains beyond him, for God already prophesied that Israel's family will live in Egypt and eventually return to the promised land. Pharaohs, kings, queens, dictators, and democratically elected leaders are still used by God to bring about God's will. As Proverbs makes clear: "The king's heart is a stream of water in the hand of the LORD; [who] turns it wherever [God] will" (Prov. 21:1). Humans may sit on thrones and believe they are determining the fate of God's chosen people, but the biblical text insists that it is the one who sits on the heavenly throne who decides fate, in spite of whoever might sit on earthly thrones.

Israel prepares for death like his father and grandfather, without seeing the fulfillment of God's promise of land. He dies far from the land that witnessed his birth. With no promise of a Christian heaven, just the shadowy abode of Sheol, Israel dies believing in the promise, knowing God will be faithful, even though his eyes may not see the promise of land come to pass. Even though Israel does not yet possess the land promised, we are told that the "Israelites" settled in the land of Egypt—here, for the first time in the biblical text, the descendants of Abraham to whom the promise was made are called Israelites (46:8). Although the term was used earlier in the text, here for the first time is a group of people who are descendants of Jacob identified by this term. The nation is forming even though the land is unavailable. It is fitting that in the passage recording the last requests of a dying Israel, who got to enjoy seventeen additional years of life in Egypt, the genesis of the nation of Israel occurs. A shift occurs from a family story to a national history. Genesis ends where Israel, the landless nation, begins. To ensure that there will eventually be a nation Israel, Israel the man requests that after he dies his bones be buried in the family plot in Canaan.

Joseph agrees. He may represent the prosperity of the moment, but Israel represents the promise of the future. When exile proves profitable, it is easy to forget the promise. After seventeen years in Goshen, where the family's needs were mostly met, why return to the famine-type experienced in Canaan? One common denominator known by most who have left their land behind for a foreign culture is that regardless of how hard they may try, they will always be strangers and outsiders. Joseph may be second in command, well assimilated to the dominant Egyptian culture, but the day is not far off when a new regime will arise that knows nothing of Joseph and what he accomplished for his adopted land (Exod. 1:8).

The Israelites in Egypt experienced what many non-European immigrants experienced in the United States. To be an alien, an outsider, is to never belong, regardless of how hard one may try to assimilate. For the Israelites, to live on the borders meant to live in the border region of Goshen. Similarly, for Hispanics today, to live on the borders means to literally make one's residence in the cities that are located along an artificial line, known as the scar caused by the first and third world chafing against one another. But the borderlands are more than just geographical realities; they also symbolize the existential reality of Israelites in Egypt then and U.S. Latina/os now. Most Hispanics, regardless of where they are located or how they or their ancestors found themselves in the United States, live on the borders. Borders separating Latina/os from other Americans exist in every state, every city, and almost every community, regardless as to how far away they may be from the 1,833-mile international line. Borders are as real in Chicago, Illinois; Topeka, Kansas; Seattle, Washington; or Chapel Hill, North Carolina, as they are in Chula Vista, California; Douglas, Arizona; or El Paso, Texas. To be a U.S. Hispanic is to constantly live on the border, that is, the border that separates privilege from disenfranchisement, power from marginalization, and whiteness from "colored." Most U.S. Hispanics, like Israelites of old, exist in the borderlands regardless of where they physically live. Joseph, in all his power and regalia, will learn this lesson, asking, like his father, to have his bones returned to the promised land when all of Israel's children return home to Canaan.

As Israel prepared for death, he called his family together to dispense blessings. He begins by having Joseph's sons, Manasseh the older and Ephraim the younger, brought to him. Israel adopts Joseph's sons, making them as much his as his eldest sons Reuben and Simeon, who ironically cease to be landholding tribes when Canaan is conquered by the Israelites. Joseph maneuvers the boys so that Israel's right hand (customarily signifying a greater portion of the blessing) lies on the elder's head. But true to biblical form, Israel crisscrosses his arms so that the right hand falls on the head of the younger. Once again, the younger is privileged over the older, a pattern begun with the first brothers, Cain and Abel. Because Israel is at the age of failing eyesight, reminiscent of when he stood before his blind father and tricked him out of the greater blessing, Joseph attempts to correct his father. But Israel insists that the younger should be favored.

The Joseph narrative began with Israel's foolishness of showing favoritism to the young Joseph. His outward bias wrecked the family, fed hatred toward the young lad, and denied him witnessing the young Joseph grow into manhood. Now, in his advanced years, he continues in his earlier folly. Once again the younger child (Ephraim) is chosen over the firstborn (Manasseh), just as Judah will soon be chosen over Reuben, Simeon, and Levi. This practice will come to be explicitly forbidden when the law is codified (Deut. 21:15–17), even though it is ignored in the time of the monarchy.

We know that Ephraim will historically surpass Manasseh; but for now the story is silent as to how Ephraim and Manasseh handle the blessings. Maybe, due to their Egyptian upbringing, they have not fully understood what appeared to them as strange, foreign, and yet quaint rituals. Most who have experienced multigenerational migration are all too aware of the communication and cultural gap between the grandparents who initially migrated and the grandchildren born into the dominant culture.

Israel asks that the God who has been his shepherd increase their numbers on the earth. For the first time in the biblical text, God is characterized as a shepherd. Eventually, King David would sing songs to the Lord who is his shepherd, leaving him with nothing to want (Ps. 23); and for Christians, Jesus would refer to himself as the good shepherd who will lay down his life for his sheep (John 10:11). By describing God as a shepherd, Israel tells us something about the character of the God whom he follows. Israel's God, like the good shepherd, guides the flock toward good pastures and protects them from the ravaging animals of prey, always willing to offer up his or her life for the good of the flock. The God of Israel loves.

After Jacob adopts and blesses Joseph's sons, he turns his attention to the twelve tribes of Israel. Jacob gathers his sons before him to offer them individual blessings, although "blessing" may very well be a misnomer. For several of the pronouncements, the references are incomprehensible and the idioms obscure. As ambiguous and murky as Israel's "blessings" may be, we can still make certain observations. The comments made by Jacob have less to do with the individuals standing before his bed, and probably have more to do with tribes that will eventually settle the conquered land on Canaan.

Jacob starts with the oldest, Reuben, who because of his grab for power by mounting his father's bed will cease to be foremost. No important figure, judge, king, or prophet will come from the tribe of Reuben. Reuben is followed by Simeon and Levi, the next two oldest, who are also passed over. They find no forgiveness for the treachery in which they participated against the men of Shechem to avenge the rape of their sister Dinah. Although Simeon will be allotted land within the territory of Judah, it appears that with time they will be absorbed by Judah (Josh. 19:9). Levi is given no land, mainly because the tribe becomes a priesthood (Num. 18:20–24)—although this connection is not explicitly stated in Jacob's deathbed "blessing."

Judah is treated as the firstborn, given the greater portion of the blessing. From Judah the scepter and mace, symbols of government, will not pass until *shiloh* comes, a difficult, cryptic term to decipher. It probably can be translated as "to whom it belongs," a possible reference justifying the Davidic line that will eventually sit on the throne. In later years the term was given a more messianic significance. The "blessing" goes on to state that Judah will tie his donkey to the vine, an act no one would commit lest the beast devours the fruit of the vine—unless the author wishes to indicate that such fruit are so plentiful that they are no longer valuable, a possible reference to some messianic existence.

The remaining comments concerning Zebulun, Issachar, Dan, Gad, Asher, and Naphtali are somewhat difficult to understand. With the exception of Issachar and Dan, these blessings might have to do with the lands where these tribes eventually settled. The reference to Issachar seems to indicate their refusal to engage in battle, while Dan's reference might show how a small and weak tribe, like a snake, can bring down a greater foe. Like Judah, much attention is given to Joseph, indicating its preeminence; but again, what these verses mean remains unclear. The oracle ends by celebrating Benjamin's predatory practices. What is significant about the oracle is the absence of blessings for women, as in the case of Dinah, who while also needing to be blessed, unfortunately disappears from the pages of Scripture.

Shortly after the blessing is given, Jacob dies. He is honored as if he was a pharaoh, complete with an official embalming and seventy days of mourning. Pharaoh's servants and palace dignitaries join Joseph as he journeys to Canaan to bury him in his family plot. Israel the man lay in what will become Israel the land. After the funeral, Joseph's brothers become concerned that now that their father is dead, Joseph might attempt to exact revenge for the wrong they did him so many years ago. So they prostrate themselves before Joseph, hence bringing to fruition Joseph's childhood dream. They offer themselves up as slaves, pleading that before their father died, he instructed Joseph to forgive them. But Joseph already had forgiven them. At times it is hard to accept the forgiveness already given.

We do not know if Israel actually said these things to Joseph's brothers. After all, shouldn't he have said them directly to Joseph? Either way, the entire episode troubles Joseph, bringing him to tears. Joseph responds by asking if he could put himself in God's place, maybe indicating that it is God, and not him, they should be concerned with. Then Joseph makes a profound theological statement that undergirds the entire book of Genesis. Although the brothers planned evil, God's design turned it to good. Hence Genesis ends with a truth concerning how God operates. God uses human sin to bring about God's will. Joseph experienced the sin of jealousy harbored by his brothers that led them to sell him into slavery, the sin of lust and pride held by Potiphar's wife that got him thrown into jail, and the sin of forgetfulness demonstrated by the chief cupbearer that kept him in jail. Yet, in spite of all these sins perpetrated against him, Joseph still saw God turn his circumstances into good. Biblical scholar W. Sibley Towner continues:

> Let [Joseph's] remarkable theological claim simmer in your mind while you conjure up pictures of the slave trade and the Indian wars, Auschwitz, and atomic explosions. . . . Can one and the same event be both evil and, in God's hands, good? . . . God does not want the brothers to do what they do. God does not order them to do what they do. Yet when they do it, God does not walk away and leave Joseph alone. . . . God is not defeated by what they do. They do it; God uses it.[15]

Toward the beginning of Genesis, Cain asks God, after murdering his brother Abel, if he is his brother's keeper. Genesis ends by answering this question in the affirmative. We are all responsible for our brothers and sisters, who are all descended from Adam and Eve. Still, evil happens, but the theological claim being made by Joseph is that in the midst of the trials and tribulations faced, Emmanuel, God is with us. Even when there is no happy ending, as so often is the case with the disenfranchised, we are not alone.

> But now the time has come to go away. I go to die and you to live; but which of us goes to the better lot, is known to none but God.
>
> —Socrates
>
> Plato, *Apology* 42a.

Joseph, like Israel before him, also dies away from the promised land. The promise may not have been fulfilled in his lifetime; nevertheless, he dies believing it—asking that when Israel's children leave Egypt, they take his bones with them. Genesis ends with the hope of the promise unfulfilled. Even in death, the book trusts in the future, as should we.

---

15. W. Sibley Towner, *Genesis*, Westminster Bible Companion (Louisville: Westminster John Knox Press, 2001), 290.

Epilogue: Ending Beginnings

Genesis, the book of beginnings, comes to an end. For over a year I have wrestled with this book, seeking the face of God. At times, when I was able to glimpse the reflection of God, I was awestruck; at other times, I was horrified and terrified. To encounter God is never what one expects. The person of faith that I was when I began this project is a different person today. Although I leave Genesis with a deeper faith, I also leave limping, realizing how much I still do not know or understand.

My reading of Genesis was unapologetically subjective. Rejecting the mythology of objectivity, I purposely wrote this commentary with a keen awareness of the margins of society, seeking the voices of those who the academy and the dominant culture seldom hear. Making a preferential option to read Genesis from the social location of the dispossessed and disenfranchised, over and against the powerful and privileged, meant getting to a deeper understanding of the text, not because the marginalized are holier or smarter, but because their reality encompasses multiple levels of consciousness. Not only must the marginalized know the worldview of those whom society privileges, they must also be cognizant of their own reality, à la W. E. B. Dubois's double consciousness.

I have tried to move beyond how many academics, Bible scholars, ministers, and priests have normatively read the Bible to consciously or unconsciously legitimize the interpretations that resonate with the dominant culture because it protects their privilege. Instead, I have endeavored to interpret these texts in such a way that they would resound with those seeking liberation from oppressive social structures through implementing justice-based praxis, aligning myself with those few scholars and church leaders who share my commitment to liberationist concerns. To accomplish this task, to read Genesis from the margins, is to engage in a subversive reading. Reading ceases to be solely for the sake of reading. Reading encompasses challenging and changing what we have come to accept as reality, regardless of how oppressive reality is. To engage in a subversive reading of Genesis is to upset the precious equilibrium on which the dominant culture rests. Only then can the possibility of change occur.

Recently, I published a short article dealing with a particular Genesis interpretation.[1] I received feedback from several friends and colleagues from within the dominant culture who questioned the methodology I employed in interpreting the passage. This should not be surprising. How the marginalized interpret Scripture will seldom make sense or seem correct to those who benefit because of their involvement or complicity with the minoritization of marginalized communities. Likewise, the reason and logic employed by the dominant culture's gatekeepers of proper exegesis fall short for those relegated to the underside of their history. During this past year, as I wrestled with this text, I concluded that normative readings from the dominant culture fail to resonate with me, and I suspect also with disenfranchised communities. For Genesis to come alive, to have meaning, to be transformative, requires those of us from marginalized communities to read the text with our own eyes, situated within our own social location, surrounded by our own community of faith. And what about those from the dominant culture who also seek to read Genesis with new eyes? The hope of their salvation rests in a humbling reading with the disenfranchised, willing to learn from those who they may have difficulty accepting as having anything relevant to add.

Employing this methodology has brought Genesis alive for me. It ceased being a stale ancient text because I found my story, and the story of my people, in its verses. I discovered that Adam and

---

1. Miguel A. De La Torre, "Your Invitation to Be a Born-Again Vegan," *EthicsDaily* (September 2, 2010): http://www.ethicsdaily.com/news.php?viewStory=16614

Eve, like me and my people, were refugees. Against their will, they were forced to leave the land from which they came, prohibited from ever returning. The angels visiting Sodom, like me and my people, were taken advantage of. While the townspeople tried to physically rape them, townsfolk in the places we settled have tried, with many succeeding, to economically rape us. Abraham, like me and my people, was an alien who wandered from place to place on a land where he would never belong or be accepted. Jacob, like me and my people, worked hard, enriching his host even though the host continuously tried to trick and take advantage of him. And Joseph, like me and my people, was a faithful servant only to be stereotyped as a rapist and thief to face an unjust legal system. The testimonies found in Genesis are our testimonies, and hence they have something very important to say to those struggling to survive today, struggling to achieve life and life abundantly.

Although we have come to the end of Genesis, in a sense our subversive reading of the biblical text has created an opportunity for our own new beginnings. If reading Genesis from the margins of society raised our consciousness, the exercise was meaningless if we refuse to allow our struggle with the text to transform us—a change that cannot occur as long as we refuse to engage in justice-based liberation praxis. Reading Genesis remains an academic process if our wrestling with the text changes nothing in us or in our society. Therefore, as we come to the end, we are forced to ask, where do we begin?

For Further Reading

Adam, A. K. M. *Postmodern Interpretations of the Bible: A Reader*. St. Louis, MO: Chalice Press, 2001.

Backer-Fletcher, Karen. *Sisters of Dust, Sisters of Spirit: Womanist Wordings on God and Creation*. Minneapolis: Fortress Press, 1998.

Bellis, Alice Ogden. *Helpmates, Harlots, and Heroes: Women's Stories in the Hebrew Bible*. Louisville: Westminster John Knox Press, 1994.

Boer, Roland, ed. *Marxist Criticism of the Bible*. New York: T & T Clark International, 2003.

Bonhoeffer, Dietrich. *Creation and Fall: A Theological Interpretation of Genesis 1–3*. Trans. John C. Fletcher. 1937. Repr. New York: Macmillan, 1959.

Brenner, Athalya. *I Am . . . Biblical Women Tell Their Own Stories*. Minneapolis: Fortress Press, 2005.

Brueggemann, Walter. *Genesis*. Interpretation. Atlanta: John Knox Press, 1982.

Ceresko, Anthony R. *Introduction to the Old Testament: A Liberation Perspective*. Maryknoll, NY: Orbis, 1998.

De La Torre, Miguel A. *A Lily Among the Thorns: Imagining a New Christian Sexual Ethics*. San Francisco: Jossey-Bass, 2007.

_____. *Reading the Bible from the Margins*. Maryknoll, NY: Orbis, 2002.

DeYoung, Curtiss Paul. *Coming Together in the 21st Century: The Bible's Message in an Age of Diversity*. Valley Forge, PA: Judson Press, 2009.

DeYoung, Curtiss Paul, Wilda C. Gafney, Leticia A. Guardiola-Saenz, George "Tink" Tinker, and Frank M. Yamada, eds. *The Peoples' Bible: New Revised Standard Version with the Apocrypha*. Minneapolis: Fortress Press, 2009.

Dube, Musa W. *Postcolonial Feminist Interpretation of the Bible*. St. Louis, MO: Chalice Press, 2000.

Ekblad, Bob. *Reading the Bible with the Damned*. Louisville: Westminster John Knox Press, 2005.

Essex, Barbara J. *Bad Girls of the Bible: Exploring Women of Questionable Virtue*. Cleveland: United Church Press, 1999.

Felder, Cain Hope, ed. *Stony the Road We Trod: African American Biblical Interpretation*. Minneapolis: Fortress Press, 1991.

Fewell, Danna Nolan, and David M. Gunn. *Gender, Power, and Promise: The Subject of the Bible's First Story*. Nashville: Abingdon Press, 1993.

Frankel, Ellen. *The Five Books of Miriam: A Woman's Commentary on the Torah*. New York: Putnam, 1996.

González, Justo L. *Santa Biblia: The Bible Through Hispanic Eyes*. Nashville: Abingdon Press, 1996.

Goss, Robert E., and Mona West. *Take Back the Word: A Queer Reading of the Bible*. Cleveland: Pilgrim Press, 2000.

Gottwald, Norman K., and Richard A. Horsley, eds. *The Bible and Liberation: Political and Social Hermeneutics*. Rev. ed. Maryknoll, NY: Orbis, 1993.

Guest, Deryn, Robert E. Goss, Mona West, and Thomas Bohache, eds. *The Queer Bible Commentary*. London: SCM Press, 2006.

Katz, Michael, and Gershon Schwartz. *Lessons for Everyday Living: Searching for Meaning in Midrash*. Philadelphia: The Jewish Publication Society, 2002.

Luther, Martin. *Luther's Works*. Volumes 1–8: *Lectures on Genesis*. Ed. Jaroslav Pelikan. St. Louis: Concordia Publishing House, 1958–1966.

Miranda, José Porfirio. *Marx and the Bible: A Critique of the Philosophy of Oppression*. Trans. John Eagleson. 1971. Repr. Maryknoll, New York: Orbis, 1974.

Newsom, Carol A., and Sharon H. Ringe, eds. *Women's Bible*

Commentary. Expanded ed. Louisville: Westminster John Knox Press, 1998.

Nissinen, Martti. *Homoeroticism in the Biblical World: A Historical Perspective.* Minneapolis: Fortress Press, 2004.

Noth, Martin. *A History of Pentateuchal Traditions.* Trans. Bernhard W. Anderson. Englewood Cliffs, NJ: Prentice-Hall, 1972.

Pardes, Ilana. *Countertraditions in the Bible: A Feminist Approach.* Cambridge: Harvard University Press, 1992.

Pixley, Jorge, and Clodovis Boff. *The Bible, the Church, and the Poor.* New York: Hyperion Books, 1994.

Pobee, John S., and Barbel von Wartenberg-Potter, eds. *New Eyes for Reading: Biblical and Theological Reflections by Women from the Third World.* Oak Park, IL: Meyer Stone Books, 1986.

Rad, Gerhard von. *Genesis: A Commentary.* Trans. John H. Marks. Rev. ed. OTL. Philadelphia: Westminster Press, 1972.

Ruether, Rosemary Radford, ed. *Religion and Sexism: Images of Woman in the Jewish and Christian Traditions.* New York: Simon & Schuster, 1974.

Scholz, Susanne, comp. *Biblical Studies Alternatively: An Introductory Reader.* Upper Saddle River, NJ: Prentice Hall, 2003.

Schroeder, Joy A. *Dinah's Lament: The Biblical Legacy of Sexual Violence on Christian Interpretations.* Minneapolis: Fortress Press, 2007.

Schüssler Fiorenza, Elisabeth. *But She Said: Feminist Practices of Biblical Interpretation.* Boston: Beacon, 1992.

Segovia, Fernando F. *Decolonizing Biblical Studies: A View from the Margins.* Maryknoll, NY: Orbis, 2000.

Stone, Ken, ed. *Queer Commentary and the Hebrew Bible.* Cleveland: Pilgrim Press, 2001.

Sugirtharajah, R. S. *The Bible and the Third World: Precolonial, Colonial and Postcolonial Encounters.* New York: Cambridge University Press, 2001.

_____. *Postcolonial Reconfigurations: An Alternative Way of Reading the Bible and Doing Theology.* St. Louis, MO: Chalice Press, 2003.

_____, ed. *Voices from the Margins: Interpreting the Bible in the Third World*. Maryknoll, NY: Orbis, 1995.

Towner, W. Sibley. *Genesis*. Westminster Bible Companion. Louisville: Westminster John Knox Press, 2001.

Trible, Phyllis. *God and the Rhetoric of Sexuality*. OBT. Philadelphia: Fortress Press, 1978.

_____. *Texts of Terror: Literary-Feminist Readings of Biblical Narratives*. OBT. Philadelphia: Fortress Press, 1984.

van Wijk-Bos, Johanna W. H. *Making Wise the Simple: The Torah in Christian Faith and Practice*. Grand Rapids: Eerdmans, 2005.

Williams, Delores S. *Sisters in the Wilderness: The Challenge of Womanist God-Talk*. Maryknoll, NY: Orbis, 1993.

Index of Ancient Sources

Index of Subjects